LOCOMOTIVES OF THE
LIVERPOOL
AND
MANCHESTER
RAILWAY

LOCOMOTIVES OF THE
LIVERPOOL
AND
MANCHESTER
RAILWAY

ANTHONY DAWSON

PEN & SWORD
TRANSPORT

AN IMPRINT OF PEN & SWORD BOOKS LTD.
YORKSHIRE – PHILADELPHIA

First published in Great Britain in 2021 by
PEN AND SWORD TRANSPORT
An imprint of Pen & Sword Books Ltd
Yorkshire - Philadelphia

ISBN 978 1 52676 398 3

Typeset in Sabon LT Std 10/12.5 by
SJmagic DESIGN SERVICES, India.
Printed and bound in India by Replika Press Pvt. Ltd.

Pen & Sword Books Ltd incorporates the Imprints of Pen & Sword Books Archaeology,
Atlas, Aviation, Battleground, Discovery, Family History, History, Maritime, Military, Naval,
Politics, Railways, Select, Transport, True Crime, Fiction, Frontline Books, Leo Cooper,
Praetorian Press, Seaforth Publishing, Wharncliffe and White Owl.

For a complete list of Pen & Sword titles please contact
PEN & SWORD BOOKS LIMITED
47 Church Street, Barnsley, South Yorkshire, S70 2AS, England
E-mail: enquiries@pen-and-sword.co.uk
Website: www.pen-and-sword.co.uk

Or
PEN AND SWORD BOOKS
1950 Lawrence Rd, Havertown, PA 19083, USA
E-mail: Uspen-and-sword@casematepublishers.com
Website: www.penandswordbooks.com

Contents

PART 5: ROLLING STOCK

Foreword

I am both flattered and delighted to be asked to write the Foreword for this splendid publication by Anthony Dawson.

Those of us that have worked with early locomotives and their replicas will welcome such an unusual, thorough and diligent assessment of the way that these primitive machines were created, how they functioned and carried out their tasks. The prime purpose of the Company purchasing and later producing such machines was to run the business of the carriage of goods and people between Liverpool and Manchester. There have been several books written in the past that cover the story of the birth of the world's first intercity railway; but what sets this work apart from the rest is the thoroughness, diligence and attention to detail that the author has applied to the task of researching and producing this volume.

The bibliographies for each chapter hint at the varied and unusual sources the author has accessed to carry out his painstaking research. He is uniquely placed by having worked and volunteered at the Museum of Science and Industry in Manchester, operating the replica *Planet* locomotive, where the story started to unfold in those heady days following the Rainhill Trials of 1829.

What particularly appeals to me as a heritage mechanical engineer is the insight and understanding that he brings to the engineering problems encountered by those early engineers concerning materials and processes that we take for granted nowadays. For example the large scale use of steel for structural components was forty years into the future. The understanding of metal fatigue that caused early steam locomotive crank axles to break so disastrously was over a century into the future.

By researching and writing this book, the author has made a significant and valuable contribution to our understanding of those heady days of early steam locomotive technology. The volume sets the record straight for those who care deeply about the technical and mechanical history of the early steam locomotive.

Richard Gibbon OBE

C Eng F I MechE
Former Head of Engineering at the
National Railway Museum 1989 to 2003

Acknowledgements

The writing of a book, although it may seem it, is not a solo task and I should like to thank all of those who have helped on the way. First and foremost Andy Mason for his shoulder to cry on, innumerable cups of coffee and his patience and assistance during research trips around the country. Secondly, the former railway staff and volunteers at the Science & Industry Museum in Manchester, in particular Matthew Jackson, Will High, Paul Dore, and Peter Brown for their friendship and encouragement over the past five years, and the unique opportunity of working hands-on with the replica *Planet* locomotive which was built at the museum and first steamed in 1992. This has given invaluable practical experience of firing, driving and maintaining an 1830s steam locomotive. Also to Matthew Jackson, David Boydell and Lauren Gradwell for the use of their photographs. Thanks too to National Museums Liverpool for the opportunity to physically examine, measure and record *Lion* – the sole surviving Liverpool & Manchester Railway locomotive – and also to staff at the NRM Search Engine. I should also like to thank Richard Gibbon OBE for peer-review of the text as well as his foreword.

Introduction

This book will chart the development of the locomotives, rolling stock and repair facilities of the Liverpool & Manchester Railway. Part one will examine the evolution of the 'standard' Stephenson locomotive; Part two experimental locomotives; Part three enginemen and firemen; Part four workshops, and Part five the rolling stock. Whilst this is a stand-alone work, it is best understood in conjunction with *The Liverpool & Manchester Railway: An Operating History* (Pen & Sword, 2020) which explores train working, safety practices and working regulations.

The Liverpool & Manchester Railway was the world's first double-track main line railway, and as such presented many operational and technological challenges, not least that locomotives hitherto had run at low speeds on relatively short colliery lines, and certainly not to a timetable. As has often been described, whilst the North East was the 'cradle of the railways' the Liverpool & Manchester was its 'nursery', particularly of the locomotive, which in the space of just over two years, was transformed from colliery engines like *Locomotion* to *Planet,* the first inter-city main line express passenger locomotive, delivered in October 1830.

The battle for the locomotive

Whilst it was one thing to build a public railway, how that railway should be run was a completely different challenge. The Board of Directors faced two challenges:

1. The type of motive power to work the railway.
2. How the railway was to be operated.

In both instances, the Board was divided, with influential opinions being sought on both sides, and in both instances they were making crucial decisions for the future development of the railway. In terms of motive power, the Board had three choices: horses, stationary engines, or locomotives. To many of the Board, the pre-1830 locomotive was crude and lumbering. George Stephenson (1781–1848), the principal engineer, had been a locomotive advocate for years and he was supported in this belief by the secretary and treasurer, Henry Booth (1789–1869). Another Board member, James Cropper (1773–1840), was decidedly against the locomotive and the Stephensons as well, eventually becoming a major opponent.[1]

'Must consume their own smoke'

The L&M Enabling Act had included references to locomotives, but the Act, however, prevented locomotives from making smoke under the penalty of a £50 fine. Hitherto all steam locomotives which had been built had been designed to burn coal; provisions of the Act meant that coke (a relatively smokeless fuel) would have to be used which presented novel engineering problems. In order to meet this new challenge, on 30 April 1827 the Board authorised Henry Booth and George Stephenson to carry out experiments:

> 'Of producing steam without Smoke … Mr Stephenson attended and having given his opinion that the Invention, if it succeeded on a large scale, would be highly important to the Company, he was directed to make any experiment requisite to decide the real merits of the scheme, it being understood that an expenditure of £100 be sufficient for the purpose.'

Stephenson reported the success of these experiments to the Board in January 1828 describing how a locomotive built with such a smoke-consuming boiler was 'likely to prove efficient and be free from the nuisance of smoke.' A drawing of the smoke-consuming boiler was presented and after much discussion, the Board agreed that 'The Engineer construct a locomotive engine on the principle and plan proposed' to be able to draw 20 tons of goods or 50 passengers; to weigh no more than 6 tons and to cost £550. This was the *Lancashire Witch*, and although being the first locomotive to be ordered by the Liverpool & Manchester Railway, it was destined never to work for the L&M, as thanks to influential Board members like Cropper who were concerned about Stephenson father and son having a monopoly, in April 1828 it was transferred to the Bolton & Leigh Railway. *Lancashire Witch* did, however, briefly return to the L&M for six months in late July 1829 to assist with ballast duties. She returned to the Bolton & Leigh in January 1830 to substitute for a broken-down *Sans Pareil* (Part 2). Thereafter her history is obscure.[2]

Lancashire Witch was the first coke-burning locomotive, and was also the first Stephenson locomotive with direct drive from the cylinders to the wheels. She was also the first locomotive built with inclined, rather than vertical cylinders which helped mitigate against the 'hammer blow' effect which damaged early track. This also allowed the fitting of springs to both axles to further prevent track damage. The wheels were wooden with cast iron hubs and a wrought-iron crank ring. Henry Booth's initial boiler design was of a 'double return flue'. In order to increase the heating surface, the main large diameter boiler flue branched into two smaller flues which ran parallel to the main flue on their return. There were two chimneys, and a single firebox which was fed alternately with coal and coke, so that the volatile gases given off by the coal would be properly burned by the coke fire and thus prevent smoke. Within the main flue were two water tubes, further increasing the heating surface. *Lancashire Witch* could also be worked expansively to use the steam more efficiently. In order to keep the through-put of gases high, Stephenson adopted existing technology from the smithing hearth or blast furnace: bellows. They were placed under the tender and driven by eccentrics, but as Braithwaite and Ericsson and Marc Séguin were also to discover, the bellows absorbed

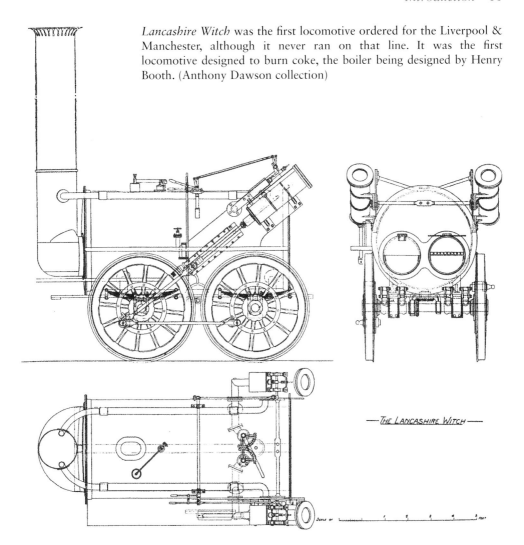

Lancashire Witch was the first locomotive ordered for the Liverpool & Manchester, although it never ran on that line. It was the first locomotive designed to burn coke, the boiler being designed by Henry Booth. (Anthony Dawson collection)

most of the power output of the locomotive. Although the use of bellows to provide a blast of high pressure air has been suggested to show that the Stephensons did not use nor were aware of the effect of the 'blast pipe', it is clear that they did. Crucially, the use of bellows, and a relatively soft blast characteristic, meant that *Lancashire Witch* worked with 'not the least noise about it.' This was an important consideration to prevent locomotives being seen as a 'nuisance' by influential and often anti-railway landowners along the line. Reduction of noise had also been a key consideration of George at Killingworth where he reduced the blast characteristics 'as far as practicable.' By burning coke and using bellows rather than a sharp blast characteristic, Stephenson was attempting to remove, or at least mitigate against the two nuisances of smoke and noise. And thereby placate the anti-railway, or anti-locomotive, lobby. *Lancashire Witch* was ultimately built with a twin flue boiler (each with its own firebox), which united to form a single chimney and the bellows were subsequently dispensed with. Exhaust steam was directed into the chimney with two up-turned 'eduction pipes.' She first ran on the Bolton & Leigh Railway on 1 August 1828 when she was named by Mrs Hulton, wife of the Chairman of the B&L.[3]

Some doubts were raised about the viability of locomotive traction when suggestions were made that the Stockton & Darlington were about to lay off locomotives in favour of horses in the summer of 1828. The Stockton & Darlington Railway had opened in 1825 with a fleet of four locomotives supplied by Robert Stephenson & Co.; although numbered and not named the four were later to be known as *Locomotion*, *Hope*, *Black Diamond*, and *Diligence*. They were small 0-4-0s with a large diameter flue tube running through the boiler and vertical cylinders. Even though the ruling gradient favoured loaded trains heading towards Stockton, they were often short of steam and the fires clinkered easily – something confirmed by experience of the replica of *Locomotion No 1*.[4] These locomotives were maintained by Timothy Hackworth (1786–1850), the superintendent of the stationary and locomotive engines. Hackworth was amongst the most experienced locomotive engineers in the country.

The L&M Board, however, had full confidence in Stephenson and indeed during April 1828 increased his salary to £1,500, the Board therefore not only expressing confidence in their Chief Engineer but by extension a locomotive-worked railway. Yet the Board could still not agree on how their railway was to be worked. Thus, in September 1828 they ordered:

'[From] the various and contradictory accounts which prevailed with respect to the power and relative economy of Locomotive Engines … considered desirable that one or two of the Directors, accompanied by the Treasurer, should proceed to Darlington to ascertain as correctly as practicable the results of the experience of that line, taking into account first cost, wear & tear, both of Engines & Road, and as far as possible all the circumstances involved in the question.'[5]

Henry Booth and James Cropper – representing both sides of the arguments of locomotives versus rope haulages – were deputed to Darlington, accompanied by John Moss the deputy chairman. Cropper submitted a report on the relative cost of moving goods by locomotives or fixed engines a week later, and which was passed to Stephenson for further comment but sadly this has been since lost. Further lengthy discussions took place during October. The Board also approached Nicholas Wood (1795–1865) of Killingworth Colliery to provide expert counsel on the matter but he declined unless he was able to carry out a personal inspection and receive more information on the matter. Booth and Cropper finally reported at the end of the October in favour of stationary engines, which was supported by a separate report presented to the board by Benjamin Thompson (1779-1867) of the Brunton & Shields Railway, although his report may have been biased by the fact he had recently (1821) taken out a patent on stationary engines and rope haulages. Thompson and George Stephenson had clashed before over locomotive versus stationary engines on the Stockton & Darlington. George Stephenson immediately produced his own report on the matter, which he presented to the Board on 5 November 1828, in which he repudiated many of the points made by Cropper and Booth:

'That locomotive engines will be found to do much more work upon the Liverpool & Manchester Line of Road than they can possibly do on the

Darlington Line, and that the wear and tear of Engine made on the improved plan [i.e. *Lancashire Witch*] will not be one half at present.'[6]

In his report Stephenson further reputed the claims that stationary engines and rope haulages were more efficient and cheaper; stationary engines required more capital outlay than locomotives, and the ropes were dangerous, especially where they crossed a public highway. Moreover, locomotives were more flexible in terms of operation; if one locomotive broke down traffic could continue, but if a single stationary engine broke down then traffic would have to be suspended until it was repaired. It was also cheaper to purchase additional locomotives rather than stationary engines. The smoke nuisance noted by Cropper and Booth had been successfully dealt with through the development of coke-burning boilers; the high cost of wear and tear on the S&D suggested that the L&M would have to use heavier rails and also pursue a six-wheel locomotive policy in order to reduce axle load. The only question to which Stephenson did not have a satisfactory answer was over the great weight of locomotives and trains sinking into Chat Moss, and proposed dividing trains in order to traverse it. He concluded:

'When these observations have been duly considered by the Directors, they will perceive that in point of convenience and dispatch the two systems [rope haulages versus locomotives] do not bear a comparison.'[7]

His report was discussed at the next Board meeting, and tempers may have become frayed between advocates of locomotives or rope haulages, with Stephenson steadfastly advocating the locomotive.[8] The Board was faced with a major decision and investment in expensive plant which it could not afford to get wrong.

Twin Sisters

Against this heated background is the order and delivery of *Twin Sisters*. This, the second locomotive ordered by the Company – but the first under its ownership – was under construction in December 1828. A note in the Board Minutes adds that on 26 November a delegation consisting of Robert Benson, James Cropper and James Bourne:

'inspect[ed] a coke boiler on <u>a new construction</u> which Mr Robert Stephenson got made at Wallasey, & which raised steam abundantly, without smoke – The Experiment appears satisfactory – H[enry] B[ooth].'[9]

Robert Stephenson also reported to Michael Longridge at Bedlington that 'we have had my new boiler tried at Mr Laird's' and that the experiment was completely successful, and even won over 'the enemies to the locomotive'.[10]

In order to expedite progress building the line, in March 1829 – i.e. a month before the proposal of the Rainhill Trials – the Board 'thought it desirable to work part of the line between the Marle Cutting at the West of Olive Mount and the Broad Green Embankment with a Locomotive Engine.' George Stephenson was 'directed to provide

Twin Sisters aka the *Liverpool Coke Engine* was the L&M's second locomotive. It gained its name from its unusual appearance with twin boilers and twin chimneys. (Liverpool & Manchester Railway Trust)

an engine for this purpose' which he reported would be ready in six to eight weeks. It had two vertical boilers and two chimneys (no doubt hence the *Twin Sisters* name); 9 x 24 inch cylinders mounted at 39° driving six coupled wheels four feet in diameter, developing about 12hp. The locomotive had arrived on or by 13 July 1829 and was at work by the middle of that month on the Olive Mount contract, where it did the work of 'about 10 horses' on construction duties, and was capable of moving the prodigious load of 54 tons at about 8mph. The boiler was refilled with warm water, heated by boilers placed at intervals along the line. *Twin Sisters* won fulsome praise from the local press who declared her 'the best … we have ever seen.' In early August 1829 *Twin Sisters* was used by George Stepehnson to carry out experiments into the best position of the 'exasrting pipe', and later in the month to carry William Huskisson and other VIPs on a tour of inspection of the as yet unfinished line. Having viewed the Sankey Viaduct, and the Rainhill Skew Arch, at Broad Green Huskisson and his party (numbering around twenty) took their seats in a waggon fitted with seats. This was coupled to the front of the engine and 'eight waggons contained upwards of 100 workmen were attached behind.' With this load *Twin Sisters* managed a speed of 10mph and conveyed the party through the Olive Mount cutting to Edgehill arriving with 'hearty cheers'. George Stephenson wrote to Michael Longridge how: '…The New Locomotive Engine works well and makes no Smoke – We had a grand day last Friday – Huskisson visited the greater part of the Line with the Directors – of course I was one of the party … at Olive Mount we were met by the Locomotive Engine which took the whole party amounting to about 135 through the deep cutting at the rate of 9 miles an hour to the great delight of the whole party. The Engine really did well.' She was still at work in February 1831 when she was involved in a fatal accident at Manchester. Like *Lancashire Witch*, she was never numbered or formally taken in stock, and was broken up in December 1831 and one of her cylinders used to work a water pump at Manchester.[11]

Walker and Rastrick Report

At the heated Board meeting of 6 November 1828, it was resolved to approach Benjamin Thompson with a view of sending a second deputation to the North East to observe a railway worked by stationary engines and ropes in action. Via James Cropper, John Braithwaite of London provided his expert opinion that the line should be worked by fixed engines. Richard Miles (latterly of the Stockton & Darlington) however reported in favour of locomotives. Thus far, the odds were greatly stacked against Stephenson and the locomotive. Cooler heads prevailed, however, and the Board resolved to seek the counsel of two prominent engineers, James Walker (1781-1862) of London and John Urpeth Rastrick (1780-1856) of Stourbridge:[12]

'To undertake a Journey to Darlington, Newcastle, and the neighbourhood, to ascertain by actual inspection & investigation the comparative merits of Fixed Engines and Locomotives as a moving power on Railways, and especially with reference to the Liverpool & Manchester line.'[13]

Walker and Rastrick were in Liverpool in January 1829 where they received their instructions from the Board, to ascertain 'the comparative expense of conveying Goods on a Railway' by locomotive or fixed engine, which included a minimum stipulation of 8mph for passenger trains. The two engineers were to ignore the clause in the Company's Act which forbade the emission of smoke, as none of the railways they were to visit had to operate under such a clause. In the meantime, during December 1828 George Stephenson had travelled the North East, to 'Darlington and the Collieries in the Neighbourhood of Newcastle' to make his own study. He was accompanied by Joseph Locke and the pair carried out experiments 'relative to the working of Locomotive and Fixed engines.' He reported his findings to the Board at the end of the month, and a printed version was presented on 5 January 1829, including costs and estimates of working the Liverpool & Manchester 'on the two systems'. Reports were also received from Benjamin Thompson in favour of rope haulages. Thompson noted that the cost of working the L&M by his patent system was 0.2134 penny per ton per mile compared to 0.2787 of a penny per ton per mile worked by locomotives; as a result the Board thought in terms of '*economy, dispatch, safety,* and *convenience*… [the] *stationary reciprocating system the best*' and, according to Thompson, the Board recommended its adoption in 'very decided terms.'[14] However, George Stephenson, Henry Booth, and Charles Tayleur (representing the locomotive interest) visited the Shutt End Colliery Railway of Lord Dudley in late August, where one of John Rastrick's engines was at work, upon which they reported favourably to the Board. This was *The Agenoria* (now preserved at the National Railway Museum in York): 'the engine moved smoothly from 9 to 12 miles per hour with about 20 tons of coal in 6 waggons. The Engine made very little puffing noise so common in Locomotive Engines.' *Agenoria* 'exhibited the practicality of moving at a speed from 10 to 12 miles per hour with ease and smoothness.' They were very impressed by the use of a gauge glass for measuring the amount of water in the boiler.[15]

Walker and Rastrick reported back to the Board in March 1829 also in favour of stationary engines and rope haulages. Thus it seemed that the stationary engine would carry the day, but in April the Board requested Stephenson make his own reply to Walker and Rastrick, which he was to submit in writing.[16] Stephenson wrote to a friend that he believed that locomotives 'will ultimately get the day ... locomotives shall not be cowardly given up. *I will fight for them until the last.* They are worthy of a conflict.' Robert sought the counsel of other locomotive advocates including Hackworth, who was convinced that the Liverpool & Manchester would be best worked by locomotives:

> 'Stationary engines, are by no means adapted to a Public line of Railway. I take here no account of the great waste of Capital but you will fail in proving to the satisfaction of one not conversant with these subjects, the inexpediency of such a system – it never can do for coaching – passengers cannot be accommodated – if endless ropes are used, there will be both danger and delay.'[17]

Hackworth provided technical information from the day-to-day operation of the Stockton & Darlington which helped refute Rastrick and Walker, describing how locomotives could pull a useful load, and up an incline. Hackworth concluded by telling Stephenson:

> 'I hear the Liverpool Co. have concluded to use fixed Engines. Some will look on with surprise; but as you can well afford it, it is all for the good of science, & the trade, to try both plans. Do not discompose yourself, my dear Sir, if you express your manly, firm, and decided opinion, you have done your part, as there [sic] adviser. And, if it happen to be read someday in the newspaper – whereas the Liverpool & Manchester Railway has been strangled by ropes, we shall not accuse you of guilt in being accessory either before or after the fact.'[18]

This clearly placed the Board in a quandary. Although Rastrick and Walker had argued in favour of fixed engines, it was not the 'knock out' blow that opponents to the locomotive such as Cropper had hoped for. Stephenson had mobilised his fellow locomotive advocates and provided a skilful riposte: locomotives could climb hills, were cheaper, and more flexible in operation – the whole system would be paralysed if a single stationary engine broke down, but not so by locomotives.[19] Fortunately there was a strong pro-locomotive lobby on the Board led by Henry Booth who seized upon Stephenson and Locke's report.[20] Furthermore, Rastrick and Walker had offered an optimistic suggestion for a way of breaking this apparent impasse:

> 'To enable you to take advantage of improvements which might be made [in steam locomotion]; with a view to encourage which, and to draw the attention

of Engine makers to the subject, something in the way of a premium … might be held to the person whose Engine should, upon experience, be found to answer the Best. The Rainhill [stationary] Engines would at the same time enable you to judge of the comparative advantages of the two systems.'[21]

Finally at the Board meeting of 20 April 1829, and after much discussion, it was resolved to postpone the debate on locomotive versus rope haulage until the *Twin Sisters* had been delivered and an actual comparison made. Furthermore, in order that the Board could benefit from any 'mechanical improvements in the conveyances of Carriages on Railways which may hereafter take place' they offered a premium of £500 for the:

'Locomotive Engine which shall be a decided improvement on those now in use, as respects to the consumption of smoke, increased speed, adequate power, and moderate weight.'[22]

Thus, in order to ascertain the type of motive power to be used on the railway, the Rainhill Trials were held in October 1829. The Rainhill Trials were not only to help aid the choice of the best means of motive power available, but also to allow other engineers to showcase their work, to challenge what men like James Cropper feared would be a Stephenson monopoly on the L&M. The Rainhill Trials were as much a forum for the locomotive as it was for George and Robert Stephenson.

Of the 'multifarious schemes' entered, four locomotives were finally selected: *Rocket* by George and Robert Stephenson and Henry Booth; *Novelty* by John Braithwaite and Captain John Ericsson; *Sans Pareil* by Timothy Hackworth and *Perseverance* by Timothy Burstall. The winner, of course, was *Rocket* which showed the triumph of the locomotive over rope haulages and stationary engines for working a timetabled public railway for passengers and goods.[23]

Civic opposition

Having won over a sceptical Board to the merits of locomotives, the final hurdle was the civic authorities in Liverpool and Manchester. The Liverpool Common Council forbade the working of locomotives within the town limits, which meant that the passenger station at Crown Street was on the edge of town. The steep (1:48) incline down from Edge Hill to Wapping also precluded the use of locomotives and the line down to Wapping was worked by rope haulage until the 1890s. The extension to the more central Lime Street (opened in 1836) was also cable worked due to the bar on locomotives and the steep incline; locomotive working at Lime Street commenced only as late as 1870.[24] In Manchester Miss Eleanora Byrom, who owned land where the Liverpool Road terminus was built, similarly forbade the passage of locomotives over the Irwell or over her property without written consent. This agreement was enshrined in the 1829 Act, so too the clause inserted by the Byroms that 'engines must consume their own smoke.' The Manchester town council only agreed to the use of locomotives so long as such use was approved by the surveyor of highways and the police commissioner, and so long as locomotives were used on railway-owned land.

However, the tour of inspection on 28 August 1830 caused Miss Byrom considerable consternation as a locomotive had been worked over the Irwell and into Manchester without her consent. John Moss visited Miss Byrom to apologise for the transgression and, via their respective legal counsel, came to an understanding whereby locomotives were able to work into the Manchester terminus, 'which would afford the opportunity of ascertaining whether the Engines, on their present improved construction, were at all objectionable to the neighbourhood.' In case an agreement could not be reached the Board considered the option of terminating trains at Ordsall Lane and hiring 'a competent person' and a number of 'Hackney Coaches' to take passengers forward to Liverpool Road. Happily as locomotives did not prove to be a nuisance and an agreement was reached, locomotives could cross the Irwell.[25]

Working the line

As with choice of motive power, the Board were similarly divided as to how the railway would be operated; whether to lease the operation of the line to a separate company; whether to lease the operation of the line but to own the locomotives (and perhaps the rolling stock); or whether to operate the line themselves owning all the track, locomotives, rolling stock and warehouses. There were two working models to inform the Board: the canals where a single company owned all the infrastructure and route-way but leased its operation to one or more individual companies; or the turnpikes, which were open to all users.

Despite the Act authorising the Company to operate as a carrier in its own right, thanks to anti-monopoly, free-trade Directors such as James Cropper and his Quaker Allies (Robert Benson and William Rotherham) the prevailing opinion of the Board was to lease the operation of their line, rather as the canals did. Leasing the line also found favour with the likes of John Moss who noted that doing so would save the Company a considerable outlay of capital. By the summer of 1828 this decision had seemingly been reversed with the Board agreeing that the Company *would* act as a carrier and would also provide warehouse space at each end of the line. In order to do so, a further £127,000 had to be raised through the sale of additional shares. The board swung back towards leasing operations in autumn 1828 and overtures were made to existing carriers such as stage coach proprietors Lacey & Allen of Manchester to work the passenger side of the business, and the New Quay Company, water-borne carriers from Liverpool to Manchester, to work the goods side. By leasing the goods side of the business to the New Quay Co. the railway company could forego all the costs of providing its own warehouses, and in the opinion of John Moss, leasing operation of the goods side would be more profitable than working it by the Company itself. Furthermore, unlike the Company, the New Quay Co. had considerable experience of organising and running a transportation business. In its proposed agreement with the New Quay Co. the Company would provide the locomotives and rolling stock, for which the New Quay Co. would pay a hire fee, a situation somewhat similar to the present privatised network in Britain where one company owns the track and infrastructure whilst a train operating company tenders for the right to operate trains and hires locomotives and stock to do so. In February 1830, however, neither the Liverpool & Manchester nor the New Quay Co. had been able to come to a final agreement and thus the Board took the decision that the Railway Company would become common carrier on its own line: it would own all the infrastructure, locomotives and rolling stock and work its own trains. The Liverpool & Manchester were not to enjoy a monopoly on their line, as from May 1831 the Board agreed to allow other railway companies to run over its metals, as well as privately owned waggons and locomotives, such as those owned by the Haydock Colliery.[26]

Locomotive department

As this author has previously described, the Liverpool & Manchester Railway was formed into four operating departments: Engineers'; Coaching; Carrying; Coal. The Engineers' Department was by far the largest and costliest. It was headed by the principal engineer of which the L&M had three between 1826 and amalgamation in 1845:

> George Stephenson 1826–1831 (to 1833 as 'consulting engineer')
> John Dixon 1833–1836
> Edward Woods 1836–1845 (resigned from the L&M section of the LNWR in 1852)

Beneath the 'principal engineer' were on-the-spot resident engineers, including the aforementioned John Dixon (1795–1865), William Allcard (1809–1861) and Joseph Locke (1805–1860). In other words the engineers who had supervised the construction of the line were also expected to exercise a supervisory role over the purchase, maintenance and operation of the locomotives owned by the Company when it commenced operations. Locke resigned in 1830 but the rest of this team remained in place until May 1833 when each submitted a letter of resignation, probably following a very public dispute with Dr. Dionysius Lardner concerning the alleged Stephenson monopoly of the L&M. Edward Woods (1814–1903) was appointed as principal engineer at the tender age of twenty-two with the equally youthful William Barber Buddicom (1816–1887) as his assistant.

The principal engineer had control over both the civil and mechanical engineering of the Company, and in the latter was assisted in the day-to-day running and maintenance of the locomotive fleet through the locomotive and shed foremen. At first job specifications seem to have been vague and overlapped. The first locomotive foreman was Anthony Harding. He was sacked for gross misconduct in 1833 and replaced by John Melling (1782–1856), the foreman of the repairing shops, who assumed the twin duties of locomotive and workshop foreman. Melling is perhaps the 'unsung hero' of the Liverpool & Manchester as it was to him that responsibility for keeping the trains moving fell between 1833 and January 1840. He was of an inventive turn of mind and patented several of his ideas. Finally, John Dewrance (c.1803–1861) was appointed as locomotive superintendent, and together with his chief Edward Woods completely renewed the locomotive fleet by the time of the Liverpool & Manchester's amalgamation with the Grand Junction Railway in summer 1845.[27]

PART 1

THE STEPHENSON LOCOMOTIVE

CHAPTER 1

From *Rocket* to *Northumbrian*

The success of *Rocket* at the Rainhill Trials of October 1829 resulted in the Board ordering four locomotives 'on the principle of the 'Rocket'' from Robert Stephenson & Co on 26 October 1829; the *Manchester Courier* proudly announcing the purchase. But this should not be seen as a fait accompli for the Stephensons as James Cropper and his allies challenged the perceived Stephenson monopoly by, albeit unsuccessfully, promoting locomotives by Goldsworthy Gurney of London. At this date the Company had only four locomotives: *Lancashire Witch*, *Twin Sisters*, *Sans Pareil* (see Part 2) and *Rocket*. Of these, *Lancashire Witch* was on temporary loan from the Bolton & Leigh Railway, and where *Sans Pareil* was also on hire because it would not burn coke, eventually being sold to that line in March 1832. This left only *Rocket* and *Twin Sisters*, both of which were used on ballast and other permanent way duties: *Twin Sisters* at the Liverpool End and *Rocket* on ballast and other permanent way duties: *Twin Sisters* at the Liverpool End and *Rocket* on

the Chat Moss section. Edward Bury's *Dreadnought* (see Part 2) was also reported to be at work on permanent way duties, probably on hire.

Immediately after Rainhill, *Rocket* was used in a series of 'public relations' exercises, and on 19 October 1829 *Rocket* was put on the Chat Moss contract working ballast trains. It was on Chat Moss in November 1829 that a local publican, Henry Hunter, was killed when *Rocket* was derailed whilst propelling a train of ballast waggons. One of her carrying wheels broke on New Year's day 1830 during experiments across Chat Moss, and a new pair was quickly substituted. The Press reported that the wheel which had broken had been 'previously injured' and the axle bent. *Rocket* was involved in yet another accident in February 1831 when one of her wooden driving wheels broke in Olive Mount cutting; the existing wheels and axles on the locomotive probably date from this accident. She was hired to the Wigan Branch Railway, and

Origin of the species: *Rocket (No. 1)*. Remains of the original *Rocket* returned to Liverpool Road station, Manchester, during 2018. (Ian Hardman)

then subsequently laid up as a 'stand by' engine until 1833 when she was used as the test-bed for Lord Dundonald's unsuccessful rotary steam engine.[1]

As soon as the next batch of locomotives were delivered, *Rocket* was obsolete; *Rocket* was in effect a proof of concept, rather than a production locomotive and underwent various in-service modifications to improve her operational flexibility, including provision of a buffer beam and lowering the cylinders during a very brief working life on the L&M. Edward Woods noted in the 1880s that 'the Rocket was not frequently used, and rarely, if ever, in the service of the ordinary traffic on the line. It was, in fact, not sufficiently powerful for the service.'[2]

The next four locomotives were 'production locomotives', but were still in effect dynamic prototypes as lessons were still being learned by Robert Stephenson and his team at Forth Street during a frenetic 33-month period of locomotive development. Given the long absence of Robert Stephenson from Forth Street, it is likely much of the development was led by Phipps, the chief draughtsman, and William Hutchinson, the foreman. Indeed the Liverpool & Manchester Railway provided a ready test track which meant that the Stephensons could see their locomotives at work and modify them in the light of experience gained in operation.

These four locomotives incorporated: Henry Booth's revolutionary multi-tubular boiler and a separate, water-jacketed firebox; cylinders with a direct connection to

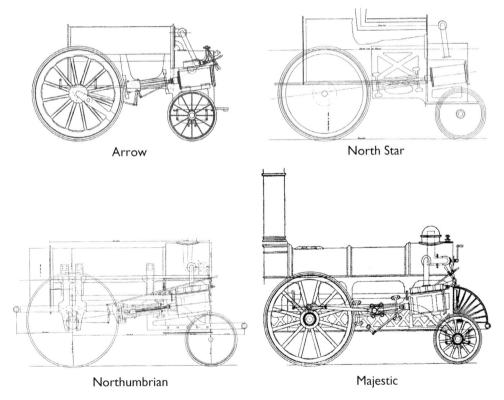

Arrow   North Star

Northumbrian   Majestic

Evolution of the 'Rocket Type': *Arrow* delivered January 1830; *North Star* (August); *Northumbrian* (July) and *Majestic* (December) all drawn to the same scale, showing a gradual increase in size, and strengthening of the frames and cylinder mounting. (After Warren, 1923)

the driving wheels; and a blast pipe in the chimney. These new locomotives were not to exceed five tons in weight and were to be delivered in three months from the date of order. The *Manchester Courier* announced that with 90 boiler tubes these new locomotives would be 'swifter, more powerful, and compact' than *Rocket*. The first delivered was *Wildfire* aka *Meteor*, outshopped from Forth Street 7 January 1830 and tried in the yard at Forth Street 'before a large party' of gentlemen and their ladies; *Comet* followed on 21 January; *Arrow* on 4 February and *Dart* on 25 February. *Wildfire* and *Comet* had arrived at Liverpool by 1 February 1830, when they were duly named by the Board, who also ordered that trials be carried out to 'ascertain the power of the Engine, and the quantity of coke consumed.'[3]

Wildfire made a spectacular debut:

> 'The Cylinders are larger, and placed almost horizontally, and the diameter of the wheels is four inches greater … These alterations are expected to give the new engine greater speed, and to make its motion more regular and steady. There had also been an improvement made in means of stopping it, by which it may be brought to a stand still almost instantly … it exhibited a grand and imposing sight … and, as the engine was approaching its maximum velocity, it continued to vomit out from the top of the chimney sparks, and masses of blazing coke, which gave the machine the appearance of a moving volcano, scattering fire-balls and red-hot cinders as it darted along the road, illuminating the air and throwing a transient glare on the countenances of the astonished bystanders … aptly enough illustrated the name of "Wildfire" which is given to it.'[4]

In order to increase the heating surface in a boiler 6 feet long and 3 feet diameter, the number of tubes was increased to 88 of 2 inches outside diameter (those of *Rocket* were 3 inches)[5], although other sources indicate 90 tubes (*Meteor*) or 92 tubes (*Arrow*).[6] Cylinders were 10 x 16 inches (compared to 8 x 16½ of *Rocket*) and the valve chest was now on top of the cylinder; those of *Rocket* had been underneath due to fears of condensation or water being carried over. The wooden driving wheels had cast iron hubs, wrought-iron tyres and in lieu of wrought-iron crank ring, a wrought- iron strap supported the spherical crank pins. These wheels were 5 feet in diameter (those of *Rocket* were 4ft 8½ins) which would become the standard on the L&M, with two exceptions, until 1845.[7] The use of 5 feet diameter driving wheels was inherited from the road coach tradition where experiments by General Desauliers in the 1770s had shown that a 5 foot wheel was the optimum size at speeds from 10–12mph. Stability of the locomotive, especially at speed, was achieved through lowering the cylinders from 38° to 8°. The replica of *Rocket* has a pronounced 'waddle' because of the position of the cylinders, and a high centre of gravity. Experience from the replica suggests that the cylinder mounting plates flexed, and as a result keeping everything steam-tight became a major issue. Although stipulated to have a maximum weight of 5 tons, upon delivery *Arrow* was found to weigh 5 tons 14 cwt 2 qr. *Rocket* was subsequently modified to conform (where possible) with these later locomotives, including lowering and inverting the cylinders (January 1831) and provision of a smokebox (probably in February 1831). She was also provided with a front buffer beam to improve operational flexibility and the original somewhat flimsy bar frame strengthened with additional bracing. *Arrow* underwent trials in June 1830, organised by Hardman Earle. On the footplate with George Stephenson was Rev. William Scoresby FSA (1789-1857), scientist and arctic explorer, who timed the run. With a gross trailing load of 33 tons she ran from Liverpool to Manchester in 1 hour 46 minutes, having been assisted up the Whiston incline by *Dart*. She attained a maximum speed of 25mph.[8] *Meteor* was involved in an accident when working in December 1830. As was the custom after dark, a Pilot Engine was run head, but it ran too far ahead of *Meteor* and her train. At Rainhill some platelayers attempted to cross the line with their lurry. Despite the Constable on duty waving his red lamp *Meteor* crashed into the lurry, and came off the rails and one wheel was broken. No passengers were hurt. *Rocket* which had been at work on ballast duties near by was used to take the train forward to Liverpool.[9]

Phoenix and *North Star* were ordered by the Board in February 1830; *Phoenix* was delivered in June 1830, and *North Star* in August, both costing £600.[10] Both were larger than the four preceding locomotives; their boiler barrels were 6 inches longer and cylinders increased in size to 11 x 16 inches which would become the standard for the next few years. They also used 'double slide valves' whereas the early locomotives had used a single slide valve. Double slide valves would be standard practice until May 1832. The pair were also provided with a steam dome, steam riser and internal steam pipes to help prevent priming and to improve thermal efficiency; despite the 1979 replica of *Rocket* being so provided, provision of a steam dome etc. was a later modification in November 1830.[11] Colburn (1871) states there were 90 copper tubes in the boiler, 2 inches diameter and 6 feet 6 inches long, providing a heating surface of 306 square feet; the firebox added a further 20 square feet. *Phoenix* was able to evaporate 41 cubic feet of water per hour, whereas *Arrow* could evaporate 34.4 cubic feet of water per hour. This larger heating surface meant *Phoenix* burned less coke per ton per mile than *Arrow*: 0.67lb compared to 0.78lbs.[12] In order to ease maintenance, the pair were provided with the first proper smokebox – a forward extension of the

Phoenix (No. 6) (June 1830) as depicted in a lithograph by Crane, in company with the 'curtain coach' *Queen Adelaide*; the central compartment had drop-light windows whilst the end two had leather curtains. (Anthony Dawson collection)

Ackermann's beautifully observed drawing of *North Star (No. 8)* (August 1830); note the name and star motif painted on the tender water cask.(Anthony Dawson collection)

boiler barrel, enclosing the blast pipe and end of the tubes, with a narrower ash box below.[13] This was a marked improvement on *Rocket et al* where the metal ducting at the base of the chimney was found to rapidly clog with ashes, and had to be removed to both empty out the ashes and char but also sweep the tubes.

One of *North Star*'s tender axles broke on Sunday 17 October 1830 when she was the 'Pilot Engine' – sent ahead about a quarter of a mile, carrying a large 'lamp with powerful reflector' to ensure the way was clear for the passenger train which was following close behind. As she was crossing Chat Moss close to Manchester an axle broke, so the locomotive crew uncoupled the stranded tender, lifted it off the rails and continued to Manchester without it.[14] This was one of several accidents involving the breaking of tender wheels or axles, all of which had been made by Michael Longridge at Bedlington Iron Works. The Board instructed George Stephenson to prepare new wheels with wooden spokes and fellows and a wrought iron tyre instead of the all-iron ones hitherto in use. A letter of complaint was also sent to Bedlington. The matter was passed over to the Coach Committee who reported in November that the broken wheels and axles sent from Bedlington had been inspected by two competent blacksmiths who found them to have been made from 'inferior iron.' A copy of the report was sent to Bedlington.[15] George Stephenson complained to Michael Longridge about the quality of iron, welding and workmanship, and recommended the use of 'Foreign Iron [i.e. Swedish], or perhaps the best Low Moor' for the tyres ('hoops') which should be at least quarter of an inch thicker.[16]

Phoenix was involved in an accident in March 1831 at Broad Green:

'The *Phoenix* engine, assisted by the *North Star*, was conveying merchandise towards Manchester, the wheel came into contact with a plank [left across the rails], and the engine was thrown off the rails. A young man named Thomas Wright, about eighteen years of age, who was acting as fireman to the *Phenix* [sic.], and standing on the engine at the time of the accident, was thrown off; and the water cask falling upon his head crushed it to atoms... His brother was the overseer of the workmen, through whose carelessness the misfortune was occasioned.'[17]

William Allcard arranged a series of trials between three different generations of locomotives during the week between 28 November and 6 December 1830, concluding that *Planet* was the most efficient: *Planet* was burning on average 19¾lbs of coke per mile; *Phoenix* 27lbs; *North Star* 28¾lbs; *Arrow* 24lbs; *Meteor* 22lbs, clearly showing the advantages of *Planet*'s larger boiler, firebox and general arrangement.[18]

Northumbrian

The final evolution of the 0-2-2 'Rocket' type were *Northumbrian* and *Majestic*. *Northumbrian* represented a considerable advance on the earlier designs; a 'modern' locomotive boiler with a smokebox at one end and firebox within the boiler barrel at the opposite, inside plate frames and the use of proper horns and guides for the driving wheels. She was delivered in late July 1830 (a fortnight before *North Star*) at a cost of £700. *Majestic* followed on 20 November for £800 and was 'put to work' in January 1831.[19] The increased cost of *Northumbrian* was, reported Robert Stephenson, due to a rise in the price in copper and 'superior workmanship of the Engines.' She arrived at Liverpool by sea in early August 1830. Two additional locomotives incorporating the 'latest improvements' and to weigh no more than 5 tons had been ordered on 21 June 1830 from Stephenson & Co., and two more were ordered a couple of weeks later.[20] In working order *Northumbrian* weighed 7 tons 6 cwt 3 qr, (only just within the maximum weight stipulation of the L&M Act of 8 tons) of which 4 tons 1 qr was carried on the driving wheels. She was 14 feet long overall, and the width between cylinder centres was 5ft 8in and 12ft 6in from the railhead to the top of her chimney. *Northumbrian*'s boiler was 6 feet 6 inches long, 3 feet in diameter and contained 132 copper tubes 1 5/8inch diameter; her grate area was 6.11sq ft, providing a heating surface of 32.75sq ft and the tubes a further 379sq ft. Warren estimated her to have a tractive effort of 1,100lbs.[21] Whilst *Rocket*, *Arrow et al* had used bar frames composed from wrought iron bar 4in x 1in, *Northumbrian* used a primitive form of plate frames, using 1inch thick iron plates on edge. This would have been stronger under compression than the simple bar frames of *Rocket*, which demonstrate several, although not necessarily always successful, attempts to stiffen them. They were joined fore and aft by a rolled iron tube through which passed a threaded iron bar and the whole assembly was bolted together. Horn guides and cylinder mounting plates were then riveted to the plate frames. The boiler was supported on two brackets at each end of the barrel and the cylinder mounting plates were supported by the firebox. The

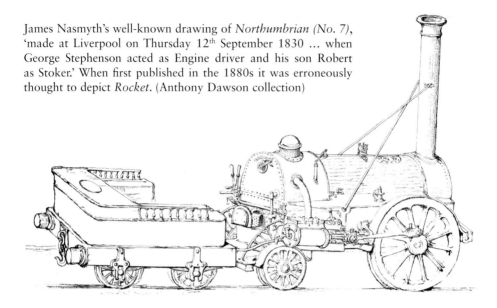

James Nasmyth's well-known drawing of *Northumbrian (No. 7)*, 'made at Liverpool on Thursday 12th September 1830 ... when George Stephenson acted as Engine driver and his son Robert as Stoker.' When first published in the 1880s it was erroneously thought to depict *Rocket*. (Anthony Dawson collection)

wheels were an improvement on earlier designs, having a cast-iron egg-shaped hub which carried the crank pin, and into which the wooden spokes were fitted, similar to those wheels now carried by Rocket.[22]

Northumbrian's delivery and performance trials coincided with that of Braithwaite and Ericsson's *William IV* and *Queen Adelaide* – despite the praise sung by the biased *Mechanics' Magazine*, both were failures, and a considerable war of words erupted between the supporters of Braithwaite and Ericsson and those of Robert Stephenson.[23] The performance of *Northumbrian* was observed by two Scottish engineers, Messrs. Grainger and Buchanan, on 16 and 17 September 1830. They estimated her to be 14 horse power, and with a gross trailing load of 20 tons she achieved a maximum speed of 25mph on the level. The *Mechanics' Magazine* sought to repudiate these claims, by grossly underestimating the weight of loaded passenger carriages at only 1¼ tons, to argue that *Northumbrian* was inferior to the engines of Braithwaite and Ericsson.[24] *Majestic* followed in December 1830, and in light of the various accidents involving broken wheels and axles, had both locomotive and tender wheels made from wood, 'which is found to be less liable to accidents than metal'. In January 1831 *Majestic* is recorded as having run six times between Liverpool and Manchester in one day, the total load carried being 140 tons.[25] The regular driver of *Majestic* was Jack Haslan, who is recorded when a heavy train stalled on Sutton Incline, as having 'screwed the spring-balance down, did not say a word to the fireman but walked up the line and shouted to the engine "Come on your beggar!". Upon reaching the summit, he jumped on board and shut the regulator. A similar story is told by Mark Wakefield about the *Rocket*.[26] Just as the locomotive developed apace, so too did tenders. The Board ordered that, in order to increase the range of the locomotives, that George Stephenson come up with some plan of carrying more water. He did so by introducing iron tanks in lieu of the wooden water casks and such tenders are shown by Ackermann. The tenders of *Northumbrian* and *Majestic* were the next step in development, incorporating a

C-shaped iron water tank which enclosed three sides of the tender, with a coke space between both 'wings.' This design was later adopted by the Planet class.

It was with these eight locomotives that the Liverpool & Manchester was opened on 15 September 1830, with *Northumbrian* pulling the Ducal carriage. With the introduction of the suite of Planet locomotives from October 1830 these engines rapidly became obsolete. *North Star* or *Majestic* (which were presumably then not in front-line service) were loaned to the St Helens & Runcorn Gap Railway in November 1831 for £20 per month, 'to be returned in good working order.'[27] A year later *Comet* was sold to the railway contractor William Mackenzie (1794–1854) for £250 and *North Star* for £275 in 1833. *North Star* was subsequently sold on by Mackenzie to the Leeds & Selby Railway in October 1834 for £350. The L&S were in crisis as only a single locomotive, *Nelson* (Fenton, Murray & Jackson), had been delivered, three additional locomotives ordered from Edward Bury in Liverpool not arriving until the end of November:

> 'The N. Star Locomotive Engine & Tender complete, £350; Carriage of same from Wapping to the Leeds & Liverpool Canal, £2 15s; loading at Wapping 10s; extras getting engine down to Wapping and loading on to road £1 12s 6d. A Total of £354 17s 6d.'[28]

The engine was paid for in instalments, and Mackenzie made a profit of £75 on this transaction.[29]

A new pair of wooden driving wheels was purchased for *Dart* in November 1830 costing £42.[30] She was out of service by summer 1832 and the Board offered her to 'Mr [John] Ward, Patentee of Gurney's Steam Carriage' as the test-bed for a locomotive based on Goldsworthy Gurney's (1793–1875) patent boiler. Gurney had first been introduced to the Board by his fellow Quaker, James Cropper, in 1829, offering the suggestion that he build them a locomotive. Gurney had sold rights (worth £32,000) to Ward to build and operate his patent steam coach between London and Liverpool in 1826; Gurney had been forced to close down his loss-making steam carriage manufactory in 1831, and this attempted move into the locomotive market appears to have been an effort to restore some of his business. Instead of utilising a rebuilt *Dart*, Ward contracted to supply a complete locomotive, 'equal in all respects' to the *Victory*, but despite lengthy negotiations no locomotive was ever built.[31]

Arrow was laid up in Manchester in 1834, as in June of that year one James Naylor tried to steal 'a spring balance and other brass work … worth all together thirty shillings' from the locomotive. He was brought before the magistrates and sentenced to two months' hard labour.[32] During 1832 it was proposed to rebuild *Phoenix* as a Planet type, but she was instead dismantled and parts of her used in the feed water apparatus for the Edge Hill tunnel engines.[33] But what of *Northumbrian* and *Rocket*? Both were sold in 1836, having been out of use for some time. *Northumbrian* was offered for sale as a ballast engine to the London & Birmingham Railway for £450 in January 1836 but the offer was declined and she was probably broken up soon after. *Rocket* was sold in October 1836 to James Thompson of Carlisle for £300, to work on the Kirkhouse Colliery Railway owned by the Earl of Carlisle. She was withdrawn from service around 1840 before eventually passing to the Patent Office Museum (now the Science Museum) in 1862.[34]

Table 1: Rocket-type (0-2-2) locomotives on the Liverpool & Manchester Railway

Locomotive	Date	Cylinders	Boiler	Tubes	Size	Notes
Rocket (1)	September 1829	8 x 16½ins	6ft x 3ft 4ins	25	3ins outside diameter	Sold October 1836 to James Thompson.
Wildfire alias *Meteor* (3)	January 1830	10 x 16ins	6ft x 3ft	90	2ins outside diameter	
Comet (5)	January 1830	10 x 16ins	6ft x 3ft	88	2ins outside diameter	Sold 1832 for £250.
Arrow (2)	February 1830	10 x 16ins	6ft x 3ft	92	2ins outside diameter	Out of service by 1834 Sold 1840 £50.
Dart (4)	February 1830	10 x 16ins	6ft x 3ft	88	2ins outside diameter	Out of service by 1832.
Phoenix (6)	June 1830	11 x 16ins	6ft 6ins x 3ft	90	2ins outside diameter?	Dismantled 1832.
Northumbrian (8)	July 1830	11 x 16ins	6ft 6ins x 3ft	132	1 5/8ins	Offered for sale January 1836 £450.
North Star (7)	August 1830	11 x 16ins	6ft 6ins x 3ft	90	2ins outside diameter?	Sold 1833 for £275.
Majestic (10)	December 1830	11 x 16ins	6ft 6ins x 3ft	130	1 5/8ins	

CHAPTER 2

The Planet class

For all the success of *Rocket* and her kin in working the first timetabled passenger trains between Liverpool and Manchester, if the service was to expand both in frequency of trains, and in their gross load, faster and more powerful locomotives were required. The answer lay in Robert Stephenson's Planet class of which the L&M would have sixteen examples; *Planet* was the first 'inter-city express passenger locomotive', and as members of the class arrived during 1831, they revolutionised passenger and goods travel.

The titular member of the class, *Planet* was completed on 3 September 1830, just twelve days before the Liverpool & Manchester Railway was to be opened by the Duke of Wellington. She was delivered, by sea, to Liverpool on 4 October 1830 when she was named '*Planet*'. She underwent running trials during October and November. *Planet* represents the first 'modern' locomotive, and incorporated design features which would become standard on locomotives for the next 130 years.[1] As Dr. Michael Bailey has stated the delivery of *Planet* was the culmination of:

'An extraordinary period of research and development by Robert Stephenson and his close colleagues in the 33 months between January 1828 and September 1830.'[2]

The working replica of *Planet (No. 9)* was built by the Friends of the Museum of Science & Industry in Manchester, and first steamed in 1992. (Anthony Dawson)

Over forty members of the class were built, principally by Robert Stephenson & Co., but also by other makers under licence, including Charles Tayleur & Co. of Newton-le-Willows, and Fenton, Murray & Jackson of Leeds. A similar number was built in the United States, and examples were also built in France. The major innovations of *Planet* included:

- A boiler with an inner firebox as part of the boiler shell.
- A proper smoke box.
- A steam dome, steam riser, and internal steam pipe.
- Cylinders set low down at the front of the locomotive, working a cranked driving axle.
- The use of sandwich frames.
- The use of leaf springs, horns, and horn guides.

Moving the cylinders to a near-horizontal position at the front of the locomotive made the locomotive far more stable. The *Manchester Guardian* opined that:

'Though the engines constructed in this manner were found to be very much more effective than any that had been previously in use, they still laboured under one obvious defect, by which their power was obviously impaired. As the two engines [cylinders], working out by alternate strokes, and communicated power to the *outsides of* the carriage, each stroke had a tendency to move that side of the carriage to which it was applied, at a quicker rate than the opposite side; the alternate advancing of the fore-wheels caused considerable unsteadiness of motion, which entirely disappeared when the steam was off ... In consequence of this defect, Mr Stephenson ... determined to try the effect of placing the cylinders beneath the boiler, and communicate the power to the wheels by means of two cranks in the axle ... This plan was reduced to practice in the construction of the *Planet*, and its consequences were immediately apparent in the steadiness of motion, and the very great working power of that engine ... We believe it was estimated that her effective power was nearly one-third greater than that of other engines of equal size, but made on the old principle.'[3]

By placing the cylinders beneath the smoke box, Stephenson increased their thermal efficiency, helping to reduce the formation of condensation by keeping them warm. But there was considerable later controversy arising from this decision.

Whilst the boiler design of *Planet* was based upon that of *Northumbrian* incorporating a firebox as part of the boiler and having a proper smokebox, the revolutionary part of the design was the cylinder position and crank axle. The use of a cranked driving axle was not new; George Stephenson had proposed using a cranked axle and coupling rods on his patent locomotive of 1814. Braithwaite and Ericsson's *Novelty* (1829) had a cranked driving axle, so too did the steam road coaches of Goldsworthy Gurney and Trevithick. Indeed, Robert Stephenson had mused in a letter to Michael Longridge of New Year's day 1828 about adopting a crank axle and general layout based on Gurney's steam coach. This, however, did not stop a bitter James Kennedy (1797–1886) from accusing Robert Stephenson of stealing the idea from himself and his late business partner Edward Bury (1794–1858), and that their locomotive *Liverpool* (see Part 2) was the first to use a crank axle and horizontal inside cylinders:

"Liverpool' was started on the 22nd of July, 1830, by Mr Edward Bury ... The 'Planet' ... was not started until four and a half months afterwards ... The late Mr George Stephenson had told both Mr Bury and Mr Kennedy, after having seen the 'Liverpool' engine ... that his son, the present Robert Stephenson, had taken a fancy to the plan of the 'Liverpool' engine, and intended to make, immediately, a small engine on the same principle.'[4]

To this claim, Robert Stephenson rejoindered:

"Planet' ... had been made ... and constructed under my direction, without any reference or knowledge of the 'Liverpool' ... Neither was there any analogy between the two machines, for the 'Planet' had a multi-tubular boiler, the fire being urged by a blast-pipe, and the cylinders, which were nearly as horizontal as their position would permit, were fixed between the frames ... with the cylinders in the smoke box a cranked axle was indispensable, and there was not anything new in its use in locomotives.'[5]

It would appear that Stephenson, Timothy Hackworth and Bury were independently trying to solve the same problem of stability and came to the same conclusion; the Stockton & Darlington Railway had ordered Hackworth's *Globe* – which had horizontal cylinders under the firebox working a crank axle – to be built at Stephenson's Forth Street works in March 1830; the Stockton & Darlington to 'finding the wheels, axles ... and boiler plates for the body of the boiler.' *Globe* was not delivered until 4 October 1830, a month after *Planet*, which supporters of Hackworth claim was deliberate sabotage. Bury and Kennedy's *Liverpool* (in its first form with return flue boiler) was probably being designed and built when *Globe* was ordered; *Liverpool* first steamed in July 1830, whilst *Planet* was still on the drawing-board.[6]

Delivery and performance

The *Manchester Courier* on Saturday 9 October 1830 reported the arrival of *Planet* and the rumour that she had run the 30 miles between Liverpool and Manchester in a record-breaking time of 32 minutes, suggesting a speed of around 60mph. This is unlikely given that she is recorded on 23 November 1830 having made the same run light-engine in only 58 minutes:

'Liverpool to Manchester in One Hour – It has often been a subject of doubt whether the distance from Liverpool to Manchester could be travelled by a Locomotive engine in the space of one hour; this extraordinary feat was performed on Monday morning by the *Planet*, one of Mr Stephenson's most approved engines, the time occupied being only 60 minutes, of which 2 minutes were taken up in oiling and examining the machinery about midway. There were no carriages attached to the Engine, the only persons on the Tender being the Engineer, the Fireman, and Mr Williams, the Principal Clerk, in Crown-Street Station. The occasion of this rapid passage was the necessity for the Engine being in Manchester by nine o'clock a.m., it having been engaged by Mr Ewart's Committee to bring down the Duke's train with the Manchester voters, and some alteration in her machinery being unexpectedly required, she was prevented setting out until the latest moment, and the Engines at the other end were all occupied with the regular business of the road.'[7]

Weighing in at 8 tons, *Planet* was at the maximum weight stipulated by the L&M Act; her later sisters would easily breach that legal stipulation. The Directors ordered on 29 November 'A trial of the power of the '*Planet*' Engine be made with a load to be conveyed from Liverpool to Manchester.' Robert Stephenson was 'to make the necessary arrangements.'[8] The *Liverpool Mercury* (Friday 10 December 1830) reported:

'Extraordinary Performance on the Railway. On Saturday last, the Planet locomotive engine (one of Mr. Stephenson's) took the first load of merchandise which has passed along the Railway from Liverpool to Manchester. The train consisted of some 18 waggons, containing 135 bags and bales of American cotton, 200 barrels of flour, 63 sacks of oatmeal, and 35 sacks of malt, what weighing altogether 51 tons 11 cwt 1 qr. To this must be added the weight of the waggons and oil cloths, viz. 23 tons 8 cwt 3 qrs; tender, water, and fuel 4 tons, and of 15 persons upon the inter train, 1 ton, making a total weight of exactly eighty tons, exclusive of the engine, about six tons. The journey was performed in 2 hours and 54 minutes, including three stoppages of five minutes each (one only being necessary under ordinary circumstances) for oiling, watering, and taking in fuel; under the disadvantages also of an adverse wind, and of a great additional and friction in the wheels and axles, owing to their being entirely new. The train was assisted up the Rainhill Inclined Plane, by other engines, at the rate of 9 miles an hour, and descended the Sutton incline at the rate of l6 miles an hour. The average rate on the other parts of the road was 12 miles an hour, the greatest speed on the level being 15 miles an hour, which was maintained for a mile or two at different periods of the journey ... Taking this performance as a fair criterion, which there is no reason to doubt, four engines of the same class as the Planet, (with the assistance of one large engine, constructed for the purpose, up the inclined plane) would be capable of taking upon the Railway all the cotton which passes between Liverpool and Manchester.'[9]

Even the anti-Stephenson *Mechanics' Magazine*, grudgingly reported:

'We understand that the journey on Saturday would have been performed in less time, had not the engineer, when passing over Chat Moss, allowed the fire to burn too low; and afterwards, when he found the steam was falling off, thrown a large quantity of coke upon it, which greatly reduced the temperature, and caused the loss of a considerable time, before the proper speed could be regained. The consumption of coke was, we believe, about two-thirds of a pound per ton per mile.'

Hardman Earle reported the results of the load trials with *Planet* to his fellow Directors on 6 December 1830:

'The first load of Merchandise by the Railway from Liverpool to Manchester had been sent by the 'Planet' Locomotive in 18 Waggons, on Saturday the 4th instant ... the Nett Weight chargeable with freight was 51 Tons 1 cwt; the Gross Weight drawn by the engine, including Waggons, Tender and Passengers, being about 80 tons. The journey was accomplished in 6 minutes less than 3 hours, including stoppages for water and oiling.'[10]

Planet was obviously a success and orders were placed with Robert Stephenson & Co for two additional 'large locomotives': *Mercury* which was delivered early in January 1831, and *Mars* in late February 1831. Stephenson & Co. reported to the Board that 'after the 1st of January, they could engage to supply an Engine every fortnight' and furthermore, that they had also approached Messrs. Fenton, Murray & Jackson of Leeds 'for a further additional supply.'[11] The *Preston Chronicle* noted *Mercury* and *Mars* were at work during the second week of February 1831. Furthermore 'The powers and capabilities of each new engine ... exceed those of its predecessors':

'On Thursday week, the Mars left Liverpool with a load of passengers at ten o'clock; arrived at Manchester at exactly 28 minutes past eleven; having performed the journey, including all stoppages, and with a heavy load, in an hour and 28 minutes! She returned to Liverpool the same day, in *an hour and a quarter!*'[12]

During trials in April 1837, *Planet* drew a load of 22 waggons of 96 tons gross, at an average speed of 20mph, using 808lbs of coke or 0.28lbs per ton per mile and 580 gallons of water, the tender tank having been filled with hot water 'before starting.' On a later trip, with four passenger carriages (c.20 tons gross) she achieved a maximum speed of 29.5mph and burned 781lbs of coke or 1.3lbs per ton per mile.[13]

The next six members of the class were all Forth Street products, but because they were over-stretched, Fenton, Murray & Jackson of Leeds supplied two as well. The first, *Vulcan*, 'made under the direction of Robert Stephenson & Co.', arrived by the end of May 1831, whilst *Fury* arrived in August.[14] The *Chester Chronicle* recorded her delivery:

'A Beautiful new locomotive engine, "The Fury", of Mr Stephenson's construction, was "launched" at Liverpool on the Liverpool & Manchester Railway on Wednesday week, making the number now in operation amount to eighteen; and the number of passengers during the present week, has averaged about 2,000 per day!'[15]

Vulcan differed from the usual Stephenson practice by having a steam dome on the first ring of the boiler, with an external steam manifold and main steam pipe. She was fitted with wooden wheels supplied by Robert Stephenson & Co. at a cost of £60.[16] *Vulcan* broke her crank axle in October 1831 and Dixon was to write to the Leeds firm requesting 'particulars as to the description of the Iron used, the mode of

The first locomotive supplied by Fenton, Murray & Jackson was *Vulcan* (No. 19). Note the steam dome on the first ring of the boiler and the external regulator and steam pipes; a modification observable on Planet locomotives built for the London & Greenwich Railway, on John Bull in the USA and on Planets built by Le Creusot in France. (Science & Society Picture Library)

its construction' and any other information which would be 'useful with reference to the future.' They replied a week later that 'The cranked axle of the "Vulcan" had been carefully made out of the best scrap iron' and that they would be willing to tender for the supply of further locomotives.[17]

The Stockton & Darlington offered the L&M two of its Planet class engines in November 1831, but the Board declined to purchase them, and instead forwarded their particulars to John Hargreaves, lessee of the Bolton & Leigh, who was then 'in want of Locomotive Power.'[18] A third engine was purchased from Leeds in November 1832 for £780. Dixon reported in December to the Directors:

'He had been to Leeds and purchased ... a Loco-Motive engine similar in power and quality of workmanship as the Vulcan ... to be delivered to Manchester in 6 weeks from the 27th November.'[19]

She 'commenced running' in early January 1833 and at the Board Meeting of 4 February 1833 was aptly named *Leeds*.[20] Fenton, Murray & Jackson offered to

Fury (No. 21) was the second Planet locomotive supplied to the Liverpool & Manchester from Leeds. Note the beautifully detailed oil pots, and the sombre dark green livery with black lining and black boiler bands. (Anthony Dawson collection)

supply further locomotives in February 1834, costing £1,000 each, to be delivered in six or seven months, but their offer was declined.[21] By September of the same year *Leeds* was in need of a new firebox, the iron one having burned out, and the Management Committee ordered a copper firebox making and fitting in Manchester, work which John Dixon estimated would take two months.[22] *Vulcan* was sold out of service to Mr Thomas Pearson for £424 in 1840, and *Leeds* for £414 2s 2d.[23]

Four Planet-type locomotives were ordered on 12 May 1832, but the order was amended in October to only three. *Pluto* was built using the boiler and cylinders from an uncompleted order for an Atlas class 0-4-0 luggage engine (see below). *Ajax* followed in November. *Firefly,* the last Planet to be delivered by Stephensons, was despatched in March 1833 and like *Pluto* utilised the boiler from a cancelled order for an Atlas class locomotive.[24]

Service life

In service, the Planet class proved to be fast, reliable and fuel efficient; by 1 April 1833 *Planet* had run 41,400 miles, far more than other members of the class. The Management Committee Minutes note that *Planet*, because of her larger heating surface compared to the earlier Rocket types, burned 19¾lb of coke per 30-mile trip whilst *North Star* was burning ten pounds more. A trial made of *Planet* in

April 1837 showed that with twenty loaded merchandize waggons, making a gross trailing load of 96 tons, she ran from Liverpool to Manchester in a time of 1 hour 29 minutes; evaporated 580 gallons of water and burned 808lbs of coke, or 0.28lbs per ton per mile. Hardman Earle carried out trials with *Saturn* in April 1832: *Saturn*, with a load of 76 tons gross (51 tons net), and assisted up the incline plane by *Atlas*, made the run from Liverpool to Manchester in 1¾ hours, burning 557lb of coke or 16lb per mile.[25]

Experiments were carried out using the newly-delivered *Victory* in May 1832. On 5 May 1832:

'This engine drew from Liverpool to Manchester … in 1 hour, 34 minutes, 75 seconds, twenty loaded waggons, weighing gross, 92 tons, 19 cwt, 1 qr; consumption of coke 929lbs net; was assisted on the Rainhill incline plane 1½ mile by the Samson. The fire-place was filled with coke at the starting (not weighed), and was again filled with coke on arriving at Manchester; the coke used in getting the steam up was not used in the above estimate.'[26]

With this load, *Victory* achieved a speed of 20mph on the dead level; rose to 25mph on a falling gradient and on a rising gradient she achieved 17mph. On 8 May with a load of twenty waggons weighing 90 tons 7 cwt 2 qrs gross, *Victory* made the same trip in 1 hour 41 minutes including a lengthy stop of 11 minutes for water and oiling round. Despite a severe head wind, she made a maximum speed on the level of 17.7mph but one of her big-end bearings ran hot, and 'upon arriving at Manchester, pistons were found so loose in the cylinder that steam blew through.' William Allcard reported to the Management Committee in July 1832 that during the trials between *Planet* and *Victory*, each making five trips per day, six days a week that *Planet* had conveyed 1,744 tons and burned just over 52 tons of coke (or 0.45lb of coke per ton per mile) compared to *Victory* hauling 1,975 tons at the same fuel consumption. Comparisons between the two engines for ten days commencing on 23 June 1832 showed *Victory* to be marginally more fuel efficient, burning 0.49lbs of coke per ton per mile compared to *Planet*'s 0.51lbs.[27]

Results from trials with the 1992 replica suggest that she has maximum tractive effort of circa 1,300lbs at 90% and 1,200lbs at 75% cut-off; starting tractive effort at 90% cut-off was a theoretical 1,670lb at maximum boiler pressure (100psi) suggesting *Planet* is capable of starting a train of 150 tons on the level, which is comparable to historical data which shows the heaviest load attributable to a member of the class, *Fury* which on 15 August 1834 started a load of 134 tons away unassisted from Liverpool Road, Manchester. Trials with the replica show the engine was capable of 78 Indicated Horsepower and 58 Equivalent Draw-Bar Horsepower which was attained with a load of 54 tons up a rising gradient of 1 in 176. The locomotive has a sustainable tractive effort of 1,200lbs at 24mph and 75% cut-off.[28] During the 'Golden Oldies' Gala at the Great Central Railway, Loughborough, *Planet* was tasked with propelling a permanent way train two miles up the 1 in 176 from Loughborough to Quorn with a load of 50 tons, which, despite firing problems, was achieved with only 45psi 'on the clock' at Quorn. Shunting movements at the Science & Industry Museum in Manchester with the demonstration freight train and a 'dead'

Bolton Battery Electric shunter show that she is 'seemingly happy' shifting loads of 50–60 tons on the level, which compares well with known weights of trains in the early 1830s.[29]

These little engines were worked very hard: only two-years old, *Saturn* was offered for sale to the Leeds & Selby Railway in August 1834 for £600. The L&S was facing something of a motive power crisis as the engines they had ordered from Edward Bury of Liverpool would not be ready for opening day. *Saturn* was one of two engines offered to the L&S – one being on loan – but upon examination it was found that *Saturn* required £260 to £300 of repairs and the offer was wisely declined; the purchase of *North Star* (above) partially solved this problem. *Saturn* was sent to the Vulcan Foundry in December 1834 for a rebuild, but upon initial dismantling was found to be worn out (no wonder the Leeds company wouldn't buy her). John Dixon didn't know what to do with her as 'she was in worse condition than he expected, and in consequence at a loss how to proceed.' Henry Booth was of a similar opinion that she 'was in so defective a state that he did not think it advisable to attempt to repair her.' She was therefore ordered to be scrapped and two new coaching engines were purchased from the Vulcan Foundry. *Mars* was also sent to the Vulcan Foundry, where the cost of repairs totalled £900 – the price of a new engine – but the final bill came to £104 1s 8d following deductions for 'Sundry Materials furnished by the Company'.[30]

Table 2: Planet Class (2-2-0) Locomotives on the Liverpool & Manchester Railway

	Builder	Date	Cylinders	Boiler	Tubes	Size	Weight	Notes
Planet (9)	Robert Stephenson & Co.	October 1830	11 x 16	6ft 6in x 3ft	129	1 5/8in	7t 3cwt (wood wheels)	In service 1840.
Mercury (11)	RS &Co.	January 1831	11 x 16	6ft 6in x 2ft 9in	84	1 5/8in	6t 2cwt (wood wheels)	Rebuilt as 2-2-2 Dec. 1833.
Mars (12)	RS & Co.	February 1831	11 x 16	6ft 6in x 2ft 9in	76	1 5/8in	7t 9cwt 1qr (iron wheels)	Rebuilt 1834; sold 1839 £358 12s.
Jupiter (14)	RS & Co.	February 1831	11 x 16	6ft 6in x 2ft 9in	79	1 5/8in	6t 8cwt (wood wheels)	'done with' 1833.
Saturn (16)	RS & Co.	April 1831	11 x 16	6ft 6in x 2ft 9in	87	1 5/8in	?	Scrapped 1834.
Sun (17)	RS & Co.	April 1831	11 x 16	6ft x 2ft 9in	93	1 5/8in	6t 15cwt 3qr (iron wheels)	Sold 1835 for £200.
Venus (18)	RS & Co.	May 1831	11 x 16	6ft 6in x 2ft 9in	62	2in	?	'done with' 1833.
Vulcan (19)	Fenton, Murray & Jackson.	May 1831	11 x 16	6ft 3in x 3ft	102	1 5/8in	6t 12cwt 3qr	Sold 1840 £424.
Etna (20)	RS & Co.	June 1831	11 x 16	6ft 6in x 3ft	97	1 5/8in	?	Sold 1835 for £250.
Fury (21)	FM & J.	August 1831	11 x 16	6ft 3in x 3ft	102	1 5/8in	6t 14cwt 2qr	In service 1839.
Victory (22)	RS & Co.	September 1831	11 x 16	6ft 6in x 3ft	97	1 5/8in	9t 12cwt 3qr	In service 1839.
Vesta (24)	RS & Co.	November 1831	11 x 16	6ft 6in x 2ft 8.5in	80	1 5/8in	7t 12cwt 2qr (iron wheels)	'on sale' 1836.
Pluto (27)	RS & Co.	July 1832	12 x 16	7ft 8in x 3ft 2in	104	1 5/8in	9t 11cwt 1qr	Rebuilt as 2-2-2 1832; in service 1839.
Ajax (29)	RS & Co.	November 1832	11 x 18	6ft 8in x 2ft 9in	62	2in	11t 4cwt 3qr	In service 1839.
Leeds (30)	FM & J.	January 1833	11 x 16	6ft 3in x 3ft	102	1 5/8in	?	Sold 1840 £414 2s 2d.
Firefly (31)	RS & Co.	March 1833	11 x 16	7ft 4½in x 3ft	109	1 ½in	8t 14cwt 3qr	Fitted with Melling's coupling wheel 1836; In service 1840.

CHAPTER 3

Engine Building

The development of the locomotive in the early 1830s was perhaps ahead of the technology and materials with which they were being built. Crank axles, for example, were hand-forged, and wooden wheels, whilst suitable for the low power outputs and speeds of colliery engines, would soon prove to be unsatisfactory for an intensive main line service. In particular, developing and maintaining the first fleet of main line locomotives presented numerous technological challenges, particularly metallurgical with regards to wheels, axles, boiler tubes and fireboxes, especially as the Stephenson Works at Forth Street in Newcastle lacked much in the way of up-to-date machine tools or testing facilities.

Crank axles

At this period, the forging of crank axles was difficult; before James Nasmyth developed the steam-hammer which could handle such large wrought-iron forgings, they had to be forged by hand. There were five ways of producing such an axle: an axle built-up from components and pressed together; a built-up axle where successive layers of plate were built-up to form the crank throws and then machined; a built-up axle made in two halves and then welded together; an axle cut from a solid slab of iron and then heated and twisted so that the cranks were 90° apart; an axle which was forged into shape from a single piece of iron which preserved the grain of the iron.[1] Stephenson & Co., however, lacked many machine tools, and it is likely that the workshops of the Liverpool & Manchester were better-equipped and had more up-to-date machinery than the Forth Street Works.[2] Crank axles were therefore forged by Longridge at the Bedlington Foundry, who also undertook boiler work for Stephenson & Co. In order to give the maximum support to his crank axles, Robert Stephenson took a 'belt and braces' approach; the axle was provided with outside bearings carried by the sandwich frames, but was also supported by four inside frames, which also served to carry the slide bars. Each of the inside frames carried a bearing so that the crank axle was supported on each side of the crank throws, relieving it of horizontal stresses, but only the outside bearings were sprung, with the inside bearings simply being able to move vertically in guide boxes. The design of the inside frames rapidly evolved; at first they were wooden, but with the delivery of *Mars* iron 'radius rods' were used to support the inside bearings. These 'radius rods' resembled coupling rods and were hinged at their leading end allowing the crank axle bearings to move vertically, but apparently they didn't carry any load. The first locomotive fitted with 'inside iron frames with wedges for the bearings' was *Pluto* and they 'answer[ed] very well.' From *Pluto* onwards, the inside bearings were also sprung, suggesting that they actually carried some weight.[3]

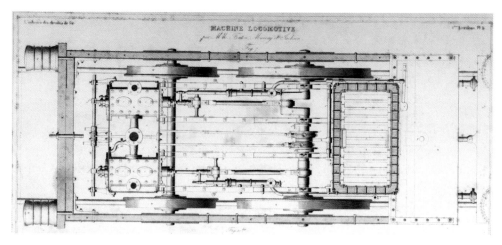

Frames, axles and valve gear of a typical Planet type as depicted by Armengaud et Armengaud, showing the outside sandwich frames and the four intermediate plate frames (which also carry the slide bars) giving maximum support to the crank axle. (after Armengaud & Armengaud)

The very first Planets suffered from a spate of broken crank axles. *Planet*'s crank axle is shown as being only 4 inches in diameter and 3½in at the crank pin; that of *Ajax* was thicker, 4¾ inches diameter. George Stephenson wrote a concerned note to Longridge complaining about the quality of the crank axles supplied by him:

> 'This says very ill of your Blacksmith's work and alarms me very much about the axletrees; for should one of them break you are quite aware of how serious an accident it would be. It is the cranked axletrees of the Engines to which I refer. The [cranked] axletrees should all be numbered at your works, and the name of the Maker inserted in a book.'[4]

Sadly George's worries came true when the crank axle of *Etna* broke in September 1831, resulting in the Management Committee recommending the use of new stronger axles, and Booth hoped that that the 'thicker and stronger' axles would meet with 'perfect success.' The report on the failure of *Etna*'s axle was passed on to George Stephenson, who recommended that the axles be made of a larger diameter, and made 'either of Swedish Iron or of English Iron smelted with Wood charcoal.' English iron was traditionally made from coking coal, and was therefore brittle due to having a sulphur content of 1% or more. Conversely, Swedish iron was traditionally smelted with charcoal so had zero sulphur content and was therefore more durable and less brittle. Smelting iron with charcoal was also traditional in the Kentish Weald. These new crank axles were 'very heavy' and expensive, but Stephenson was requested by the Board to take such steps as he thought fit to 'secure the best iron for the purpose.'[5] The crank axle of *Fury* broke in December 1831 whilst heading a first-class train on the embankment at Glazebrook near Bury Lane. The axle broke 'about 20 yards over the bridge … the Engine was precipitated over the south side of the embankment, dragging two of the carriages after her which were thrown on their sides.' The passengers were able to escape through the windows, both of the guards Howell and Rothwell being praised for their conduct in helping the passengers to escape before the carriages slipped further down the embankment.[6] The *Liverpool Mercury* cast blame for the accident on the Liverpool & Manchester Railway for using a locomotive on a passenger train that had not been fitted with a new, stronger crank-axle which 'would have been ready in a week.'[7] *Fury* had run some 8,000 miles in three months (2,666 miles per month) before the axle broke whilst that of a sister engine was reported to have lasted for 22,000 miles in ten months (or 2,200 miles per month) before it broke. The new axles had been increased in strength by 'two thirds' and 'all but two or three locomotives' had been so fitted.[8] Anthony Harding and Thomas Worsdell were awarded five guineas each by the Management Committee for their 'exertions in getting home the Engine and Carriages on the night' after the accident.[9] John Gray attended the Management Committee meeting of 7 December 1831 and was able to report that '7 of the Engines had been supplied with Cranked axles of two-thirds additional strength.' As a result, the Management Committee ordered: 'That in future, an Engine not having the Stronger axle be not allowed to go with the Coach Trains.'[10] As a result of this order, *Planet* – which had broken her crank axle whilst crossing Chat Moss, and even though she had been fitted with a stronger replacement – was not allowed to 'go with the coach trains' because it had been manufactured from 'inferior iron' and the Board were concerned that it too might fail.[11] Crank axle failure was not just limited to Planet type engines on the L&M; the crank axle of *Nelson* (Fenton, Murray & Jackson, 1834) on the Leeds & Selby also failed after around twelve months' operation in December 1835. A replacement axle cost £63 10s 9d.[12] Despite the introduction of new, 'very heavy' axles which were 5 inches diameter and costing £50 each, Anthony Harding reported in April 1832 that *Mercury* had a 'bent axle.'[13] The increasing size of crank axles is shown in a note of 12 May 1832 which records that 'In future the crank-axles for 5ft coupled wheels not to be less than 4 7/8 inches and 4ft 6in wheels 4¾ [inches] finished.'[14] Following the failure of *Pluto*'s crank axle in June 1833, the Directors expected 'a guarantee of the soundness of the wheels and axles for twelve months' from Stephenson & Co.[15]

These failures were due to poor axle design; it had not been realised that cracks were most likely to occur where changes in diameter occurred. Stephenson's axles stepped down for insertion into the wheel hub, and further stepped down for the outside bearing journals. This meant that several changes in diameter had been introduced, including at the most critical place, at the nave of the wheel. Unfortunately, the radii on the shoulder of the axle, where the axle stepped down in diameter to enter the wheel hub, were too small and thus prone to stress fractures. No provision had been made either to machine stress-relieving grooves into the axle. Replication repeated history as the replica *Planet* suffered from two broken axles, with stress fractures caused in exactly the same location as the originals.[16]

The Chevalier de Pambour in 1835 indicated that even stronger crank axles had been introduced by that date, and that the axle increased from 5 inches diameter to 5½ inches diameter where it passed through the wheel hub. De Pambour also shows collars fitted to each end of the crank axle. These collars were to prevent lateral spread of the horn guides as the locomotive travelled around sharp curves. The 1992 replica of *Planet* originally displayed this same problem, especially in reverse, so collars were subsequently fitted to the axle in order to cure this lateral spread. In his design for his

Patent Locomotive of 1833 (see below), Robert Stephenson introduced and patented flangeless driving wheels in order to 'obviate or diminish' the lateral spread on the crank axle horn guides, by allowing greater lateral movement of the driving wheels.[17]

Wheels

The Liverpool & Manchester standardised maximum wheel diameter at 5 feet; George Stephenson thought any larger would be dangerous, largely as a result of an accident involving Edward Bury's locomotive *Liverpool* which had wheels 6 feet in diameter. Stephenson blamed this accident solely on the large size of her wheels. The *Manchester Guardian* (30 July 1831) took umbrage with the Directors of the Liverpool & Manchester for allowing what they considered to be a dangerous locomotive onto the line and putting public safety at risk. The L&M Directors accepted this report, much to the chagrin of Bury, and subsequently passed a by-law which stated 'In the future no locomotive Engine shall be allowed to be introduced on the Railway with wheels of a larger diameter than five feet.'[18]

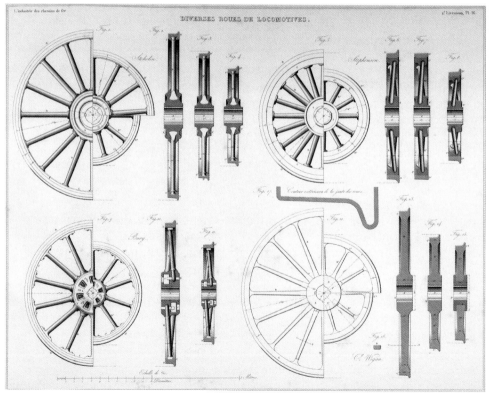

Different types of wrought-iron wheel: Stephenson 'gas pipe' (top right); Bury's (bottom left), both of which used cast-iron hubs and wrought-iron spokes. Those of the Haigh Foundry (bottom right), were forged and fire-welded from individual components. Bury's wheels were ordered to replace the 'gas pipe' type of Stephenson. (after Armengaud & Armengaud)

The wheels of *Planet* were initially of composite construction: cast iron hub with ash spokes and oak felloes with a shrunk on wrought-iron tyre. Whilst these wheels had been successful enough on *Rocket* and *Northumbrian*, they were a failure on the earliest *Planet* types, which suffered from a series of broken wheels, often co-incident with a broken axle. Between January 1830 and April 1831 some 11 pairs of locomotive wheels and axles were purchased from Robert Stephenson & Co.[19] Continuing distrust of the wheels provided by Stephenson & Co. resulted in the Management Committee ordering that the next two engines from Newcastle be 'despatch[ed] without wheels, the <u>Company</u> to provide wheels on their arrival.'[20] *Pluto* was delivered without wheels but was fitted with 'strong wood wheels' by the company, but *Ajax* (delivered November 1832) had iron wheels.[21] Such was the on-going problem with locomotive wheels, that the Board ordered a 'Return to be made of all the engine wheels received from Newcastle' listing how many were currently in use, and how many had failed in service.[22] As an alternative to wooden wheels, in January 1832 the Management Committee ordered that Mr Edward Roscoe 'supply a pair of his Improved Forged Iron Engine Wheels' for trial purposes, and in March 1832, the Board of Directors ordered that 'the big wheels be not provided until the Company has had further experience of the kind most likely to answer.'[23]

These composite wheels were replaced by early wrought-iron 'gas pipe' wheels which will be discussed later. These too were not a success as there was another spate of broken wheels, notably those of *Firefly* where one wheel collapsed, causing the locomotive to come off the rails. Thereafter, the Directors recommended the wheels made by Edward Bury & Co. of Liverpool or the patent wheels of Richard Roberts & Co. of Manchester, which seem to have solved the problem of wheel breakages. The durability of Bury's patent iron wheels is open to debate, however, given the high rate of failure of such wheels on the Leeds & Selby Railway after less than six months. The Leeds & Selby eventually received a guarantee from Bury as to the 'soundness' of his wheels for at least six months.[24] Roberts had patented his locomotive wheel in April 1832 using wrought-iron spokes and a cast iron hub:

'The nave is of cast iron, and has a rabbet at each end to receive wrought iron hoops, the rabbets are a little taper toward the middle of the nave to hold the hoops in their places. In the direction of the axis of the nave there are grooves for the reception of the inner end of the spokes ... and are fitted accurately ... in to the grooves in the nave, the shouldered portions of them filling those parts of the grooves which are within the circular surfaces of the rabbets; the spokes are firmly held in the nave using hoops let on hot over the ends of the rabbets of the nave and T ends of the spokes. The outer ends of the spokes are spread on both sides in the direction of the circumference of the wheel, and are riveted to the ... felloe. The tire is put on and secured into the felloe in the usual way.'[25]

Edward Bury's wheels were similar, including the use of T-shaped spokes which slotted into a cast iron hub. The spokes were off-set around the nave, like those on a bicycle wheel. The wheels in use on the Liverpool & Manchester in 1835 are described as having 'cast spokes and hub and wrought iron rim and flange' which were thought to be the safest 'under the high velocities which are attainable.'[26] The replica of *Planet* uses cast steel wheels, without tyres, machined to BR main line tolerances.

Making steam

As with heavy forgings, Robert Stephenson & Co. out-sourced production of boilers and fireboxes to the Bedlington Ironworks. Due to quality control problems at Bedlington, however, the boiler of *Rocket* had been made from best Staffordshire plate, but presumably some of these problems had been overcome, with Stephenson & Co. renewing their dealings with Bedlington after 1829. That said, however, some of these issues such as the uneven thickness of boiler plate don't appear to have gone away. There were problems with getting boilers steam-tight: when *Pluto* was steam-tested she was found 'rather leaky' whilst *Ajax* was also found to leak badly under test on 10 and 11 October 1832 due to poorly peened-over rivet heads. A third steam test on 26 October found her 'very nearly tight.' *Firefly*'s boiler also leaked.[27]

Planet's boiler design was based on that for *Northumbrian*: 6 feet 6 inches long and 3 feet diameter, containing 129 copper tubes, 1 5/8 inch outside diameter.[28] By using so many tubes, Stephenson had taken the idea of maximising heating surface to its logical extreme, but in fact the boiler design was a failure as so many tubes restricted water circulation within the boiler. Not only did the high number of boiler tubes impede water circulation (and therefore heat transfer), it also reduced the amount of steam

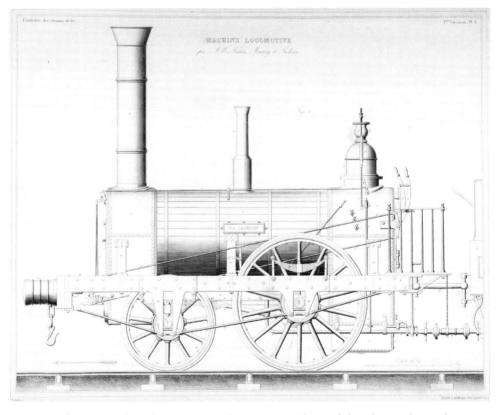

Elevation of a typical Planet locomotive, in this case *La Jackson* of the Chemin de Fer de Paris a Saint-Germain-en-Laye, built in Leeds by Fenton, Murray & Jackson. (after Armengaud & Armengaud)

space available despite the use of a steam dome over the firebox. Having the main steam pipe bifurcate in the boiler would not have helped matters; Colburn's analysis of data presented by de Pambour concluded that Planet type locomotives were prone to priming as a result of this. By using a larger diameter boiler barrel and fewer tubes (under 100) solved this problem. The firebox had an area of 37¼ square feet and the tubes provided a heating surface of 370 square feet: 407¼ square feet in total, making an excellent steam generator. De Pambour (cited by Colburn) notes that between 6.6lb–7.7lb of water was evaporated for every pound of coke burned, and the replica has a maximum steaming rate of 3,000lbs per hour.[29]

Boilers grew larger with each locomotive delivered: that of *Planet* was 6ft 6in long and 3 feet diameter with 129 tubes whilst that of *Pluto* was 7ft 9in long, with 104 tubes, although the boilers of *Mercury*, *Mars*, *Jupiter* and *Saturn* were smaller, only 6ft 6in long and 2ft 9in diameter. The grate area also increased from 6.50 square feet of *Planet* to 7.31 square feet of *Pluto*. The boiler of *Venus* only had 60 tubes, but they were two inches diameter. This meant there was a consequential increase in weight – *Planet* weighed 8 tons whilst *Pluto* was 9 tons 11 cwt 1 qr. The boiler of the replica is 6 feet 9¾ inches long and 3 feet ½ inches diameter, with 92 tubes.[30]

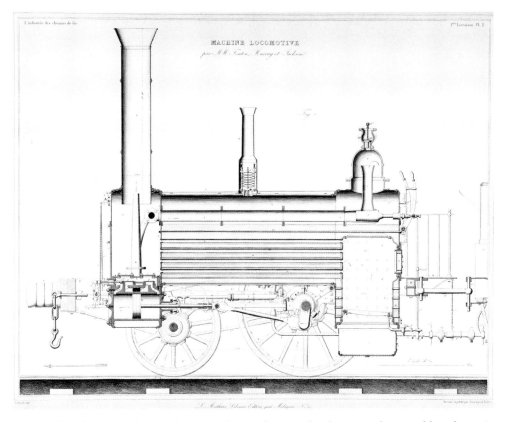

Section of a Planet type locomotive: note the regulator under the steam dome and lengthy main steam pipe. The long blast pipe reaches into the base of the chimney and double slide valves are used. (after Armengaud & Armengaud)

Even though Stephenson had provided outside 'Sandwich frames', the boiler was considered to be a major structural element of the locomotive and was rigidly fixed to the frames, and was therefore unable (or at least restricted) in its ability to expand when it was pressurised. Furthermore, the drag pin – to which the tender is coupled and takes the entire load of the train – was riveted directly to the rear of the firebox shell which meant that the load was passed not through the frame but the boiler. This was a major design flaw, resulting in the only boiler explosion on the L&M – that of *Patentee* in 1838 (below). Due to the limitations of forging large wrought iron plates, the boiler and outer firebox were made from more than twenty iron plates 3/8-inch thick and measuring 4ft 1in by 3ft 1in. By the later 1830s Bedlington was able to produce boiler plate 6ft 6in x 3ft. The boiler plates were lap riveted together; where the smokebox and firebox shell met the boiler barrel, angle irons were used.[31]

Fireboxes and tubes

Because of the high cost of copper and thus the difficulties of acquiring high quality copper plate, the inner fireboxes of the first Planets were iron, but they were very rapidly found to 'burn out'; firebox tube plates are recorded as having caused considerable trouble, including buckling due to over-heating. This was probably due to poor water circulation around the inner firebox due to the build-up of scale and sludge, especially between the tube plate and the front of the outer fire box shell. Water space around the inner firebox was around 2¼ inches, but in September it was proposed to increase this to a full 4 inches. Unusually, this was not provided with any mud hole doors or wash-out plugs to enable that part of the firebox to be cleaned out. Experiences with the replica *Planet* show this area is very prone to scale and sludge deposition for a similar reason. Some locomotives such as *Fury* had gone through three iron fireboxes in only two years; the first firebox lasted for 21,330 miles and the second – from Low Moor iron – a mere 6,060.[32] Clearly, iron fireboxes were not the way forward. The Management Committee ordered on 9 February 1832, that despite the increased cost: 'The Engines should be fitted up with a Boiler End and Firebox of Copper instead of Iron, as being more likely to wear well, and be more economical in the end.'[33] The matter was to be referred to Stephenson for perusal and in May 1832 specifications were issued for copper fireboxes, copper boiler tubes and 'syphon boxes.'[34]

Problems with copper boiler tubes first started to appear during 1831, which John Dixon blamed on the use of gas coke. Tubes were failing at an alarming rate: 'almost constant failing in one or other of the engines, and which caused great inconvenience and loss of time' as well as 'much expense.' The copper tubes of *Pluto* had weighed 11¼lbs when new but after only running 7,170 miles had lost some 4¾lbs of metal due to abrasion from coke particles. Other locomotives fared no better, suffering burst tubes after only 3,000 miles. In order to improve circulation around the boiler, *Ajax* was provided with a long copper pipe 'from the bottom of the boiler near [the] smokebox to the bottom of the firebox.' A similar tactic was tried with *Pluto* which had '3 circulating pipes put into the firebox.' The high number of small (1 5/8 inch) tubes impeded water circulation and from the use of dirty water were quickly coated with scale and over-heated. Thus the number of tubes was reduced and their diameter

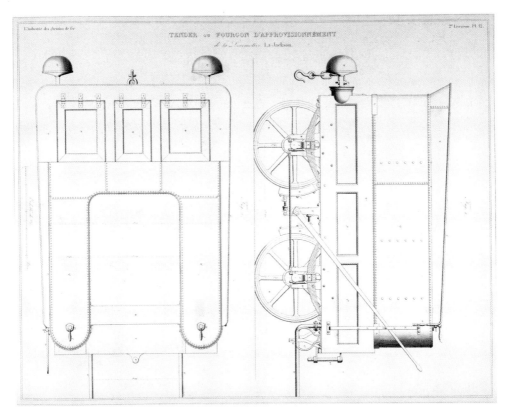

The tender of *La Jackson*. The tender of the replica *Planet* was built with reference to that of *Patentee* (1833). Note the unusual hitch-down wagon-type hand-brake. (after Armengaud & Armengaud)

increased with *Ajax* being delivered with 62 tubes of 2 inches inside diameter, of which '59 open and [the] 3 at bottom plugged up.'[35]

The 'excessive expenditure' on locomotive maintenance, especially the renewal of fireboxes and tubes, was commented upon at the 1833 General Meeting. Iron fireboxes had been found to 'burn very rapidly away' and copper tubes wore out equally as quickly. There were a few exceptions to this rule, but the Directors felt this problem (and expense) was 'not insurmountable' and that experiments 'on the material of the tubes and fire-places, and on the circulation of water' were being taken earnestly forward by their engineer. They also welcomed input on the problem from 'scientific men on the subject.'[36]

John Dixon went about this problem methodically; initially the Board approved the use of Perkins' patent circulators to improve the flow of water around the boiler and firebox and *Vesta* was so fitted along with a copper firebox (below). Dixon's next approach was to examine where the tubes had burst, and found that they had 'burned through' approximately 12 inches from the firebox end. Thus, Dixon used brass ends brazed on the copper tubes, so that the last 18 inches or so of the boiler tube, where it inserted into the tube plate, were brass. These did not prove successful as the copper part of the tube still 'burned 'away' but the brass section was 'wholly uninjured.'

'Supposing that the failure was owing to the copper being still too near the fire' Dixon then made tubes one half brass (firebox end) and one half copper (chimney end) but the copper tube still failed, even when he made the boiler tubes almost entirely of brass but with only the last 6 inches being made from copper. Clearly, copper tubes were not the way forward and he had *Firefly* delivered from Newcastle in March 1833 with 57 copper tubes and 52 brass tubes 'so placed as to be equally exposed to the action of the fire.' After only running 3,000 miles 'she began to burst tubes, and by 15 May when she had run 4,900 she had burst 8 or 10 <u>copper</u> tubes.' Dixon therefore decided to retube *Firefly* with a complete set of brass tubes, and 'since that time not one of her tubes … has failed.'[37]

Dixon also carried out experiments with various thicknesses of copper and brass boiler tubes to find a more durable solution; the Management Committee ordering that *Sun* be retubed at Liverpool whilst 'one of the other Engines at Manchester' be retubed with copper tubes, 'half the tubes to be light, and half heavy tubes'.[38] *Victory* was fitted with 'thick brass tubes', one of which was removed in July 1832 in order 'to ascertain the wear' and whether thicker tubes were an improvement over the thinner tubes.[39] Dixon was not necessarily in favour of using thicker copper tubes. He wrote to the mechanically-minded Hardman Earle that:

'The Jupiter was the first to get an entirely new set of tubes in her (12lbs instead of 6lbs). It took 60lbs copper and several tubes have burst and the extra weight has been useless. Heavy tubes cost £60 extra, add 1,000lbs to the weight and do no good, and I consider they injure the boiler ends.'[40]

In his reply to Dixon, Earle noted he had initially been 'in favour of heavy tubes' but later changed his mind:

'The Planet first shook my faith in heavy tubes. She has light ones (6½lbs. Some I find now shrunk to 4lbs) but she has double what the Jupiter has. I consider she is better because she has a large boiler, has more tubes, and a larger firebox and blast pipe.'[41]

Earle considered that the reason why tubes were burning out so quickly was due to poor water circulation in the boiler, and he proposed an experiment with the *Phoenix*: 'Let us transfer Pheonix [sic] into the Planet class, put copper ends to her boiler, copper into her firebox. And 140 tubes, one half copper, the rest iron with copper ends.'[42] The Management Committee agreed to this suggestion, and that *Phoenix* should be rebuilt as a Planet and 'such other experiments that they may think likely to be advantageous' take place with her. The results of this experiment are unknown.[43] *Phoenix* was eventually dismantled and her boiler used as part of the 'feed apparatus' of the boiler of the tunnel engine at Edge Hill.[44]

So many locomotives were out of action due to leaking tubes, that *Comet*, the 'spare engine' based at Rainhill, was ordered 'to be provided with an Engineman and kept with her steam up, ready for contingencies' in September 1832.[45] Boiler tubes were initially made from lengths of copper, individually formed around a mandrel and then soldered. To ensure they were completely cylindrical, the finished tube was passed through a series of rollers and an iron or steel mandrel passed through the centre. Drawn, seamless tubes – where a cast cylinder of brass or copper was forced, using a hydraulic press, over an iron mandrel to make a tube – were 'perfected' in 1838 by Charles Green in Birmingham, suggesting that the Liverpool & Manchester were early-adopters of this new technology when John Dixon carried out a series of experiments with them in 1832.[46] He reported to the Management Committee in October 1832:

> 'Mr Dixon exhibited two pieces (cross sections) of Copper Tubes taken out of the Mars. One, a common tube, worn as thin as paper. The other a drawn tube, without seam or joining, appeared sound and strong as when first put in. The tubes had been in equal times.'

As a result of this, Dixon was authorised to get a 'complete set of drawn tubes' for experimental purposes.[47] The Directors refused to accept *Firefly* due to a fault with the firebox, 'owing to a cross steam at the lower part of it'. Henry Booth was to liaise with Stephenson & Co. who were to put this right at their own cost.[48]

A new boiler and copper firebox was ordered to be made for *Vesta* in August 1832 at the Liverpool engine shops, 'under Melling's superintendence'.[49] In April 1833 she was 'new tubed' with brass tubes by means of comparison with copper tubes and was ordered to have her 'cylinders fresh-bored.'[50] Evidence of this re-boring comes from de Pambour who describes her cylinders as 11 1/8th inches bore.[51] The opportunity was also taken to fit her with the experimental firebox patented by Jacob Perkins (1766–1849) 'for promoting the better circulation of the water' by means of comparison with both the Stephenson and Bury type fireboxes then in use. Perkins was an Anglo-American inventor, best known as the father of refrigeration from his studies on heat transfer. His patent 'circulator' was an early attempt at a thermic siphon, using 'a number of 2-inch diameter copper pipes' as 'steam risers' to provide 'a definitive circuit or path from the sides and the crown of the firebox.' *Vesta* 'began work' with the circulator on 24 October 1832 and by 4 January 1833 had run 6,510 miles, and when some of the tubes were withdrawn for inspection 'looked very well'. By February 1833 Vesta had run 20,000 with Perkin's circulator fitted and the tubes were 'without the slightest appearance of wear' and 'free from corrosion.' There was also a reported saving of fuel. But this would prove to be false hope.[52] Perkins reported to the Board in April 1833 about the 'operation of the Circulator in the Vesta Engine' and as to 'the deposit of mud' in the boiler barrel. Henry Booth was ordered to write to Perkins enquiring about 'his terms on which he would be willing to allow the company the use of his patent circulator.' Five locomotives were eventually fitted with his patent 'circulator' but the results were not all that the Directors had hoped, leading to a lengthy and sometimes acrimonious correspondence with Perkins and his co-patentees for the next few years, the relationship between the Board and Perkins (or his co-patentees) deteriorating to such a state that 'The Directors must decline any further correspondence … on the subject of the circulator.' John Dixon was ordered to provide a comprehensive report, to 'ascertain the merits of the circulator, taking in to account the effect, if any, on the state and condition of the Engines' as well as fuel consumption. He reported to the Board on 21 October. So did Mr Alfred King 'the engineer of Liverpool Gasworks' who had also made experiments with Perkins' device concluding 'the general result of which was very little difference between the Boilers with the Circulator, and those without.' As a result of both reports, the Board declined to adopt Perkins' Circulator.[53] John Dixon noted that instead of prolonging the life of copper boiler tubes, the use of the Patent Circulator had in fact reduced their working life, and they 'gave way even before the usual time.'[54]

In March 1833 John Dixon recommended that some 'angle iron be introduced into the boilers just under the bottom of the tubes' to take the ends of boiler stays. And again at the recommendation of Dixon, the Management Committee ordered in the April that 'the Engine yet to come from Newcastle have a copper lining to her fire-box' and be provided with brass tubes. In order to improve water circulation in the boiler it was also ordered 'the Tubes be placed further apart than what they have usually been'.[55] Dixon was also instructed to purchase 'a fresh supply of Brass for the tubes … for the several engines that would want tubing', some '200 strips of brass' being ordered at the end of April 1833.[56] By way of experiment into their potential to resist corrosion, *Mars* was re-tubed with copper tubes 'coated with zinc inside and out' for 2s per tube in May 1833; *Milo* was re-tubed with brass tubes in June and *Leeds* was fitted with a copper firebox in September.[57] Finally, from December 1833 brass tubes were adopted in place of copper. The new tubes were to be fitted as the copper ones wore out and locomotives required a complete re-tube. The brass tubes were secured using steel ferrules. One of *Ajax*'s brass tubes burst, and was reported by Henry Booth in January 1834, as being 'burnt or worn very thin, as were the copper tubes used previouslyfrom the scouring action of abrasive coke particles.'[58] The company accounts show that for the half-year ending 30 June 1834, some £409 7s 11d was spent on 'Brass & Copper for Tubes and Fire-Boxes'.[59] Brass tubes and the method of making and fitting them had become the norm by summer 1835 when the Dublin & Kingstown Railway wrote to the L&M Board in something of a panic, requesting 'A few dozen brass tubes, as they were apprehensive their railway would be completely stopped if they did not get an immediate supply.' Henry Booth agreed to help and a 'few dozen' rolled brass tubes were sent to Dublin.[60]

Venus received a new boiler and firebox built by Edward Bury & Co. at the Clarence Foundry in Liverpool in December 1832 after being in service only twelve months. By May 1833 John Dixon reported to Stephenson & Co that she had only run 8,000 miles and that the tubes were bursting at a rate of '3 or 4 a day' and she would have to be re-tubed.[61] *Mercury* was fitted with a copper inner firebox by Bury & Co. in March 1833,[62] and *Saturn*, *Ajax* and *Milo* were ordered to be fitted with new copper fireboxes in October 1834 whilst undergoing a 'thorough repair' by Charles Tayleur & Co., Edward Bury & Co., and George Forrester & Co. respectively.[63] The copper fireboxes of *Vulcan* and *Jupiter* had to be replaced in April 1834. Henry Booth reported to the Board (7 April) 'That the copper Fire Boxes of Vulcan and Jupiter had failed, a few inches below the Fire Door, where the substance of the copper was burnt or corroded almost through.' It was proposed to 'protect the present Fire Boxes with paint' and 'to endeavour with respect of new Fire Boxes to give them a coating of hard solder or Brass.' The issue of iron fireboxes was also discussed. They had been found to quickly wear out, but it was uncertain whether this was due to 'combined action of the Fire and Sulphur' or their material. The D-shaped inner firebox of *Liver* was ordered to be immediately fitted with stays, and Henry Booth was instructed to liaise with Edward

Bury 'to ascertain the present quality and texture of the Iron, or to make it safe.'[64] Booth reported that Bury had 'some holes drilled through the *Liver*'s Fire Box' to ascertain the quality of the iron, 'which he found (as far as he could judge) fresh and good.' He also recommended alterations to the staying of *Liver*'s firebox which the Board approved, and the alterations and repairs were carried out by Bury & Co. in Liverpool in July 1834.[65]

Whilst the conversion from iron to copper fireboxes was taking place, the inventive John Melling presented a model of an 'improved firebox for loco-motive engines' which used hollow, water-filled fire-bars and 'ash-pit constructed so as to form part of the boiler' – design features which would form part of his 1837 patent. The Management Committee ordered that a full-scale trial take place, and his 'model firebox' be installed in *Experiment* 'to be constructed under the Superintendence of the Committee.'[66] Dixon recommended – and the Management Committee agreed – in March 1833 that it would be useful to have three or four copper inner fireboxes made and kept as stock 'ready as the occasion might require.' [67] Thus by 1834 the conversion from iron to copper inner fireboxes and brass rather than copper tubes was complete. The increasing cost of copper (and therefore brass), led to the Management Committee investigating the possibility of returning to iron fireboxes and even iron tubes. John Dixon was instructed in June 1836 'that iron tubes be put in the next engine that wants retubing.' [68] Unsurprisingly, iron tubes were not a success: 'They occasioned more coke to be burnt; and the steam was not raised so rapidly as with copper or brass, but they were more durable, not being so liable to burst.'[69] As a result, the use of iron tubes was therefore ordered to be discontinued as being 'undesirable' and brass tubes remained the standard.[70]

Boiler fittings

The regulator was a simple rotary plug valve located under the dome (mounted over the firebox) and the main steam pipe ran the length of the boiler. Unusually, it branched to supply steam to both cylinders within the boiler barrel, rather than in the smokebox. This was simply due to lack of space within the small smokebox of the Planet (and Samson) classes.

The boiler was fed with two cross-head driven feed pumps, which meant that water could only be put into the boiler whilst the locomotive was moving. In order to overcome this disadvantage the 0-4-0 Samson types delivered to the Glasgow & Garnkirk Railway were fitted with a hand pump to inject water into boiler when the locomotive was stationary, and Rastrick notes that Stephenson & Co. supplied a portable forcing pump to the Warrington & Newton Railway, again presumably to refill boilers.[71]

Planet – and all other locomotives on the Liverpool & Manchester – had a usual maximum working pressure of 50psi; two safety valves were provided. One of 'Salter' type which also acted as a crude pressure gauge, and a second spring-loaded valve placed out of reach of the engineman, locked up in a brass casing: 'To prevent him from overloading this valve, as he is often tempted to do so in order to obtain from the engine a greater effect, even at the risk of danger.'[72] A change in the design of the lever safety valve was introduced in May 1832 at the behest of Allcard using a short lever so that '1lb on the lever may equate to 1lb pressure on the valve.'[73] Some of the enginemen must have been in the habit of tampering with the safety valves as William Allcard was instructed to:

> 'By actual experiment prove the correctness of the Safety Valves on all the Locomotive Engines, and that he lock-up and retain the key of one of the Valves on each Engine; and that he make a report to the Directors stating the name of the several Engines and the dates when they shall have been tested.'[74]

In the opinion of the Chevalier de Pambour, the calibration of these valves was often imperfect:

> 'It sometimes happens that … the pressure is declared to be 50lbs per square inch, whilst it really is 60 or 70lbs. Moreover, the calculation of the pressure is generally so incorrectly made, that any dependence cannot be placed upon it.'[75]

Lawson 'engineman of the *Sun*' was reprimanded by the Management Committee for having set his safety valves to 60psi – albeit with the authority of Ralph Hutchinson from Robert Stephenson & Co. Lawson was ordered to be more careful in the future.[76] De Pambour also states that an L&M fireman was not thought to be doing his job properly unless the safety valves were constantly blowing off, wasting a quarter of all the steam generated. He quite rightly thought this very wasteful, and Zerah Colburn ascribes the high fuel consumption on the L&M to 'extravagant firing' and suggests that L&M locomotives were burning 10lbs of 'best coke' per indicated horse-power per hour, but upwards of 4lbs of coke was actually going to waste.[77]

Valve gear

The valve gear on *Planet* was based on that used by *Rocket* (and her successors): slip-eccentric with manual override. As with *Rocket*, a pair of eccentrics are sandwiched between a pair of cheek plates on the crank axle. These are free to move laterally on the axle between a pair of driving dogs. These dogs were at first clamped to the axle; those of *Vesta* worked loose in February 1832 resulting in a collision at Manchester when the driver lost control.[78] A year later (April 1833), at John Melling's recommendation it was ordered:

> 'That the Excentric Drivers should be tapped fast into the Axle Shaft, so that once set right, they might not be liable to get wrong, as they frequently did, either from accident or design.'[79]

The 'driving dogs' of the replica are similarly pinned to the axle.[80] Each of the cheek plates has a slot into which one of the driving dogs engages; the whole eccentric assembly is shifted from left to right via a yoke, controlled from the footplate by a pedal. When the pedal is pushed down, the yoke shifts to the right, engaging forward gear. When it is disengaged, the yoke moves to the left engaging reverse gear. Conversely, in the locomotives built by Fenton, Murray & Jackson, fore-gear was selected when the pedal was released and back-gear when the pedal was depressed.[81]

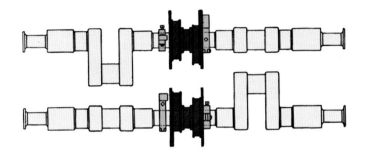

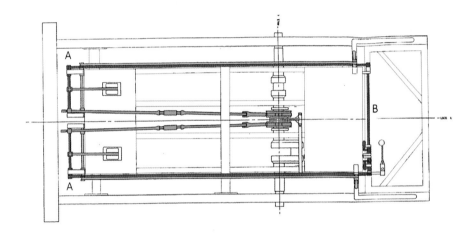

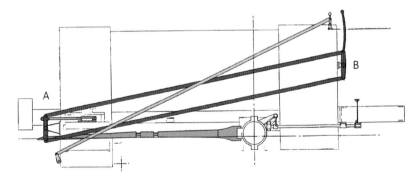

The valve gear of the Planet and Patentee type was of slip-eccentric with manual override. The eccentrics (red) are free to slide laterally between two fixed 'driving dogs' (light blue). The eccentrics are shifted by a yoke worked by a foot pedal (yellow). The eccentric rods (orange) terminate in drop-hooks which can be raised or lowered via the lifting links (cyan) from pins on the front rocking shaft (A) which in turn drive the valve spindles (green). The movement of the valves is mirrored by those of the valve handles (purple) and rocking shaft (B).With the drop-hooks unlocked (raised from the rocking shaft), this means the valves are worked manually independently from the eccentrics. When locked, the valve handles constantly wag backwards and forwards when the engine is in motion. (Andrew Mason)

The foot pedal was originally kept in place with a J-spring but the short length of the running line in Manchester, which necessitated frequent changes of direction, led to the weakening of a coil spring which kept the locomotive in fore-gear, leading to drivers experiencing difficulty in keeping the locomotive in gear. Prof. Bev Pardoe of the University of Salford replaced the spring with a torsion-bar, which has since proved simple, effective and reliable. Stephenson described this arrangement in great detail:

> 'Two eccentrics ... fixed together at right angles to each other, and placed loose upon the centre of the cranked axle ... and a driver with a projecting stud is fixed on the axle on each side, just clearing the eccentrics, a hole being made in each side of the eccentrics to fit the studs. The eccentrics can be shifted along the axle to either side by means of a lever, to make the stud in the driver on that side drop into the hole on the eccentric when it comes opposite to it in revolving, and cause the eccentric to turn with the axle and work the slides. The stud of the driver is put on the opposite side of the axle to the corresponding hole in the eccentric; so that when the eccentrics are shifted to the other side by the lever, they have to stop half a revolution before the driver catches hold of them, and are then fixed exactly opposite to their former position, and reverse the engine; in their intermediary position, when they touch neither of the drivers, they are stationary and cease to work the slides.'[82]

Instead of using a foot pedal to change gear, Isaac Dodds (1801–1884) devised a simpler method using a wrought-iron lever which pivoted to the left or right, and via toothed gears, shifted the eccentric cluster. Dodds observed that in moving the eccentrics over, one of the slide valves 'moved the length of the lap', no doubt a useful insight for his later 'sliding wedge' expansive valve gear. It was first fitted to *Pluto* in May 1832 and was considered by Hutchinson to be an easier method of changing gear than the foot pedal system. This method of selecting fore- or back-gear appears to have been adopted by Tayleur & Co. as two French authorities describe: 'In the engines of Mr Tayleur, the forward-gear is when the eccentrics, and the lever, are to the right; and in back-gear they are to the left.'[83]

The eccentrics drive a pair of eccentric rods – one per cylinder – which pass forward between the cylinders. Each of the eccentric rods terminates in a drop hook. These drop hooks engage with a pin on the forward rocking shaft which drives the valve spindles. The drop hooks can be raised and lowered from the footplate via a lifting link so that they are either engaged and locked in place, driving the rocking shaft, or disengaged, leaving the valve gear free to be worked by hand.

When unlocked, the valves can be worked manually from the footplate using two 'valve levers' on the left-hand side of the footplate. These control the front rocking shaft; the left hand lever controls the left hand valve and the right hand lever the right hand valve. Furthermore, the movement of the levers follows that of the valves themselves: when the lever is pushed forward, the valve moves forward. In order to start the locomotive it was usual to drive the locomotive 'on the handles'. Driving 'on the handles' provides 100% cut off, in other words, maximum boiler pressure to the pistons in the cylinders. There is a lot of skill and practice required in driving the locomotive in this way. When the locomotive has begun to move and gained momentum by being driven manually, the eccentrics can be engaged; the drop hooks

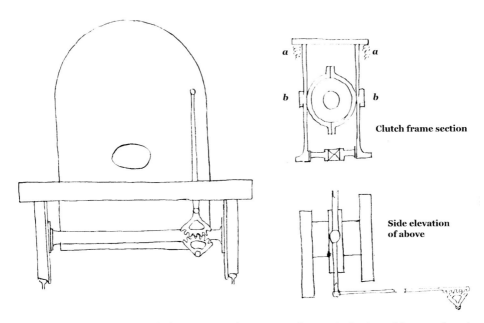

Clutch frame section

Side elevation of above

Isaac Dodd's modified form of Planet type valve gear used a vertical, pivoted lever rather than a foot pedal to shift the eccentrics between fore- and back-gear. It was approved by William Hutchinson and fitted to *Pluto* in 1832. It was later adopted by Charles Tayleur & Co. (Author, after ROB 2-1-1)

can be lowered on to the drive pins on the front rocking shaft and the locomotive will run on its own. Isaac Watt Boulton said of this valve gear:

> 'My old friend, whom I had known as a lad, from stationary winding engine driver, then as a fireman, and he soon became engineman, then night foreman, and at the time I spoke to him, as second-in-command of the locomotive department … I saw this old friend get on [the] locomotive with two loose excentrics and hand gear … He tried hard for a long time to get it to move, but had to give it up. He could not get her to move in either direction. When another old friend – Old Bill [William Holmes, the driver of *Planet*] – who did understand the hand gear, got on, and off she went in a jiffy. I have often started a load with the loose-excentric gear, while the same engine could not start it off with the fixed-excentrics. You could give the engine the steam, full on the piston, the *instant* the crank passed the centre – that is, if you knew how.'[84]

In order to stop the locomotive, the regulator is closed, shutting off steam. As the locomotive drifts to a halt, the reverser pedal can be disengaged (if the locomotive is travelling forwards) to put the locomotive into reverse. Because the locomotive is still moving forward, but with the regulator closed and valve gear in reverse, steam can be gently admitted into the cylinders, creating back-pressure in the cylinders and slowing down and stopping the locomotive. With skill and practice a locomotive can be gently brought to a stand and be held stationary on the regulator. Although the replica of *Planet* has a modern air-brake system, her drivers take pride in being able to stop and start her in 1830s style.

CHAPTER 4

Luggage Engines

Samson and *Goliath*

Whilst the delivery of *Planet* and her sisters had revolutionised passenger transport on the Liverpool & Manchester Railway, what was needed was a larger, more powerful locomotive to enable the carrying of freight. Braithwaite & Ericsson's *William IV* and *Queen Adelaide* (Part 2), had not lived up to their promise to enable the Company to carry freight in any meaningful way. It was only after the delivery of *Samson* and *Goliath* that freight carrying could begin in earnest.

These two 'large' luggage engines were ordered from Stephenson & Co. on 20 September 1830; the *Liverpool Mercury* reported in December 1830, 'new and powerful' locomotives were soon to be delivered from Newcastle and that the freight carrying would begin in earnest in New Year 1831. Stephenson & Co. reported to the Board in December 1830 that 'two large locomotive engines' would be ready by the first week of January 1831.[1] *Samson* was delivered in New Year 1831 and *Goliath* by March 1831. These two locomotives took the development of the Planet design one step further: in order to maintain the same short wheelbase (5ft 2in), to enable them to negotiate sharp curves and switches, as well as use the short turn tables, the 5 foot driving wheels and 3 foot leading wheels were replaced by four 4ft 6in coupled wheels, creating a heavy-weight 0-4-0 'luggage engine' with total weight available for adhesion. Sadly, after less than twelve months operation, *Samson* broke her crank axle in December 1831.[2]

Both engines carried somewhat larger boilers than *Planet*; the diameter of the barrel was increased from 3 feet to 3ft 6ins and the length from 6ft 6ins to 7 feet. The number of tubes was increased to 140 (*Samson*) and 132 (*Goliath*), but as with *Planet* this high number of tubes hindered free circulation of water in the boiler. The firebox was also increased in size to 7½ square feet giving a total heating surface of 457 (*Samson)* and 447 (*Goliath*) square feet respectively. Cylinders were also increased in size to 14 inches by 16 inches stroke. They also used double slide valves. This brought the weight of *Samson* up to 10 tons 4 qr of which 5 tons 11 cwt 3 qr was carried on the driving wheels. The crank pins for the outside coupling rods on the driving wheels were spherical (to allow the maximum play to the crank axle) whilst those on the leading wheels were cylindrical.[3] The *Preston Chronicle* reported the delivery of *Samson*, by sea from Carlisle to Liverpool on 12 February 1831. The pair 'are to be placed at Rainhill and Sutton, to assist the other engines in ascending the inclined planes at those places.'[4]

The *Manchester Guardian* (26 February 1831) reported the 'extraordinary performance of Mr Stephenson's engine':

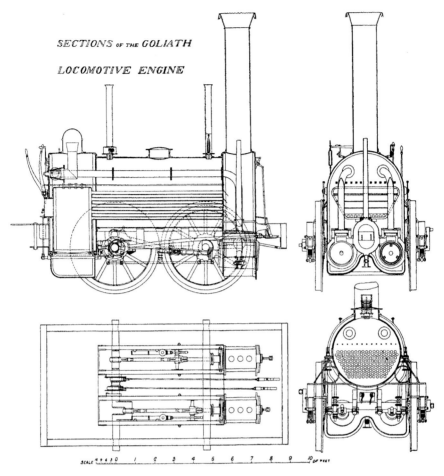

SECTIONS OF THE *GOLIATH* LOCOMOTIVE ENGINE

SCALE OF FEET

Samson (No. 13) and *Goliath (No. 15)* were the first 'luggage' (i.e. goods) engines delivered to the Liverpool & Manchester in New Year 1831. They had 4ft 6in coupled wheels and were the most powerful locomotives on the line when new. (After Warren, 1923)

'Yesterday morning, Mr Stephenson's engine, the Samson, started from the station at Liverpool with 30 waggons, carrying the following load:-

	Tons	Cwt
23 waggon load of oats	82	10
7 waggon load of merchandize	24	15
Total Nett Weight	107	5
Tares of the 30 Waggons	42	15
15 persons	1	0
Making the gross weight of	151	0 (besides the weight of the tender, with its coke, water, &c.)

With this enormous load, the Samson moved off at ten minutes past eight, and proceeded to the foot of the inclined plane, at the rate of about 20 miles an hour. It was assisted up the incline plane by three other engines (the Mars, the Mercury, and the Arrow), and arrived at the top in 38 minutes after leaving the station. As the assisting engines pushed behind the load, whilst the Samson tugged in front, it was easy, by observing where the connecting chains were tight, and where slack, to ascertain what portion of the work was done by each, and it was found that the Samson generally drew sixteen waggons, the gross weight of which would be about 80 tons; on arriving at the top of the inclined plane, the Samson stopped for five minutes to take in water, and then proceeded to Park-Side, where it arrived at 29 minutes past nine, stopped there eight minutes for water, and arrived at Manchester at sixteen minutes before eleven. The whole time of the journey was, consequently, two hours and thirty-four minutes, the net time of the travelling was two hours and twenty-one minutes.'[5]

The *Guardian* added:

'From the performance of the Samson on the Inclined Plane, no doubt is entertained that it would draw 200 tons on a perfectly level rail way. The quantity of coke consumed ... was 1,726lbs (12 cwt 1 qr 4lbs), being not quite one-third of a pound per ton per mile.'[6]

The *Manchester Guardian* continued in a similar vein in March 1831, describing how the exploits of *Samson* had completely 'thrown into the shade' those of *Planet* at the end of the previous year. *Samson* had:

'Repeatedly, without assistance, taken from fifty to sixty tons of goods up the Huyton inclined plane (an elevation of one in 96), and an average speed of about ten miles an hour; a performance which was previously supposed to be beyond the powers of a locomotive engine of any moderate or manageable size.'[7]

Samson probably had a maximum output of 40–50 horsepower; the *Mechanics' Magazine* reported that Joseph Locke described how on 19 April 1831 *Samson* drew a load of 44½ tons gross at 'about eight miles per hour' up the incline plane at Rainhill, which equated to '39 horse-power.' Another account describes *Samson* and *Goliath* as being of 'about 50 horse-power'. On 2 April 1831 *Samson* and *Goliath* worked a train of a thousand bags of New Orleans cotton from Liverpool to Manchester: starting at 8 am, *Samson* 'dragging a train of 30 loaded waggons, and Goliath 27.' Upon reaching the foot of the Whiston incline:

'The Goliath was detached from its load, and assisted the Sampson [sic] up the inclined plane. The latter then proceeded on its journey and arrived at Manchester at half-past eleven. A considerable number of spectators had assembled to witness its arrival. The Goliath, being left without assistance, carried its load up the inclined plane in three trips, and did not reach Manchester until half-past one, having been delayed a considerable time by a slight accident to the machinery.

The progress of both machines was very considerably delayed by a strong north-east wind, which blew right against them, and by the extreme slipperiness of the rails, which had been wet by several slight showers of rain in the course of the morning.

The total number of bags of cotton brought by the two engines was 1,035. Of these the Sampson [sic] brought 549. The precise weight of each load has not yet been ascertained; but as each bag of American cotton averages four cwt., the following may be considered a correct estimate of the Sampson's load:-

	Tons.	Cwt.
549 bags of cotton, at four cwt each	109	16
Tares of 30 waggons	42	15
Weight of the guards and other persons on the train	1	
Weight of the Engine	8	1
Total	161	11[8]

The load hauled by *Goliath* was probably in the region of 120 to 130 tons. A trial of *Samson* in May 1832 with a load of 150 tons gross showed that she could reach a maximum speed of 12mph, having taken 2 hours 40 minutes to cover the distance from Liverpool to Manchester, despite heavy rain earlier in the day, and a strong wind:

'The rails very wet, but the wheels did not slip, even at the slowest speed, except at starting, the rails being at that place soiled and greasy with the slime and dirt to which they are always exposed at the stations.'[9]

Goliath broke her crank axle in summer 1834; it was replaced at the Vulcan Foundry when the opportunity was also taken to lengthen the throw of the crank 'as much as the cylinders will allow' from 16 inches to 'an 18-inch or 19-inch stroke.'[10]

Atlas and *Milo*

Although like *Planet* before them, suffering with some 'teething trouble', the Samson Class were obviously a success, as two more were ordered from Robert Stephenson & Co.: *Atlas* was delivered in October 1831, and *Milo* in February 1832. Sadly, neither were initially successful locomotives.[11] *Atlas* was apparently the first locomotive to be fitted with piston valves, and drawings certainly exist showing such valves, although Robert Stephenson & Co. describe her fitted with 'double slide valves'. Her unreliability was, however, probably due to being fitted with pistons valves, with problems being experienced keeping them steam-tight, and the experiment was not repeated.[12] *Atlas* and *Milo* had cylinders 12 x 16 inches and whilst *Samson* and *Goliath* had wheels 4ft 6ins diameter, *Atlas* and *Milo* had wheels 5 feet diameter. In working order *Atlas* weighed 11.4 tons and 8 tons 19 cwt 2 qr empty. Her fully loaded tender added an additional 5.5 tons. De Pambour shows that her boiler had a heating surface of 274.9 square feet (217.88 square feet from the tubes and 57.06 from the firebox) and was capable of evaporating 50 cubic feet of water per hour. He estimated that *Atlas* had a tractive effort of approximately 2,400lbs and was capable of hauling loads

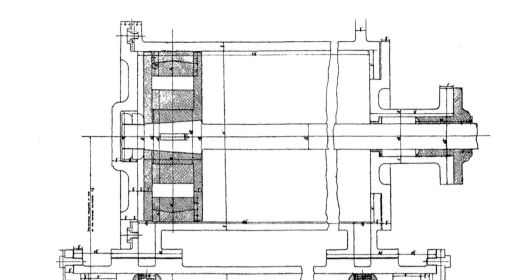

Atlas (No. 23) was fitted with a very early form of piston valve – Richard Roberts of Manchester had devised a piston valve at about the same time – but problems in keeping it steam-tight resulted in a high failure rate. (After Warren, 1923)

of 60 tons or more.[13] De Pambour notes the heaviest load *Atlas* shifted was a whopping 190 tons. On 23 July 1834, she departed Liverpool:

> '...with a train of 40 waggons weighing exactly 190 tons, and, including the tender, 195 tons. The help of two other engines was necessary for the moment of starting. On the Whiston incline plane the train was helped by four engines; viz.: two in front of the train, the Atlas and the Experiment, and two behind, the Sun and the Goliath. Drawn thus by five locomotives the train went away up the plane without a moment's delay; and once at the top the Atlas resumed alone the haulage.'

She reached a maximum speed of 15mph but slowed to as little as 4½mph ascending the Whiston incline. Boiler pressure was constant, never dropping below 51psi. Whilst hauling this massive load, she burned 1,596lbs of coke or 0.28lbs per ton per mile.[14]

The Board had never been happy with the performance of *Milo* since her delivery in February 1832:

> 'The treasurer stated that a new Engine of the Atlas Class had arrived from Newcastle ... But ... that the Cranked Axle was of insufficient strength being

only 4½ inches diameter in the crank pin, they declined to receive the Engine till refitted with a stronger Axle.'[15]

A letter from Robert Stephenson dated February 1832 shows that *Atlas* had been converted to a six-wheeler by that date, the additional wheels being able to be lifted from the rails, an innovation of John Melling, to aid adhesion by throwing all the weight of the engine on the coupled driving wheels, the reverse of his coupling wheel innovation.[16] De Pambour notes:

'The locomotive Atlas … has six wheels, of which four are of equal size, and are put in motion through the movement of the pistons. The two others are very small and have no flanges, can be raised from contact with the rails by the action of steam in a moveable cylinder. This disposition prevents these latter wheels being embarrassed in their revolutions.'[17]

But this innovation of John Melling, however, does not appear to have been a success as the Directors ordered on 11 May 1835 that Melling was to remove it and 'devise some plan for making the small pair of wheels under the *Atlas* bear their proportion of the weight.' A month later, *Atlas* was ordered to be taken out of traffic 'until the springs of the hind wheels were so adjusted as to make it impossible for the engineman to put them in and out of play.'[18] There is a reference to the ability to raise and lower one pair of wheels from the rails in a report on the Liverpool & Manchester Railway made by the Scottish Engineer Thomas Grainger for the Arbroath & Forfar Railway, dated October 1837, and Grainger recommended the adoption of such a system for use on the A&FR.[19]

In April 1832 both *Atlas* and *Milo* were reported 'as requiring repairs although New Engines, owing to their original Defective Construction.' The pair were ordered to be put right at Stephenson & Co's expense.[20] Because of the unreliability of both engines, the Management Committee ordered in May that: 'The Samson and Goliath be the Engines to be regularly employed at the two Incline Planes, and that the Milo and the Atlas be the spare ones, for those stations.'[21]

John Dixon was instructed to report to the Board as to the cost of putting *Atlas* into 'repair and efficiency', including the cost of work already carried out on her 'over and above the ordinary wear and tear' of daily service. John Dixon reported on the state of *Atlas* to the Board on 11 June 1832; a week later he presented his costing for the 'extraordinary repairs' of *Atlas*, *Milo* and *Vesta*, which were all suffering from boiler problems. Dixon considered the boilers being 'inferior … as compared to the other engines.'[22] The final cost of the repair work to *Atlas* and *Milo* was £212 11s 3d which was to be paid for by Robert Stephenson & Co.[23] In September 1832 *Milo* was sent to Messrs. Foster & Griffin of Liverpool for such repairs and alteration that William Allcard thought fit, including a new iron firebox.[24] But by 1 April 1833 John Dixon records that the firebox had 'shown symptoms of blistering, &c. before it has worked a month' and recommend she be fitted with a copper firebox. He also noted that *Atlas* had only run 8,850 miles, whilst *Milo* had run a little more, 8,880 miles. In October 1834 *Milo* was sent to George Forrester & Co. of Liverpool for thorough overhaul, but upon dismantling was found to be in such a poor state as to be beyond economic repair.

She was 'so defective in her principal parts – Fire Box, Chimney End, Cylinders, Wheels & Axles' that Forresters thought it more expedient to build a replacement. The Board hoped that they would take *Milo* (valued at £250) as part of the payment for a new engine (which Forrester quite rightly declined); instead a new engine was ordered for £860.[25] It was reported to the annual meeting held in February 1835 that during the past six months 'three new and powerful engines' for merchandise trains had been delivered whilst a fourth had been entirely reconstructed 'with new materials ... with the exception only of the cylindrical boiler.' This was presumably *Milo*.[26]

Titan and *Orion*

Despite the teething trouble with *Atlas* and *Milo*, the overall success of the Samson type led to the Management Committee instructing Robert Stephenson & Co. 'the engines which they should send, in future, would have coupled wheels like the Atlas.'[27] *Samson* and *Goliath* appear to have been particularly hard-worked; both were out of action in late September 1832 and John Dixon was instructed to hire the recently completed experimental locomotive *Caledonian* from Messrs. Galloway of Manchester to partially solve the motive power shortage.[28] The worn-out state of *Goliath* is shown that she was sold in September 1835 for as little as £100 to one Samuel Ellis; *Sun* and *Etna* (2-2-0 Planet types) were in marginally better repair and sold in the same month for £200 and £250 respectively, *Etna* finding her way to the Dowlais ironworks in South Wales.[29]

The success of the railway, resulting in an increased number (and weight) of trains being run, meant there was a locomotive shortage at the beginning of 1834. Tenders had been invited in December 1833 for two new luggage engines with copper fireboxes, brass tubes and five-foot driving wheels. Fenton, Murray & Jackson responded in February 1834 quoting £1,000 each, and Edward Bury & Co. £1,140. Neither of these quotes were accepted, and instead Henry Booth wrote to Hick & Co. of Bolton and Charles Tayleur & Co. for two luggage engines 'with coupled wheels, 11-inch Cylinder, and 20-inch stroke', the tender going to Tayleur & Co for £950 each, the first to be delivered in five months, and the second in seven 'from the date of the order.' Both engines were to be 'of the same pattern' so that parts were interchangeable. The Management Committee was also ordered to 'consider the best means of putting the Locomotive Engines into complete Repair, with as little delay as possible.'[30]

The next pair of 'heavy coupled engines' were *Titan* and *Orion*. They were delivered in September and October 1834 as four-wheelers, with 5 feet coupled wheels and cylinders 11 x 20 inches. They were supplied with 'one spare cranked axle, one straight axle and one set of wheels.'[31] Both were quickly converted to six-wheelers (0-4-2) 'to improve riding', the Directors ordering in May 1835 'an additional pair of wheels to be placed under the heavy end of *Orion*'. This was done through the provision of frame extensions to support an extra pair of carrying wheels.[32] Tayleur & Co. reported to the Board in March 1835 the cost of the spare axles and wheels for the two engines, and at the same time recommended increasing the size of the cylinders to 12 inch bore which could be done for £130.[33] Mather, Dixon & Co. had offered to supply the Company with one of their new engines in January 1835 for £850, but because

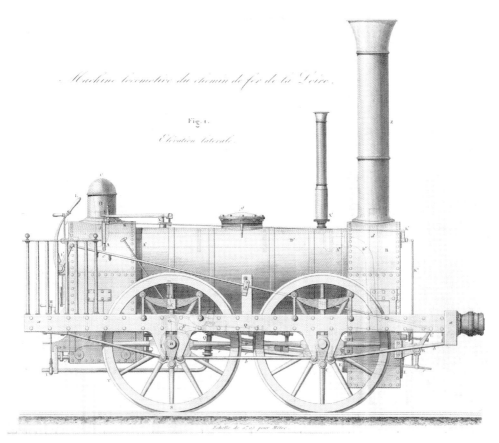

A French depiction of a typical member of the Samson Class, supplied to the Chemin de Fer de la Loire. (Anthony Dawson collection)

'it was not constructed upon the Plan which they preferred as best', i.e. with outside frames and bearings, it was not purchased. Two engines, however, were subsequently purchased from Mather, Dixon.[34] *Titan* was damaged by the GJR engine *Warrington* which ran into her at Edge Hill in January 1838: the cost of repairs came to £12, paid by the GJR. [35]

Planet: 'Perfection'?

The Planet class (and its Samson class derivative) was the first mass-produced 'class' of locomotives and was the progenitor of the main line steam locomotive for the next 130 years; to paraphrase former NRM Director Colonel Steve Davies, *Planet* was the space shuttle to *Rocket*'s *Apollo 11*. Hardman Earle thought that with the *Planet* design the steam locomotive had come as close to perfection as it was then possible (1832): 'she comes nearer to what we consider perfection (relative, of course) than any which have succeeded, but her form and general construction has never been improved upon.'

Table 3: Samson Class (0-4-0) Locomotives on the Liverpool & Manchester Railway

	Builder	Date	Cylinders	Wheels	Boiler	Tubes	Size	Weight	Notes
Samson (13)	Robert Stephenson & Co.	January 1831	14 x 16	4ft 6in	7ft x 3ft 6in	140	1 5/8in	10t 1qr (iron wheels)	Sold by 1839.
Goliath (15)	RS & Co.	March 1831	14 x 16	4ft 6in	7ft x 3ft 6in	132	1 5/8in	10t 8cwt 2qr	Sold 1835 for £100.
Atlas (23)	RS & Co.	October 1831	12 x 16	5ft	7ft 4in x 3ft	98	1 5/8 in	11.4t (iron wheels)	Rebuilt as 0-4-2 February 1832; rebuilt 1842; sold 1852.
Milo (25)	RS & Co.	May 1832	12 x 16	5ft	7ft 4in x 3ft	98	1 5/8 in		Scrapped 1834.
Titan (34)	Charles Tayleur & Co.	October 1834	11 x 20	5ft	8ft 4in x 3ft	88	1 3/4in	13t 7cwt 2qr (iron wheels)	Rebuilt as 0-4-2 May 1835 & cylinders re-bored 12 x 20 inches. In service 1839.
Orion (35)	CT & Co.	November 1834	11 x 20	5ft	?	89	1 3/4in		Rebuilt as 0-4-2 May 1835 & cylinders re-bored 12 x 20 inches. In service 1839.

CHAPTER 5

The Patentee Type

Track problems

The six-wheeled Patentee type locomotive grew out of serious problems with the L&M permanent way. As the late Andrew Dow has described, the railway is a transport machine:

> 'one part of which is the movable, consisting of the rolling stock, and the other part fixed, comprising the permanent way and its auxiliaries ... The several parts are dependent upon one another, and together they constitute the railway transport machine.'[1]

In other words, no matter how good the locomotive or rolling stock, if the track system was unable to support the weight and speed of the trains running on it, then the whole system would fail. This was something which George Stephenson understood; he was a great 'systems integrator' taking a 'system scale' view of a problem, 'regarding the road and the locomotive as one machine, speaking of the rail and the wheel as "man and wife."'[2]

The origin of the six wheeled locomotive was due to the permanent way not having been designed for an axle load greater than 4½ tons: half a ton less than the load on *Planet*'s driving wheels. By November 1833 the maximum axle load was stated to be 5 tons.[3] Faults with the permanent way (track, chairs and blocks) had begun to occur from the beginning of 1831, and by spring 1832 serious problems were beginning to manifest. The line had been initially laid with wrought-iron fish bellied rails weighing 35lbs per yard for the most part laid on stone blocks. George Stephenson had optimistically estimated that the rails would last for 60 or 70 years before needing replacing, but later had to revise this down to 30 years, but this too was wildly optimistic.[4]

As a result of the number of broken rails and stone blocks, in April 1832 the Board resolved that the maximum axle load for any locomotive was 4 tons 16 cwt and in the following month George Stephenson was asked to report on the condition of the permanent way. In fact John Dixon was amazed as to how the very lightweight 35lb rail can 'carry the present Engines at the present velocities without being all ruined or spoilt in a week.'[5] Breakage of the rails was 'a daily occurrence' and it was estimated some 2.5% of all the rails had in fact broken and had been replaced, with '5 miles of the whole 30 relaid with stronger rails.'[6] Breakage of rails was due to the weight of the locomotives passing over them, but also because there was no elasticity in the track, and from the shape of the rails. George Stephenson and other engineers of his generation believed the track should be absolutely solid, whilst a younger generation of men such as John Dixon, Edward Woods and others were of the opinion that having a solid permanent way was 'highly deleterious' to both the iron rails and vehicles using the railway.[7] The line was partially relaid with heavier 60lb parallel rails in 1835, and following an inspection by Professor Peter Barlow, the entire main line was relaid with 75lb rails 1837–1838.[8]

In November 1832, George Stephenson suggested to the Board that in order to reduce axle load, they adopt six-wheeled engines, by adding an extra pair of wheels behind the firebox to relieve some of the weight on the driving wheels and crank axle. He estimated that out of the 10 or so tons a locomotive then weighed, more than half, about 5½ tons, was on the driving wheels, higher than the 4½ tons axle loading the L&M track had been designed for.[9] Thus, the provision of extra carrying wheels would relieve the track of some of this weight and hopefully mitigate against further damage until heavier rails could be laid. *Atlas* had been rebuilt as a six-wheeler in or by February 1832; *Meteor* was rebuilt as a 2-2-2 in December 1833, whilst *Titan* and *Orion* were converted to 0-4-2s in May 1835; the Directors' Minutes hint that *Firefly* had also been converted to a 2-2-2 by 1835. Richard Roberts notes in 1841 that *Mars* and *Hercules* were also converted to six-wheelers.

In February 1833 a second discussion took place regarding the state of the permanent way and the best means to reduce the axle-load of locomotives. The introduction of six-wheeled locomotives was again raised:

'A Discussion took place as to the expediency of recommending to the Board a large 6-wheel engine which Robt Stephenson & Co. were making which they recommended as one which would do less injury to the rails, and by having more Boiler room, would wear longer.'[10]

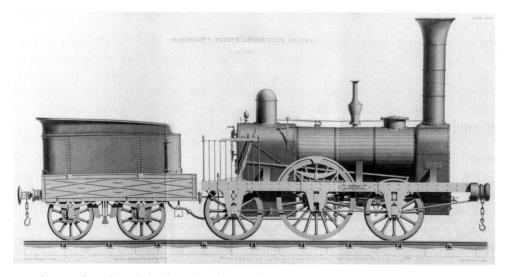

In order to reduce the axle load on the relatively light-weight permanent way, the Board ordered the use of six wheels. The 2-2-2 coaching engine became the mainstay of passenger traffic for most of the nineteenth century. (Anthony Dawson collection)

John Dixon expressed his doubts as to whether an engine with such a long fixed wheelbase would be able to negotiate the points and crossings, and he was instructed to liaise with Messrs. Stephenson on the matter.[11]

Development of the six-wheeled luggage engine was somewhat tortuous, as it was thought that the addition of a pair of carrying wheels behind the firebox would reduce adhesion, hence no doubt why when John Melling introduced carrying wheels on *Atlas*, he contrived a system whereby they could be raised or lowered from the rails, in order to 'throw the weight' on the driving wheels when needed. Opponents to the six-wheeler argued that 'The additional wheels appear objectionable by increasing the weight to be propelled'; the additional wheels increased the rolling friction of the locomotive; and a longer wheel base required larger turn-tables and switches.[12] Edward Woods was of a similar opinion: whilst he did not consider the weight of additional wheels and axles to be 'of much importance' he thought six-wheel engines were more prone to slipping due to having 'less adhesion than four-wheeled engines'; he was concerned about 'the difficulty of "taking the points"' and 'the tendency to strain and friction in passing round curves' because of the longer wheel-base. Due to a longer wheelbase, Woods also thought them more damaging to the track, especially going round curves, causing track spread.[13]

With the relaying of the line with 60lb rails in 1835 the opportunity was taken to raise axle-loads to 6 tons, a 1 1/2 ton increase on the previous limit. A six ton axle load was confirmed by the Board in December 1835 who added that:

'The Directors reserve to themselves now and at all times the power to require additional or third pair of wheels to be placed under any engine working on their line, for the purpose of giving steadiness to the motion, where the same shall be deemed necessary or expedient by the Company's Engineer.'[14]

Even with the main line laid with 75lb rails, excessive axle load still remained a problem. John Hargreaves' locomotive *Utilitis* (see Part 2), albeit carried on six wheels, was reported to the board to weigh 15 tons and as a result was 'very damaging' to the track. The Board ordered therefore 'that the Engineer prevent the *Utilitis* running on the Liverpool and Manchester Line' and no locomotive heavier than 15 tons was allowed to run. Indeed, Whishaw shows that the majority of L&M engines were small and weighed less than 15 tons – only *Samson* and *Goliath* (Hick & Co., 1839) weighed over that mark.[15]

Patentee

Robert Stephenson & Co had built their six-wheel engine speculatively and first offered it to the Liverpool & Manchester in spring 1833. Dixon reported on her in April 1833, and the issue of the locomotive damaging the track, particularly the wooden switches (which he had predicted), was discussed. As a result, the Management Committee 'did not feel prepared to recommend the use of such engines at present.'[16] The locomotive was originally fitted with flanged driving wheels, which were found to damage the permanent way, in particular the switches. She was offered to the

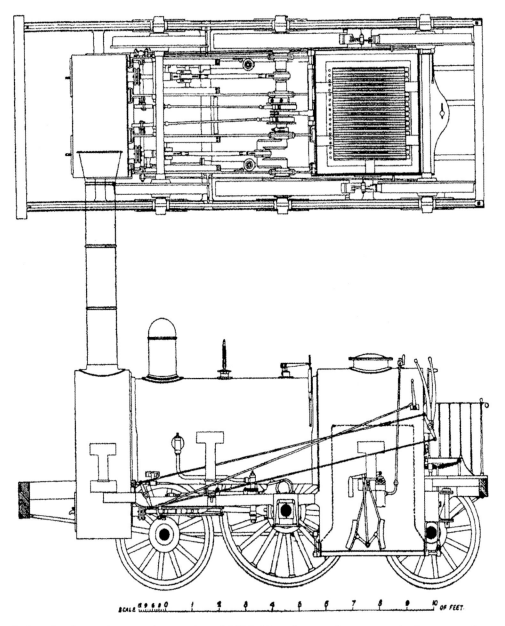

Robert Stephenson's patent locomotive of 1833. Note the prominent steam brake mounted on the firebox. (After Warren, 1923)

Liverpool & Manchester for £1,000 in May 1834 on the condition that she be fitted with 'new cylinders and frame work' ('to strengthen the fastenings of her interior framing'), with 'Stephenson & Co. being responsible for any repairs that might be suggested.' As a result, she was sent to Charles Tayleur & Co. for modifications and following these was accepted in to stock in September 1834, at a cost of £700 – the £300 difference being the alterations carried out.[17]

In December 1833 Tayleur & Co. were 'desirous' that their six-wheeled engine should also undergo trials. Hardman Earle recommended:

'That a trial be made of Chas. Tayleur & Co.'s 6 wheel Engine to run with the Luggage trains between Liverpool and Manchester, and an account be kept of her consumption of coke.'[18]

Henry Booth was instructed to liaise with Tayleur & Co., and 'that the trial might be arranged under Mr Dixon's orders.'[19] Dixon reported back to the Management Committee on Boxing Day 1833:

'He had been along the line, from Liverpool to Manchester. The centre wheel, from its increased breadth, rubbed hard against the check rails and the wood switches, so much so that he did not consider it safe for it to be run in its present state. Mr Dixon, however, was of the opinion that the breadth of the wheel might be diminished without detriment to the engine.'

The Management Committee resolved that if Tayleur & Co. were willing to carry out the alterations to the locomotive suggested by Dixon, then they would accept it into stock and Dixon was 'instructed to communicate on the subject with the Vulcan Foundry accordingly.'[20] At the committee meeting of 4 February 1834, it was reported by Dixon that Tayleur's six-wheel engine 'had been tried again' but again had not proved successful due to poor weight distribution:

'From the difficulty of adjusting the weight on the bearing wheels, the adhesion was very incomplete, and consequently the Engine was unable to take above 9 or 10 loaded waggons. He had therefore sent it back to the Vulcan Foundry.'[21]

Stephenson's *Patentee* was an unlucky engine, and had a chequered career: on 29 March 1836 she ran into the *Leeds* which was crossing out of the 'pig siding' at Manchester. A month later her front axle broke near Bury Lane whilst she was working the 5pm first class train and she ran off the rails.[22] Henry Booth was instructed to investigate and concluded that the accident had been made worse because of the driving wheels lacking flanges which meant that they could not hold the locomotive on the track.[23] John Gray wrote in 1841 that 'such a causality was anticipated' and that in fact a pair of flanged driving wheels for her 'were actually in progress' at the time of the accident. Thereafter *Patentee* (and all other 2-2-2 coaching engines) were fitted with flanged driving wheels.[24]

1838 was an 'annus horribilis': in January *Patentee* collided with *Phoenix* on the Whiston Incline as the result of a 'vague signal' and in April her fireman, Daniel McVie, was crushed to death whilst disconnecting the tender water hoses. In October she was involved in a fatal accident at Newton Junction. Finally, in November she exploded whilst working a goods train up the Whiston Incline, killing both of her crew. Early on Monday 12 November 1838 *Patentee* had been pilot engine coupled to *Fury* (the train engine) at the head of a heavy train of 43 loaded goods waggons (around 200 tons) assisted (Banked) from the rear by the newly arrived *Lion* driven by Joseph Greenall. Whilst toiling up the incline, *Patentee* blew up with an explosion 'which ... resembled the firing of a cannon, was heard at Prescot and other places, more than a mile distant.'[25] According to the *Manchester Courier:* 'The Engine was shattered to pieces, and the tubes were totally destroyed.' The Engineman, Charles Warburton, was found:

> 'Forty yards distant ... his right leg was broken, and his head terribly mangled ... The Fireman ... Samuel Jones, a lad of not more than eighteen years of age ... was found in the opposite direction. His left leg was literally severed from his body, and lay two yards distant from it.'[26]

At the inquest, John Melling was called as witness and could not account for the explosion: the lead plug had not melted, suggesting the water level had not dropped dangerously low; the boiler plates were found to have been sound; and he dismissed the idea that the crew had tampered with the safety valves as 'Warburton was an old and experienced engineer.' Even if he had tampered with the Salter-type safety valve, the spring-loaded lock-up valve would have prevented such a failure. Warburton had, as per regulation, wanted to divide the train to run it up the bank, but had been persuaded not to by Greenall. A verdict of accidental death was recorded and a Deodand – a medieval custom of placing a fine on any property that had taken human life – of 20s was placed on *Patentee*.[27] It is likely that the cause of the explosion was due to a fault inherent in the design as the drag-pin was riveted directly to the back of the firebox wrapper, rather than to the frames, so when under extreme load the firebox could be literally ripped apart. Following the explosion the Directors recommended the examining of all locomotives on the line, ensuring that 'the staying of the Fire Box above the Fire Door and Boiler End next the Chimney were strong.' This suggests the cause of the explosion lay not with the boiler but the firebox, and the drag-pin being riveted to it. In light of the findings of the inquest, however, the Board also ordered that 'in all new Engines, the safety valve at the front end of the boiler be made larger than those now in use' as a fail-safe, to release more steam in case of the other being tampered with.[28] Although blame was cast upon Warburton the engineman, it transpired that the back plate of the firebox had not been secured to the firebox using angle irons, but instead the edge of the plate had been turned over to make a flange, but this flange was too short and in the opinion of the civil engineer Charles Hulton Gregory 'its fibre had probably been damaged' during that process. This resulted in a weak spot, which under load from the drag-pin had given way.[29] Thus it was a combination of unique events which resulted in the death of Warburton and Jones: *Patentee*'s firebox back-plate had been badly manufactured and was a major weak-point; there was an excessive load placing extra strain on an already poorly made or designed component which then failed. *Patentee* had run (other than breaking an axle) quite safely since 1833 and no other L&M locomotive – despite having their drag-pins riveted directly to the firebox back-plate suffered a similar catastrophic failure – even working a load in excess of 100 tons. Despite the tragedy, *Patentee* was repaired and was in use working luggage trains 1839–1840.

Boiler and firebox

Robert Stephenson had early on recognised that the power of the locomotive was dependent entirely on its heating surface, and that the most steam was generated around the hottest part of the boiler, the firebox. By introducing an extra pair of wheels behind the firebox, this meant that Stephenson could more properly balance the weight of the locomotive, and furthermore use a 'larger boiler than hitherto used':

> 'By virtue of my improvement, a larger boiler is used, containing more heating-surface than heretofore, a less intense excitement of the combustion will be required in order to produce the necessary quantity of steam ... Increasing the magnitude of the boiler, giving a larger extent of heating surface thereto, and working the enlarged boiler with a more moderate intensity of fire ... will save fuel.'[30]

A larger boiler and firebox therefore made the locomotives more economical to run, and as Stephenson noted in his patent specification (No. 6484 of 7 October 1834) he was already becoming aware that the hot gases had not given up all their energy in passing through the boiler tubes, leading to 'rapid burning of the metal of the boiler' – an observation which would lead to the 'Long Boiler' locomotives of the 1840s where Stephenson attempted to find a better ratio between boiler length and diameter, to get the maximum amount of heat from the gases passing through the tubes.

Patentee had a boiler 7ft 1 in long and 3ft 6in outside diameter. The firebox exploited the maximum width available between the outside frames, measuring 3 feet 11¼ inches by 4 feet 1 inch with the inner copper firebox measuring 36½ inches by 3 feet 3 inches. It had a surface area of 9.9 square feet. There were 106 brass tubes, 1 5/8 inches outside diameter, 1/13 of an inch thick. Each of the tubes was made from 'the best rolled brass' and individually rolled and soldered. Total heating surface was 364.36 square feet.[31] A larger smokebox enabled the main steam pipe to bifurcate outside of the boiler barrel, in the smokebox, presenting less of a maintenance problem. Also aiding maintenance was a smokebox door: in order to gain access to *Planet*'s smokebox, a heavy oval plate has to be unbolted, a two-man job, and which made access to the smokebox a lengthy task. With his Patent Locomotive, Stephenson introduced:

> 'A large door ... for the purpose of affording access to the cylinders and tubes; there is a ledge fixed around the opening, against which the door is closely pressed by four finger nuts ... There is also a small door, near the bottom of the smoke-box door, for the purpose of clearing out the cinders and ashes that collect in it.'[32]

Both of these doors had to be an air-tight fit so as not to destroy the vacuum created by the blast pipe. A damper was also fitted at the base of the chimney, to regulate the flow of gases through the boiler.

Running-in trials were conducted by John Dixon in May 1834 to assess not only her fuel consumption but also her characteristics when fired with Gas coke or Worsley coke. He reported that she burned 0.49lb of Worsley coke per ton per mile, and 0.78lb per ton per mile of Gas coke. He also noted that 'some alteration' had been made in her firebox, but does not elaborate as to what that was. Following these trials it was ordered that engines with copper fireboxes use Worsley coke 'or coke of that description' with Gas coke being restricted to those with iron fireboxes.[33] Worsley coke was a hard foundry coke with far fewer volatiles than coke used for gas making. It was the preferred fuel, despite being more expensive than Gas coke, because it burned hotter (about 12%) and cleaner. The extra cost in purchasing Worsley coke compared to Gas coke, however, could be off-set because the locomotives burned less Worsley coke. The use of colder Gas coke in locomotives with iron inner fireboxes suggests an attempt to prevent them from overheating and 'burning out.'[34]

Wheels and axles

The larger firebox, and therefore weight behind the driving wheels, meant that 'there was an excessive pitching motion, which makes them rise on the springs of the front wheels' which was 'considered very dangerous when running very fast.' Thus, the extra carrying wheels 'support[ed] the fire-box, and prevent this [pitching] action.' The larger firebox also meant the wheel base was extended from 9 feet of the converted four-wheelers, to 10 feet, and the weight was distributed as follows:

Leading-wheels	4 tons 10 cwt
Driving-wheels	4 tons 6 cwt
Trailing-wheels	2 tons 13 cwt
Total	11 tons 9 cwt[35]

In his patent specification, Stephenson described:

'The additional small wheels which I apply beneath the hinder end of the boiler, will sustain the extra weight of a larger boiler than hitherto used, without distressing the rails; and bearing-springs are to be used … and the said springs will cause all the six wheels to apply and bear fairly on the rails, and ease all joints and concussions; the relative weights or portions of the whole weight of the engine, which shall be borne by each of the six wheels being regulated by the strength and setting of their respecting bearing-springs. The main-wheels which are to be impelled by the power of the engine being in all cases left loaded with as much of the weight of the engine as will cause sufficient adhesion of those wheels to the rails to avoid slipping thereon.'[36]

Weight distribution was a problem with the Patentees, with too much weight being taken on the leading axle. Stephenson introduced his composite wrought- and cast-iron 'gas pipe' wheels for his Patent Locomotive. This utilised hollow, wrought-iron spokes, off-set like those on a bicycle, around a cast iron nave, which was poured around them:

'The rims of the wheels are cast iron, four inches and a half wide and two inches and a half deep; they are cast with a groove round them outer side to diminish the weight; the bosses are cast on the inner side, where the spokes are inserted.

The spokes are wrought iron tubes one quarter of an inch thick and tapering from two inches and a quarter to two inches in diameter, and they are cast into the nave and rim. The spokes are inclined to the plane of the wheel ... and they are inclined alternately in opposite directions ... for the purpose of increasing the lateral strength of the wheels ... The spokes are laid into the moulds in which the wheels are cast, and the wheels cast around them, the ends of the spokes being first plugged up ... the rims of the wheels are cast first ... before the naves are cast because they contract more in the cooling than the naves, being of a larger diameter, tending to force the spokes nearer to the centre.'[37]

The wheels were turned on a lathe and wrought-iron tyres were rolled and shrunk on. The tyres were then bolted in place with three countersunk bolts. The driving wheels lacked flanges, in an attempt to reduce lateral strain on the crank axle. These wheels did not prove durable in service and were prone to breakage. The Directors' minutes of 3 June 1833 note:

'That in consequence of the complete failure of several of the Engine wheels on their patent principal, & the partial failure of the Pluto's crank axle, the Directors would expect ... a guarantee of the wheels and axles for 12 Months; and that the Engine should be sent without wheels & Axles.'[38]

In February 1834 the patent wheels of *Firefly* collapsed. As a result the Board ordered the use of Stephenson's patent wheels to be suspended for engines then being built, and the patent wheels of Richard Roberts & Co. of Manchester or of Bury of Liverpool to be adopted.[39] Charles Tayleur jnr. attended the Board Meeting of 3 March 1834 'recommending a trial' of their wheels 'on the Principles of Mr Stephenson's patent ... offering to guarantee the stability'. The Board were hesitant, and only accepted them so long as Tayleur could guarantee them for 50,000 miles.[40] Despite this guarantee, the wheels of *Eclipse* and *Star* – both by Tayleur & Co. – failed in spring 1836, having only run 5,600 and 3,200 miles respectively. The Board considered 'the wheels to have been improperly manufactured, or made of unsound materials' and that the 'makers ought to put them immediately into working order' at their own expense.[41] The enterprising Theodore Jones of London suggested the Directors purchase a set of his 'patent wheels under his guarantee for durability' but they declined this offer, suggesting instead that a comparative trial be made of them instead.[42] Jones' patent wheels resembled bicycle wheels; they used a wrought-iron rim and cast-iron hub into which off-set wrought-iron spokes were secured.[43] They had been successfully used by Braithwaite and Ericsson on *Novelty* at the Rainhill Trials (see part 2). As an added precaution, spare wheels and axles were ordered for *Orion* and *Titan,* and at the Management Committee meeting on 19 February 1835 a long discussion 'took place as to the expediency of limiting the weight to be allowed by the Company to be placed on one pair Locomotive Wheels.'[44] The scale and cost of the problem is shown through the company accounts: £246 5s 11d was spent in the second half of 1834 on 'New Wheels, Cranked Axles &c.'; £576 18s 7d in the first half of 1835 and £221 1s 6d for the second; over £1,000 was spent from January to June 1836 on replacement wheels and axles.[45]

Valve gear

Patentee was provided with the same slip-eccentric valve gear as *Planet*, but unlike *Planet* where the front rocking shaft was ahead of the cylinders, it was squeezed in behind the cylinders, below the boiler barrel. This also meant that the lifting links for the drop-hook ended eccentric rods were also beneath the boiler, the entire valve gear being somewhat inaccessible within the frames.

Stephenson had already appreciated the expansive action of steam in the cylinder with *Lancashire Witch* (1828), and with *Patentee* he introduced a degree of lap lead to the valves; lap is the amount by which the valve overlaps the steam port at the middle position of each valve. The lead of a valve is the amount by which the steam port is open when the piston is at dead-centre, and is particularly useful on locomotives intended to work at high speed, when the valve events are in quick succession, giving a free exhaust:

> 'The principal advantage by giving lead to the slides is in beginning to get rid of waste steam before the commencement of the stroke; so that when the piston commences its stroke there is but little waste steam before it to resist its progress, the steam beginning to be let out of the cylinder before it has driven the piston to the end of the stroke ... For this reason, an advantage is obtained by letting out the steam before the end of the stroke ... The lead given to the letting out of the steam is made greater than the steam lead ... The steam is shut off a little before the end of the stroke in consequence of the lead of the slide, and acts expansively for that portion, saving so much of the steam.'[46]

Steam brake

Locomotives such as *Planet* or *Samson* had no brakes, but with *Patentee* Stephenson introduced not only brakes on the locomotive but a fast-acting powerful steam brake. This consisted of a vertical cylinder mounted on the left-hand side of the firebox, working wooden brake blocks on the rear of the driving wheels and front of the carrying wheels. The tender was also provided with the traditional hand brake. In his patent specification, Stephenson stated:

> '[The steam brake] which consists in applying the force of a small extra steam-piston fitted into suitable cylinders, which by turning a cock can be supplied when required with steam from the boiler, in order to act upon a double brake, or a pair of clogs, which are applied to the circumferences of the tires of the said main-wheels without flanges and of the two additional small wheels.'[47]

Coaching engines

Rapid and *Speedwell* were 2-2-2s delivered from Tayleur & Co. in 1835 with 5 feet driving wheels and cylinders measuring 12 x 18 inches (*Rapid*) and 12½ x 18

(*Speedwell*). The Directors resolved to order four new six-wheeled coaching engines in August 1835, 'two be delivered in six months from the date of order and two in nine months.' At the suggestion of Edward Woods, they were to be ordered with a 'short stroke' but, in order to off-set the loss of tractive effort from the shorter stroke, with 'an increased diameter of the piston'. Increasing the diameter of a cylinder is more effective than increasing its stroke, and with a short-stroke cylinder is a very effective means of increasing output force. Furthermore, the piston travels less distance and less quickly, thus reducing wear. Thus, Woods had these two locomotives built to assess whether short-stroke engines were faster runners, more fuel efficient, with lower maintenance costs. At a time when the balancing of the power strokes or reciprocating masses of a locomotive was unheard of, or at best little understood, Henry Booth correctly thought that reducing the stroke would reduce piston velocity and thus also 'diminish the reciprocating motion' of the engine, making it more stable at speed. The Management Committee agreed to order four new coaching engines on 6 August 1835:

> 'The four new engines should be of the Planet Class, 14 inch stroke instead of 16 as at present, and the diameter to be increased so as to make the Engines of the same power as the two last Engines, the Rapid and the Speedwell – which would require a cylinder from 13 to 13½ inches diameter; the new Engines to have 6 wheels according to the present arrangement of the Fire Fly's; Copper Fire Boxes 2 feet inside from front to back, with the latest improvement in every other respect.'[48]

Four days later the Board approved the purchase of four new locomotives, but instead of ordering four with 14 inch stroke, two were ordered with 'the usual stroke of 16 inches' and two with a stroke of only 12 inches. A tender of £850 from the Haigh Foundry was accepted for two engines with a 16 inch stroke and Booth was authorised to enquire whether they would build a third for the same price, which they agreed to for £950; Charles Tayleur & Co. built one 'short stroke' engine (*Star*) for £1,050.[49] Edward Woods notes that the 'short stroke' engines were fast runners, 'establish[ing] … a quicker rate of travelling than had before been known on the line' but also with an 'extravagant increase in the consumption of coke.' At the time it was thought to be due to the 'mechanical disadvantage of the short stroke' and no further experiments took place.[50] That said, however, the design was of sufficient success to result in an order of a further six 'short stroke' locomotives which were to be 'the same size and description' as *Star*.[51] Works drawings show *Star* had a distinctive six-pointed star mounted above her nameplate. She had cylinders measuring 14 x 12 inches.[52] Of these six short-stroke engines, four were to be built by Tayleur & Co. for £1,150 each and two by Mather, Dixon & Co. for £1,120. They were to be delivered in September, October, November and December 1836.[53] The three six-wheeled coaching engines from the Haigh Foundry were *Vesuvius* (February 1836), and *Lightning* and *Cyclops* (both June 1836). All three had cylinders 12½ x 16 inches; two more 'bank engines' were ordered by John Dixon in the same month.[54]

Messrs. Robert & William Hawthorn of Newcastle contracted to build two coaching engines *Sun* and *Venus* (alias *Vesta*), in 1836 for £1,150 each. *Sun* was delivered in spring 1837, and the Directors' minutes record she began work on 27 March.

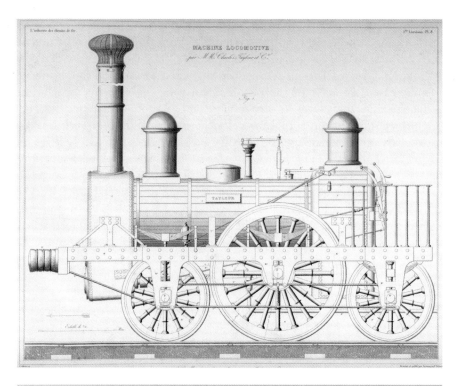

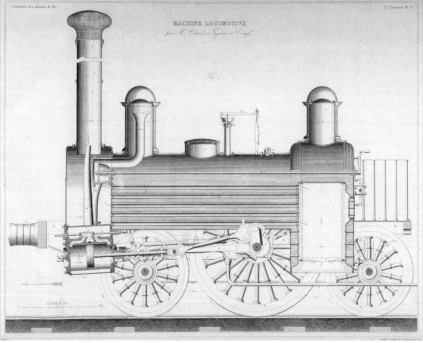

Charles Tayleur of the Vulcan Foundry also developed a six wheel 2-2-2 coaching engine. Note the use of two steam domes to increase the amount of steam space in a relatively small boiler. (After Armengaud & Armengaud)

The Newcastle press was full of praise for her; the *Newcastle Journal* noted she was 'destined to run with the first-class passenger trains' and was 'about 40 horses' power'. Much attention was drawn to her 'architectural details' including the two steam domes. Her overall appearance was 'in good taste, being chaste, yet attractive.' She was fitted with Hawthorns' radial valve gear which meant that she could be 'instantaneously' reversed using only a single reversing-lever on the footplate, which, in the opinion of the press, would lead to greater railway safety. In June 1838 *Sun* made the run from Manchester to Liverpool in 41 minutes, or 45mph – clearly in breach of regulations.[55]

A month later, however, Hawthorns, 'request[ed] to be released from their contract to furnish a second engine similar to the "Sun"', but the Board did not think it 'expedient' to do so. *Sun* and *Venus* were the only engines on the L&M from Hawthorns: in April 1838 John Melling travelled to Newcastle to inspect two engines which had been 'built to go abroad, but the money not being forthcoming were now on sale.' Despite the urging of Melling, the Board declined to purchase them, being 'sufficiently well supplied [with locomotives] for the present year.'[56]

Table 4: Patentee-type (2-2-2) Locomotives on the Liverpool & Manchester Railway

	Builder	Date	Cylinders	Boiler	Tubes	Size	Weight	Notes
Patentee (33)	Robert Stephenson & Co.	1833	12 x 18	7ft x 3ft 4in	106	1 5/8in	11t 9cwt	Boiler explosion 1838; rebuilt; in service 1841.
Rapid (37)	Charles Tayleur & Co.	1835	11 x 16	8ft x 3ft	89	1 5/8in		In service 1840.
Speedwell (38)	CT & Co.	1835	12 ½ x 16	7ft 9in x 3ft	89	2in		In service 1840.
Vesuvius (43)	Haigh Foundry Co.	1836	12 ½ x 16	7ft 6in x 3ft 3in	94	1 5/8in		In service 1840.
Lightning (43)	HF Co.	1836	12 ½ x 16	7ft 6in x 3ft 2in	94	1 5/8in	11t 11cwt 1qr	In service 1840.
Cyclops	HF Co.	1836	12 ½ x 16	7ft 5in x 3ft 2in	94	1 5/8in	12t 8cwt	In service 1840.

Table 5: Short-stroke coaching (2-2-2) Locomotives on the Liverpool & Manchester Railway

	Builder	Date	Cylinders	Boiler	Tubes	Size	Weight	Notes
Star (41)	Charles Tayleur & Co.	February 1836	14 x 12	?	71 21	1 5/8in 2in		
Milo (47)	CT &Co.	November 1836	14 x 12	7ft 5in x 3ft	103	1 5/8in	12t 11cwt 2qr	
Dart (48)	Mather, Dixon & Co.	December 1836	14 x 12	7ft 5in x 3ft	100	1 5/8in		
Phoenix (49)	CT & Co.	December 1836	14 x 12	?	100	1 5/8in		
Majestic (50)	CT & Co.	December 1836	14 x 12	?	104	1 5/8in	12t 9cwt 1qr	
Etna (51)	CT & Co.	January 1837	14 x 12	7ft 5in x 3ft	103	1 5/8in	13t 2qr	
Arrow (52)	MD & Co.	February 1837	14 x 12	7ft 5in x 3ft	100	1 5/8in	10t 13cwt 1qr	
Sun (53)	R & W Hawthorn	March 1837	14 x 12	?	107	1 5/8in	12t 12cwt	Rebuilt with Melling Radial Valve gear.
Meteor (54)	MD & Co.	March 1837	14 x 12	7ft 5in x 3ft	100	1 5/8in		
Comet (55)	MD & Co.	March 1837	14 x 12	7ft 5in x 3ft	100	1 5/8in	12t 1cwt 12qr	
Vesta (56)	R&W H	March 1837	14 x 12	7ft 5in x 3ft	107	1 5/8in	12t 12cwt 2qr	

Large Samson class

As with the Planet class, the 2-2-2 Patentee type was a free runner capable of handling passenger trains; but a locomotive with more weight available for adhesion for working goods trains and banking loads up the Whiston and Sutton Inclines was necessary. Just as it had been a logical evolution to convert a 2-2-0 to an 0-4-0 wheel arrangement, so too the evolution from 0-4-0 to 0-4-2, creating a locomotive with more weight available for adhesion and via the carrying wheels, better able to support a larger firebox to better mitigate the phenomenon known as 'hunting'.

Due to the increasing loads of luggage trains, early in December 1834 Henry Booth ordered specifications for a new 'Engine calculated to take 20 waggons up the Whiston Incline Plane.' The plans and specifications were prepared by 15 December 1834 for an engine with 16 x 18 inch cylinders and 4ft 6in coupled driving wheels, 'calculated to draw 100 tons up the Whiston Incline Plane.' The issue of inside versus outside bearings ('the same as Samson and Goliath') was passed to the Sub-Committee to discuss and feedback.[57] As a result of their deliberations, a revised specification was issued later in the month, for locomotives with 5 foot driving wheels, and cylinders 12½ x 16 inches. Both engines were to be built to a common pattern so that the parts were interchangeable.[58]

At a meeting of the Management Committee in January 1835 it was reported that the existing luggage engines were struggling to cope with ever-heavier loads on the Sutton and Whiston Inclines, and John Dixon was ordered to view the new six-coupled luggage engine working on the Leicester & Swannington Railway and ascertain whether an 0-6-0 would be useful for the L&M. He reported on the 8 January 1835 that the locomotive weighed some 15 tons, and whilst powerful with cylinders measuring 16 x 20 inches 'was very slow in its movements, and did not appear to be much approved of on that line.'[59] Instead of ordering several of these big 0-6-0s to work the Whiston and Sutton Inclines, Dixon set out a specification for new 'bank engines':

'A small Bank Engine would be more generally useful to this company – Namely an engine to weigh <u>10</u> to <u>11</u> tons, <u>15</u> inch cylinder, 18 inch stroke, 4 coupled wheels of 5 feet diameter each.'[60]

Tenders were invited for these engines in February from Tayleur & Co., Edward Bury, George Forrester & Co. and Mather, Dixon & Co.; that of Mather, Dixon & Co of £880 being accepted, but with wheels 4ft 6in diameter as opposed to the 5 feet diameter originally specified, and cylinders 15 x 16 inches.[61] *Hercules* had been delivered as an 0-4-0 in December 1835 (above), but was almost immediately rebuilt as an 0-4-2. *Thunderer* (delivered as an 0-4-2) followed early in the following year, the first six-wheeled luggage engine to be delivered.[62] The delivery and performance of *Hercules* was described by the contemporary press:

'Among the number of improvements in steam carriages ... which tends to insure the safety of passengers and to protect the rails ... Is effected by the addition of a small pair of wheels placed under the after part of the carriage – not for the purpose as they were formerly used to increase adhesion to the rails by connecting all the wheels together, but to relieve the very great weight on the cranked axle, caused by the firebox and the overhanging weight of the after part of the frame. The effect has been

Evolution of the six-wheeled Stephenson luggage engine: take an 0-4-0 'Samson' class locomotive (top); provide a frame-extension and pair of carrying wheels behind the firebox (middle) to create the 0-4-2 'Large Samson' class. (Anthony Dawson collection).

satisfactorily ascertained in a fine and powerful engine called the "Hercules" lately constructed by Messrs. Mather, Dixon and Co., which was first worked with four wheels as usual, and then without any other alteration. The improvement in this and every other case where it has been tried was very evident, and promises to remove all the objections which can be made against it. It was feared, that by relieving the weight from the cranked and driven wheels, the adhesion to the rails would not be sufficient to allow the engine to be worked to its full power without slipping.'[63]

Hercules underwent running-in trials during February 1836, and took a load of 170 tons gross from Manchester to Liverpool 'without once slipping, though the day was not favourable for such a trial.' The advantages of the six-wheeler were thought to outweigh any disadvantage due to increased weight or needing to re-lay switches or purchase new turn-tables:

'As regards the rails, it is of the utmost advantage, by distributing the load more equally over them … the next point to be stated, and one to which the public are feelingly alive, is the great increased safety, by the adoption of six wheels, that should the cranked axle break, the engine will still be borne on four [wheels] … Some engineers argue that a cranked axle properly made, will not break, but experience teaches that it is impossible to guard against defects in the iron … The additional wheels also renders the motion of the carriages smoother, which must considerably diminish the friction both to the engine and the rails.'[64]

Two 0-4-2 locomotives were purchased from Tayleur & Co. in November 1835, the company reportedly 'having two to dispose of, which were nearly finished, with 12 inch cylinders, 18 inch stroke, coupled wheels' at a 'reasonable price.'[65] Each locomotive cost £1,050 each; the first, *Eclipse*, was delivered in December 1835, and *York* in January 1836.[66] They had 12 x 18 inch cylinders, 5 feet driving wheels, 3 feet carrying wheels, and weighed 12.5 tons. The wheels of *Eclipse* collapsed in May 1836, after only having run 5,600 miles; Tayleur & Co. were ordered to put her into full working order at their own cost.[67]

In response to the breaking of rails due to the weight of the engines, especially those operated by John Hargreaves, and after having sought the opinion of John Dixon, the Board resolved in December 1835 to introduce six-wheel locomotives:

'[The maximum weight they] would allow on one pair of wheels … not more than 6 tons be allowed, including the average quantity of coke & water in the Firebox & Boiler – and that the Directors reserve themselves and at all times the power to require an additional, or third, pair of wheels to be placed under any Engine working on their Line, for the purpose of giving steadiness to the motion where the same shall be deemed necessary or expedient by the Company's Engineers.'[68]

One newspaper reported that the Board had adopted six-wheelers as 'standard', and would only allow six-wheeled engines to work on their line: 'The directors are so satisfied … that they do not willingly allow the large size engines to draw without them.' It was 'much to the credit of the directors of the Liverpool and Manchester Railway Company' that they had adopted six-wheelers much to the public safety.[69]

Table 6: Large Samson class (0-4-2) Locomotives on the Liverpool & Manchester Railway

	Builder	Date	Cylinders	Boiler	Tubes	Size	Wheels	Weight	Notes
Eclipse (40)	Charles Tayleur & Co.	December 1835	12 x 18	?	107	1 5/8in	5ft	12.5 tons	Rebuilt with Melling's valve gear.
Hercules (39)	Mather, Dixon & Co.	December 1835	15 x 16	?	98	1 5/8in	4ft 6in	?	Delivered as 0-4-0; rebuilt 0-4-2 January 1836.
York (42)	CT & Co.	January 1836	12 x 18	7ft 9in x 3ft	78	2in	5ft	12.5 tons	
Thunderer (44)	MD & Co.	February 1836	15 x 16	8ft 3in x 3ft 3in	97	1 5/8	4ft 6in	?	

CHAPTER 6

Melling's Patent Locomotives

During the first few years of his tenure in his twin roles as 'Superintendent of the Engine Shops' and 'Locomotive Foreman', John Melling had been faced firstly with a lack of motive power, and secondly escalating costs of running and maintaining the locomotive fleet. These increasing running costs were raised at the half-yearly meeting of the Company in June 1836, and also by Henry Booth at a meeting of the Management Committee in November 1836. A 'discussion took place as to the practicality of improving the system on which the Company's very large expenditure' could be amended. The suggestion of reducing expenses through contracting-out the construction, running and repair of the locomotives, carriages and waggons was raised. Edward Woods was instructed to prepare a costed return of all the staff employed in the locomotive department as well as the 'joiners, fitters, and Other workmen' employed by the company.[1] A draft contract for a prospective contractor was drawn up and published, stipulating that the successful contractor would supply the motive power needs of the company for a period of three years and that:

> 'They must make use of the Company's present stock of locomotive engines, which they must keep in complete repair and efficiency, providing all materials and workmen necessary for the purpose, and taking on himself the maintaining of the required Locomotive power at a fixed rate per ton.'[2]

This proposal was unsuccessful in finding any potential signatories, and as a result in May 1837 the Board decided to re-organise the motive power department and its workshops. It was considered that it was 'advisable to concentrate the Repairing Establishment at Liverpool' at Brickfield, and to reduce that at Manchester. John Melling was promoted and was responsible 'for the whole of the locomotive establishment', and because his assistant, his son Thomas Melling, had left to work for the Grand Junction Railway, John Melling's wages were increased to six guineas per week. His pay was increased the following year to £400 per annum.[3]

The locomotive fleet was renewed between 1836 and 1838: six new locomotives were ordered to be purchased in 1836; ten more locomotives were purchased in 1837 at a contract price of £11,780; and four more in 1838. This represented a considerable outlay of capital: £3,950 was spent on new engines for the second half of 1836; £7,399 9s 1d during the second half of 1838 and £5,568 4s in the first half of 1839.[4]

As part of this heavy capital outlay, Henry Booth had suggested to the Board in August 1837 that they purchase eight new locomotives in order to handle an expected increase in traffic. The Directors agreed with Booth, and ten new locomotives were ordered in October 1837:

'2 October 1837.

The treasurer stated that in conformity with the instructions of the Board he had contracted for Ten Locomotive Engines, viz. With Todd, Kitson & Laird of Leeds, for -

2 Luggage engines with 11-inch cylinder, 20 inch stroke to be delivered on the 30th April 1838 £1,100 each.

2 Coaching Engines with 11½ inch cylinder, 18 inch stroke. 5' 6" wheels. To be delivered on the 30th June for £1,060 each.

2 Bank Engines with 13-inch cylinder, 20 inch stroke, to be delivered 30th September 1838 for £1, 1130 each.

With Benjamin Hick of Bolton for -

2 Luggage engines. 11 inch cylinder, 20 inch stroke. To be delivered 30th June 1838 for £1,350 each.

With Rothwell & Co, for -

2 Coaching Engines. 11 inch cylinders, 18 inch stroke.
1 to be delivered by the 31st May
1 to be delivered by the 30th June 1838 for £1,250 each.'

The Directors also thought it desirable that John Melling should 'from time to time' inspect the engines whilst they were being constructed.[5] Four more locomotives were ordered in October 1838 and two luggage engines were purchased from Thomas Banks & Co. of Manchester in December, one of which had been running on the L&M 'for about a fortnight on Trial' and had proved satisfactory, for £1,450. These two locomotives were perhaps those which Banks & Co. had advertised for sale in October 1838 having 'six wheels ... strong copper firebox, seventy-eight 2-inch brass tubes in [the] boiler, and all made of the best material.'[6]According to Melling's list, twelve of these locomotives included his 'patent improvements.'[7]

Melling's Patent Application (No. 7410 of 26 July 1837) included six different inventions; three of which he had previously developed and tested on the Liverpool & Manchester. The earliest was his firebox which was first used on the experimental locomotive *Experiment* built by Sharp, Roberts & Co. of Manchester in summer 1832. Melling's patent firebox used hollow water-filled fire-bars and there was a water tank beneath the fire grate which acted as a form of pre-heater for the feed water. In his patent application Melling described:

'A shallow tank, or water ash-box, which is suspended beneath the grate, bars, or furnace, of the engine, the interior of which communicates by means of the hose pipes with the tender, and by [another] pipe also communicates with the

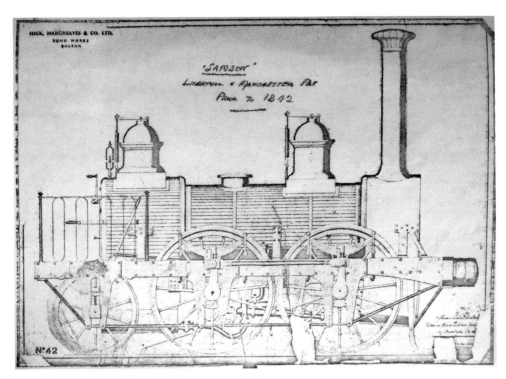

Samson (No. 66) built by Hick, Hargreaves & Co of Bolton was ordered by the Liverpool & Manchester in October 1837 as part of the same order for *Lion*. She gives a good impression of what later 1830s luggage engines – including *Lion (No. 57)* – would have looked like when first built, with twin steam domes and a slightly raised outer firebox. (Old Locomotive Committee)

pumps that supply the boiler. Now, it will be seen that the falling cinders from the furnace, as they are caught by this water ash-box, will heat the water therein: this heating process is also materially assisted by the steam, which at fifty pounds pressure will raise the ball-valve contained in the valve-box, and immediately escape through the pipe into the tank, and there being condensed will be found to effect a great saving in of fuel as it is evident that the boiler may always be supplied with hot water.'[8]

His second innovation (which he did not patent) was a hollow 'double axle' which allowed one wheel to rotate at a different speed to the other when traversing curves, which he presented to the Directors in July 1833.[9] Robert Stephenson had included a similar idea for a sleeved axle in his patent application of March 1831 for improvements in wheels and axles for rail vehicles running on edge rails.[10] Melling's third 'improvement' was a 'Coupling Wheel' which did away with the need for outside coupling rods, and helped increase adhesion with a heavy load or when rails were 'in a wet or greasy state.' A third, smaller wheel, which could be raised or lowered via a steam cylinder, was placed between the driving and leading wheel. In its lowered position, it coupled both wheels together. This did away with the need for coupling rods, but also meant additional adhesion was available when required through the coupling of the extra wheels. He first presented his idea to the Management Committee in January 1833. He informed them that he had 'invented a contrivance by which he could get the adhesion of <u>4</u> wheels on the Incline Planes or whenever it was necessary, without all the wheels being coupled together which occasioned much strain and friction.' The Committee ordered he supply working drawings of his idea.[11] In his Patent Specification, Melling noted that:

'The contrivance is very advantageous in comparison with the ordinary previous mode of coupling between any two wheels, because, if the rail be dry or the adhesion sufficient, the anti-friction wheel may be lifted off and remain idle,

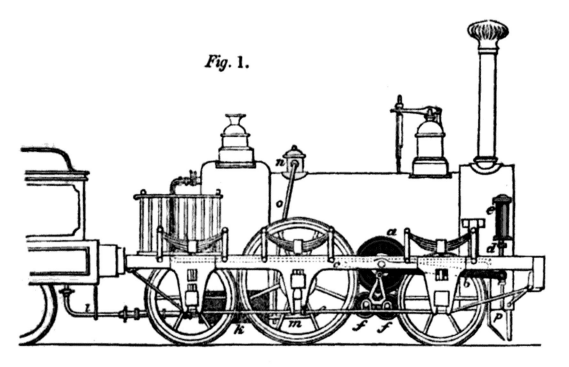

Fig. 1.

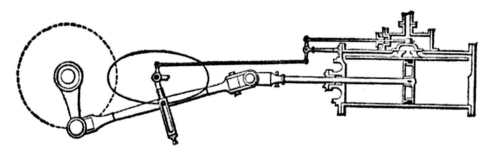

John Melling's patent of 1838 including his 'coupling wheel' (red) and associated brake (blue) which could be raised and lowered via a steam cylinder (orange). A feed water heater tank was placed beneath the firebox into which waste steam could be diverted (yellow). Bottom, Melling's radial valve gear. (Andrew Mason)

while the ordinary system of outside cranks and connecting rods must always continue working, and thus, at certain times, act as an incumbrance. Another important feature … is the smoothness with which the engine works … compared to engines coupled in the ordinary manner. The improvement is effected by transmitting a considerable portion of the weight from the cranked or driving axle to the straight or independent axle, which entirely prevents the tremulous lateral motion of ordinary locomotive engines.'[12]

The wheels could thus be coupled or uncoupled at will, and 'at any rate of running.' The first locomotive to be so fitted was *Firefly* in Autumn 1836. The *Durham County Advertiser* (18 November 1836) reported:

'On the morning after the Fancy-Ball in Liverpool, a train, loaded with guests, left the railway [station] at half past five o'clock, and was drawn by the Firefly locomotive engine, to Manchester in fifty minutes, being ten minutes under the hour. After arriving at Manchester, it immediately returned with a load of goods, and arrived at Liverpool at eight o'clock, being only two hours and a half in performing the two trips, including stoppages in Manchester. This beautiful engine has lately been repaired, and some new invention applied to it by one of the company's engineers.'

Following this success, the Board ordered that a full-scale trial take place, under the direction of Edward Woods in February 1837:

'Mr Melling's contrivance of the Adhesion Wheel, worked by a steam-cylinder, being now completed on the Firefly engine, it was Ordered that Mr Woods make a full experiment of the efficiency of the same, and that he ascertain the extent of the Impeding Friction produced by the Adhesion Wheel when in full operation by running the Engine down a portion of the Sutton Incline Plane by its own gravity, both with and without the application of the adhesion wheel, marking the distances traversed in each case.'[13]

Robert Stephenson had previously expressed doubts over the utility of coupled wheels, and thought there was a 'considerable loss of power.' Edward Woods also shared Melling's dislike of coupling rods and outside cranks; in his opinion they were 'undesirable, not only as tending, by the irregular motion they produce, to injure the wheels and axles' but also 'prove[d] injurious to the road.' He further notes that coupling rods increased the rolling friction of a locomotive and for 'want of proper adjustment' could lead to unequal tyre wear; then there was the risk of the connecting rods breaking which was 'not of uncommon occurrence. Engines have been occasionally thrown off the rails by the end of the connecting rod striking the ground'; they were unsuitable for high-speed running; if a coupled-engine slipped the rods were liable to break and the engine 'subject to a very violent side motion, and great strain is thrown upon the wheels … the cranks and the rods'; by having four-coupled engines with inside cylinders the weight carried on the leading axle was increased and finally, if the rail were 'clean' and level, coupling was unnecessary. Woods carried out a series of five experiments with *Firefly*, on a 'slippery part of the road' over a measured distance of 320 yards to ascertain the degree of adhesion that was generated via coupling the leading wheels. Woods concluded that the 'coupling wheel' was 'effective in a great degree' in increasing adhesion and preventing slipping. In his patent application, Melling also showed that there was considerably less wear to uncoupled wheels than coupled, and provided evidence through several wheel profiles. The great locomotive designer Patrick Stirling (1820–1895) described coupled engines as akin to a 'laddie runnin' wi' his breeks doon' and indeed limited experimentation carried out by Richard Gibbon and Richard Lamb conclude Stirling (as well as Stephenson, Melling, *et al* before him) were correct in their observations.[14]

The Chevalier de Pambour similarly thought the 'coupling wheel' was useful for helping heavy loads up the incline planes, when the extra adhesion from four wheels was deemed necessary.[15] In his second edition (1840) he describes the coupling wheel as 'a very ingenious arrangement':

'By means of which an engine may be made to adhere by all its wheels, notwithstanding the differences of their diameters. It consists of a friction wheel which can be let down at will between the two pairs of contiguous wheels, and which connects them so one cannot turn without moving the other with it. By these means, locomotives can have coupled wheels which are of unequal diameter, and this is very advantageous to the proper construction of the machinery, and does not put all the wheels in communication, other than the moment when necessary, without stopping the engine.'[16]

Melling's next invention was similar: a brake which used two small wheels, which could be raised or lowered by steam between the driving wheel and another wheel-set. As the two small wheels ran in opposite directions a braking effect was produced. Another was to use a steam jet 'for the purpose of cleansing the rails from snow, grease, or sand...'[17]

His most successful innovation was his radial valve gear. The Grand Junction engine *Lynx* was the first locomotive equipped with it in autumn 1837, and underwent full-scale trials supervised by William Allcard.[18] Further trials were made between *Lynx* and *England* in autumn 1839 between Liverpool and Birmingham. To ensure the comparative data was fair 'precisely the same 14 waggons, weighing 84 tons 4 cwt gross' were used on both days. They were made in the presence of Henry Booth, Hardman Earle, Captain Cleather (GJR) and Walter Gwynn (1802-1882) of the Baltimore & Ohio Rail Road. *Lynx* made the run to Birmingham in 2 hours 51 minutes and the *England* in 3 hours 19 minutes; *Lynx* being faster by 2 minutes, but as she passed milepost 92 one of the wheels of the waggons broke, causing the waggon to derail, it taking a valuable eight minutes to set things right. Edward Wood noted *Lynx* had achieved a maximum speed of 36mph.[19]

Because of the limited space between the frames, Melling dispensed with the use of eccentrics to drive the valves. Instead the drive for the valve spindle was derived from a pin in the centre of the connecting rod working in a slotted link. According to D. K. Clark:

'Mr Melling ... made a stud fast in the middle of the connecting rod, which by the nature of the connecting-rod motion, described a species of elliptical curve ...

The stud worked in a slot formed in a lever, of which this axis was placed in the centre of the oval. This arm the pin carried round with it, and on the same axis a small crank worked the valve-rod, like an ordinary eccentric.'[20]

John Scott Russell thought Melling's valve gear ingenious, but perhaps overcomplicated, and furthermore the valve timing was far from perfect:

'The scheme is so much more complex than the eccentric, that it can scarcely have less friction; and it unfortunately causes a much greater proportion of the motion of the valves to occur while the piston is in the middle of the stroke, than the eccentric does.'[21]

Both Clark and Nicholas Procter Burgh describe the valve-timing as being 'lumpy' because of the elliptical motion of the stud on the connecting rod, which meant the valve was moving at its slowest when it should have been moving at its quickest (when supplying and cutting off steam at the end of each stroke) and moving quickest in the middle of the stroke.[22]

Melling explained his valve gear in more detail in his patent application:

'Studs fixed on the connecting rods, and carrying small rollers, these rollers work in the morticed links or levers, and as the connecting-rods vibrate by the motion of the crank-shaft, a rotary motion is also communicated to the morticed levers, these levers being mounted fast upon the end of a smaller cranked shaft, cause that shaft to revolve, and consequently vibrate the four small connecting-rods (which are of the same throw as the traverse of the valves). Now as these rods receive an alternate reciprocating motion at every revolution of the crank-shaft, the forked ends of the rods vibrate short levers upon the shaft, which being their fulcrum, causes the most effectual opening and shutting of the slide valves by means of the connecting links which are attached to the valve rods.'[23]

The motion of the connecting rod stud turned the slotted link, and thus rotated the crank shaft to which the slotted link was fixed. Essentially, Melling had replaced the four eccentrics on the crank axle with a crank shaft running between the inner plate frames. This provided the reciprocating motion for the 'small connecting rods.' The 'small connecting rods' were gab-ended with upward-facing V-shaped gabs which engaged with a pin on a rocker arm. The engine was reversed by a single reversing lever on the footplate which simultaneously raised one pair and lowered the second pair of the 'connecting rods.' Like Stephenson, Melling also introduced a small amount of lead into his valves to reduce back-pressure. Melling's radial valve gear inspired that made by Hawthorn of Newcastle introduced in the following year. Unlike Melling's gear, it used an X-gab and could be worked expansively.[24] Not part of his patent application was Melling's invention of the ball-clack, which according to de Pambour had revolutionised the working of the L&M as the pumps no longer went out of order as frequently.[25]

Melling, however, had not been entirely honest with both the Liverpool & Manchester and Grand Junction Boards, having only informed them that he had patented his valve gear, *after* they had ordered new locomotives so fitted upon his recommendation!

On 11 December 1837 Henry Booth noted that Melling had 'stated to him verbally that he should not charge this Company for his Patented Improvements.' Booth was instructed to get this in writing, signed by John and Thomas Melling. John Melling attended the Board Meeting a week later where he was admonished by the Chairman, who also requested 'a distinct and legal agreement' between the Board and Melling assuring them of the free use of his patent. Melling replied that he 'did not want a farthing' for his improvements, and would not charge them for as long as he was in their employ. He was unwilling to sign such a document there and then, but presented a written agreement to the Board in January 1838. Melling declared he would allow the Liverpool & Manchester to use his patent improvements on further locomotives without the payment of royalties for as long as he was employed by them. The Board made a generous gift of 100 guineas to Melling for the use of his patent on eleven locomotives then building, and he was 'requested to name his terms on which he will allow his Improvements to be applied to the other Engines belonging to the Company.' In reply, Melling allowed the use of his patents at 50 guineas per engine.[26] The Grand Junction had ordered ten locomotives fitted with Melling's valve gear before they knew Melling had patented it. The Grand Junction Board refused to pay 50 guineas per engine and instead 'offered a present of 200 guineas for the permission to apply the invention to Ten Engines' which was twice the fee offered by the Liverpool & Manchester. In total the Grand Junction had 31 locomotives fitted with his patent improvements by April 1839 with a further eight under construction by Sharp Roberts, Hawthorns, and Bury.[27] By December 1838 Melling had granted patent rights at £52 10s each on some eighteen locomotives, totalling some £1,181 5s.[28]

The trial of the valve gear was obviously a success as on 1 March 1838 it was resolved to have *Pluto* and *Swiftsure* rebuilt and fitted with the patent valve gear and some half-dozen locomotives constructed with the new valve gear, suggesting that the fitting of Melling's radial valve gear to *Lion* and her sisters was perhaps a late change to the design.[29] By 1839 *Pluto* had been rebuilt as a six-wheeler with carrying wheels 3ft and 3ft 6in diameter, the rebuild probably occurring at the same time as the fitting of new valve gear.[30] The Management Committee resolved on 16 March 1838:

> 'That it would be desirable that when Engines had to undergo a thorough repair, they should be refitted with the patent improved gearing, the Charge for which this Company on the part of the Patentee was 50 Guineas an Engine, which would comprise (if it were thought proper to adopt them) the patent coupling wheel and the water tight ash pan.'[31]

This resolution does appear to have been carried in to effect: two fitters at Manchester shed were paid 18s in May 1839 for 'fitting up friction wheels', which also involved 44lbs of iron (costing 11s). The cost of a brass 'self-acting steam valve complete with union joints &c. &c. for conveying Surplus Steam from the Boiler into the ash box tank' cost £6 in June 1838, again suggesting that Melling's feed-water heater had been adopted. Five locomotives were thus fitted by August 1838.[32] Indeed, Edward Woods instructed locomotive crews when standing idle to 'turn the [waste] steam … into the tender tank, to warm the feed water' in order to save fuel, so 'the heat produced during the interval of rest is turned to full account'.[33]

A list of locomotives fitted with his patent valve gear was drawn up by Melling on 10 April 1839 and records fifteen locomotives on the Liverpool & Manchester had it.[34] Other locomotive engineers attempted to emulate Melling; Timothy Hackworth on the Stockton & Darlington introduced his own unsuccessful version of the coupling wheel, whilst James McConnell on the Birmingham & Gloucester produced a version of Melling's feedwater heater using waste steam from the safety valve.[35]

The first of the locomotives carrying Melling's 'patent improvements' to be delivered was *Lion*, the *Leeds Times* of Saturday 4 August 1838 announcing:

'Messrs. Todd, Kitson & Laird, of this town, have just completed their first locomotive engine manufactured for the Liverpool & Manchester Railway. The engine was exhibited to a number of respectable gentlemen on Tuesday last, who spoke in the most flattering terms of the excellence of its manufacture.'

The *Leeds Mercury* of the same date added:

'New Loco-Motive Engine. We witnessed the trial on Monday last of a new and very powerful locomotive engine, built by Messrs. Todd, Kitson & Laird of this town, for the Manchester and Liverpool Railway. Benjamin Gott esq. and T. B. Pease esq., and several other gentlemen connected with railways in this neighbourhood, were present, and expressed, in the highest terms, their admiration of the excellent workmanship and appearance of the engine.'

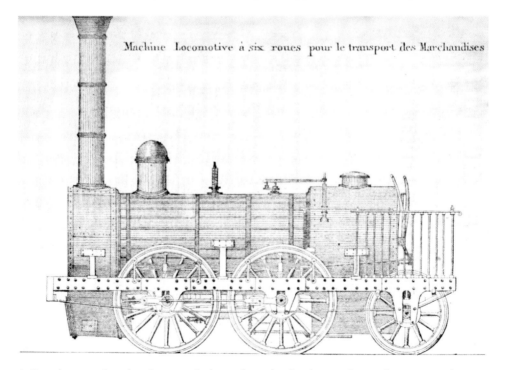

A French engraving showing a typical member of a Stephenson Large Samson type luggage engine, dated 1838. (Anthony Dawson collection)

Until *Elephant* and *Buffalo* had been delivered early in 1839, *Lion* and *Tiger* were used as the banking engines on the Whiston and Sutton Incline Planes, as described by the *Manchester Courier* in November 1838:

> 'New and Powerful Locomotive Engine, built by Messrs. Todd, Kitson & Laird of Leeds, has been placed on the railway, to work as a "help-up" Engine on the Whiston Incline Plane, where it is hoped it will do the work of two Engines. It is shortly to be joined by a second Locomotive of the similar type.'

It was whilst employed as the Whiston banker in November 1838 that *Lion* was involved in the tragic explosion of *Patentee* which had only just re-entered service after having been repaired following a fatal accident at Newton Junction in October.

In March 1839, *Lion* and *Tiger* were put on the more mundane duties of hauling goods trains. *Lion* is recorded in summer 1839 as regularly working loads of 14 or 15 goods waggons from Liverpool to Manchester and back, and being able to work

Lion (No. 57) as she was when discovered in the 1920s. Often described as having a 'haycock' firebox, she doesn't: instead the boiler – which dates from 1865 – has a high-crowned waggon-top firebox. The ornamental brass cover so distinctive of the restored locomotive was a controversial addition by the LMS in 1930. (Old Locomotive Committee)

them up the Whiston and Sutton inclines without any assistance. Francis Whishaw (1839) describes goods waggons weighing 2 tons, and being able to carry 4 tons of load (making 6 tons gross),[36] which suggests a maximum probable load of 80–90 tons. *Lion* is recorded as being 'at work' – and in 'full steam' – for over sixteen hours per day, but was only doing seven hours of 'useful work' in making four full trips from Liverpool to Manchester (120 miles in total), burning 12 cwt 1 qr 8lb of coke, of which 2 cwt was going to waste keeping her in steam whilst she was standing idle! On average, she burned 39.4lbs of coke per mile, or about half a pound of coke per ton per mile. *Mammoth* (Banks & Co) burned 45.6lbs of coke per mile with a load of seventeen waggons (100 tons gross).[37] J. G. H. Warren in 1930 estimated a tractive effort for *Lion* of 2,100lbs at 50 psi boiler pressure, whilst modern calculations have put this somewhat higher at around 3,325lbs, being capable of pulling a load of 100–110 tons.[38] Calculations using the equation for tractive effort presented by the Chevalier de Pambour, suggests that with her original cylinders (11 x 20 inches) *Lion* had a tractive effort of 2,016lbs and with her present cylinders (14 x 18 inches) 2,940lbs. These figures are supported by contemporary data presented by Edward Woods showing that *Lion* was capable of handling tons of upwards of 100 tons weight; indeed Edward Woods stated that 100 tons was the maximum allowable load per engine. He also shows that these engines were in steam for upwards of 20 hours per day.[39] Woods' figures also show that *Tiger* was perhaps the marginally better engine handling heavier loads and burning less coke:[40]

Week Ending	Engine	Miles Run	Trips	Load	Weight	Coke/Trip	Coke/Mile
26.10.39	*Lion*	540	18	14	84 tons	13cwt 14lb	49.0lb
	Tiger	420	14	13	78 tons	12cwt 1qr 18lb	46.8lb
16.11.1839	*Lion*	540	18	14	84 tons	13cwt 2qr 4lb	50.5lb
	Tiger	360	12	15	90 tons	12cwt 1qr 5lb	45.9lb
23.11.39	*Lion*	120	4	12	72 tons	14cwt 1qr 4lb	53.7lb
	Tiger	60	2	16	96 tons	11cwt 1qr	46.7lb
30.11.39	*Lion*	180	6	11	66 tons	12cwt 3qr 19lb	48.2lb
	Tiger	420	14	15	90 tons	11cwt 2qr 22lb	43.7lb
7.12.39	*Lion*	360	12	13	78 tons	14cwt 1qr 25lb	54.0lb
14.12.39	*Lion*	360	12	12	72 tons	13cwt 3qr 12lb	57.7lb
21.12.39	*Lion*	120	4	11	66 tons	15cwt 2qr 14lb	58.3lb

In comparison the coaching engines *Panther* and *Leopard* were running similar distances with a much lighter load, and thus burning less coke. Coaching engines were on average making twelve trips of thirty miles per week (total mileage for twelve engines on 26 October 1839 was 4,320) whilst luggage engines were making nine trips. Edward Woods demonstrates for the same period:

Week Ending	Engine	Miles Run	Trips	Load	Weight[41]	Coke/Trip	Coke/Mile
26.10.39	*Panther*	300	10	6	30 tons	10cwt 1qr	38.3lb
16.11.1839	*Panther*	240	18	5	35 tons	8cwt 3qr 17lb	33.2lb
23.11.39	*Panther*	180	6	6	30 tons	11cwt 5lb	41.2lb
	Leopard	420	14	6	30 tons	2cwt 1qr 24lb	35.3lb
30.11.39	*Panther*	120	4	6	30 tons	10cwt 3qr 21lb	40.8lb
	Leopard	360	14	7	36 tons	9cwt 10qr 19lb	34.2lb
7.12.39	*Panther*	360	12	6	30 tons	10cwt 3qr 9lb	40.4lb
	Leopard	570	19	6	30 tons	9cwt 1qr 10lb	34.9lb
14.12.39	*Panther*	300	10	6	30 tons	10cwt 2qr	39.2lb
	Leopard	630	21	6	30 tons	9cwt 5lb	33.4lb
21.12.39	*Panther*	360	12	6	30 tons	11cwt 1qr 19lb	42.6lb
	Leopard	540	18	6	30 tons	10cwt 2qr 14lb	39.6lb

Francis Whisaw carried out experiments on the L&M in Autumn 1839, which show that the 'Melling Patents' were as good runners as those fitted with conventional valve gear:

Date	Locomotive	Load	Vehicles	Average Speed	Maximum Speed
9.11	*Milo*	39 tons	9	21mph	40mph
11.11	*Arrow*	27 tons	6	28 ½mph	35mph
11.11	*Milo*	22 ½ tons	5	30 ½mph	50mph
11.11	*Roderick*[M]	26 tons	6	28mph	44mph
11.11	*Rokeby*[M]	32 ½ tons	8	20 ½mph	47mph
11.11	*Vesuvius*	23 ½ tons	6	20mph	33 ½mph
25.11	*Comet*	30 ½ tons	7	25 ½mph	not recorded
25.11	*Rokeby*[M]	15 ¼ tons	4	20 ½mph	43 mph
27.11	*Roderick*[M]	28 tons	7	22mph	34mph
28.11	*Roderick*[M]	28 ½ tons	7	26mph	36mph
2.12	*Panther*[M]	18 ½ tons	5	20 ½mph	40 ½mph

Note: 'M' indicates a Melling Patent

Clearly these engines were fast runners, making good times between Liverpool & Manchester. They also didn't lack 'slogging power'; on one run, *Roderick* was able to work her load of 24 tons up the Whiston Incline of 1 in 96, maintaining a speed of 25mph from bottom to top. In March 1840, Liverpool & Manchester coaching engines with a load of six carriages are recorded as burning 33.5lb of coke per mile; luggage engines burned on average 44lbs of coke per mile – *Mammoth* with a load of 22 waggons burned 52.5lbs whilst *Milo* with only twelve waggons burned 43.3lbs per mile.[42] *Panther* is recorded in 1842 having run from Manchester to Liverpool in 40 minutes:

'Quick Travelling. The Panther locomotive engine, made at the Railway Foundry in this town – Thompson, engine driver; Ashton, guard, left Manchester on Thursday, the 22nd instant, at twenty-two minutes to one o'clock, and arrived at Liverpool at eighteen minutes past one, completing the journey in forty minutes! We believe the distance has never before been done in so short a time since the opening of the railway. It was a special train, engaged by Lord Eglinton's trainer, who, we understand, was on the racecourse within an hour and ten minutes of the time he left Manchester, a distance of forty miles.'[43]

John Gray records that *Panther* was involved in an incident where a cokeman – for reasons unknown – managed to start *Panther* and jumped off in fright. A driverless *Panther* 'passed Patrecroft [sic] with the greatest fury' and managed to run as far as Parkside before running out of water, where she presumably dropped her fusible plug.[44]

Leopard was damaged in an accident at Liverpool Road in February 1842 when her fireman Emanuel Knight attempted to move her, but whilst crossing over the main line was rammed by the GJR engine *Basilisk*. Knight was immediately dismissed.[45]

As a prelude to building their own locomotives, the Directors ordered on 1 October 1838 that the wheels, axles, frame and valve gear of the next four locomotives to be built were to be made 'in house' (suggesting that the Brickfield workshops were capable of undertaking such work) under the direction of Melling at Edge Hill, and only boilers, fire boxes, and tubes be contracted for.[46] Written specifications for boilers were issued by Edward Woods: barrels were to be constructed from Low Moor iron, consisting of four narrow plates, each the full length of the barrel, with longitudinal joints, lap-riveted together, a type of boiler known as 'long plate' boilers:

'The boiler to be cylindrical, 7ft 6in long outside, between the smoke-box and the outside casing of the fire-box, below the tubes. To be 3ft 3in diameter inside.

To be made of four plates, of equal breadth, of the best Low Moor iron, each plate the whole length of the boiler, and five-sixteenths of an inch thick. The End next the chimney to be made of one Low Moor plate, of best quality, five-eighths of an inch thick, in which must be drilled, square through, without countersink, 130 tube holes, one inch and three-quarters diameter, and three-quarters of an inch from each other; the upper surface of the top row of tubes to be 14in from the top of the boiler.

The boiler plates to be put together with best 5/8in rivets, and to be fastened to the chimney end and outer casing of the fire-box by 3½in angle iron and double rows of ¾in rivets; the whole to be well caulked inside and out. Care must be taken that the proper side of the plates be kept *upwards* in punching the rivet holes, so that when put together the *smallest diameter* of the rivet holes in each plate shall be next to each other at the joint, the rivet heads on each side; and for this object, the dies used in punching the rivet holes should be one-eighth of an inch more in diameter than the punch.

The smoke-box or chimney end to be made of the best Low Moor plates, three-sixteenths of an inch thick, chimney one-quarter thick, to be made and completed with doors and fastenings, similar to the chimney ends, &c., on the Lion and Tiger engines belonging to this company, and in conformity with a drawing to be furnished.'[47]

This boiler was probably at the limit of existing technology; in October 1838 the largest boiler plate rolled at Bedlington (for example) was 7ft 6 in x 7ft.[48] The inner firebox was to be made from the best copper plate, 7/16ths of an inch thick, other than the tube plate which was to be 5/8ths thick. The tube holes 'must be drilled square through, without countersink, 1 5/8in diameter, and 7/8in asunder.' Furthermore:

'The roof, which must be 1 in and a half above the top row of tubes, must be firmly supported by six cross-bars, 3 in in depth, having each 7/8th bolt holes, tapped and rivetted on the underside in the usual way. A five-eighth lead plug to be tapped into the roof, without a head upon it. The two sides, front and back, to be stiffened with ¾in copper stays, tapped and rivetted, and holding firmly together the inner and outer casing; the stays to be 4½in asunder, from centre to centre of each. The inside width of the fire-box to be 3ft 4in, and the length from front to back 2ft 6in. The depth from the underside of the roof to the upper surface of the fire-bars to be 3ft 3in. The fire-door to be circular, with a clear opening of 12in diameter. The closing joint of the doorway to be formed of a ring of pure cast copper, 2in broad and 3in thick, filling up the water space between the inner and the outer casing, the same being fastened to this ring, or closing with 7/8th copper bolts, firmly rivetted and countersunk on the outside.'[49]

The outer firebox was to be made from Low Moor plates, 3/8ths of an inch thick, leaving a water space of 3 inches at the sides and back and 4½ inches along the tube plate:

'One plate front and back; the whole neatly and firmly riveted together, and the top must not rise above the top of the cylindrical boiler more than is necessary … eight 2in iron plugs to be tapped and screwed into the outer casing at the lower corners of the water space, the plug holes to be opposite each other, so that a rod may be passed completely through in each direction, for the purpose of cleaning out the bottom of the water space. There must be a clear water space 4 in in depth below the upper surface of the fire-bars or grate, and into this part of the fire-box eight iron studs must be tapped and screwed, two on each side, to support the fire grate. A circular hole to be cut for the regulator above the fire-door, near the top of the outer casing.'

The boiler was to be provided with two steam domes: one above the firebox and the second 'one third of the distance between the smokebox and the fire-box.' They were to be made from Low Moor plates 3/16th of an inch thick, 14 inches diameter and 22 inches high. A Salter safety valve was to be carried in the dome over the firebox whilst a second safety valve was mounted behind the chimney 'and supported on a neat brass pillar.' Both valves were to be 2 inches diameter and calibrated to lift at 60psi. The domes were to be 'neatly cased with brass.' Finally, Woods noted that:

> 'The whole to be manufactured and finished in a neat, substantial and workmanlike manner; as complete in all respects, both as to materials and workmanship, as the boilers of the Lion and Tiger Engines on the Liverpool & Manchester Railway.'[50]

Despite being specified as being cylindrical, due to their mode of construction they were not true cylinders and indeed Francis Whishaw notes the boilers of *Lion* and *Tiger* to have been slightly oval in cross section, no doubt because of this. He also notes that they had 128 tubes rather than the 130 specified by Woods and were 7ft 4in long.[51]

John Melling reported towards the end of October 1838 that because of the poor condition of the locomotives at the Liverpool end of the line, five or six new locomotives would have to be purchased together with new/additional machinery in his workshops – a new stationary engine being authorised on 29 October 'to work the lathes and other machinery.' Four locomotives were to be sent 'to the Viaduct or Vulcan foundry' for thorough repair.[52] Two new luggage engines were purchased from Thomas Banks & Co. of Manchester (to be named *Mammoth* and *Mastodon*).[53] Melling and Fyfe were ordered to prepare reports on the states of the locomotives at each end of the line, and Edward Woods reported the same to the Board in June 1839; four engines at the Manchester end (*Swiftsure, Atlas, Ajax, Pluto*) were under heavy repair, and in reply to his request to start building engines, as soon as they had been 'turned out, in complete repair' Melling was granted permission to start building locomotives at Edge Hill.[54] The Board advertised for sale by auction 'Wheels, axles, cylinders, pistons, eccentrics, brasses, pumps and various other parts of Locomotive Engines' at Edge Hill in June 1839.[55]

Many of John Melling's 'Patent improvements' were seemingly Heath-Robinson in nature; hollow, water-filled fire bars had first been proposed by George Stephenson in 1827 but had been quickly found to choke with sediment and burn out, yet Melling had clearly not learned that lesson. The use of the 'coupling wheel' and a similar method of braking was ingenious and later found another advocate in Francis Webb of the LNWR in 1882, who like Edward Woods and Patrick Stirling before him, objected to the use of coupling rods. By dispensing with coupling rods, Webb had hoped to minimise the 'great wear and tear' from the weight and friction of a coupling rod, especially at speed. By reducing the friction, Melling and Webb had hoped to produce a freer-running locomotive which was easier on the track. Melling's radial valve gear was one of several contemporary designs which sought to make driving a locomotive easier by having fore- and back-gear controlled from the footplate, compared to Robert Stephenson's flying reverse. It was the first radial valve gear in commercial use, but was perhaps over-complicated, with poor valve-timing, and following the introduction of Buddicom's gab gear in 1840–1841, and then the Stephenson link, would have rapidly been obsolete. Melling was certainly an innovative locomotive engineer, and credit must also be given to the Board for taking on his many suggestions and adopting them in their locomotive renewals in the latter part of the 1830s, continuing their railway's role as the 'Grand Experimental Railway'. It was to John Melling that the day-to-day operation, maintenance, and management of the products of Forth Street or the Vulcan Foundry fell and it is a testimony to him and his men that the Liverpool & Manchester Railway was able to maintain a fast, and efficient timetabled service despite often being hampered through lack of essential machinery, and a Board of Directors who, whilst they were continually looking for means of cost-saving innovations, were also reluctant to spend money on tools and equipment. Under John Melling, the locomotive fleet was entirely replaced 1838–1839 largely with locomotives carrying his patent improvements, which also saw a move toward standardisation and simplification, which would be continued under his successor John Dewrance.

As Dr. Michael Bailey has identified, the Stephenson outside-framed six-wheel locomotive, either as its 2-2-2 Patentee or 0-4-2 Large Samson variant, inspired the 'standard' form of British locomotive during the first-half of the nineteenth century. The type also appeared as an 0-6-0 and 2-4-0. Valve gear had been improved, from the 'flying reverse' of *Planet* to the gab gear of Buddicom.[56] Where experimental work had taken place on the L&M, it was within the design envelope established by Stephenson – and the Board – which included outside sandwich frames; 5 feet driving wheels; and an axle load of no more than 4½ tons (1832) later rising to 6 tons (1835). This experimental work had been to further refine the Stephenson locomotive, by improving its efficiency and therefore lowering working costs.

Lion was restored by the LMS at Crewe 1929–1930 with input from historians J. G. H. Warren and E. A. Forward of the Science Museum who elected to restore her to an 1840s appearance. They were given *carte blanche* by Sir Henry Fowler of the LMS. The tender was built in 1930 using parts from three ex-Furness Railway tenders by the LMS at Crewe. (David Boydell)

Table 7: Melling Patent Locomotives on the Liverpool & Manchester Railway

	Builder	Date	Type	Cylinders	Boiler	Tubes	Size	Wheels	Weight
Pluto (27)	Robert Stephenson & Co.	1832	2-2-2						
Eclipse (40)	Charles Tayleur & Co.	1835	0-4-2						
Sun (53)	R & W Hawthorn	1837	2-2-2						
Lion (57)	Todd, Kitson & Laird	August 1838	0-4-2	11 x 20	7ft 4in x 39in x 42in	126	1 5/8in	5ft	?
Tiger (58)	TK&L	November 1838	0-4-2	11 x 20	?	128	1 5/8	5ft	14t 9cwt 2qr
Rokeby (59)	Rothwell & Co.	1838	2-2-2	11 x 18	?	125	1 5/8in	5ft	14t 15cwt 2qr
Roderick (60)	Rothwell	1838	2-2-2	11x 18	?	125	1 5/8in	5ft	14t 13cwt 2qr
Mammoth (61)	Thomas Banks & Co.	March 1869	0-4-2	12 x 18	8ft 1in x 36in x 41in	78	2in	5ft	13t 19cwt
Leopard (62)	TK&L	March 1839	0-4-2	11 ½ x 18	7ft 5in x 39in x 42in	127	1 5/8in	5ft 6in	13t 13cwt
Mastodon (63)	TB & Co.	March 1839	0-4-2	12 x 18	8ft 1in x 36in x 41in	78	2in	5ft	14t 5cwt 2qr
Panther (64)	TK&L	March 1839	2-2-2	11 ½ x 18	7ft 5in x 39in x 42in	127	1 5/8in	5ft 6in	13t 4cwt
Elephant (65)	TK &L	March 1869	0-4-2	14 x 20	?	128	1 5/8in	5ft	?
Samson (66)	Benjamin Hick & Co.	March 1839	0-4-2	11 x 20	?	127	1 5/8in	5ft	15t 3cwt 2qr
Buffalo (67)	TK &L	March 1839	0-4-2	14 x 20	7ft 4in x 39in x 42in	127	1 5/8in	5ft	?
Goliath (68)	BH & Co.	March 1839	0-4-2	11 x 20	7ft 5in x 39in x 42in	127	1 5/8in	5ft	15t 3cwt

CHAPTER 7

Edge Hill Comes of Age

In August 1838, the Directors were again considering ways of reducing the heavy expenses associated with the locomotive department. Henry Booth was instructed by the Board to visit London for a week to observe the different systems in use in and around the capital.[1] During autumn 1839 the Management Committee were considering their options for running the locomotive department, and for reducing its cost. At a joint meeting between L&M and GJR Directors on 23 September 1839, they discussed ways of running the motive power department, and based on the experiences of the London & Birmingham Railway which had contracted the supply of its locomotives to Edward Bury, they discussed the 'expediency, or otherwise, of entering into Contracts for the supply of Moving Power for the two Railways.' But this route was not taken up. After a lengthy meeting they resolved firstly that the L&M and GJR motive power departments work closely together in order to reduce costs; secondly that given the GJR was still as yet an unknown quantity it was not desirable to contract for motive power; thirdly given the expense involved in purchasing and maintaining their own locomotives, it was therefore best to maintain the current system. Perhaps as censure of Melling senior and junior who had charge of the L&M and GJR engine shops respectively, they resolved:

In John Dewrance, the Liverpool & Manchester had a competent and forward-looking Locomotive Superintendent who had an excellent working relationship with the chief engineer, the young Edward Woods. (After Marshall 1930)

'It was desirable for each Company to engage a Principal Superintendent of the Locomotive Engine Department of first-rate mechanical acquirements, and of higher station than the foremen who had hitherto had charge of that Department, whose business it would be to introduce the most beneficial systematic arrangement into each branch of Locomotive Expenditure, and to exercise over the whole that close personal supervision which would enable him to either bring down the Expenditure in the Locomotive Department ... or to give to the Directors a satisfactory explanation why so desirable a result was not accomplished.'[2]

At the following meeting of the L&M Management Committee, it was felt desirable to appoint 'a competent Superintendent.' A draft contract was drawn up for the position of L&M Locomotive Superintendent and ordered to be advertised.[3] James Kitson, of Kitson & Laird of Leeds, wrote speculatively to the Board in January 1840 whether the 'Directors were disposed to contract for their motive power.' Henry Booth was instructed to reply that 'the Company were not at present' so disposed.[4]

Henry Booth was empowered by the Board to re-organise the locomotive department in December 1839, and he gave Melling three months' notice to quit. All mechanical work was to be centralised at Edge Hill which was to be considerably expanded. The workshops were to be re-organised, and Edward Woods was appointed 'acting Manager of the Mechanical Department, for the whole line … with full authority' on a salary of £800 per annum.[5] Finally, John Dewrance was appointed as 'Locomotive Superintendent and Foreman of the Engine Shops' in January 1840.[6]

Boiler pressure

In order to improve the power output of his locomotives, John Dewrance proposed raising boiler pressure to 70psi in September 1841. He believed that the engines could be safely worked at a higher pressure, and indeed many unofficially were. He explained how this higher pressure was safe, 'that the pressure was proportionate to power' and would therefore make the locomotives more powerful and thus more efficient and cheaper to run. The Management Committee, however, were aghast at this revelation and 'could not sanction the Company's Engines being worked in the smallest degree higher than was consistent with perfect safety' and would not sanction a raise in boiler pressure.[7] He must have got his way, as by 1845 boiler pressure was 70psi and 'when the steam is blowing off strongly, there is 80lbs to the square inch.'[8]

Bearings

Bronze bearings with oil lubrication were in use until 1843, and Edward Woods had reported to the Parliament the year before that he had adopted standardised axle boxes and journals; the main journal was carried on the outside frame and that crank axles 'of [the] most modern construction' were supported by sprung bearings carried on the inside plate frames.[9] Beginning in 1843 experiments were made with Babbitt's 'soft metal' or 'Britannia metal' bearings. Britannia metal is an alloy of tin, antimony and copper, first patented in the United States in 1839 by Isaac Babbitt and has a lower coefficient of friction than bronze bearings. Edward Woods had John Dewrance fit them to the *Ostrich* for trial purposes, reporting to the Board on 16 November 1843 that:

'By the use of which, a saving of about three-fourths of the oil ordinarily consumed by a Locomotive Engine; besides a still more important saving in labour owing to the very small wear and tear which appeared to take place with the new bearings ... [the] connecting Rod and axle bearings belonging to the "Ostrich" Engine which had just run ... 4,680 miles with scarcely any perceptible wear.'[10]

Babbitt had informed the Company that he would allow them to use his patent bearings for £500, and whilst the Board agreed to this in principle, they thought the matter required further consideration, and passed it back to the Management Committee.[11] Edward Woods was requested to communicate with Francis Trevithick of the GJR for further information on Babbitt's bearings, and in December 1843 was instructed to enquire as to the 'validity of the patent', and ultimately the Board agreed to pay for Babbitt's patent bearings, with a down-payment of £250 to Babbitt's agent and a second payment of £250 'provided he substantiated his right to the patent, and obtained such permissions from other Principal Companies as should place the Liverpool and Manchester Company on an equality with the most favoured position.' In other words, give the L&M preferential treatment![12]

Valves and valve gear

Edward Woods and John Dewrance appear to have had an excellent working relationship, and both men carried out an intensive series of experiments on valves and valve gears in order to improve the efficiency (and therefore reduce running costs) of the locomotive fleet. For the first eight years of the L&M, locomotives used short-travel slide valves with no lap or lead, and with a fixed cut-off. Lap is defined as:

> 'The amount by which the valve overlaps the steam port at the middle position of each valve ... "steam lap" is the amount by which the valve overlaps the port on the live steam side; similarly the "exhaust lap" is the amount by which the valve overlaps the port on the exhaust side.'[13]

Whilst 'lead' is the amount by which the steam port is open which the piston is at front or back dead centre. 'Cut-off' refers to the point in the stroke at which the steam-port

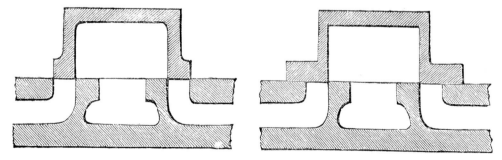

The 'lap' of a slide valve is defined by how much the valve overlaps each steam port in the mid-position. Left, a slide valve with no lap; right the same valve but with lap equal to the exhaust passage. (Anthony Dawson)

closes allowing the steam in the cylinder to work expansively.[14] A cut-off of 90% appears to have been the norm for early locomotives. The replica *Planet* locomotive has a fixed cut-off of 75%, in other words steam is admitted into the cylinder for 75% of the stroke, but when being driven 'on the handles' has 100% cut-off (steam admitted for the entire stroke) which is useful for starting heavy loads from a standing start.

Robert Stephenson first introduced a small degree of exhaust lap in his patent locomotive in 1833; by opening the exhaust port earlier he reduced back-pressure in the cylinder and gave a freer exhaust, essential for fast running, but it was only in the second-half of the 1830s that any interest was shown in valves and using steam expansively in the cylinder largely to reduce running costs, especially in the coke bill. Woods notes that the existing valves were 'altogether unsatisfactory' because whilst there was a small amount of lead, the exhaust port only opened at the end of the stroke, resulting in high back-pressure in the cylinder made worse through the exhaust port being restricted in size. Thus, in 1838 Woods modified the valves and exhaust port of the *Lightning*:

'Its original valve … placing the valve on the ports, so as to allow the exhausting passage to be 3/8th of an inch open, the steam port would at the same time be ¼ inch open. This space was therefore closed by adding to the length of the valve at each ¼ inch … the amount by which the valve at each end overlaps the steam ports, when placed exactly over them [i.e. dead centre], is technically termed the "lap". The lap of the Lightning's valve being then 3/8ths of an inch, the exhausting passage was about 3/8th of an inch open when the stroke was finished.'[15]

The length of the valve was increased by ¼ inch at each end. Thus, lap of 3/8ths of an inch equate to the exhaust port being opened by the same amount at the end of the stroke. The eccentric was also shifted on the axle. *Lightning* began running in this modified state in March 1838, seeing a reduced net consumption of coke (i.e. coke burned whilst running), 'evidently obtained from the earlier exhaustion of steam' but still 'little better than the best performances at the end of the year 1830.'[16]

Further experiments were made in 1839 with *Rapid* and *Arrow* which had modified valves with 3/8th of an inch lap, again seeing reductions in coke burned. The valves of *Arrow* were altered again in February 1840 to have '3/4th of an inch instead of 3/8ths of an inch lap at each end', the valves only opening 7/8th of an inch 'at full port'. As important as lap and lead was the timing of the valve. By cutting of the admission of the steam earlier, and consequently opening the exhaust port earlier steam was used expansively in the cylinder and back-pressure was reduced from having a freer exhaust, meaning the engines used less steam and therefore fuel and water. Woods states 'an immediate reduction of nearly 8lbs per mile was the result' of this modification representing a saving of 20% in fuel consumption but with 'no injurious effect … upon the power, but rather the reverse.'[17]

John Dewrance continued to experiment with valves 'early in the year 1840', soon after his appointment at Edge Hill. Dewrance recommended that the exhaust port should, at the end of the stroke, be 'nearly wide open' which he accomplished by making the lap equal to the width of the steam port. Furthermore, he proposed to increase the travel of the valves. Once again the valves of *Rapid* were modified with one inch lap and were made to travel a full 4¼ inches:

'The result of this arrangement, was, that the exhausting passage was one inch open at the end of the stroke, and ... the steam was cut off at 79[%]; it expanded from 79[%] to 95[%]; at 95[%] it began to be released, and was escaping into the atmosphere from 95 to 100.'[18]

This early cut off and expansive use of steam, together with the exhaust port opening early, and generous steam passages, reduced the consumption of coke from 36.3lbs per mile to 28.6lbs per mile, 'a saving of one-fourth of the fuel.' Dewrance therefore proposed that new valves with a 1 inch lap, and 4 inch travel (elsewhere he states *Rokeby*'s valves travelled 5 inches[19]), be introduced across the entire locomotive fleet. Due to the design of existing steam chests, however 'in many cases there was no room in the steam chest for valves of greater lap; in others, that it was impossible to increase the length of travel' and thus new cylinders and steam chests would be required. Thus Dewrance had to replace 'the cylinders, steam chests, working gear, and inside framing of several engines' in order to carry this out; Woods hoped the cost of rebuilding these engines would be recouped from fuel saving later on.[20]

In addition to the study of valves and the use of steam expansively in the cylinder, Woods carried out experiments on the size of blast-pipe orifice in Autumn 1839, and in 1842 Woods and Dewrance carried out experiments to measure the evaporative capacity of the different parts of a locomotive boiler; they had one built where a 5ft 6in long boiler barrel was 'divided into six compartments by vertical diaphragms.' The first compartment was six inches long, the others twelve. Woods and Dewrance found that most steam was generated around the hottest part of the boiler (the firebox) 'the evaporative duty of the first compartment was about the same per square foot as that of the firebox; that of the second compartment about a third of that value; that of the remaining compartments very small.' They concluded that the 'first six inches' of the boiler did more work than the 'remaining 60 inches of tubes.'[21]

These experiments with valves were also taken up by John and William Gray, the latter developing an early form of 'link' motion, known as the 'Horses' leg Motion', which allowed the cut-off to be varied, and fitted to *Cyclops* in summer 1839. Gray offered the Liverpool & Manchester board 'the free use of his patented improvements in locomotive engineering' at the rate of £20 per engine in December 1839. The Board accepted his offer and suggested they would be willing to fit it to such engines 'from time to time might think fit to apply the improvements.' Despite this offer, no L&M locomotive was ever fitted with Gray's patent valve gear.[22] Edward Woods notes that in the fitting of Gray's valve gear:

'[The] Alteration consisted in the adaptation of particular mechanism for working the valves, whereby the engine-man was enabled, without disturbing the regulator, to vary at pleasure the quantity of steam admitted to the cylinder within the limits of a range extending from 46 to 82 per cent. Of the length of the stroke, allowing the steam to act expansively after being cut off.'[23]

Cyclops had 5 feet driving wheels, and cylinders 12 x 16 inches. Her firebox provided a heating surface of 42.02 square feet and the boiler tubes 248.29 square feet. The steam was cut off 'after the piston has travelled through the space of 6, 7, 8¼, 9½,

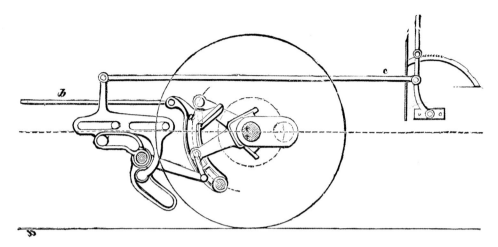

John Gray was the first locomotive engineer to come up with a variable-expansion valve gear and apply it to a locomotive. His complicated 'horses leg' gear was trialled on the Liverpool & Manchester, but they did not adopt it. It was adopted by the Hull & Selby Railway, of which he was locomotive superintendent. (Anthony Dawson collection)

10¾, 12 and 14 inches, equating to a cut-off of 37.5%, 43%, 51%, 59%, 67%, 75% and 87%. Trials were held with *Cyclops* on the Liverpool & Manchester to ascertain fuel and water consumption; comparative speed between fixed and variable cut-off locomotives and overall performance between 'the best engines hitherto in use on the Liverpool & Manchester' and *Cyclops*. The amount of coke burned, water evaporated (included water lost to priming) and the cut-off were recorded for six first-class trains (i.e. only making one stop between Liverpool & Manchester) and six second-class, or stopping, trains over the same distance. *Cyclops* was also worked under observation on two luggage trains. Edward Woods reported to the GJR Board that:

> 'Experience has shown that the Rokeby & other Engines fitted with similar valves, can be made to do the same amount [of] work as Engines with Mr Gray's patent Gearing, with an equally small consumption of fuel, but it hitherto has been a matter of doubt whether the Rokeby Class of Engines can compete with the patent ones, when employed in drawing very heavy loads, the one being able to command an admission of steam of 91 per cent of the stroke, the other an admission of only 72 per cent.'[24]

Thus trials between *Rokeby* and *Cyclops* were held under Woods' supervision. Twelve merchandise waggons with 'low sides' were loaded with 'scrap iron, bricks, stones, &c. so that each weighed exactly 5 tons gross.' The total train weight was 60 tons gross. The safety valves of both engines were set and locked-off at 70psi and 'the same thermometric pressure gauge was used for observing the pressure of steam in the boilers.' The incline was staked out at twelve intervals of 220 yards the first stake being '40 yards distant from the foot of the [incline] plane.' The engines were then run up the incline, 'starting from a position of rest made the best of their way, with full steam on.' *Cyclops* and *Rokeby* each ran up the incline and their time taken, speed, and boiler pressure were recorded. *Cyclops* could work its load up the incline in 8 minutes 12 seconds whilst *Rokeby* was marginally quicker, taking 7 minutes 4 seconds, and indeed achieved a higher speed than *Cyclops* (30mph compared to 28.1mph) and was able to maintain a higher boiler pressure. Contemporary opinion was that the introduction of an earlier cut-off would reduce the power of a locomotive.[25] Woods was eager to dispel this. Whilst working in full forward gear, he recorded that *Cyclops*:

> 'With 91 per cent of the steam is brought to a par with the old Engines with respective to its tractive force. The Old valves with ¼ inch lap at each end cut off at 95 per cent & exhausted at 98, the steam being used expansively. The close correspondence exhibited in all the results proves that the Rokeby is quite as efficient as the Cyclops in drawing the heaviest loads & that therefore no loss of power is sustained by cutting off a little earlier in order to obtain a greater freedom in the exhausting.'[26]

Experimental runs were then made with the *Cyclops* and the GJR engine *Hecate* on 16 November 1839 and 11 January 1840 between Liverpool or Manchester and Birmingham. John Melling billed the GJR £3 13s 3d for coke, cokeman as well as one horse, driver and cart for a quarter-days' work. Woods wrote to the GJR Directors that during the November trials, where both engines had the same load of 49 tons gross, *Cyclops* achieved a higher average speed over the 95 miles of 27.40mph compared to 19.79mph of *Hecate*. On the return trip *Cyclops* achieved 29.8mph and *Hecate* 21.26mph. *Cyclops* also burned more coke per mile (26.2 tons / 24.1 tons). During the January trials, *Hecate* struggled to make steam and as a result her blast pipe was 'taken off' at Birmingham 'and the orifice reduced' to increase the blast but even after this modification she 'was much detained between Warrington and Liverpool being unable to ascend the Warrington Incline without help.' *Cyclops* was also in difficulty as one cylinder cover came loose whilst running from Birmingham, and steam was lost with every stroke of the piston, meaning she lost time and had a very high fuel and water consumption.[27]

Comparison runs were made with *Rapid*, *Leopard* and *Comet*, the latter having a fixed cut-off at 100%. *Cyclops* burned between 24.5lbs and 32.1lbs of coke per mile whilst *Rapid* and *Leopard* were burning 40.7lbs and *Comet* 31.5lbs. Trials were later held over the longer and hillier Grand Junction route, which showed that *Cyclops* had the advantage in terms of fuel efficiency over *Rokeby* or *Hecate*. Woods may not have properly understood expansive working, suggesting that the great improvement in *Cyclop*'s fuel efficiency was due to the earlier release of the exhaust steam and a higher boiler pressure; both factors 'neutralised' any efficiency gained through expansive working. Colburn has suggested that Woods greatly over-estimated back-pressure in the cylinder.[28] That said, however, following the exhaustive trials with Gray's valve gear he concluded – although he did not adopt expansive working on the Liverpool & Manchester – that:

> 'The principle of using the steam expansively may be applied ... with success, and that a very material economy cannot fail to result from that application.'[29]

In September 1841 the result of the trials with *Cyclops* and Gray's expansive valve gear were reported to the L&M Management Committee; there was a saving of 2 to 3 cwt of coke per day by using steam expansively but even though it represented considerable cost-saving, the Committee did not approve of its adoption because it 'deviat[ed] to some extent from the uniform pattern and duplication of the other Engines.' It was also more complicated than the existing valve gear, and there was also the issue of royalty payments.[30]

Experiments with coal

In order to reduce working costs of his locomotives Edward Woods was eager to experiment with burning coal rather than the more expensive coke, but this was never achieved successfully. Coal, unlike coke which is nearly pure carbon (about 90%), is only about 75% carbon, and contains lots of impurities known as volatile matter: ash (10%); oxygen (8%); hydrogen (5%); nitrogen (1.5%) and sulphur. Different types of coal have different ratios of carbon to volatile matter, and best dry steam coal has been defined as containing between 9.5%–13.5% volatile matter. Welsh steam coal has a higher ratio of carbon compared to Yorkshire coal, for example, necessitating different firing techniques; Welsh steam coal being the closest to a coke fire. Indeed good Steam Coal has a similar calorific output as 'the best Worsley Coke' of around 13,300BTU. In order to burn, coal must be heated to above 400° Celsius and to do so efficiently must do so in the presence of a lot of oxygen. Furthermore, in order for the volatile matter to fully combust so as not to form black smoke, the combustion products must be heated to well over 1,000° Celsius and be supplied with sufficient oxygen.[31] It was this problem of properly burning the volatile matter – and therefore preventing smoke – which gave many early locomotive designers a headache.

The first attempt to burn coal efficiently on the Liverpool & Manchester had been made by John and William Gray in the boilers of the stationary engine at Crown Street Yard. The Grays proposed a 'double firebox', using a horizontal water filled mid-feather to divide the two, one above the other. The lower firebox was fed with coal, and the upper with coke, the combustion products (and volatile matter) from the coal fire rising and passing through the coke fire in the top of the firebox where it was hoped they would be completely burned, thus preventing smoke. The design was similar to John Chanter's patent firebox of 1834, and indeed Chanter was co-patentee with the Grays.[32] John Gray attended the Board meeting on 30 November 1835 with a model of their 'double grate firebox for burning coal':

> 'After some conversation, and explanation on the part of John Gray, it was agreed by the latter that the Company should have the liberty of constructing and using as long as they pleased, two of the Fire Boxes, on any Locomotive Engines, to which they should adapt them, without any charge, on the score of patent right. The Board therefore consented to construct one and try one of the propose Fire Box – it being at the same time understood, that by so doing, they give no opinion, and made no admission, as to the validity of the Patent.'[33]

The Board ordered that Gray's firebox be fitted to *Liver*, and experiments 'be tried with burning coal … to ascertain the Comparative Consumption of Coke and Coal' by the locomotives. Edward Woods reported to the Board that he had experimented with burning coal in the *Fury* and *Swiftsure*, but the results were not satisfactory, and had even resulted in damage to *Fury* probably due to the volatile gases from the coal burning in the tubes or even the smokebox:

> 'The Chimney end … was a good deal burnt, and the joints of the steam pipes injured with excessive heat. Mr Woods was making some alteration in the fire bars to remedy this evil, and would proceed with the experiment.'[34]

Further experiments took place with *Patentee* and *Star*. Woods was of the opinion that if coal were to be a useful fuel, it would have to be screened before use to remove the slack and shale. Even after screening, the engines burned about 25% more fuel with Haydock coal than with best Worsley coke; contemporary observers suggest that Worsley coke burned between 20%–30% hotter than some coals.[35] After the attempts at burning pure coal, Woods next ran trials with *Liver* using coke and coal 'in the proportion of 3/4th coal and 1/4th coke.' Whilst 'The smoke was not altogether destroyed' it had been 'very much mitigated' and Woods thought modifications to Gray's firebox, and different proportions of fuel, might result in coal being burned more effectively. Hardman Earle reported very favourably on trials held with *Liver* at the end of November. Thanks to greater familiarity with the new type of firebox, 'and with care and good management' smoke could be almost completely avoided. He recommended the fuel load be half coke and half coal. The only downside with the firebox was the water-filled mid-feather dividing the two fireboxes and hollow water-filled fire-bars, 'which leaked considerably'.[36] Sadly, this mid-feather burst in January 1837; the engineman John Darbyshire was severely scalded, and the fireman William Wood had his thigh broken. The Board ordered the Management Committee to investigate, and John and William Gray attended their meeting of 19 January 1837. The investigation into the accident concluded that the fault lay in the construction of the mid-feather – being a casting of 'an alloy of copper with a Portion of Tin and Zinc' – rather than being sheet copper. The Management Committee 'declined to sanction the reconstruction of the Liver's Fire Place' and instead proposed to sell her 'in her present state' and that *Patentee* be seconded for experimental purposes.[37] John Chanter wrote to the Board expressing his intention of purchasing *Liver* for £900 and 'proposing that in the mean time the Hollow Fire Bars and Water Chamber be taken out at his expense.' The Board was initially reluctant, the minutes noting '[they] were willing to wait a week for Mr Chanter's decision but declined having anything done at the Fire Box in the meantime.' Chanter wrote again in February, being 'desirous of making some slight alteration in the Liver's Fire Box which he thought would affect the consumption of smoke without the water chamber.' He proposed to make these alterations at his own expense and the 'Directors judge the result.'[38] This work was completed by April 1837 and the Directors ordered further trials take place under the Direction of Woods.[39] Finally, Chanter proposed to purchase *Liver* for £500 in September 1837 but this offer was declined as being much too low, and Henry Booth was authorised to dispose of her 'to obtain what he should deem a fair value', being sold to the Messrs. Mullin & MacMahon, contractors of the North Union Railway for £700 in October 1837.[40] Experiments with Gray and Chanter's 'Patent Firebox for the prevention of Smoke' continued into the following year, when in July 1838 Edward Woods reported on the performance of 'the Prince George', a locomotive owned by Messrs. Melly Prevost & Co. for export. The experiment was not a success, the engine burning a far higher amount of fuel 'compared with that of the Company's Engines with Fire Boxes of the ordinary construction' and with the emission of black smoke.[41]

James Slater (c.1809–1874), machine and chain maker of Salford, offered the company the use of his patent boiler for 'the consumption of smoke' in May 1837 and the matter, together with a renewed offer from Chanter, was discussed by the Management Committee.[42] Henry Booth entered the coal-burning debate by essaying his own boiler in April 1837. In his boiler design, Booth used a sloping grate, with carefully screened coal being fed into the fire from a hopper. Lecount of the London & Birmingham Railway described how fuel was fed from this hopper into the firebox through a 'long narrow aperture extending the whole width of the furnace' rather than through a narrow firebox door, so that each load of coal was put over the full width of the firebox:

> 'The furnace is charged with coal and lighted in the ordinary way; the furnace door then being shut; the coal-box is then charged with the fuel, which lays on fire-bars, forming an inclined plane; on this the coal gradually descends into the furnace. The coal-box is kept constantly filled-up a few inches above the bottom of the water space, or outer casing, under the fire door, along the whole width of the furnace. When the fuel is properly ignited in the furnace, if the engine is in motion, the shaking of the boiler, furnace, and coal-box, assisted by the inclined position in which the coal lies on the plane, will partially supply the furnace with fresh fuel.'[43]

It was thought that the burning coal at the bottom of the sloping grate would 'coke' the fresh charge of coal as it moved down the grate, so that the volatile gases would be driven off and burned, the coke thus produced burning in the usual way.[44] Although patented (No. 7335 of 4 October 1837) there is no evidence to suggest Booth's firebox ever got beyond the theoretical stage.

Due to the increasing cost of coke, the Board invited one Edward Oliver Manby (1816–1864), an engineer from South Wales who had experience of using anthracite and Welsh coal as a fuel for smelting, to carry out experiments with burning anthracite in locomotive fireboxes in July 1838. Anthracite is a form of hard coal with a very high carbon content (c.73%), and very few impurities (c.30%) and because of this it was hoped it would burn cleanly without making smoke. Successful trials were carried out with *Vulcan* 'one of the smaller ones used for conveying goods' under the superintendence of Edward Woods. The first experiment was with *Vulcan* running light engine from Huyton Colliery without any difficulty. Returning with a train of empty coal waggons she achieved a maximum speed of 21mph:

> 'The experiment was highly satisfactory, the fuel burning nearly without dust from the chimney, and entirely without smoke. The speed of the engine was

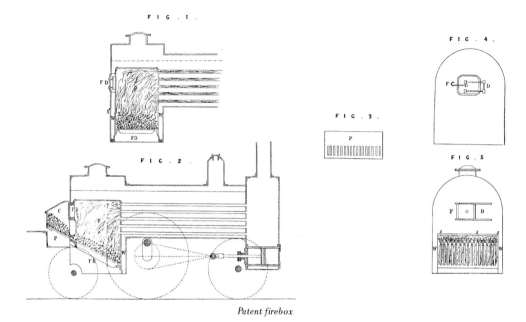

Patent firebox

Henry Booth, the General Superintendent, had an inquisitive mechanical mind and was in part responsible for the boilers for *Lancashire Witch* and *Rocket*. He patented this coal-burning boiler in 1836 but there is no evidence one was ever made. (Anthony Dawson collection)

twenty-one miles an hour, which is about that of the Vulcan with the usual coke. Another trial was made in the evening of the same day. The consumption of anthracite was only five and a half cwt although a large portion was wasted from the fire-bars being too wide apart for economical use of this fuel. The engine would have used upwards of seven and a half cwt of coke for the same journey, and for the same load.'[45]

One newspaper hoped that because of the rise in coke prices, the use of anthracite would be 'a most important public benefit' and would present a 'saving of thirty to forty percent' compared to coke. That said, however, experiments with anthracite on the London & Birmingham Railway carried out in the same year were not successful, the firegrate becoming clogged and engines running out of steam.[46]

Samuel Hall (1781–1863) carried out experiments on the firebox of *Star* with an improved version of his patent apparatus for destroying smoke – which had been used with limited success on the Leicester & Swannington Railway in 1841, and later on the North Midland Railway during 1842.[47] Hall's apparatus had been patented in 1836 and 1841, using jets of heated air in the firebox 'like an argand burner', in order to promote the better consumption of the volatile gases in coal. Long iron pipes lead from the front of the smokebox (the openings of which could be varied using a damper), along the inside of the boiler barrel, heating the air, before being ejected into the firebox. Rather than introducing heated air, cold air was sucked through the tubes, leading to firebox and tubeplate problems.[48] The trials on the L&M had 'signally failed in producing the desired effect' largely because it introduced cold air into the firebox which lowered firebox temperatures making the production of smoke more likely and also damaged the copper firebox. Furthermore, Charles Wye Williams CE (1779–1866) of Liverpool claimed that Hall had stolen the idea from him, which he had patented in 1841.[49]

Next to take up the challenge of burning coal was John Dewrance, who adopted a double firebox design remarkably similar to that of Gray and Chanter. Dewrance noted that his coal burning firebox was based on the thinking of Williams (above) 'applied by me on Locomotive Engines of the Liverpool and Manchester Railway, by Mr Williams' permission.' Late in life Dewrance noted that he used a single firebox, divided into two using sloping firebars 'placed (step fashion) one above the other' but also introduced a baffle plate in order to slow down the heated gases leaving the firebox, and admitted air via a metal plate 'closely perforated with holes'. The firehole door had a 3 inch diameter hole, which could be closed with a flap, for the admission and regulation of 'secondary air' above the burning coal.[50]

In his first boiler design, (as noted above) Dewrance used a double grate; the lower for burning coke and the upper for coal, separated by sloping, water-filled firebars as a partition. In order to slow down the speed of the volatile gases leaving the firebox, and therefore increase combustion time, Dewrance used a transverse mid-feather in the upper part of the firebox in front of the bank of tubes, which acted as a brick-arch. There was a short combustion chamber within the boiler barrel to ensure the volatiles were completely burned. Both fireboxes had their own dampers so that air could be carefully controlled to ensure complete combustion and therefore smoke. He enrolled his patent application in April 1845, and it was granted in October 1845 for 'constructing locomotive and other boilers, with a box, chamber, or chambers, in addition to the ordinary fire-box, into which additional chamber or chambers the combustible gaseous products ... are made to pass, and therein mixed with atmospheric air and consumed.' Trials were successfully carried out with the *Condor* that autumn.[51] The following year, Dewrance designed a second patent boiler with a combustion chamber above the firebox, and within the outer firebox wrapper, which increased the combustion time leading to complete combustion of the volatile gases.[52]

Whilst the original L&M locomotive *Lion* and the replica *Planet* locomotive will quite happily steam on coal despite neither having a brick arch, without making [much] smoke, the problems encountered in the mid-1830s with burning coal effectively was less likely to do with coal as a fuel *per se* but the type of coal being burned. Whilst *Planet* thrives on Welsh Steam Coal (which is nearly pure carbon), the coal the L&M were trying to burn in the 1830s came from the Haydock Colliery of Turner & Evans which was described in the later nineteenth century as 'not fiery in nature' and giving off a lot of gas, suggesting it possessed a high percentage of volatile matter, and was therefore prone to making smoke. The problem of the proper combustion of coal in order to prevent smoke would persist for the next few decades, and was only cured in the 1850s by Matthew Kirtley (1813–1873) who had been apprenticed to Robert Stephenson & Co. and for a short time had worked on the L&M. He successfully introduced a brick arch and deflector plate in the firebox in 1856, which directed air onto the burning coal, and slowed down the passage of the combustion products through the firebox so that the volatile matter could be completely burned.

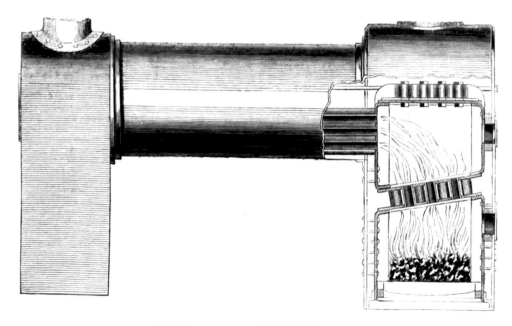

DEWRANCE'S PATENT BOILER.

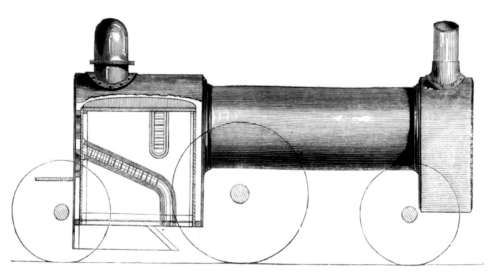

John Dewrance also tried his hand at designing and building coal burning boilers. His first design borrowed from that of Gray in having two grates, one above the other. A subsequent design still used two grates but separated by a water-filled mid-feather.(Anthony Dawson collection)

New locomotives

Following the success of his experiments on valves and valve gears, Edward Woods was determined to build new, more efficient locomotives and to rebuild existing locomotives (where possible) as a stop-gap. The new long-travel long-lap valves represented a saving of 25% in fuel compared to the older short-travel valves with limited (or no) lap and lead. Whilst admiring the efficiency of Gray's 'horse leg' valve gear, Woods found it complicated and 'it was considered more desirable to delay proceedings until the simpler method was fully tested', ultimately settling on the gab valve gear developed by Buddicom at Edge Hill for the GJR. Adopting new valves was 'no easy task':

'On close examination it was discovered that, in many cases, there was no room in the steam chests for valves of greater lap; in others, that it was impossible to increase the length of travel. Therefore it was necessary to prepare, in the first instance, for the sacrifice of at least the cylinders, steam chests, working gear, and inside framing of several engines then needing repair, and eventually, as resources would permit, for replacing the Company's entire stock with new engines, all built according to one model.'[53]

The Board of Directors agreed with Woods, and the cost of rebuilding the locomotives was 'only relative, not actual … the saving in the cost of fuel and repairs' covering the cost of the rebuilds.

Woods notes that between 1840 and 1842 some twenty-four new engines were built at Edge Hill and 'broke up as many old ones' yet at the same time the actual expenses of the Locomotive Department fell from £51,580 in 1839 to £25,732 in 1842.[54] He further notes:

'Some engines, such as the Vesta, Swiftsure, Phoenix, Etna, Rokeby, Meteor and Sun were altered at a trifling expense, so as to approximate towards the improved principles, and thus tended to keep down the consumption of coke, whilst more perfect engines were in the course of formation. The York was several months under repair, and did not come into action until 1841.'[55]

New standard cylinders were adopted: 12 x 18 inches for 'coaching' engines and 13 x 20 inches for 'luggage' engines. Woods was able to report to the Gauge Commissioners in 1845 he had twenty-eight coaching engines and eighteen luggage engines with cylinders of those dimensions.[56]

Woods reported to the Chairman on 16 December 1842 that locomotive construction had commenced at Edge Hill, and that the existing locomotives were 'in excellent condition, and in working order, and indeed none immediately require any serious repairs.' He had organised the locomotive fleet into three categories:

'1. The "New" Engines are those which have been built entirely by the Company, and, which from the uniformity observed in their construction, rank *first* in value.

2. The "Rebuilt" Engines are such of the old Engines as have had all their parts renewed with the exception perhaps of the boiler, firebox and framing, and rank *second* in value.

3. The "Repaired" Engines are such of the old Engines have undergone thorough repair without altering the cylinders, gearing, etc. to conform with the most approved models, and rank *third* in value.'[57]

Now that Melling had left the L&M, royalty payments were now due, and faced with relatively new engines but with peculiar valve gear and other patent 'improvements', those built to Melling's designs were rebuilt to the standards established by Woods. Melling's patent radial valve gear was replaced by the gab gear developed by William Barber Buddicom for the Grand Junction Railway in 1840 and it is with this valve gear which *Lion* is still equipped. Buddicom used four fixed eccentrics on the crank axle.

Right: Dewrance introduced new gab valve gear designed by William Buddicom at Edge Hill in 1840. It used opposed V-shaped gabs engaging on pins on a rocker arm to drive the valve spindles, as seen here on the preserved *Lion*.

Below: Buddicom's gab valve gear, from which the Stephenson–Howe link valve gear was an obvious evolution: A, reversing lever; B, reach-rod; C, eccentrics; D, back-gear eccentric rod; E, fore-gear eccentric rod; F, lifting-links; G, rocker-arm; F, valve spindle.

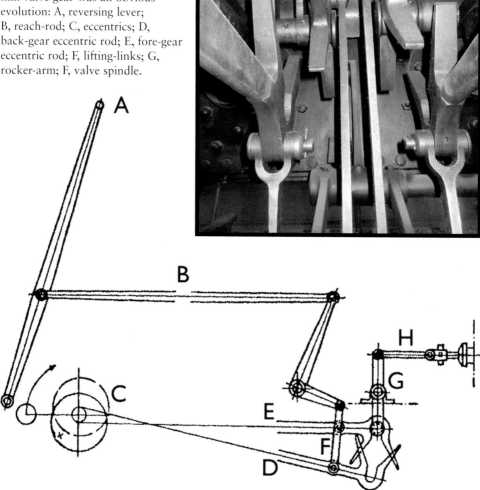

The eccentric rods terminated with opposed V-hooks, which could be engaged on a pin working a rocking shaft which in turn drove the valve spindles. This valve gear has a few idiosyncrasies: in order to engage fore-gear, the reversing lever has to be pulled backwards. Apprentices at Ruston Diesels Ltd. (where *Lion* was restored to steam in 1979) found that it was impossible to change gear when *Lion* was stationary and could only be achieved whilst the locomotive was coasting, with the steam shut off. This also meant that *Lion* could be driven like her predecessors, using back-pressure in the cylinders as a brake to bring the locomotive to a stand.

The process of rebuilding as locomotives came in for repair took several years to achieve. In a report to Charles Lawrence at the end of 1842 Edward Woods noted that thirteen locomotives – *Ajax, Eclipse, Etna, Fury, Hercules, Majestic, Milo, Patentee, Phoenix, Sun, Thunderer, Vesta* and *Victory* – had already been scrapped and a further six (*Dart, Cyclops, Mammoth, Rapid, Speedwell, Swiftsure*) were 'worn out' and were not scheduled for rebuilding. Of the 'rebuilt' and 'repaired' locomotives, Woods presented the following completion dates:[58]

Date Completed	Coaching Engines		Luggage Engines			Ballast Engines
	Rebuilt	Repaired	New	Rebuilt	Repaired	
25 January 1840						*Titan* (34)
11 September 1840		*Rokeby* (59)				
11 December 1840						*Star* (41)
29 January 1840		*Panther* (64)				
3 February 1841				*Goliath* (68)		
5 March 1841					*York* (42)	
6 March 1841				*Samson* (66)		
6 April 1841				*Lion* (57)		
14 May 1841				*Tiger* (58)		
15 July 1841	*Roderick* (60)					
22 July 1841	*Lightning* (45)					
29 September 1841		*Vesuvius* (43)				
1 October 1841		*Arrow* (52)				
14 October 1841				*Elephant* (65)		
19 October 1841				*Buffalo* (67)		

Date Completed	Coaching Engines		Luggage Engines			Ballast Engines
	Rebuilt	Repaired	New	Rebuilt	Repaired	
25 February 1842				Mastodon (63)		
3 June 1842	Pluto (27)					
2 September 1842		Comet (55)				
1 November 1842			Atlas (81)			
31 December 1842		Meteor (54)				
31 December 1842		Leopard (62)				
Total	3	7	1	7	1	2

By the end of 1842 Woods could inform the Chairman that:

'In the course of two years … 19 of the old Engines have been entirely thrown aside, and their place supplied by the new or rebuilt Engines.'

Of this stock of locomotives as of 31 December 1842, Woods predicted that *Panther, Rokeby, Star, Titan, Vesuvius* and *York* would be 'expected to become unserviceable by the end of the year 1843' and that he had accordingly ordered six locomotives to replace them, to be ready at the end of 1843.[59]

As Woods noted, this rebuilding process resulted in basically new locomotives, but crucially for accounting purposes they did not appear as capital expenditure. The totality of this work is shown with the cost of the work. For example, *Mastodon* and *Pluto* were being rebuilt during January to July 1842 at a cost of £889 12s 10d and £874 3s 2d. In both cases the 'rebuild' was more expensive than building a new Bird class locomotive at Edge Hill (£647 13s 6d each). Three more (*Leopard, Comet, Meteor*) had under gone heavy repairs, costing £706 14s 10½d.[60] *Atlas* was rebuilt at a cost of £961, leaving very little of the original hence being re-numbered as part of the new stock.[61]

The programme of rebuild and repair was completed by December 1843 when Edward Woods notes that 'every engine belonging to the Company has the improved valve' with 1-inch lap, 4-inches travel and with wider steam ports. 'Great care' was taken in the casting of new cylinders to 'enlarge the area of the passage of exhaustion' to reduce back-pressure in the cylinders as much as possible. Cylinder sizes were standardised across the fleet: 13 x 20 inches for luggage engines and 12 x 18 inches for coaching engines. Oddly, however, both *Lion* and *Tiger* were rebuilt with cylinders 12 x 18 inches as for coaching engines.[62] The valves of *Lion* have a travel of 3 13/16th inches, the cut-off being 81%. The lead is 3/32th in and the lap 13/16th in, so slightly less than the figure quoted by Woods, but probably acceptable to 1840s tolerances.[63] Finally, Woods was able to demonstrate that his new valves and valve gear, together with careful firing, had reduced the coke bill of the Liverpool & Manchester from 12,604 tons in 1838 to 3,103 tons at the end of 1843.[64]

Those 'old' locomotives which survived the Edge Hill 'cull' still at work at the end of 1844 included:

Coaching Engines	Luggage Engines	Jobbing Engines
Roderick (64)	*Elephant* (65)	*Atlas* (23)
Pluto (27)	*Buffalo* (67)	*Mastodon* (65)
Comet (55)	*Lion* (57)	*Rokeby* (59)
Meteor (54)	*Tiger* (58)	*Leopard* (62)
Vesuvius (43)		*Star* (41)
Lightning (45)		*Samson* (66)
Arrow (52)		

The oldest pre-Edge Hill locomotive still in service was *Pluto* (Stephenson, 1832) although substantially rebuilt. Clearly *Rokeby*, *Star*, and *Vesuvius* had earned a reprieve since December 1842, whilst *Panther*, *Titan* and *York* had all been broken up. Some twenty-two Bird class locomotives were in service.[65]

The Bird class

The result of this extensive period of research and development was Dewrance's Bird class. The class was designed as a 'standard' locomotive, with the same boiler, cylinders, valves, valve gear, and wheels, shared between 2-2-2 coaching engines and 2-4-0 luggage engines. They were relatively small locomotives: the boilers were only 9 feet long. The firebox provided 48 square feet of heating surface and the boiler tubes 458 square feet. Woods notes that they were capable of running at 45mph with a load of 30 or 40 tons gross. Boiler pressure was 80psi and the maximum evaporation rate was 11cubic feet per hour. According to I. W. Boulton who purchased six survivors in the 1860s, boiler barrels were 8ft 6in long, 3ft 6in diameter with 125 brass tubes of 2in outside diameter. The inner firebox was copper: 3ft 3½in wide by 2ft 6in long and 4ft deep, the roof and tube plates ¾in thick and the sides 1/2in. The first eight were delivered by June 1842, and work had commenced on three more; the total cost being £5,181 19s 4d. Twenty-four had been delivered by the end of 1842, at a cost of £650 each, completely renewing the locomotive fleet.[66] Ten new engines were delivered during the second half of 1844 at a cost of £4,052 18s 6d and £473 1s 4d for new tenders.[67]

The Bird class saw, for the first time, a standardised locomotive fleet, which promised reductions in working cost and repairs and maintenance through interchangeability of parts, a common design and design ethos. Indeed, the Bird class saw a reduction in operating costs of the locomotive fleet. According to figures presented by Edward Woods, for the six months ending 20 December 1844, the new Bird class 'coaching' engines were burning on average 17.6lbs of coke per mile whilst the older rebuilt locomotives were burning on average 22lbs per mile: varying from 19.4lbs per mile (*Vesuvius*) to 22.8lbs per mile (*Comet*). The heavier 2-4-0 'luggage' engines were burning far more coke, however, than the 2-2-2 'coaching' engines, averaging 25.4lbs of coke per mile;

In the Bird Class, the Liverpool & Manchester Railway had its first standard fleet of locomotives: 2-2-2 (shown here) for passenger working and 2-4-0s for goods ('luggage'). (Anthony Dawson collection)

Crow burned the least coke (22.4lb per mile) and *Petrel* the most (28.2lb per mile). The rebuilding programme of the older 'luggage' locomotives was obviously a success, as their fuel consumption of 25.6lbs of coke per mile was only fractionally more than the newly-built locomotives. The reduction of the fuel bill for these engines was quite dramatic: prior to being rebuilt in 1841, *Lion* and *Tiger* were burning 49.0lb and 46.3lb of coke per mile, but at the end of 1844 this figure had fallen to 24.9lb and 24.3lb of coke per mile, representing a cost-saving of nearly 50%. As Colburn has rightly noted, however, this reduction in the weekly coke bill was not only down to improved valves and valve events, but also due to the coke bonus scheme instituted by Woods which rewarded the economical working of locomotives.[68] That said, Woods' belief that the rebuilt locomotives would certainly recoup the capital expenditure on their rebuilding process through fuel saving does appear to have been well-founded. The rebuilt locomotives cost far more in repairs however: during the last half of 1844, repair work on *Goliath* came to £46 17s 8d; *Lion* £19 9s 2d and *Mastodon* £22 4s 3d compared to less than £10 for engines of the Bird class. Overall running costs were between 5d and 7d per mile per locomotive, although for some of the older, rebuilt, locomotives like *Goliath* this was as much as 11.79d per mile. Average running costs for the locomotive fleet as a whole was 6.75d per mile. The cost of repairs in 1844 was 1.17d per mile, a considerable reduction from 13.1d per mile (or 0.34d per ton per mile) in 1834. The Bird class was clearly a success in traffic and met the design criteria established by Woods and Dewrance for

Compared to their contemporaries, the Bird Class were relatively small and lightweight, with low pressure boilers. Twenty-six were built between 1841 and 1845 at Edgehill. (Anthony Dawson collection)

the class.[69]Across the entire locomotive fleet, the average amount of coke per ton per mile by December 1844 was 21.4lb, or 2.02d per mile run; including consumables and enginemen's wages locomotives cost 11.63d per mile. By Summer 1845 Edward Woods had 41 locomotives at work. In the first half of the year they had run 282,416 miles or about 38 miles per day per engine. The new fleet of locomotives significantly reduced running expenses, something of great import at a time of falling receipts.[70]

Locomotive livery

Although the canary yellow carried by *Rocket* at Rainhill is well-known, the locomotives of the Liverpool & Manchester were far more sombre in their day-to-day operation. Accounts show that green and black paint together with 'whiting' and varnish were purchased at Edge Hill.[71] Green paint was probably chrome green, described during the early nineteenth century as being hard-wearing, and not liable to change colour in the presence of heat, water or sulphides, making it an ideal choice for locomotive livery. Black paint was probably 'lamp black' which was made using soot collected from oil lamps, and was thus not a 'true' black. Varnish would have been vegetable-based and would have given a brown tint to the underlying colour.

Contemporary iconography, particularly that by Rudolph Ackermann or Thomas Talbot Bury, shows the locomotives and tenders painted dark green with black frames, buffer beams and lining. Ackermann also shows the number painted in white on the front buffer beam and numerals carried on the chimney – a feature confirmed by the letter books of Nasmyth Gaskell & Co. when the London & South Western Railway requested brass similar numerals 6½ inches high on the chimneys of their locomotives.[72] Brightwork was painted with 'black varnish'.[73]

The replica of *Planet* is painted Brunswick green with black frames, lining and buffer beam. The oak boiler cladding is varnished and the boiler bands polished brass but it is possible that both were painted in the 1830s. Ackermann shows boiler cladding either a golden brown – perhaps meant to represent varnished timber – and also green with black boiler bands. T. T. Bury also shows green boiler cladding with black bands, so too a colour wash drawing of *Vulcan*. *Lion*, now in Liverpool Museum, has been painted a variety of shades of green since its restoration at Crewe in 1930: the earliest paint scheme included 'red-brown' frames, black smokebox and chimney, and quite a bright green for wheels, splashers, tender, etc. reputedly using very old stocks of LNWR paint.

Table 8: Bird Class Locomotives built at Edge Hill for the Liverpool & Manchester Railway

	Date	Type	Cylinders
Swallow (69)	September 1841	2-2-2	12 x 18
Martin (70)	December 1841	2-2-2	12 x 18
Kingfisher (71)	September 1841	2-2-2	12 x 18
Heron (72)	November 1841	2-2-2	12 x 18
Pelican (73)	December 1841	2-2-2	12 x 18
Ostrich (74)	March 1842	2-2-2	12 x 18
Owl (75)	March 1842	2-4-0	13 x 20
Bat (76)	June 1842	2-4-0	13 x 20
Stork (77)	May 1842	2-2-2	12 x 18
Crane (78)	October 1842	2-2-2	12 x 18
Swan (79)	October 1842	2-2-2	12 x 18
Cygnet (80)	December 1842	2-2-2	12 x 18
Pheasant (82)	January 1843	2-2-2	12 x 18
Partridge (83)	June 1843	2-2-2	12 x 18
Bittern (84)	April 1843	2-4-0	13 x 20
Lapwing (85)	October 1843	2-4-0	13 x 20
Raven (86)	December 1843	2-4-0	13 x 20
Crow (87)	January 1844	2-4-0	13 x 20
Redwing (88)	March 1844	2-2-2	12 x 18
Woodlark (89)	March 1844	2-2-2	12 x 18
Penguin (90)	January 1845	2-4-0	13 x 20
Petrel (91)	July 1844	2-4-0	13 x 20
Linnet (92)	July 1845	2-2-2	12 x 18
Goldfinch (93)	July 1845	2-2-2	12 x 18
Bullfinch (94)	July 1845	2-2-2	12 x 18
Chaffinch (95)	June 1845	2-2-2	12 x 18

PART 2

BREAKING THE MOULD

The Liverpool & Manchester railway was dominated by the designs, and products, of Robert Stephenson & Co. and this naturally drew criticism from the local press and nationally, including a missive in the *Edinburgh Review* by Dr. Dionysius Lardner (1793–1859). Lardner's criticism was based on the familial relationship between George and Robert Stephenson as chief engineer and locomotive manufacturer and that the Board were somehow enthralled by them. Lardner also claimed that the Stephensons were holding back locomotive development through what we'd now describe as a restrictive 'design envelope' which precluded alternative 'form[s] of engine.' The Board penned their own reply to Dr. Lardner, noting that they had welcomed locomotives from other manufacturers on their line and that there was no 'unfair play.' It was simply that the Stephenson locomotives as defined by *Planet* worked, and despite their several flaws (see Part 1) were capable of operating a daily timetabled service, which locomotives such as *William IV* (by Braithwaite and Ericsson) were not. On the back of this diatribe, and criticism at Board level by anti-monopoly directors such as James Cropper or Theodore Rathbone (who would become a major thorn in the side of Robert Stephenson on the London & Birmingham), George Stephenson resigned from the Company in 1833, and locomotives were no longer purchased from Stephenson & Co. In turn this stimulated local engineering firms to supply locomotives for the L&M.[1]

No doubt thanks to the innovative Henry Booth, the Directors of the L&M were open to any suggestion which could improve the running and efficiency of their railway, especially if it led to cost-saving. They also welcomed suggestions from their own engineers, including that of a multi-tubular boiler by Joseph Locke, and a valve gear by John Dixon who attempted to introduce 'a steam cylinder and piston, immediately above the slide and connected therewith by a rod' to work the valves in order to relieve them 'from the very heavy steam pressure on the slides.' A similar idea had also occurred to John Gray.[2] A suggestions for 'improved' patent locomotive came from Herr Johann Kollmann recommended his brothers' locomotive for their consideration. William Crawshay II of Cyfartha Iron Works in South Wales called the Boards' attention to his own 'heavy engine' in March 1830 and Timothy Burstall of Edinburgh proposed to built a locomotive for the Company in May 1830. James E Anderson also wrote to the Board, proposing that they pay the cost of patenting his 'improved locomotive carriage, in consideration of which the Liverpool & Manchester Co. might use his invention at one half the price charged other Companies'. The Board declined as it was 'contrary to their Established Rule not to take any share or interest in Patents.'[3]

Whilst the outside-framed inside-cylinder Stephenson locomotive had quickly come to dominate the motive power of the Liverpool & Manchester Railway, between 1830 and 1834 the Board accepted eight experimental locomotives on to their line for trial, four of which were taken into stock:

Liver (26) by Edward Bury.
Experiment (32) (although only after substantial modifications) by Sharp, Roberts & Co.
Caledonian (28) by Galloway & Bowman of Manchester.
Swiftsure (36) by George Forrester of Liverpool.

Those locomotives not taken into stock included *William IV* and *Queen Adelaide*, Edward Bury's *Liverpool*, and Galloway & Bowman's unsuccessful first attempt, *Manchester*.

CHAPTER 8

Braithwaite and Ericsson

Novelty by John Braithwaite (1797–1870) and John Ericsson (1803–1889) had been the 'people's favourite' at the Rainhill Trials. Yet, despite the vociferous support of the *Mechanics' Magazine* and its allies including Charles Blacker Vignoles and James Cropper, *Novelty* had not been a conspicuous success and had been dogged by mechanical faults, not least the failure of the boiler feed pump, causing the boiler to run dry and part of the flue to collapse. Whilst her boiler was theoretically brilliant, it could not meet the demand for steam. Furthermore, although her cylinders could generate about 6hp, the bellows which provided the forced-draught for the fire required 6.5hp to work them. In other words, *Novelty* was using more energy to work the bellows than propel herself.[1] A month after Rainhill, Henry Habberly Price from Neath Abbey, who had been present at the Rainhill Trials, informed the Board he was about to

In 1929 a full-size static replica of *Novelty* was built by the Science Museum using all four original wheels and one of the original cylinders, which had been preserved by John Melling and his descendants. (Anthony Dawson)

build 'a loco-motive Engine, to combine Mr Braithwaite's and Erickson's principle, with alterations and improvements.' The Board replied that they would be prepared to purchase the engine so long as it 'should appear to possess those advantages which Mr Pryce [sic] anticipated.'[2] Not accepted by the L&M, the locomotive was worked by Thomas Prothero, a South Wales coal merchant, and named *Speedwell*.

But *Novelty*'s story did not end in defeat at Rainhill. Braithwaite and Ericsson carried out modifications to her, the most notable being the provision of a third cylinder to work the bellows which were so vital to her performance. The boiler and blowing mechanism was also modified. This work also increased her weight, and therefore adhesion. In this rebuilt state *Novelty* underwent further trials in the winter of 1829. They took place on the Rainhill Level, involving waggons 'on those of Mr Stephenson's and those on Mr [Ross] Winan's principle.' One of these load trials ended in tragedy when one Towlerton, the Company Overlooker at Sutton fell from a waggon on which he was riding and was run over and killed. The Board gave £50 to his widow. Thereafter the Board ruled that no further experiments be made with *Novelty* 'except under the immediate instruction of the Directors, or the personal superintendence of Captn. Erickson.' Novelty was also prohibited from propelling a load at more than 4mph. With her bellows worked by steam, *Novelty* was found to be able to move a load of 35 tons at a speed of 12.5mph; the anti-Stephenson *Liverpool Courier* hoped that 'as soon as Novelty has a space of five or six miles to proceed upon, so that the full momentum may be acquired and kept up, the velocity will be greatly augmented.'[3] The *Lancaster Gazette* reported that these trials had been a success:

> 'The Novelty, which has been materially improved by the alterations it has undergone, was exercised on the railway at Rainhill. It is stated to have drawn 31 tons gross at a speed of 12 miles an hour; the distance traversed was a mile and a half. A supplementary cylinder has been added to this engine, for the sole purpose of blowing the bellows, and the two cylinders are independent of each other.'[4]

Indeed, the apparent success of these trials was reported in the engineering and national press, reporting verbatim from the *Mechanics' Magazine*.[5] Further trials took place, supervised by William Daglish jr. of Wigan, on 26 January 1830. With a load of 28.5 tons *Novelty* ran at an average speed of 8mph, and burned 84lbs of coke an hour. With her improved blowing apparatus, *Novelty*:

> 'Carried nearly ten times its own weight, with the adhesion of only two wheels, which is certainly something extraordinary, though I am aware it will not do it in all seasons of the year.'[6]

The result of these trials were communicated to the Board on 1 February 1830, on which date a proposal from Ericsson was read, offering to 'Furnish a Locomotive Engine, weighing five tons, to draw a hundred tons, at fifteen miles per hour.' The Board agreed to the proposal, and authorised the construction of a single locomotive by Braithwaite and Ericsson.[7] *Novelty* was eventually acquired by Charles Blacker Vignoles who had hoped to use her for the opening of the Wigan Branch

Railway, but she had a distressing tendency to keep de-railing so *North Star* (on hire from the L&M) was used instead.[8]

A fortnight later Ericsson attended the Board meeting in Liverpool, where further details were thrashed out for two identical locomotives:

'The weight of the engine not to exceed Five tons. The gross weight to be drawn by each, to be Forty tons, with the best constructed waggons in use on the railway at the time of the trial – to be conveyed from Liverpool to Manchester in two hours; assistance to be provided by the Company up the Whiston Incline Plane, or allowance to be made for loss of speed on that part of the Line – the pressure of the steam in the Boiler not to exceed 50lb per square inch; the engine not to consume more than ½lb of coke per ton drawn per mile … to be delivered in Liverpool not later than the 15th June next, and be kept in repair by the builders for twelve months. The price to be One Thousand pounds for each engine.'[9]

The final delivery of both engines was delayed, and Ericsson suggested a revised delivery date of 15 July, but even this proved optimistic. The delivery date came and went, and on 19 July Henry Booth was instructed to write to Messrs. Braithwaite and Ericsson concerning the non-delivery of their locomotives. It transpired the delay was due to legal problems in getting the boiler design patented; Ericsson assured the Board that both engines would be completed by the beginning of August and that they would be despatched from London on 27 July and delivered to Liverpool 'on or before the 7th August.'[10] But once again, delivery was postponed. An apologetic Braithwaite wrote to the Board (who met on 2 August) stating that the first engine had been despatched 'from London Saturday last', but a fortnight later (15 August) the two engines had still not been delivered. They finally arrived in Liverpool sometime around 23 August, together with Ericsson 'who had gone to Manchester to superintend the fitting up of his Engine.' Ericsson was 'refitting the <u>Novelty</u>, which he would engage to take 30 passengers from Liverpool to Manchester in <u>one hour</u>.' *Novelty* was expected to arrive in Manchester around 12 September. Ericsson also proudly reported that the two locomotives had, with Royal permission, been named *William IV* and *Queen Adelaide*. Booth organised formal running trials, but George Stephenson found objection to the tender having wheels loose on the axle, which 'he considered improper and dangerous.'[11] All was not well; Ericsson once again had to write to the Board that the running trials of *William IV* would be delayed, and that he expected *Queen Adelaide* to be delivered in time for the opening on 15 September. It wasn't until the end of September that *William IV* was apparently ready to undergo running trials; she arrived in Liverpool on 22 September and 'was witness exercising there on the evening of the 23d.' The *Mechanics' Magazine* reported:

'On Tuesday, the William the Fourth … made its appearance at the Manchester end of the line, and exercised for two or three hours. On Wednesday it made the trip to Liverpool in two hours and twelve minutes (including stoppages); and on Thursday evening again exercised, as at Manchester, between Edge Hill and Olive Mount.'[12]

Braithwaite and Ericsson's second attempt: *William IV* and *Queen Adelaide*. Although theoretically brilliant, using a fan powered by exhaust steam to draw the fire, they were a dead-loss. There is no evidence *Queen Adelaide* ever steamed. (Anthony Dawson collection)

William IV was estimated to be 'an engine of about twenty horse power' with two vertical cylinders 12 x 14 inches. Her driving wheels were five feet in diameter, and apparently uncoupled. As with *Novelty*, the final drive was via bell-cranks, but unlike *Novelty*, the driving wheels were positioned beneath the cylinders resulting in shorter connecting rods. Whilst *Novelty* had been a well tank, *William IV* propelled a tender carrying her coke and water. Boiler pressure was 50psi, and was a joint patent between Braithwaite, Ericsson, Vignoles and the Scottish engineer Alexander Nimmo. It was designed to be a 'closed system' and consisted of both a vertical element containing the firebox surmounted by a 'steam chamber' and a horizontal section (the boiler proper) through which a copper flue tube passed five times before entering the 'exhausting chamber' sat on top of the vertical boiler element. Within this 'close box or chamber' was a rotary fan which span at an estimated speed of 52mph. It was driven by steam exhausted from the cylinders. The fan was intended to draw all the combustion products 'through all the turns of the boiler … through the other five turns of the flue … and finally was drawn through the exhausting chamber and passed into the atmosphere' via 'a short tube above the exhausting chamber.' The patentees hoped that the boiler design would produce a 'saving of at least 120 per cent in the cost of fuel.'[13] The idea of using a fan to draw the hot gases through the boiler, and later to use a steam powered blower to provide the draught through the fire grate, was studied in great detail by Brunel in the early 1840s, concluding that a continuous flow of air on a coke fire did reduce fuel consumption, but the introduction of variable cut-off valve gear probably ended Brunel's experiments.[14]

The formal running trials, which were held on 24 September, proved Stephenson right over the expediency of not having wheels loose on the axle as *William IV* derailed on the Sankey Embankment and had 'been all but precipitated over … the embankment,' causing considerable disruption to the ordinary traffic of the line. The anti-Stephenson Mechanics' Magazine dutifully blamed the Liverpool & Manchester for this accident. Braithwaite and Ericsson wrote to the Board 'expressing their regret' for this disruption.[15]

Braithwaite and Ericsson wrote to the Board 'requesting leave' for further trials of *William IV* between Eccles and Manchester. Just in case there was another accident it was considered expedient for them to take place 'after the last train shall have started for Liverpool.' The Directors agreed to this, and John Dixon was instructed to superintend the trial.[16] The *Manchester Courier* reported that *William IV* 'did not entertain the expectations' of her builders; the *Manchester Mercury* thought much of the reportage surrounding *William IV* was 'fallacy'; whilst the *Liverpool Chronicle* thought the reports of their success were wildly exaggerated with little basis in fact. The *Mechanics' Magazine* (16 October 1830) immediately sprang to their defence, claiming that an 'erroneous' and 'absurd notion' had 'gone abroad' that the two engines were 'unequal to the task'. It did admit, however, that 'The Adelaide has not, up to this moment ... been tried at all.'[17]

Braithwaite and Ericsson continued to work on both engines during the winter of 1830; Ericsson wrote to the Board at the end of January 1831 noting he required more time to get *William IV* in order, but 'would be ready for the final trial about the end of the month.' The Board obviously allowed him this extra time, but also sent 'a gauge showing the distance which the Engine wheels should be apart' further suggesting that the reason she had derailed in September 1830 was due to problems with the wheels, and them keeping true to gauge.[18]

Formal trials were held between 14 and 17 January 1831 which the *Mechanics' Magazine* claimed proved that the efficiency of Ericsson's boiler was not in doubt: *William IV* evaporated 'twenty-four cubic feet of water ... in thirty minutes, in a boiler one-fifth the size ordinarily required to produce such an effect.' *William IV* was reported as drawing a load of 40 tons gross – the weight stipulated in the design brief – but when she got to the Whiston Incline 'the resistance was such that the wheels went round, striking fire with the rail' so the load was taken forward by a Stephenson locomotive. The trailing load was increased to 60 tons for the trial on 17 January and *William IV* apparently managed to handle this load at an average speed of 9mph, which several commentators thought unlikely.[19] The *Manchester Guardian* and other Manchester 'papers noted *William IV* had struggled to move its specified load of 40 tons at anything approaching the 10mph Braithwaite and Ericsson had 'positively contracted for' and *William IV* had 'given up its task before it had reached half way.' The *Mechanics' Magazine* replied that the *Guardian* was guilty of spreading pro-Stephenson falsehoods; it had never been intended for *William IV* to proceed any further than Rainhill; that the load 'taken in hand' by *William IV* had had to have been taken on by two Stephenson locomotives demonstrated their lack of power; finally the trial was not a failure but rather it had been arranged to demonstrate the evaporative power of the boiler which 'was placed beyond doubt.'[20]

On the morning of 18 February 1831 further formal trials were held. The *Preston Chronicle* reported how *William IV* ran, light engine, between Liverpool and Manchester in just over two hours. On the return leg, 'there was a trial of power between it and one of Mr Stephenson's engines (the *Mars*)'. *Mars* with a load of 30 tons gross departed after *William IV* which was running light engine, and 'overtook it near Newton' and 'from thence pushed [*William IV*] all the way to Liverpool.' A further trial was held later the same evening with pretty much the same results.[21]

An optimistic Braithwaite and Ericsson determined to continue the trial runs on the following day (19 February). *William IV* left Manchester at '17 minutes before 9 o'clock' with a trailing load of five loaded goods waggons, gross weight 20 tons 6 cwt. Given her previous performance *Meteor* had been placed on stand-by 'to follow close behind in case any assistance being required.' Which it duly was.[22] *William IV* was only able to make about 8½mph, and that on a descending gradient. The speed often dropping so low that 'some of the labourers on Chat Moss ran along side, and the fireman of the Meteor got off the tender, ran as far as the King's load, and returned again.' The trial was abandoned at Parkside, but because the 10am passenger train was then due, *William IV* was shunted by hand into the refuge siding to let it pass. *Meteor* then took forward the five waggons, *William IV* finally reaching Liverpool at 1pm.[23] The *Manchester Guardian* reported that despite incredibly high water consumption, 'it was very obvious that the engineer *could not succeed in keeping up an adequate supply of steam.*' The *Guardian* concluded: 'their engines will not work – at all events not to any useful purpose, whilst those of Mr Stephenson perform their allotted task in admirable manner.'[24]

Despite the assertion of the *Mechanics' Magazine* that Braithwaite and Ericsson's patent boiler was an efficient steam generator, which 'exceeds the most sanguine expectations of the patentees' *William IV* was 'almost at a stand still whenever the force-pump was on' from lack of steam. One correspondent to the *Register of Arts* concluded:

> 'The gentlemen who had the honour of petitioning our beloved sovereign for permission to call these engines King William IV and Queen Adelaide, may be proud of the appropriate choice, and these appear no exception to the Royal rule.'[25]

The *Guardian* hoped that their comparative performances 'will, at any rate, put an end of the system of petty detraction which has so long and so incessantly levelled at Mr Stephenson' by a 'little knot of pseudo-mechanics' led by Vignoles and Robertson. The *Guardian* opined that the reporting of the *Mechanics' Magazine* was a 'system of puffing and misrepresentation' and by reporting in detail the various failures of *William IV* was hoping to set the record straight. One Birmingham 'paper thought that both engines were 'found defective ... and will not be used on the railway' and the *Manchester Guardian* 'was threatened with action by the solicitors of Messrs. Braithwaite and Ericsson' because of their reportage.[26] But what of *Novelty*? After 'languishing' disused in the 'corner of a warehouse' in Manchester 'forsaken and neglected', she was acquired by Robert Daglish jnr of Wigan who rebuilt her in 1833 with a new multi-tubular boiler containing 58 1 3/8inch diameter brass tubes; the firebox was an upright dome-topped cylinder after the manner of Edward Bury. New wheels 4 feet diameter were fitted, as were new cylinders measuring 6 x 16 inches. He presented the old cylinders and wheels to John Melling. *William IV* and *Queen Adelaide* were failures; indeed later in life Ericsson referred to them as being

ERICSSON'S CALORIC ENGINE.

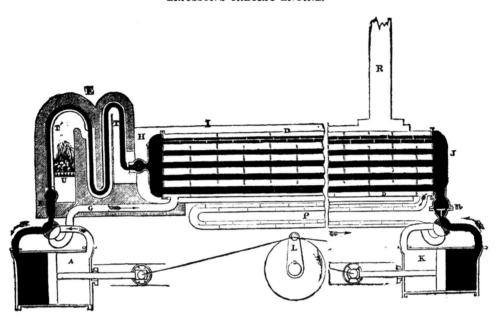

John Ericsson designed and patented a hot-air, or 'caloric', locomotive which used expanding hot-air and contracting cold-air to drive a piston in a cylinder.(Anthony Dawson collection)

'very classical' in appearance but 'miserably inefficient.' It is apparent the boiler of *William IV* was an excellent steam generator whilst the locomotive was stationary or working light-engine, but was unable to generate sufficient steam to meet the demand of the cylinders whilst working under load.[27]

Ericsson's final attempt to build a locomotive was in November 1833 when Henry Booth was instructed to communicate with Ericsson concerning details of his patent caloric (i.e. hot air) engine as adapted for a railway locomotive. He had first demonstrated a hot air engine in 1830 where it 'excited … much interest.' His second was built in 1833 and demonstrated in London that summer; it was much lauded as the successor to the steam engine, especially on safety grounds as it had no boiler which could explode. A lengthy discussion took place as to the merits of the engine, with the Directors being willing to defray any costs in producing working drawings of the engine. Ericsson's reply was swift, sending preliminary details to Liverpool in a matter of weeks; full particulars had been received by the end of the month. The matter received due attention of the Board in New Year 1834, when Mr Aggs, a friend of Ericsson who had been introduced to the Board via John Cropper jr, attended. It transpired Aggs was acting as an agent on behalf of Ericsson, and that Ericsson was not so much willing to build a locomotive for the Board but rather was intending to sell them a licence to do so. The Chairman informed Aggs that 'it was contrary to the rule & practice of the company' to do so, but 'should Captain Ericsson bring an Engine for trial, on the Rail Way, every opportunity should be afforded in proving its merits.' And there the matter ended, but Ericsson continued to develop his design, even building a hot-air engine powered ship in 1852.[28]

CHAPTER 9

Sans Pareil

Timothy Hackworth was the 'Superintendent of the Permanent and Locomotive Engines' on the Stockton & Darlington Railway, a position he enjoyed thanks to George Stephenson, and had previously briefly worked for Robert Stephenson & Co. He was an experienced and skilled engine-wright.[1] Hackworth had built his entry for the Rainhill Trials, *Sans Pareil*, in his spare time and using what limited capital he had. And indeed, even before Rainhill he approached the Board seeking re-assurances in case his entry 'should be <u>very nearly</u> as complete & good in all respects as to the one which should win the premium' and whether they would be prepared to purchase the engine. Henry Booth replied that the Board would 'deal liberally' with the 'proprietor of an Engine under those circumstances' but were not under any obligation to purchase it.[2]

Because *Sans Pareil* had been built alongside Hackworth's day job, there had been little opportunity for running trials, other than being steamed once, at midnight on the Aycliffe Level before she was despatched (by road) to Liverpool. Thus, it is not surprising that several mechanical faults were discovered at Rainhill, including problems

with the boiler feed pump which twice failed. More serious was the boiler which was found to leak, and a poorly cast cylinder. Considered by the three judges to have been overweight, and of 'a mode of construction [which] did not seem to them a sufficient value of recommendation to the directors of the company', *Sans Pareil* was withdrawn and despite Hackworth requesting a further trial once the faults had been ironed out, he was denied this.[3]

The remains of Timothy Hackworth's *Sans Pareil* are on display at Locomotion, Shildon. The boiler barrel dates from 1829; the cylinders date from 1837 as do one set of wheels. The chimney is a result of a Victorian restoration to prepare her for display. (Lauren Jaye Gradwell)

Following his defeat at Rainhill, Hackworth wrote to the Board, requesting a second formal trial of *Sans Pareil*. The problems with *Sans Pareil* had been out of his control: the leaky boiler had been made at the Bedlington Iron Works (where Robert Stephenson & Co. also sourced their boilers, but crucially the boiler of Rocket had been made from best Staffordshire plate due to quality control issues at Bedlington) and the cylinders by Stephenson & Co. These were two firms in which Hackworth had 'been compelled to put confidence … which I found with sorrow was but too implicitly placed.' Stephenson & Co had also found fault with the boiler plate supplied by Bedlington and for that reason had changed their supplier in January 1829.[4] The faulty cylinder was a 'defect … of a nature easily to be remedied' and could have been carried out at Rainhill by fitting a replacement, if permission had been granted by the judges. The Board agreed to a second series of trials at Rainhill during late October. Whilst Hackworth had requested to use the same course as used during the actual Trials, due to building 'work on the adjacent Bridge' taking place the final distance was only ¾ mile. Fitted with a new cylinder *Sans Pareil* performed faultlessly, hauling a load eight times her own weight:

> 'At half-past ten o'clock, one of your Agents weighed in 7cwt. of Fuel – the engine was kept continually in motion (save watering) til 6 at night, when a Portion of the fuel remained unconsumed – during the day the Engine ascended and descended the Inclined Plane repeatedly, with water and fuel and twelve passengers (at the agreed rate [i.e. 10mph]). Afterwards a load of 38 tons was attached to the Engine – also 15 Passengers – thus laden up an ascent (this I am informed) of 4ft. pr mile the speed maintained was 13½ miles per hour – during the Day the fire was never cleaned.'[5]

Hackworth 'had not the least hesitation' that *Sans Pareil* was up to the task of working on the Liverpool & Manchester. In terms of 'simplicity, power, and economy' she was 'unequalled' and capable (in his opinion) of moving a gross load of 60 tons at 10mph. Further trials were held on the Bolton & Leigh Railway, to ascertain her hill-climbing ability using the Daubhill and Chequerbent Inclines:

> 'Up the first, a mile and a half long, the "Sans Pareil" drew its tender with coke and water, two loaded waggons and a carriage containing passengers – making a train load of 15 tons – at an average speed of nine miles an hour. On the steeper incline, with a load of 4 tons 15 cwt, the speed was from 9 to 11 miles per hour.'[6]

The Board agreed to purchase *Sans Pareil* for £550; £50 more than the premium they awarded Stephenson & Booth for *Rocket*, the amount being settled in December. Purchase of *Sans Pareil* enabled the L&M to continue to use the *Lancashire Witch* (which they had hired from the Bolton & Leigh for a period of three months from 25 July) on ballast duties for a further three months by putting *Sans Pareil* to work on the Bolton & Leigh. The reason for this was because *Sans Pareil* was a coal burner, and 'will not work on Coke, and therefore unfit for the Liverpool & Manchester Line.' This was an observation shared by John Hargreaves, the lessee of the Bolton & Leigh. Lancashire Witch must have been worked hard, as during July 1830 Ralph Hutchinson was paid for 12 1/2 days' work on her. In November 1830, in order to extend the loan period for *Lancashire Witch*, the L&M Board ordered that the new set of wheels costing £100 'lately arrived from Newcastle' should be fitted, and for her to 'remain on her present station at Eccles for a few weeks more.' *Lancashire Witch* was clearly in poor repair, needing more than just wheels, including new eccentrics, eccentric straps, a new cross head, new regulator stuffing box and a new sprung safety valve, which were ordered from Newcastle. The arrival of *Rocket* towards the middle of the month meant that she could take over on ballast duties at the Manchester end to relieve the burden on *Lancashire Witch*.[7] The board ordered on 19 October that 'every effort should be used to complete these repairs in the shortest time possible in order that the Engine may be forwarded to the Bolton Line.' By December Sans Pareil was 'much out of repair' so Hackworth was to 'send a man over' from Darlington to oversee the work. Then, on 4 January 1830 the Bolton & Leigh requested the immediate return of *Lancashire Witch*, 'Hackworth's engine being too much out of repair to work' to which the L&M Board assented.[8]

Sans Pareil remained on loan to the Bolton & Leigh on an informal basis; at the Board meeting of 8 March 1830 David Hodgson reported that the B&L, in order to formalise the hire agreement of *Sans Pareil*, were 'desirous to know the terms on which the ... Company would let on hire "The Sans Pareil" Locomotive engine.' Henry Booth was instructed to communicate with the B&L that *Sans Pareil* would be available to hire for a period of twelve months for £20 per month, but this charge was too high for the B&L and it was reduced to £15 per month 'for three months certain', either party being at liberty to extend the hire period, or cancel the contract with one month's notice. The B&L was to keep her in good repair, and she was to be returned to Liverpool 'in good working order.'[9] The *Liverpool Mercury* records that she started working B&L passenger trains a month later:

> 'The Sans Pareil engine, with coach attached to it, and adapted for Passengers, went from Bolton to Leigh, attended by some of the Directors of the Company. On its return from the former place to Bolton, it ran, using the lower incline next to Leigh, at a rate of fifteen miles per hour, and at the higher incline at Chowbent, at the rate of eight miles an hour. The engine, including stoppages, came from Leigh to Bolton in thirty-five minutes. The distance between the two is ... eight miles.'[10]

In October 1831 Joseph Pease of the Stockton & Darlington wrote to the L&M Board requesting to purchase *Sans Pareil*. The Board considered her unfit for use on the L&M and were obviously eager to dispose of her and agreed to her sale.[11] This sale fell through, but in January 1832 the Management Committee agreed to sell her to Hargeaves of the Bolton & Leigh for £110.[12] *Sans Pareil* was rebuilt with larger cylinders and new iron wheels (replacing wooden-spoked originals) in 1837 and was finally retired in 1844, when she was used as a colliery winding engine. The driving wheels were removed and replaced by gear wheels used to work the pump gear. Here she remained until 1863, thus out-lasting both *Rocket* and *Novelty*. Her present appearance is entirely down to 'restoration' in 1864.[13]

CHAPTER 10

Edward Bury

Edward Bury (1794–1858) was perhaps the only major competitor with Robert Stephenson for the design and manufacture of locomotives in the 1830s. Bury was born in Salford and educated in Chester, and his locomotives were the first major challenge to the Stephenson type and indeed resulted in much controversy between the two men and in the national press. His business partner, the marine engineer James Kennedy, had been employed at Robert Stephenson & Co of Newcastle for eighteen months, and briefly manager at Mather, Dixon & Co of Liverpool. Of Kennedy, Robert Stephenson later wrote that he regretted that Kennedy ever been taken on: 'If Kennedy had not obtained a great deal of information from here we should have stood much higher in Locomotive Engine Makers then we do now. Bury never would have made an engine.'

Bury's first locomotive was called *Dreadnought*, which he intended to enter into the Rainhill Trials of October 1829 but the engine was not completed on time. John Bourne, writing in 1875, described how:

> 'It had two inclined cylinders working down to cranks on a shaft carried across beneath the boiler, on which the shaft wheel for pitched chains was fixed, and this wheel gave motion to a pitched chain passing over pulleys on the fore and aft axles of the carriage, and so propelled the machine. This engine was formed with side rods working down to the cranks, the same way as the 'Locomotion.' The boiler was made with a fire tube and two return tubes.'[1]

The description by Hardman Earle, one of the Liverpool & Manchester Directors, agrees with that of Bourne who notes both the chain drive and an 'accelerating wheel' whilst Bury's widow wrote that:

> 'She had the old plan of boiler and six wheels, with cylinders ten inches in diameter, two feet stroke, and two valves – one, the ordinary valve, the other the expansive valve – to allow the steam being worked expansively.'[2]

From the above it is apparent that *Dreadnought* was an 0-6-0 with inclined outside cylinders measuring 10 x 24 inches. Her driving wheels were 4 feet in diameter and with a wheelbase of 8ft 6in. The cylinders drove a crank shaft which carried the necessary toothed wheel to drive the chain. The boiler was reminiscent of the initial design for Lancashire Witch: it had a single large flue which branched to form two return flues to increase the heating surface, putting the chimney and firebox at the same end of the boiler. One description of the boiler mentions how the tubes were 'heated externally' and that the 'small [water] tubes' projected from a 'hollow fire bridge over the fire' but that the boiler could not generate sufficient steam. The boiler of *Liverpool* was apparently the same, where 'small tubes' were heated 'inside of the large tube in which the furnace was placed' suggesting the use of cross-tubes within the main flue. The draught was provided by bellows 'placed under the tender, and so constructed that the blast could be worked by hand to get up steam.'[3]

Dreadnought was used during the construction of the Liverpool & Manchester Railway 1829–1830; Lecount notes in 1839 that *Dreadnought* 'was first started ... March 12 1830', and she is mentioned as being 'now employed' by James Scott Walker in September 1830. Her later history is somewhat confused: whilst Bourne notes that *Dreadnought* was sold to 'Mr Hargreaves of Bolton, and continued in use in traffic [on the Bolton & Leigh Railway] for twenty years', Ahrons suggests that '*Dreadnought* was a complete failure'. She was too heavy for the lightly laid permanent way and frequently broke crank pins on the drive-shaft, even after she had been rebuilt with lowered cylinders and better weight distribution.[4] Far from being broken up in December 1830 (and supposedly representing a dead loss of £1,500), *Dreadnought* is recorded as being at work on the Bolton & Leigh 'conveying goods' in June 1831 when she was involved in a fatal accident. Whilst being taken to the Hope Foundry for repairs, and with the tender 'literally covered with men and boys', it was 'thrown off the line' due to the turn table at the Foundry not being correctly set, 'was thrown off the track with a considerable shock, and ran along for the space of twelve yards upon the road' before colliding with a stone wall, killing three men.[5]

Bury's second locomotive was the aptly-named *Liverpool*. Edward Woods described *Liverpool* as at first having a return-flue boiler the draught for which was provided by bellows, reminiscent of the *Lancashire Witch* which used similar technology in its coke burning boiler to prevent smoke:

> 'The "Liverpool" was a four-wheeled coupled engine with cranked axles and cylinders under the smokebox. The hand-gearing was placed in front of the smokebox, where the driver stood, the stoker being in the usual position, at the other extremity of the engine, or fire-box end ... The boiler was not multi-tubular ... but contained a number of convoluted [i.e. return] flues ... The furnace was urged by a blast from a pair of bellows working under the tender and not by the aid of the blast-pipe ... In its first stage it did not resemble any form of engine now in use.'[6]

John Bourne adds that the bellows were soon dispensed with as they 'made holes in the fire' and this was the reason for the replacement boiler, which had a 'round firebox' and an 'exhausting jet in the chimney.' Woods describes the firebox of this boiler being 'domed' and containing a 'very small internal fire-box', and Mrs Bury – eager to deny any involvement by Stephenson or their supporters – suggests it was a version of Marc Séguin's 1828 patent design.[7]

According to Bury's widow, *Liverpool* was first steamed in the yard at the Clarence Foundry on 12 July 1830, and that the Directors of the Liverpool & Manchester had been invited to attend. Lecount suggests *Liverpool* underwent trials on the L&M ten days later, and it was reported to the Board the locomotive was ready for trial at the end of October 1830. C. B. Vignoles' diary records experiments with *Liverpool* on 4 September 1830, together with *Dart* and *North Star*. Between these two dates, Kennedy notes that *Liverpool* broke its crank axle and was taken off the line to have

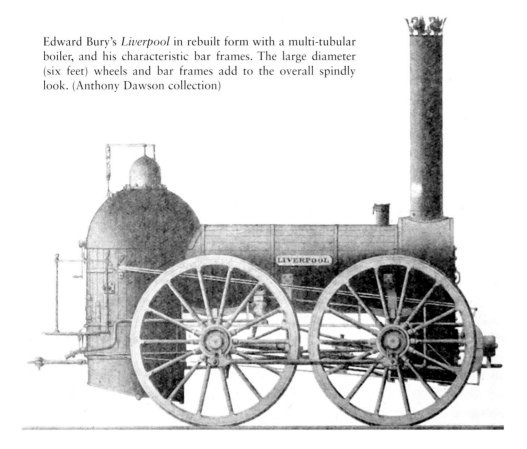

Edward Bury's *Liverpool* in rebuilt form with a multi-tubular boiler, and his characteristic bar frames. The large diameter (six feet) wheels and bar frames add to the overall spindly look. (Anthony Dawson collection)

it welded, hence a second trial being requested in October. The October trial was to be supervised by Thomas Longridge Gooch who was to 'keep an exact account of the Engine's performance; the quantity of Coke & Water used.' Sadly, Gooch's report does not survive, although judging by Bury's letter read to the Board a month later, it appears that the trial may not have actually taken place, much to Bury's annoyance. The Board ordered the trial to take place by the end of November 1830.[8]

It is possible that between November 1830 and May 1831 *Liverpool* was rebuilt, although Edward Woods notes that as the multi-tubular boiler was fitted after an accident in July 1831 it is possible the boiler was replaced in the six months preceding May 1831. Mrs Bury notes that *Liverpool* was 'started May 17th, 1831.' In June Bury wrote to the Board requesting formal trials of the rebuilt locomotive, and that it be used 'for the Conveyance of Goods between Liverpool & Manchester and a fair comparison be made' between it and a Stephenson locomotive. George Stephenson (who was in attendance), however, objected to the trial due to the large (6 feet) diameter of *Liverpool*'s wheels which he thought were unsafe; although the size of the wheels are not mentioned in Autumn 1830 it may be that they mitigated against the trials, or perhaps were changed during the period between November 1830 and June 1831. The Management Committee were requested to report on the matter and to organise a trial of the engine 'if they were of the opinion it could take place with propriety.' Stephenson was also asked to prepare a report on the relative merits of different wheel sizes which he presented to the Board on 27 June. Following a lengthy discussion the Board agreed that 'Mr Bury's engine be allowed to run with Goods between Liverpool & Manchester, taking such loads as Mr Bury may deem expedient' for a two-month trial. But so as not to interfere with the day to day operation of the line the Board thought it undesirable to 'load the Company's Engines differently from what they are now doing.' Bury thought this unfair as no direct comparison between *Liverpool* and the Company's locomotives could be made, and immediately complained to the Board; Henry Booth tried to poor oil on troubled water, but reiterated that the Board was not willing to amend the mode of trial.[9] It is unclear whether the trial of *Liverpool* took place on the Liverpool & Manchester, in July she is recorded as working on the Bolton & Leigh Railway. Sadly, whilst working a train up one of the incline planes 'with a heavy load of goods' she derailed, probably due to a wrongly placed switch. *Liverpool* overturned, killing the engineman and fireman whilst two boys riding on the tender were seriously hurt.[10]

The only locomotive by Bury to be accepted into service by the Liverpool & Manchester Railway was *Liver*, named after the mythical bird from whence Liverpool takes its name. On 1 August 1831 Bury attended the meeting of the Board of Directors, stating that he was 'desirous to make an engine for this company.' Following a discussion, the Directors noted 'that they were in want of Engines' and that Bury should make his application in writing to 'build one or more locomotives, with conditions as to keeping the same in repair.'[11] Bury's proposal was read by the Board a week later, and Henry Booth was ordered to 'consult with Mr Stephenson' and prepare a 'draft of agreement ... for the purchase of one or more locomotives from Mr Bury.'[12] The draft agreement was ready for the Board Meeting of 15 August, which Bury attended, who contrary to the agreement drawn up by Booth and Stephenson, 'Strongly recommended inside bearings instead of outside, as stipulated.'[13] After 'Mr Bury had retired' George Stephenson was interviewed by the Board, affirming his preference for outside frames 'for safety for locomotives with cranked axles.' Henry Booth was instructed to report the same to Bury, 'that in any contract for engines, the directors cannot dispense with the stipulation outside bearings.' The order was placed a week later for two locomotives costing £750.[14] In December 1831 Henry Booth reported that the crank axles for the locomotives being built by Bury were '4¼ inches diameter in the Crank Pin & made of excellent Low Moor Iron.'[15] Whilst these locomotives were building, there was a last minute change: at the request of Stephenson, the Management Sub-Committee ordered that 'double springs be put in ... as approved ... the extra cost being allowed by the Company.' In other words, the bearings of the inner plate frame were also to be sprung.[16]

Despite this alteration, the first locomotive was ready by early January 1832 and was transferred to John Hargreaves, lessee of the Bolton & Leigh Railway;[17] the second was completed by April, the pair having cost £1,488 7s, half being payable by Hargreaves.[18] *Liver*'s boiler was 6 feet 6 inches long and 3 feet 3 inches diameter. The firebox was 3 feet 7 inches wide, 2 feet 9¾ inches front to back and 3 feet 1¼ inches high. There was a water space of 2½ inches and 97 iron tubes: 73 of 1¾ inches diameter in

Liver (No. 26) was a hybrid having Bury's typical D-plan firebox surmounted by a large copper-sheathed steam dome together with Stephenson's outside sandwich frames. (Anthony Dawson collection)

the bottom of the boiler and 24 of 2 inches diameter at the top, giving a heating surface of 321½ square feet to which the firebox provided an additional 31½ square feet.[19]

Liver was named on 16 April 1832, and performance trials were held between *Liver* and *Planet* supervised by William Allcard but it later transpired that Anthony Harding, the Locomotive Foreman, had sabotaged the trials in favour of the Stephenson engine. Despite this it was noted that thanks to her larger firebox, *Liver* was the more economical locomotive, burning only 0.49lb of coke per ton per mile compared to *Planet* (0.54lb per ton per mile).[20] A trial run by Hardman Earle at the end of the year, however, showed that *Vesta* (Planet class, 2-2-0) burned only 0.28lbs of coke per ton per mile, and *Liver* 0.32lbs.[21]

Liver was something of a hybrid with outside bearings and sandwich frames favoured by the Stephensons and the D-plan, dome-topped firebox preferred by Bury, the latter resulting in considerable controversy between the two men. Stephenson reported his concerns over the use of Bury's firebox on the grounds of safety because there were no stays between the inner and outer firebox. A lengthy discussion took place over the merits of the two types of firebox at the Board Meeting of 23 April 1832 where Stephenson was ordered to 'report as to the safety' of 'circular fireplaces.' Stephenson's doubts were perhaps proved correct when Allcard reported to the Board a 'defect with the fireplace of the Liver Engine.' Despite this defect, Allcard however considered 'her perfectly safe.'[22]

Flushed with success, Bury hoped to curry favour with the Board and gain a lucrative contract to supply and maintain locomotives for the L&M:

'Mr Bury requested an order to build two new and powerful Locomotive Engines which he was confident he would make superior to any Engine now on the line, and he would engage to keep them in repair for twelve months at a fixed rate per ton to be agreed upon.'[23]

The Board decided to take up Bury's offer and that he 'be requested to pass the terms on which he should undertake to keep the Engines in repair to the Board.'[24] But the issue of fireboxes did not go away: Allcard suggested to the Board on 2 July 1832 that 'A survey by two Boilermakers be held on the fireplaces of Mr Bury's engines, to ascertain whether their mode of construction is safe.' One of the boilermakers was to be appointed by Bury, and the second by the L&M.[25] The two boilermakers were George Forrester of Liverpool and Mr Vernon from Messrs. Vernon & Guest of Smethwick, whose reports were read to the Board at the end of the month; unfortunately their correspondence does not survive.[26] Stephenson presented his report and reply to Forrester and Vernon a week later, when the Board ordered that a survey be made of all the locomotive fireboxes, their form and condition for presentation to the Board.[27] He reported to the Management Committee on 6 September that 'he considered [circular fireboxes] highly dangerous.' The Management Committee resolved to forward the report to the Board and suggested they seek the recommendation of a professional engineer on the matter. William Allcard was instructed to examine all the fireboxes in use on the railway, with a view to 'ascertain … what wear had hitherto taken place in the fireplaces.' In light of Stephenson's report, *Liver* was to be withdrawn from passenger service, and the Committee wrote to Hargreaves of the Bolton & Leigh – which ran several of Bury's engines – informing him of Stephenson's conclusion.[28]

The matter was discussed by the Directors four days later. They acknowledged Stephenson's report and his conclusion that:

'Circular fireplaces … were objectionable because they could not be advantageously strengthened by crowns stays as the square sided fire-boxes were, when an accident by bursting took place the effect would be entirely disastrous.'[29]

Because of the 'decided difference of opinion' between Bury and Stephenson, and because several of Bury's engines were running on their line, the Directors resolved to 'Request the Professional opinion of John Farey esq. of London' on the matter. Bury and Stephenson were also requested to put their views in writing.[30] A fortnight later Bury wrote to the board objecting 'to the question of the comparable merits of Circular and Square fireboxes' being referred to Mr Farey alone. He thought that there should be at least six expert witnesses, half chosen by the Board and half by himself. As a result, the Board consented to consult Mr Farey as well as 'two other impartial Engineers of acknowledged ability' to be chosen by Farey. The Board also reminded Bury to send them his personal report on fireboxes but, probably feeling that the Board was biased toward the Stephensons, he refused to submit it, unless he was 'allowed to appoint some of the arbitrators'. The Board refused to accede to his request, but Bury did finally submit his report a week later.[31] Bury must have received a boost when Allcard reported to the Board on 12 October that both locomotives built at the Clarence Foundry had been inspected and now had a 'certificate of approval ... of two Engines ... One for Mr Hargreaves, and the other, with coupled wheels, for Messrs. Bournes & Robinson.' Interestingly, Allcard had inspected and certified the locomotives in the absence of Stephenson, and as soon as the latter had returned from business in London, he raised the issue of the size of locomotive wheels to the board.[32]

The *Liverpool* had had wheels 6 feet in diameter which Stephenson had found objectionable, and the engine built for Bournes & Robinson had wheels 5 feet 6 inches diameter. In his report on *Liverpool* in June 1832, Stephenson thought that any wheel larger than 5 feet was dangerous; he re-affirmed this belief at a Board Meeting of 22 October 1832: 'A Discussion took place as to the largest wheels to be admitted on the Railway. Mr Stephenson ... recommended that 5 feet diameter be the maximum.' The Board asked Stephenson to put his observations in writing, and report back to them which he did a week later which the Board accepted. As a result a by-law was passed prohibiting the use of wheels larger than 5 feet diameter. Messrs. Bournes & Robinson were written to informing them of the Board's decisions and that their locomotive would only be allowed to run at no more than 12mph over L&M metals.[33]

Farey and Field reported their findings to the Board on 14 January 1833:

'Read Mr Farey's and Mr Joshua Field's Report on the comparative advantages and disadvantages of Round and Square Fire places for Loco-Motive Engines; and giving a decided preference for the Square Fire-Box, principally on the score of superior safety. The Considerations of the Measures to be adopted in consequence of this Report was postponed till the Directors could communicate with Mr Stephenson on the Subject. The Treasurer was instructed to acknowledge the receipt of the report and enquire of Mr Farey whether there would be any objecting a few copies for distribution, occasionally, at the discretion of the Directors. The Treasurer was instructed to inform Mr. Bury that the Report was arrived, and that he was welcome to peruse the same at the Railway Office.'[34]

A furious Bury – sensing the loss of lucrative contracts for the Clarence Foundry – attended the Board meeting a week later:

'Mr Bury Attended ... and stated that he had made an alteration and improvement in the form of his circular fire box ... and he thought if Mr. Farey had known of it he might have given a different Report ... Mr Bury was informed that if he would furnish his statement in writing, the Directors would transmit it to Mr Farey with request to be informed whether the perusal of it would induce him to alter his decision.'[35]

Bury was still not placated, and believed that incorrect drawings of his fireboxes had been sent to London:

'Mr Bury attended and stated that he called in the assistance of 10 Engineers who he expected would be unanimous in preferring the Circular Fire-Box to the

Square one. Mr Bury stated that it was evident from Mr. Farey's report that the drawing of the 'Liver' Fire Place had been incorrect.' [36]

An exasperated Henry Booth minuted:

'The Board recommended to Mr. Bury to adopt the plan before suggested, namely to state clearly in writing in what particulars the drawing appeared to have been incorrect. This statement, when furnished, the Board would transmit to Mr. Farey with request to be informed whether, in consequence thereof, he should be induced to alter his opinion respecting the comparative merits of Square and Round Fire-Boxes. Mr Bury said he must have time to consider; it would be expedient for him to adopt the course recommended by the Board.'[37]

Bury wrote to the Board a week later, 'declining to interfere further in the discussion or decision respecting Round or Square Fire-places.' In order to see fair play, the Board instructed Allcard to ascertain if there were any discrepancies in the drawings sent to Farey, and 'if any of the particulars were incorrect.'[38] Allcard reported a fortnight later that there were very minor differences between the drawings sent to London and the firebox fitted to *Liver*: 'the drawing sent to Mr Farey the round fire box there delineated was made to overhang the axle 8 inches more than the "Livers" did.'[39]

Undaunted, Bury wrote to the Board in March requesting permission to build two 'large' locomotives for 'the carrying of goods only.' The matter was passed over to George Stephenson, who reported back to the Board a month later that 'Mr Stephenson's opinion being unchanged, and the Company moreover not being in immediate want of Engines, Mr. Bury's proposal was declined.'[40]

But this was not the end of Bury's involvement with the L&M. In late December 1833 the Board wrote to him enquiring about his terms for 'building two locomotives with 11 x 20 inches cylinders and coupled wheels, with Copper Fire-Box, Brass Tubes, and other particulars to be specified.' The price for a locomotive was £950 but which excluded an additional £110 for the copper firebox; £30 for piston valves rather than slide valves; £50 for 'additional framing.' Bury's tender for £1,140 each, with delivery in seven months was, however, unaccepted, being the most expensive of those received. Instead, the lowest tender, that of Charles Tayleur & Co. at £950, was accepted.[41] Due to Robert Stephenson 'having very little time to spare', Bury was also consulted regarding the cylinders and valves of the stationary engines at Edgehill to work the trains down the new tunnel to Lime Street; the Clarence Foundry also supplied the main steam pipe for the engines.[42]

Being a one-off *Liver* was used as a test-bed for Perkin's Patent Circulator, which was fitted when she was under repair in Liverpool, requiring a new inner firebox. Her firebox was renewed in March 1833, but in April 1834 there were worries over her iron inner firebox; holes were drilled through it to ascertain the quality of the iron and it was found to be in good order, but Bury did recommend a revision to the stays of the roof of the firebox. She was repaired at the Clarence Foundry in July 1834, but in December 1834 he declined to take any more repair work from the L&M due to the 'difficulty of giving satisfaction to the Foreman and Engineer of the Company' with the quality of his work.[43] In 1836 *Liver* was fitted with yet another experimental firebox, by Gray and Chanter, in order to burn coal, being finally sold in 1837.

CHAPTER 11

Built in Manchester

Galloway, Bowman & Glasgow

Manchester, by Galloway, Bowman & Glasgow, was the first locomotive built in Manchester. The company had been established by William Galloway (1768–1836) in 1790 as a firm of Millwrights with a foundry on Great Bridgewater Street; in 1806 John Bowman (c.1768–?) joined the concern and in 1820 William Glasgow (1782–1861). Although Dendy Marshall suggests *Manchester* was delivered in 1832,[1] she was in fact completed by summer 1831, and she underwent running-in trials that September. The *Manchester Times* described her as being of 'peculiar construction':

> 'The machinery is all in sight – not stowed away under the boiler, but close to the eye and hand of the engineer. Another is that the engineer's station is at the *front* of the engine, so that no obstruction on the road can escape his notice.'[2]

Despite this first-hand description of the locomotive, the drawing presented by Dendy Marshall in *The Engineer* shows the driver's controls in a conventional position. *Manchester* had vertical cylinders, mounted on pedestals and working downwards. They measured 11½ by 16 inches and were 'placed directly over the crank axle, which has wheels of 5 feet 3 inches diameter.' The wheels were wooden with welded iron tyres, and made by John Ashbury founder of the Ashbury Carriage & Wagon Works of Manchester. Again, this press report differs from the depiction given by

Manchester, by Galloway, Bowman & Glasgow, was the first locomotive to be built in Manchester. She had vertical cylinders driving a jackshaft and an annular boiler where exhaust gases passed back toward the firebox end before exiting the chimney.(Anthony Dawson collection)

Dendy Marshall. Vertical cylinders were preferred as it was still thought that the weight of a horizontal piston would wear the cylinder bore oval. To overcome the problems associated with vertical cylinders and trying to spring both axles, Bowman & Galloway apparently adopted a dummy crankshaft arrangement which was held rigid in the frame but drove the sprung driving wheels by external connecting rods. They would use a similar arrangement with a dummy crank shaft to overcome the same problem with their later locomotive, *Caledonian*. The boiler and firebox were conventional but the chimney was located toward the rear of the boiler barrel. There were two safety valves and a steam dome on the front ring of the boiler from which steam was taken for the pair of cylinders. Hot gases from the boiler were fed through ducts toward the chimney. Exhaust steam from the cylinders' was also discharged into the chimney; the blast must have been quite fierce to help draw the fire.

Manchester underwent trials during the last week of August 1831. But there was great difficulty in getting *Manchester* to Ordsall Lane sheds; she had to be physically "barred" along the unpaved street with crowbars, taking from 6pm to 9am![3] The *Manchester Times* reported:

> 'On Monday last, a trial was made on the railway by a new locomotive engine by our townsmen, Galloway, Bowman and Glasgow. The engine had attached to it, besides carriages containing about eighty passengers, a train with goods weighing forty tons. With this heavy load the distance to Newton, fifteen miles, was done easily in fifty-eight minutes. Here some delay took place from the loss [of] a small bolt, and some further delay took place at the inclined plane till it was cleared of the *Goliath* which had been taking up its load twice. It was supposed by persons on the railway that the new engine would have to do the same thing, but it was determined to try it with the full load. The first half of the rise was gone over at the rate of seven or eight miles an hour, which gradually diminished till it fell to four or five. The engine was thus put to the severest trial and stood it creditably.'[4]

On the return-leg to Manchester, 'Mr Glasgow, perhaps grudging to see even an engine with so little to do' ordered that a 'train of carriages… loaded with some thirty tons of oak timber' be coupled to the train, and 'then this engine with this great load, came beautifully into Manchester' the whole trip taking two hours, of which twenty minutes were taken up in coupling on the timber waggons. During another run *Manchester* was damaged running 'against the points. One wheel remained on the line but the other ran off, straining the crank axle.' *Manchester* had to limp back to Parkside. Whilst most of the 200-strong party of day trippers who had taken a ride were able to return to Manchester, John Galloway and others remained overnight with the stricken *Manchester* 'to get the engine back, which we accomplished by taking out the bent axle.'[5]

The L&M did not purchase her, but did consent to Galloways hiring her to the Haydock Colliery to work their coal trains, and it was whilst on hire that *Manchester* was involved in a fatal accident on 2 March 1833 when working down the Sutton Incline. The engine had 'got away' from her driver, Daniel Baxter, and had 'jumped the road'. The brakeman was sadly 'thrown off and killed.' Brought before the Board, Baxter and his fireman Thomas Brady stated that 'the break was insufficient in the moist state of the rails – that the Engine was never safe at a great speed, she had no reverse motion, or he would have used it.'[6] William Allcard was instructed to investigate and report to the Management Committee. Ralph Thomson, engineman of the *Goliath*, was half way down the incline when *Manchester* 'was at the top'. He perceived that:

> 'Manchester was coming down very fast, and was gaining upon him – was very afraid he should have been run down – the Manchester was only 30 or 40 yards from the Goliath when she jumped the rails, and was almost broken to pieces.'[7]

It was obvious that the crew of *Manchester* had lost control: Thomas Ashton, the constable on duty, was also an eye-witness and reported 'Manchester was going too fast – never saw her going so fast before – thinks he never saw a luggage train go so fast before.' Whilst another constable, Cowan, reported 'he heard something break and the engine immediately jumped off the rails.'[8] The Inquest came to a similar conclusion: that it was due to a lack of brake power; that *Manchester* had no reverse gear; and the high centre of gravity. In a report read to the Board on 18 March Stephenson objected to the use of vertical cylinders because they raised the centre of gravity making them less stable than a horizontal cylinders locomotive, thus the L&M did not consent to purchase the *Manchester*, and sent a letter to Messrs. Galloway informing them that in future 'the Directors would object to any new Engine with Vertical Cylinders being put to work.'[9] *Manchester* was subsequently loaned to Richard Badnall for his experiments on his theory of an 'undulating railway' where she was found to be something of an encumbrance.[10]

Bowman & Galloway's second attempt, *Caledonian*, was a more conventional machine, but she too had vertical cylinders. Although Dendy Marshall considers *Caledonian* to have been a rebuilt version of *Manchester*, it is clear the two locomotives existed contemporaneously. *Caledonian* was an 0-4-0 with outside sandwich frames, vertical cylinders measuring 12 x 16 inches driving a crankshaft located centrally between both driving wheels, working with outside cranks and coupling rods. She was delivered in autumn 1832 and underwent successful running trials. The *Manchester Courier* reported how with a 'train of loaded waggons':

> 'The engine proceeded at a rapid rate from Manchester to Liverpool, and shortly afterwards returned to Manchester. We understand the experiment was highly satisfactory. Unlike the engines of Mr. Stevenson [sic], the cylinders are perpendicular, and are place on top of the engine.'[11]

John Galloway's notebooks record that on 20 September *Caledonian* took a load of 25 waggons from Manchester to Liverpool. She left Manchester at 5am and reached Parkside where she took on water at 6.30am. She stopped for 8 minutes at the foot of the Sutton incline which she surmounted at 7.02am and arrived in Liverpool at 8.08am having burned 630lbs of coke. A week later (27 September) she made the same run with 30 loaded waggons making a gross trailing load of 150 tons. Despite her vertical cylinders she was obviously a success and the Board agreed to purchase her for £800 on 29 October 1832, including a spare set of wheels.[12] *Caledonian* was involved in a fatal accident on 28 February 1835. 'Owing to the switch leading out of

Galloway, Bowman & Glasgow's second attempt: *Caledonian (No. 28)*. Often thought to have been a rebuilt *Manchester*, the two existed contemporaneously. *Caledonian* had vertical cylinders driving a jackshaft, she was much more successful than *Manchester* and taken in stock. (Anthony Dawson collection)

the St Helens Junction Line being left wrong placed' she collided with the Horsley Iron Company engine, *Star* 'which was proceeding with the train to Manchester':

'was jerked off the rails and ran across to the opposite side of the road when she came into collision with the Caledonian Engine and Tender. Ralph Thompson the Company's Engineman was thrown off and killed on the spot, a working mechanic belonging to the Horsley Company was also thrown off and had his foot badly crushed ... The Company fireman and Barnsley the Horsley Company's Engineer escaped without much injury. The engine having broke loose from the train, the Coaches kept the way, and after about ½ an hour's delay, were forwarded to Manchester by another engine.'

Caledonian was severely damaged, the 'tender was literally broken to pieces' whilst the 'Horsley Engine was a good deal damaged, and one of her cylinders and some of the steam pipes being broken.' *Star* had been designed by Isaac Dodds, who had been an early pupil of George Stephenson. According to his biography, *Star*, built in 1834:

'Had several improvements which were novel at that time, namely, the frame was a solid plate, the horn-plates being welded on; the boiler was made to expand and contract on that frame, in the manner now generally adopted; the cylinders were placed horizontally, outside, and the motion was given to the valve by a return crank, working the eccentric rod to an arc or link moving by a reversing lever, the position of the eccentric-rod in the arc, which gave the forward or backward motion, and also varied the stroke of the valves.'

Although Dodds claimed '[it] was the first engine made with a solid or plate fame' that honour may instead go to *Experiment* (below). He also claimed *Star* possessed the first reversing motion acting directly by a reversing lever, and the first arc or link motion, with fixed centres used; and also the first boiler free to expand on the frame.'[13]

Rather ironically, the Horsley Iron Co. had in fact offered *Star* to the L&M for £950 but in light of the accident, their offer was declined.[14] Henry Lawson, Caledonian's driver, was suspended on 1 June by the Board for 'carelessness ... after the Piston Rings were broken, by which the Cylinder-Cover was damaged.' *Caledonian* worked on the L&M for five years, being sold in 1837 to the London & Birmingham Railway as a ballast engine for as little as £400.[15]

Sharp, Roberts & Co.

Described by Dendy Marshall as a 'freak', *Experiment* was the first locomotive to be built by Sharp, Roberts & Co. of the Atlas Foundry, Manchester. Sharp, Roberts & Co. had been founded by Thomas Sharp in 1806. Welshman Richard Roberts arrived in Manchester penniless, fleeing from the Militia Ballot in 1814. In 1816 he established a firm of tool makers, and supplied parts for textile machinery. In 1826, Roberts entered into partnership with Thomas Sharp and Robert Chapman Sharp to form Sharp, Roberts & Co. with an international reputation for the quality of their cotton mill machinery.

Experiment appears to have been built speculatively by that firm: in mid-August 1831 Henry Booth reported to the Board that 'Mr Sharpe, of the House of Sharpe & Roberts ... intimated that the House would be glad to make one or two Loco-Motive Engines.' The Board agreed to this suggestion and that Sharp, Roberts be issued with the same 'draft agreement prepared for Mr Bury' as well as requesting particulars of the cost, and time required to build two locomotives 'of the same power' as those Bury was building.[16] Booth met with Richard Roberts the following week. Roberts proposed using vertical cylinders which Booth found objectionable and indeed the Board instructed him to write to Sharp, Roberts that they 'had a decided Objection to upright Cylinders as injurious to the Road' as well as causing an 'Objectionable motion to the Engine.'[17] Despite this, however, Sharp, Roberts proceeded with building a vertical cylinder engine 'but with such an arrangements of the Connecting parts as would obviate the objections' – i.e. the placing of the vertical cylinders mid-way between the driving and carrying wheels, mounted low down on the frame and driving upwards via bell cranks, rather as Braithwaite and Ericsson had done with *Novelty*. Having thus been re-assured, and provided that the engine be in all other regards satisfactory, the Board consented to the idea.[18] Construction was underway by autumn 1831, as in late October Sharp, Roberts enquired whether they could dispense with a cranked axle as specified in their agreement, and instead replace it with a 'straight axle to the large Wheels and outside cranks.' The matter was referred to Stephenson for further discussion.[19]

Experiment (No. 32) was the third 'freak' to be built in Manchester. Like *Manchester* and *Caledonian* she had vertical cylinders, with final drive through a bell crank. Rebuilt on conventional lines, *Experiment* was briefly taken into stock. (After Marshall, 1930)

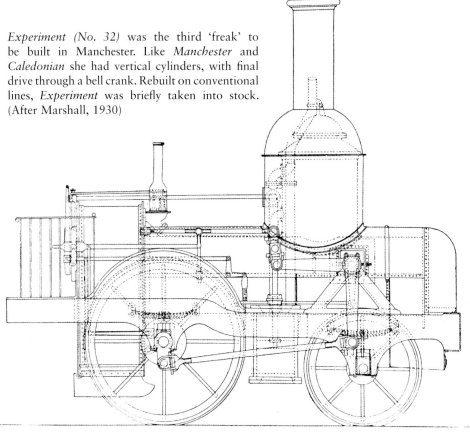

"The Engineer"   Swain Sc.

Delivery of the locomotive was incredibly delayed. Whilst *Experiment* was still under construction, in July 1832 the Management Committee, having seen a model and drawings for a firebox designed by John Melling which had 'hollow fire bars and ash pit constructed so as to form part of the boiler', ordered that such a copper firebox be made and fitted to the *Experiment* by Melling, but under the Committees' superintendence. Amongst other innovatory features were the use of plate frames for the first time; Roberts wrote in April 1861 that 'I applied the plate frame in question in 1833, to the "Experiment" (the first engine I ever made) for the Liverpool and Manchester line' which he used ever since. Experiment was also fitted with Roberts' patent type of piston valve. These were made from wrought iron and consisted of two concentric iron cylinders, one inside the other, and closed at each end. The outer was perforated to allow admission of steam to the cylinder and escape via the exhaust ports. No eccentrics were used, instead motion for the valves was derived from a pin near the fulcrum of each bell crank and 'transmitted thence, through suitable gearing, to the valve attached to the opposite side of the engine.' Problems were encountered with 'stick slip' due to lack of sufficient lubrication; and unequal expansion of the wrought and cast iron used in the valve and cylinder casting. In November 1832 Sharp, Roberts sent a drawing of the engine showing an overall width of eight feet. The design was rejected by Robert Stephenson who thought it 'very objectionable.' It was not until May 1833 that it appears to have been ready for delivery and running trials when Roberts wrote to the Board 'soliciting the attention of the Directors to their new Loco-Motive Engine.' *Experiment* had been 'working to their entire satisfaction for upwards of a week' and they 'considered it to be of a very improved construction'. The price was £1,000. Henry Booth baulked at the cost, and because the L&M was not in need of a new locomotive, but as 'the Engine was stated to possess a decided superiority in several respects' he did consent to *Experiment* undergoing running trials on the L&M. John Dixon reported the result of the trials on 7 October; he noted that the locomotive used 40% more coke than other locomotives on the line and that there were 'other objections.' The Board resolved 'it would not be expedient to purchase the Experiment' but the Board did agree to pay a 'fair price' for 'the work the Engine had at different times done for the Company.'[20]

In February 1834 it was agreed to purchase the engine for £700, and *Experiment* was eventually taken into stock in October 1834 but on the proviso that it be rebuilt with outside horizontal cylinders, and new valve gear 'to convert her into an Engine similar to those made by Forrester & Co. for the Dublin Company.' The conversion work was to be carried out by Sharp, Roberts but they were unwilling to comply and so the rebuild to horizontal cylinders with 'spring pistons' was carried out by the L&M. *Experiment* performed well under trial, but had a high fuel consumption. It was also found that the safety valves had been set dangerously high at 70psi. It's not clear whether *Experiment* ever entered revenue-earning service, and she was sold to the Grand Junction Railway in 1836, who held on to her for two years before she was sold again to the Birmingham Engine Co. in February 1838.[21]

CHAPTER 12

Outside Cylinders

Swiftsure by George Forrester & Co. of Liverpool was the final non-standard locomotive to be offered to the Company. She was ordered in November 1834 for £860, with a copper inner firebox and 11 x 18 inches cylinders, to replace *Milo* which was beyond repair. *Swiftsure* was delivered in spring the following year. She was essentially an outside cylinder Planet, which overcame many of the problems associated with the forging by hand of early crank axles (Part 1). Marc Séguin in June 1834 shows the unusual use of parallel-motion to guide the piston rod, rather than the more traditional cross head and slide bars. The valves were worked using two fixed eccentrics.[1] *Swiftsure* was rebuilt with Melling's patent valve gear in March 1838 and again by Woods and Dewrance in the 1840s.[2] She wasn't the first Forrester locomotive to have run on the L&M, as one of their engines intended for the Dublin & Kingstown Railway underwent running trials in July 1834, running light-engine between Liverpool and Manchester in 67 minutes and returning with a first-class train in 77 minutes.[3] *Swiftsure* was involved in a fatal accident at Parkside on 19 November 1835 when

Swiftsure (No. 36) by George Forrester & Co. of Liverpool was an early outside-cylinder Planet type. Three similar locomotives were built for the Dublin & Kingstown Railway and two for the London & Greenwich. They apparently rode badly due to their width, being nicknamed 'Boxers' from their pronounced lateral oscillation.(Anthony Dawson collection)

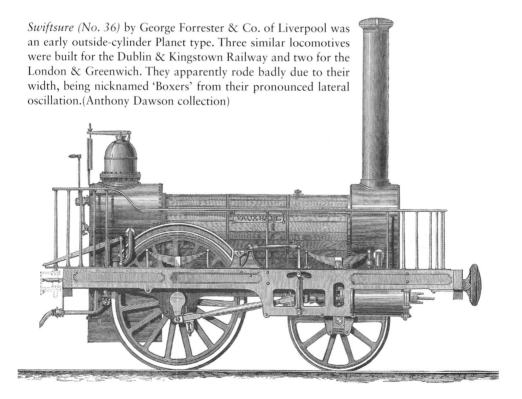

her driver, Abel Jones, a senior fireman and 'occasional engineman', collided with a stationary luggage train at Parkside. A labourer was crushed between two waggons and subsequently died. Jones was demoted from fireman to cleaner and lost his place in the 'link' for promotion to engineman.[4]

Another outside cylinder locomotive which ran over L&M metals was the *Star* built by the Horsley Iron Company, who via their agent Mr Pollock had approached the Board in November 1833 to build a locomotive, which was agreed so long as the locomotive had a maximum axle load of 5 tons. She was undergoing running trials in March 1835 when she was involved in the fatal accident with *Caledonian*. The Board declined to purchase her but did agree to pay for the cost of repairs which totalled £492 2s 8d; this work was completed by July and the Horsley Co. attempted to sell *Star* to the L&M for a second time, which was again declined. She was eventually purchased by the Dublin & Kingstown Railway.[5] *Utilitis*, designed and built by Thomas Dobson, engineer to John Hargreaves, the lessee of the Bolton & Leigh Railway, also had outside cylinders. They were 'fixed on the outside of the smokebox, and the power is directly applied to two cranks, attached to two of the large wheels, to which the other large wheels are coupled by a connecting rod.' The boiler tubes were iron rather than brass (thought to be lighter, cheaper and more durable than brass or copper), and there was a damper fixed in the chimney to regulate the flow of gases through the boiler and also act as a back-pressure regulator. *Utilitis* weighed over fifteen tons and was therefore banned from working over the L&M. By the time of Wishaw's visit in 1839 *Utilitis* had been rebuilt as an eight-wheeler to reduce the axle load.[6]

The L&M Board allowed other engineers and companies to try their engines on their line, so long as they did so 'at the entire risk of the Owners' but one such proving run ended in tragedy in January 1837 when a six wheeled engine from Charles Tayleur & Co. collided with a stationary L&M passenger train at Newton. Other non-company locomotives to have worked on the L&M included *Prince George* which was an experimental locomotive fitted with Chanter & Gray's patent firebox 'for the prevention of smoke'. Edward Woods reported on the performance of the locomotive in July 1838 and concluded that the patent firebox 'was very imperfect' in preventing smoke and that the locomotive had a high fuel consumption. Another locomotive taken on trial was the *St George* by Bourne, Bartley & Co. of Manchester upon which Woods reported favourably in April 1839.[7] Bourne, Bartley & Co. was dissolved in March 1840 and their entire stock in trade was sold at auction, including rights to their patent wrought-iron wheels, and the passenger locomotive *St David*.[8] *St George* was purchased by the North Union Railway, and *St David* by the Bolton & Leigh Railway, both of which were leased by John Hargreaves. During June 1839, there was a request from Edmund Butler Rowley 'for the loan of a 'Locomotive Boiler and Wheels' for a trial of his experimental rotary steam engine, which he would fit up at his own expense. Instead, the Board agreed to sell him 'one of the smaller old Loco motives, at a reasonable price.' Rowley's request had come with a testimonial from David Dockray of Manchester and it was also noted one of Rowley's rotary engines, made by Glasgow & Mayburn of Manchester, was already in use in a mill in Manchester driving power looms. Rowley, a half-pay Royal Navy Surgeon who had taken up practice in Chorlton-on-Medlock, Manchester, had patented his engine twelve months earlier;

he had previously patented a pneumatic telegraph. Rowley's steam engine consisted of a vertical cylinder containing a central spindle on which two, or more, impellers were mounted, and rotary motion was imparted through a steam jet. The motion thus produced was transferred to the wheels via gearing. Rowley's patent specification shows a Planet type locomotive with the rotary engine mounted in the smokebox geared to large diameter driving wheels, creating an 0-2-2. Although the press noted that construction of the locomotive was underway during June 1839, there is no evidence this unusual locomotive ever worked.[9]

In October 1839 *Soho*, the first locomotive by Peel, Williams & Peel of the Soho Ironworks in Manchester, underwent running trials on the L&M Main line. The *Manchester Courier* thought that she 'greatly excels any we have previously seen.' *Soho* was a 2-2-2 and contrary to L&M bye-laws, her driving wheels were 5ft 6in diameter and her cylinders measured 11 x 18 inches. The boiler had 85 brass tubes. The valve gear was unusual:

> 'There are no eccentrics, but in place of them two spur wheels staked onto the crank axle, driving to two other wheels of equal diameter placed immediately over them, and to preserve the distance between the centres constantly the same and unaffected by the motion of the springs. The wheels last mentioned are attached to a short axle or shaft, carrying at each end a small crank arm, which drives attached to the valve spindle.'[10]

The running trials were supervised by Edward Woods, and under trial she ran between Manchester and Liverpool in one hour nine minutes, ten minutes being taken up in 'delays'. *Soho* burned 1,064lbs of coke or 1.03lb per ton per mile. On the return trip she pulled 25 loaded waggons making 133 tons 18 cwt 2 qr gross. Woods also used the opportunity to carry out experiments on the blast pipe orifice, carrying out trials with different sized openings. An experiment carried out on 9 October with the 4.45pm first-class train from Liverpool to Manchester, which consisted of eight carriages, weighing 5 tons each (40 tons gross), taking only 52 minutes. She burned 672lbs of coke (or 0.56lbs per ton per mile) and evaporated 504 gallons of water. The result of this trial suggested to Woods that an enlarged blast pipe orifice was preferable to a more constricted one. *Soho* was 'highly creditable' to her builders but was not purchased by the L&M.[11]

The delivery of *Swiftsure* marks the end of an initial experimental phase in motive power carried out by the L&M; despite the end of this experimental phase the Board did not deter others from using their main line as a railway laboratory. It certainly lived up to the ideal of 'The Grand Experimental Railway.'[12]*Experiment*, *Caledonian* and *Swiftsure* broke the Stephenson mould largely due to the position of their cylinders, but the former was only taken into stock after it was brought more closely into line with the Stephenson ideal.

PART 3

ENGINEMEN AND FIREMEN

CHAPTER 13

Locomotive Foremen

In order to effectively operate a timetabled passenger and merchandise service, the Liverpool & Manchester Railway required an efficient, well-managed and reliable locomotive fleet. The effective and efficient management of the locomotives and the running sheds at first was down to John Dixon, the Locomotive Superintendent, who 'immediately on the opening of the railway was entrusted with the care and management of the locomotive engines', a position he filled for six years, being later appointed as 'General Superintendent of Traffic' on 4 January 1836.[1] James Forsyth was appointed as his assistant in 1833, but he was killed on the foggy afternoon of 30 December 1844 whilst walking home for dinner along the 'extension line' between 'the Mechanic's shop to his residence at Ordsall-lane, Salford.' He had been warned beforehand by his son not to walk home 'as was his custom' along the line but had not heeded his advice. A verdict of accidental death was recorded.[2]

The responsibility of the day to day management of the locomotives, the enginemen and firemen fell to the 'Locomotive Foreman' of which the Liverpool & Manchester had three between 1830 and 1845:

Anthony Harding (1830–1833)
John Melling (1833–1840)
John Dewrance (1840–1845 but with the title and status of 'Locomotive Superintendent').

Each of the running sheds – at Brickfield (Liverpool) and Ordsall Lane (Manchester) – had their own foreman – John Melling (1781–1856), and Alexander Fyfe (c.1790–1848) respectively. Melling was a local man, being born at Haigh near Wigan, and is described as 'an engineer, of Woodhouses, Wigan.' Alexander Fyfe was from Aberdeen. He was a qualified civil engineer, and had first been involved on the Caledonian Canal before coming to the attention of George Stephenson and being employed on the Stockton & Darlington Railway. Fyfe has been described as Stephenson's 'chief designer and draughtsman' and 'made all the improvements in Stephenson's time in the locomotive', including designing *Planet*. Fyfe was also involved in the construction of the Liverpool & Manchester, and had built the bridge over the River Irwell in Manchester. Fyfe was paid 'three & a half guineas per week' (somewhat more than Melling), but does not seem to have been a well man; he was absent from work for most of March 1832, and in April his wages were suspended 'until he resumes his duty.'[3] Thomas Forsyth (the son of John Forsyth) was taken on as 'foreman' of the engine shops at Ordsall Lane in December 1833 on a salary of £60 per year. Sadly, he lost a leg in a railway accident ('by having been run over by an engine') and thereafter wore a cork replacement. He was later employed as a draughtsman in the repair shops at Edgehill. In 1845 he took out a patent on a form of railway signal and was subsequently Manager of Sharp, Roberts & Co. of Manchester in whose employ he was killed in a boiler explosion in 1858.[4]

Anthony Harding was one of three brothers, and all three were personally known to George Stephenson, Anthony and Thomas having worked at the Bobby Colliery, West Moor, on Tyneside. Anthony was a qualified civil engineer. He had first worked on the Caledonian Canal and he had assisted Joseph Locke (1805–1860) during the excavation of the Wapping Tunnel, where his brother Thomas Harding was one of the contractors, whilst the third brother John Harding 'found his way' to the L&M locomotive department as assistant to Anthony, after having previously worked with Stephenson senior on the Stockton & Darlington. Anthony Harding drove *Meteor* on the opening day.[5] Anthony was paid 50s per week and John 30s, and from November 1831 both were allowed free passes on any second-class train on the line in order to visit the 'repairing sheds'.[6] Although Harding was responsible for the management and pay of the enginemen, he was not for their appointment as they had to be recommended to the Board by Allcard and Dixon, and that decision then ratified by the Directors. Surprisingly, it wasn't until April 1831 that the Management Sub-Committee ordered Harding to ascertain the exact number of men employed by him:

> 'Make a return … of the names of all the Engine-men & Fire-men, all the Engines belonging to the Company, and that no change be made in the present appointments without first being approved by the Directors.'[7]

Harding and John Melling seem to have had a fractious relationship especially as neither of their positions - Locomotive Foreman and Workshop/Shed Foreman - had been clearly defined; in March 1831 Hardman Earle reported to the Board:

> 'He had been witness to some rude & improper behaviour on the part of Melling junr to Anthy Harding on account of what Melling conceived to be an interference with his province. The Treasurer was instructed to reprimand Melling Junr. in the name of the Directors, and in order to prevent similar ground of Complaint in future, to give to the parties written statements of their respective duties.'[8]

Harding and Melling were brought before the Board only a few weeks later with regards to an accident where the *Goliath* (driven by Simon Fenwick) had collided with a Bolton engine; Harding was admonished by the Chairman for not having reported the accident or made a full and complete written report to the Board.[9]

John Harding's assistant at Edge Hill was called Walsh, who had initially been employed 'in Keeping account of the Coke, measuring out the Oil, marshalling the Carriages, and making necessary entries in the Engine and Ticket books.' There had, however, been 'scope creep' with regard to his actual duties, Walsh eventually working in the ticket office and 'in the general business' of the station. Harding was admonished by the Management Committee for making 'a change in the occupation of Company Servants' without authority from the Directors.[10] Harding was reprimanded again in January 1832 because his son – another Anthony – had let a friend travel by one of the trains 'free of charge' and without authority to do so.[11]

The management of the motive power department and workshops during the early 1830s appears to have been poor. Anthony Harding had been brought before the Board several times, and had been admonished by the Chairman for misconduct. For example, he had been reprimanded for having re-employed a workman called Hatton (without the Board's permission) who had been previously sacked for drunkenness. He also received a dressing-down from the Chairman for having ordered the enginemen during the trial between Bury's *Liver* and Stephenson's *Planet*, to screen the coke of the latter 'with a view of bettering the performance of the Newcastle engine; a proceeding exceedingly reprehensible.' Finally, he was sacked by the Board in April 1833. At a special Board Meeting of 30 April he was found guilty of gross misconduct, including fraudulently drawing more wages than he had enginemen or firemen and pocketing the difference; making fraudulent entries into the expenses account and receipt books; and in showing favouritism toward his brother regarding contracts.[12] John resigned a week later. Anthony and Thomas later appeared on the Manchester & Leeds Railway, with 'Anthony Harding of Todmorden' being resident engineer on the Summit Tunnel (1837–1839) whilst Thomas entered into business with James Copeland as civil engineers and contractors on another Stephenson line, the Leicester & Swannington in 1833. Harding and Copeland having previously worked on the L&M. The partnership was dissolved in 1837, and in 1839 Thomas is described as being a resident engineer on the Clay Cross Tunnel in Derbyshire another Stephenson project. A month later George Stephenson, together with Allcard and Dixon (altho he rescinded his) resigned largely as a result of complaints of favouritism levelled at George by Dr Dionysus Lardner in the pages of the *Edinburgh Review*. The Board denied this but the on-going relationship between Stephenson and the disgraced Hardings certainly hints at favouritism.[13]

Waggon building and repairs as well as heavy repair work and forging was undertaken at 'Millfield Station and Workshops' by the father and son team of William and John Gray – the forgetful William having previously been a foreman at Robert Stephenson & Co. until the middle of 1826. William had given three months' notice to quit the L&M in July 1832, but doesn't appear to have actually left.[14] A few months after the Hardings had departed, William and John Gray were brought before the Board on grounds of gross misconduct. It had been alleged that John Gray had misappropriated Company timber (and man-power) to make furniture for his Company-owned house. There were also discrepancies in the quantity of iron bought, and actually used. Both men appeared before the Board on 17 June 1833, and a special meeting was called the following day, which lasted four hours and involved some fourteen witnesses. The matter was finally resolved on 29 June; the case of misappropriation of Company materials was not proven but it was found that record keeping was not as accurate as it might have been. The Grays' contract was renewed in July 1836 with a joint salary of £550.[15] In the light of these two scandals, and the resignation of Stephenson, it is little wonder that in July 1833 Henry Booth was appointed as 'General Superintendent' with close supervision of the 'various Departments of the Concern.' Similarly, the suggestion from Charles Tayleur & Co of October 1833 to take over the maintenance and operation of the locomotives has to be viewed in light of these various scandals.'[16]

In place of the disgraced Hardings, John Melling was appointed to the dual role of Locomotive Foreman and 'Superintendent of the Engine Shops' on a wage of three guineas (£3 3s) per week. His younger son, Thomas (1817–1896), was employed as his assistant on £2 2s per week. In August 1832, on the recommendation of Stephenson, the Board ordered that heavy repair be focussed at the Liverpool end of the line, rather than the haphazard system previously in use where engines were repaired indiscriminately at either end of the line. The fitters in the Manchester repair shop were urged to look for alternative employment.[17]

Melling was under the direct authority of the two Resident Engineers, John Dixon (who was also Locomotive Superintendent) and William Allcard, but he always seems to have chafed under the orders of others. Melling was disciplined in December 1832 for having put unnecessary ornamental brass work on Rocket. What was required was 'good & substantial workmanship ... with as little unnecessary expence as possible.' He had obviously tried to appoint his own enginemen and firemen without consulting his superiors, as in June 1833 the Directors ordered that 'no change be made in the hiring of the Enginemen' other than with the permission of Dixon or Allcard.[18] He was censured by the Board in September 1834 for having over-stepped the mark by making comments in his 'Engine Book' regarding the management of the motive power department. Brought before the Board, Melling was cautioned by the Directors for his behaviour, where they ruled:

> 'He should confine himself in his Book, to a statement of the repairs of the Engines going on in his own shed, without commenting on the transactions or management of other departments.'[19]

Melling thought that 'improper persons' were being employed as enginemen at the Manchester end and said as much to the Board; in reply the Board warned him to only make statements 'concerning the conduct of the Enginemen (or otherwise)' directly to John Dixon. In addition, the Board ruled that 'in future no Engineman or Fire-Man be appointed without being first approved by the Sub-Committee.' An irate John Dixon wrote to the Board, complaining that their decision 'was tantamount to a vote of censure upon himself' as hitherto he had been responsible for the hiring of engine crews.[20]

Melling was in trouble again a year later for further comments made in his engine book; he claimed Peter Callan and Thomas Green were both 'incompetent', a charge which they both denied. The Management Committee decided that Melling had entirely failed to prove his case, and as such he received due caution to temper his remarks. Melling was also questioned about a report he had made to the Directors that Francis Smith, the Superintendent at Edge Hill Station, had been found in a 'state of intoxication'. Smith denied this but Melling replied that he had been informed by 'Murphy the Watchman, who had it from others' that Smith had been seen drunk on duty. An investigation into the situation took place during which it was found that Smith had a prior record of drunkenness, having been taken into custody on several occasions for intoxication. Melling was vindicated and Smith was dismissed.[21]

In 1837 Melling became Locomotive Superintendent, whilst also maintaining responsibility for the workshops and sheds. He was employed by the L&M until November 1839 when, following a major reorganisation of the Locomotive Department, he was given three months' notice, and was replaced in the New Year of 1840 by John Dewrance, from Messrs. Peel, Williams & Peel of Soho Foundry, Manchester, a long-established firm of engine builders. Dewrance was paid a salary of £250, plus the house formerly occupied by John Melling. Dewrance had an excellent working relationship with Edward Woods the Principal Engineer, and would serve the L&M until amalgamation with the Grand Junction. Charles Ritchie (an alumnus of Mather, Dixon & Co. of Liverpool) was appointed 'Foreman of Crown Street Yard' under the orders of the 'Superintendent of the Engineering Establishment' on £130 per year, and Edward Woods recommended that his assistant, William Green, be relocated from Manchester to Liverpool.[22]

John and Thomas Melling subsequently established the Rainhill Iron Works in December 1839, and requested that they be allowed to lay a branch line to the L&M and build a more substantial fence along their property at their own expense, to which the L&M Board agreed. It transpired that Melling had planted a garden orchard with trees and shrubs 'on Company ground, Brickfield Station' and following his dismissal, he sent the Board a bill for their cost (£30 4s 5d). He had also had Messrs. William Mackenzie, the contractor for the Lime Street Tunnel, to build a stout garden wall using stone excavated from the tunnel, for which he also sent a bill of £4. The Directors would not consent to the purchase of Melling's plants, but would allow them to remain until they could be safely removed ('the season for their being safely transplanted being past'). They also declined to pay for Melling's wall as Mackenzie had neither had the authority to sell the excavated stone to Melling, nor to build the wall. Melling was disappointed with this decision, but the Board 'saw no reason to alter their decision.' Henry Booth was invited to act as arbitrator, 'to make an amicable settlement of the matter' by which Melling was offered £5 'for the plants within the walled court … immediately in front of his house.'[23] As a locomotive builder, Melling was not successful, only building three locomotives for the Grand Junction at Rainhill: *Sphinx* delivered in May 1841; and *Saracen* and *Scorpion* delivered in February 1842.

CHAPTER 14

The First Enginemen

It would be highly likely that the first enginemen and firemen of the Liverpool & Manchester would have spoken with a broad Northumbrian accent, leaving their native Tyneside where they would have worked on the Stockton & Darlington Railway or the various colliery railways, at Hetton, Killingworth and Wylam. Thus, most would have been personally known to George Stephenson.[1] This influx of Geordies led to considerable resentment from the local workforce. An anonymous article in the *Edinburgh Review* (but later discovered to have been written by Dr. Dionysius Lardner) criticised the Liverpool & Manchester Directors as being enthralled by George Stephenson. The Directors publicly denied any patronage, stating of their 600 employees only 60 (the majority of the enginemen) were from Tyneside.[2] And whilst this could be interpreted as a favouritism or nepotism, the North East was the only area of the country to have experienced enginemen and firemen in any sort of number, who could be approached to work on the Liverpool & Manchester; so it was natural that George Stephenson appointed those men whom he knew personally, and who could be relied upon, as the first locomotive crews.

The list of locomotive 'directors', 'flagmen' and 'brakesmen' drawn up by Joseph Locke for the opening day in September 1830 gives the following, all of whom were 'Stephenson men' and whom he trusted as men who could be relied upon for the safe working of the railway on such an important occasion:

Northumbrian	George Stephenson
Phoenix	Robert Stephenson Jr (George Stephenson's brother)
North Star	Robert Stephenson Snr (George Stephenson's father)
Rocket	Joseph Locke (former apprentice)
Dart	Thomas Longridge Gooch (former apprentice)
Comet	William Allcard (former pupil)
Arrow	Frederick Swanwick (former apprentice)
Meteor	Anthony Harding

Amongst the 'flagmen' was William Gray (later in charge of the Crown Street Yard), and amongst the 'brakesmen' were James Scott (superintendent at Manchester) and his colleague Thomas Ilbery (superintendent at Liverpool); John Melling (future locomotive foreman) and his son; John Gray; John and James Cummings; and Thomas and John Harding (brothers of Anthony).[3]

The tradition of 'One driver one locomotive' began on the Liverpool & Manchester. During the 1830s enginemen and firemen were appointed to a single locomotive and were not permitted to drive any other; despite this one Ralph Thomson, the driver of *Mars*, was suspended by the Directors for refusing to take out *Arrow* in February 1832, despite this being at the Directors' request, but was reinstated a month later.[4]

Isaac Shaw's beautifully detailed plate of *Northumbrian (No. 7)*. The crew are wearing 'wheel' aka 'mechanics' hats with a broad, exaggerated top (which was then in fashion): short waist-length jackets, and fall-front trousers. A greatcoat is draped over the tender side. (Liverpool & Manchester Railway Trust)

Rocket men

Amongst the first enginemen employed by the Liverpool & Manchester were Robert Hope, John Dunn and Mark Wakefield who 'ballasted with Lancashire Witch' whilst Thomas George and Robert Creed worked the *Twin Sisters*. Mark Wakefield is recorded as being the 'regular driver' of *Rocket*, with Robert Hope as his fireman.[5] Wakefield and Hope, together with Ralph Hutchinson, one of the fitters sent from Newcastle to erect *Rocket*, are recorded as her crew at the Rainhill Trials:

> 'Ralph Hutchinson, of Newcastle-upon-Tyne, assisted to construct The Rocket at that place, and attended it to Liverpool, where he was invested with the management of it by the late Mr Robert Stephenson, with Mark Wakefield as his assistant, and Robert Hope as fireman, Ralph Hutchinson being at all times responsible for the efficient working order of the engine.'[6]

Family tradition suggests three brothers Hutchinson worked at Forth Street: Ralph we've already met; William Hutchinson (1792–1853) was the head foreman, whilst Edward moved from Newcastle to Liverpool to work on other railway projects in the early 1830s. The Quaker Edward Fletcher (1807–1889), a future CME of the North Eastern Railway, had been apprenticed to Robert Stephenson & Co. in 1825; he was apparently sent with *Rocket* during her running-in trials at Killingworth and was a part of 'team *Rocket*' at Rainhill; Fletcher was later the engineman of *Invicta* on the Canterbury & Whitstable line.[7] Other claims to have driven *Rocket* include Joseph Bell (c.1812–1895) who had a railway career spanning fifty years, on the Liverpool & Manchester, South Eastern & Chatham Railway, and finally the District Railway. His obituary claims:

> 'He was, in youth, engineer of the first locomotive ever constructed – George Stephenson's Rocket. He ran the Rocket at fifteen miles an hour on average; reached 29 miles an hour and on one occasion 35 miles an hour.'[8]

Charles Fox, builder of the Crystal Palace, also claimed to have driven *Rocket* at Rainhill. Fox was, however, involved with Braithwaite and Ericsson.[9] Another claimant to have driven *Rocket* is Edward Entwistle (1815–1909), who late in life described how at the age of 11 he was working as a mechanic for the Duke of Bridgewater's trustees, and volunteered to be George Stephenson's assistant (aged 16), and that he was with George Stephenson when he drove *Rocket* on the opening day – when in fact *Rocket* was driven by Joseph Locke and Mark Wakefield. His story first appeared in America in the 1890s and was repeated several times until his death, the story changing with each telling.[10] Entwistle's claim was almost immediately questioned; one correspondent to *The Engineer* describes Entwistle's account as 'ludicrous': 'Is it at all likely that Stephenson would displace the regular driver of "Rocket", and put an inexperienced boy on the footplate? It is reasonable to suppose that Stephenson had at that time a pick of drivers, and that even had the supply fallen short, he would have appointed a fireman, not an absolute novice.' Whilst a letter to *The Morning Herald* suggests the driver of *Rocket* was called White.

Mark Wakefield and his brother John had both been apprentices at Robert Stephenson & Co. Both were drivers on the L&M, with John going on to be 'locomotive superintendent of the Greenwich line.'[11] Mark Wakefield was discharged on 3 November 1831 for disobeying the orders of the Board (19 October 1831), by leaving half his luggage train standing on the main line up the Whiston Incline instead of shunting it into a siding, causing considerable delay.[12] John Wakefield resigned from the L&M on 15 May 1835 to work for the London & Birmingham Railway, and his place was taken by Peter Callan who had been employed by Messrs. Bourne & Robinson driving their coal trains. The Board, however, were unhappy with this turn of events because they had not been informed that Wakefield had been 'poached' by the London & Birmingham, and wrote to the L&B committee informing them 'in future [they] would feel obliged by receiving communication direct from the Committee … previous to the engagement of any enginemen or servants' of the L&M.[13] John Melling was also unhappy with this appointment, noting in his Engine Book that Callan was incompetent in 'the care and working of an engine.' This, however, got back to the Management Committee who admonished Melling for making what, in their opinion, was an unsubstantiated claim.[14] Robert Hope was dismissed in August 1831 for being intoxicated 'and directly disobeying orders.' He later appears as 'Foreman of the Locomotives' on the Leeds & Selby Railway; he was appointed on 9 December 1836 on a salary of £120 per annum. Hope was to remain with the L&S until 1839: his salary was increased to £170 per annum in June 1837 and his contract extended for three years from 1 July 1837. He also received £10 per annum from which to pay rent for a house.[15] Another early engineman was one John Williams who died in 1893 aged 73 and who had been 'an engine driver for 51 years, and was until about twelve months ago … in the employ of the L. & N. W. Company.' He reportedly drove the '"Ace of Trumps"[16], the fellow engine to Mr George Stephenson's "Rocket"'.[17] Another was Ralph Beeston who had migrated from the Stockton & Darlington to work on the L&M, and who died in 1904 aged 87.[18] L&M Enginemen alive in 1880 and present at a dinner held in Crewe to mark the L&M Jubilee were John Murphy (appointed 1828); Thomas Valentine (1833); Thomas Stockton (1838) and William Manners (1842).[19] It has been possible to reconstruct a list of over 60 Liverpool & Manchester Enginemen, but this list is by its nature incomplete, as it largely includes those who had been disciplined by the Board or Management Committee.[20]

Robert Kirkup, the driver of *Majestic*, became the brakesman on the Wapping Tunnel engine, and was frequently admonished for letting the trains down the tunnel at too great a speed.[21] He was subsequently employed by the Leeds & Selby Railway as an engineman.[22] There was quite a clan of Weatherburns employed, including Robert Weatherburn the elder (b.1780) and his sons including Martin (b. 1805), Robert (1811-1880) and Henry (b.1818). The family produced quite a crop of railway employees. Robert, Martin and Henry were drivers on the Liverpool & Manchester; Robert is described as being the regular driver of *Victory* and Martin of the *Mars*. Martin subsequently found work on the Leicester & Swannington Railway. According to Robert Weatherburn the younger, his father had been trained by George Stephenson at Killingworth, but 'was removed by my grandfather to Liverpool in the March of the year 1830, and was then the youngest driver in England.' He was eventually driver of one of the stationary engines at Edge Hill, and later worked for the Leicester & Swannington Railway before moving to Hunslet, Leeds, where his children were born.[23] One Thomas Weatherburn (he was probably related) was taken on as an apprentice fitter in 1835. Other early drivers included Robert Creed who drove *Northumbrian*; Poys Hall driver of *Vulcan*; and John Hall driver of *Comet*. Joseph Greenall was from Leeds and was the first driver of *Lion*; and perhaps had been originally sent as a fitter from Todd, Kitson & Laird. Thomas George – who was known to George Stephenson from his colliery days – has been described as the driver of *North Star* and was first driver of *Planet*. Isaac Watt Boulton (1823-1899) suggests her 'regular driver' was William 'Old Bill' Holmes, and recalled that:

'[In 1841] I made the acquaintance of William Holmes, better known as "Old Bill Holmes", who was engineman of the Planet from the opening, and who was for many years after, in fact to the end of his life, about the Sheffield Railway, and who ended his days with Messrs. Beyer, Peacock & Co., of Gorton. I have spent scores of hours in conversation, forty-four years ago, and up to the end of his life, with him about the Rocket and things that occurred at Edge Hill … I also was in much company with the early engine men. Dick Cunliffe, who lost one leg, and worked as an engine man with one leg for many years, on the Liverpool &

Manchester, and the Dublin and Kingstown. He sat one day doing some repairs to his engine at Ordsall Lane, with one leg across the rail, and another engine man named George Clews ... knocked his engine over his leg. He, Winstanley, Bill Tabern [sic. Taburner], John Holmes – a boilermaker at Edgehill – [and] Bill Greenhough ... I knew intimately.' [24]

I. W. Boulton also records how Holmes had a reputation for fast-running and 'had run a first-class train 31¾ miles in 40 minutes and stopped at three stations.'[25] Bill Holmes was driving the *Sun* with the 7pm train from Manchester to Liverpool when it collided with three of the 'Blue Boxes or break waggons' at Edge Hill Station on the evening of 1 September 1838. Eye-witnesses remarked Holmes had been driving at 'a very rapid and dangerous speed'; the three brake waggons 'were broken to pieces'. In his evidence before the Management Committee, Holmes noted that 'the reversing Gear was out of Order and would not act, and that the Breaks were inefficient owing to the wet which prevented him from stopping.' The Committee, however, were of the opinion Holmes had been guilty of 'gross violation of the Company's Regulations in coming at such a furious speed at Edge Hill Station.' He was dismissed, 'not to be taken again into the Company's employ.'[26] Dick Cunliffe was the Engineman of *Orion* but on the afternoon of Friday 28 April 1837 he had been repairing her at the engine shed at Ordsall Lane.

A detail from one of the Ackermann 'Long Prints'. *Jupiter (No. 14)* was in fact a 2-2-0 rather than an 0-4-0. It is likely this is in fact intended to represent *Samson* or *Goliath*. (Anthony Dawson collection)

He must have been laying or sitting down, as another engine was moved on a parallel line and ran over his leg 'fracturing it a little above the ankle, and lacerating the flesh.' He was taken to Manchester Infirmary where he underwent an amputation, and returned to work with a cork replacement.[27]

Fragments of Edward Woods' pay books show by July and August 1840 that the tradition of 'one driver one engine' was not perhaps as strictly enforced as it once was. He shows that for the week-ending 4 July 1840 he had sixteen enginemen and fourteen firemen on duty. Most of these men were assigned as regular 'mates' and to a regular engine; Driver Hendley's regular fireman was called Clarke and they spent that week working *Comet* on both passenger and goods workings. Dick Cunliffe (above) and fireman Jameson worked *Swiftsure* and *Pluto* on passenger workings. Bill Taburner (above) and fireman Hudson were also regular mates working *Etna* and *Milo*, whilst Death and Merry worked *Rapid* on passenger services and *Panther* on goods workings. Merry also fired *Panther* to Driver Purdy. Wood and Knight were regular mates working *Arrow* and *Cyclops*.[28]

Pay and conditions

Enginemen were at first paid 1s 6d on a trip basis for up to four trips (i.e. two return journeys from either end of the line), earning 6s per day at a time when the average Manchester mill operative earned 8s–11s per week, and a labourer about half that amount. By summer 1831 enginemen were working on average six trips per day, and as a result the Management Committee introduced a bonus for those engine crews making more than four trips:

> 'To pay the Engine-men 2/- per trip for every trip <u>exceeding</u> four in one day –
> Mr Harding stated that the Etna had performed 6 trips the day before – The
> regular pay was for 6 trips.'[29]

Whilst enginemen were well-paid, the firemen only were paid 8d per trip and did not receive a bonus for working more than four trips per day, or a Sunday bonus. This meant that an engineman in making six trips per day was earning as much as 10s, whilst a fireman was only earning 4s.

Whilst the first enginemen and firemen had been appointed from the north east, their successors were home-grown. The Board noted in 1834, that in appointing firemen:

> 'It was desirable to look forward to their becoming enginemen, and with this in
> view it must be an advantage to a man to have been employed in a fitter's shop.
> They wished, therefore, that when vacancies occurred, that the firemen should be
> supplied from the repairing sheds.'[30]

The enginemen and firemen were organised into what are referred to in the minute books as 'links', although whether 1830s usage mirrored later usage of the term is not clear. But certainly, there was a hierarchy amongst the ranks of firemen and enginemen, with senior firemen being promoted to junior engineman. Whilst this system allowed promotion, demotion and losing one's place in the 'link' was also used as a means of punishment too, with one senior fireman being downgraded to cleaner.[31] Good discipline was maintained through a series of fines: if an engineman or fireman was late to work they could be fined 2s 6d 'for each offence.'[32] A footplate career began as an 'Engine Boy' or 'Bar Boy' who was employed by the engineman who at the end of the day would throw out the fire by lifting one or two of the firebars (hence 'bar boy') so the fire could be disposed into a pit beneath the engine. They were responsible for cleaning the engine and lighting the fire; from there they would progress to being fitters at Melling's Shed in Liverpool, and then pass out as a fireman, first on the ballast trains, before graduating to luggage trains and finally second- and then first-class coaching trains. The process would begin again with firemen learning to drive first on the ballast or picking-up trains, then luggage trains and finally coaching trains. In order to ensure promotion was carried out fairly, the Directors ordered a tabulated list of all enginemen and firemen be made, noting their length of service, a tradition which carried on to the end of steam. In his summing up at the first Railway Conference of December 1840, Henry Booth stated:

'Every care should be taken to get steady drivers, and more care than has, perhaps, usually been exercised in the choice of stokers or firemen. This class of servant should ... be somewhat raised in importance in the scale of railway service. No fireman should be employed under 21 years of age, and a strict scrutiny in to respectability of character and steadiness of conduct should be instituted ... A man of this description, after a few years service, would be prepared by ample training in the most effectual school to take the higher place of engineman, and a steady engineman with such a fireman ... is the proper party to have charge of the engine.'[33]

Booth believed that what was required for the safety of any train was 'constant vigilance' and that no man:

'However professionally competent ought to be trusted with the charge of an engine, till he has serve an apprenticeship to the business, and has thus become familiar with the rapidity of the locomotive engine, and its consequent excitement – with its severe exposure to the weather – with the customs and practice of railway operations, and with all the contingencies of locomotive transit regarding police regulations, signals, &c.'[34]

In other words, Booth instigated the system of footplate training which would last until the end of main line steam in Britain in 1968.

Most of the engine crews lived in Liverpool, and because of this there was often a shortage of crews and locomotives at the Manchester end of the line on a Monday morning. Following a minor timetable change, the Management Committee ordered in September 1831 that:

'The Engineers be instructed to make arrangements to have one or two Engines at Manchester every Monday morning over and above the Coach Engines to start the Goods before the coach trains.'[35]

In November 1831 the Management Committee ordered, that in order for crews to change over half way so they could return home, 'on Sundays coach trains may stop to make the necessary exchange wherever they meet' doing away with an often lengthy wait at Newton so that enginemen and guards could change trains.[36] This became such a problem that in February 1832 John Dixon was instructed to ensure there were always sufficient engines and men to work them, even if it meant them moving to live in Manchester.[37] In order to achieve this, Dixon proposed building houses for the enginemen as a private venture but the Board disagreed, and did not approve of its officers being landlord to any of its employees. A row of five cottages, however, were built 'at the Brick Field Station' for 'Melling and some of the men' at the Liverpool end of the line in August 1833 at a cost of £430.[38] A further four were built a year later and John Melling requested he be allowed a larger house in summer 1839, by 'adding to it one of the smaller adjoining houses.' The Management Committee agreed, so long as Melling also paid an additional 3s 6d rent 'which was the rent of the smaller cottages.'[39] Cottages were also built at Kendrick's Cross 'at the watering-station at the top of the Whiston Incline' for locomotive crews.[40] Ultimately changing engines half-way on Sundays became part of *Rules and Regulations*:

> 'Some of the enginemen having doubted whether the practice of changing engines (halfway) on Sundays was by order, or by permission; notice is given that the enginemen are required to change (half way) on Sundays, unless by mutual agreement and consent each enginemen remains with his own engine.'

The enginemen as a whole were admonished in November 1831 for failing to stop at Warrington Junction to pick up or drop off goods waggons belonging to the Warrington & Newton Railway. It was ordered that the 'Warrington Company's People will waive their flags when they wish the Engine to take on goods.' If a waggon needed to be uncoupled at the junction it was duly noted on the waybill handed to the engineman so that 'the Enginemen will know themselves when they have waggons to leave.' In order to encourage the enginemen to stick to this new rule, a bonus of 1d per loaded goods waggon 'conveyed between Liverpool or Manchester & the Warrington Junction' was granted.[41]

In order to increase efficiency, and consequently 'reduce the number of Engines running and … Enginemen and Firemen employed,' the Management Committee ordered in April 1832, that once the 'new Heavy coupled engines' (*Atlas* and *Milo*) had arrived, trials be held with them in comparison with smaller luggage engines, the *Vesta* and *Liver*, in working the incline planes and in taking trains from Liverpool to Manchester and back.[42] The trials with the larger engines must have been a success, as a week later the committee found it 'desirable' to 'make all practicable reductions' in the number of enginemen, reducing their number from seventeen to twelve. The committee noted:

> 'One of these Mr Stephenson proposed to take to his Colliery in Leicestershire, the other four the Committee proposed should have the option of being kept as firemen and should this take place, some firemen might be dismissed.'[43]

In order to accommodate an increased frequency of trains caused by a timetable change, the number of trips per engine was increased from four to five in May 1832.[44]

Much to the displeasure of the locomotive crews, the Management Committee ordered that the bonus for extra trips be discontinued on 14 June 1832 returning wages to their old rates:

> 'The Engineers Wages … their pay by the Trip be 1s 6d without any extra allowance, either for twice going up the Incline (should that occasionally be necessary), or for any extra numbers of Trips which the engine might perform.'[45]

John Harding was ordered to take the engine cleaners on to the pay roll 'and under his management' in July 1832, as previously they had been employed by the enginemen themselves.[46] The Management Committee was still obviously in a penny-pinching mood at the start of 1833. In February, they considered that John Dixon was employing too many men in 'cleaning, coking and watering' the engines at Manchester and that he should make reductions.[47] The number of engine cleaners was probably cut too far, however, as in June of the same year Melling was ordered to 'take measures to keep the engines effectively cleaned' and to take on two or three additional cleaners if needs be.[48] The Directors also felt too much time was being wasted cleaning the engines, and ruled in February 1833 that the hand-gear and other bright work on the engines be painted with 'black varnish instead of the bright polish.'[49]

The pay of the locomotive crews also came in for scrutiny. The pay of enginemen was cut from 1s 6d to 1s 3d per trip whilst firemen were paid 10d in lieu of 1s per trip; payment for working on Sundays was reduced to 4s for enginemen and 3s for firemen. The pay of the crews of the banking engines was 'made equal to the Enginemen with Luggage trains … that is equal to 5 trips.'[50] The disgruntled enginemen wrote a letter

Planet (No. 9) with a short train of enclosed or 'glass' coaches. Train lengths were short: no more than six carriages during the early 1830s. (Anthony Dawson collection)

airing their grievances to the Directors. At a special Board Meeting on 1 March 1833, a deputation of enginemen consisting of Messrs. Scott, Dunn, and Fenwick, attended where they:

> 'Stated that they should be glad to work with the Engines, to find their own Firemen & provide Oil, Tallow, Hemp to pack their own pistons (but not to clean the engines) at 4s per trip.'[51]

The matter of the reduction of wages was then discussed, the Directors trying to settle the matter by telling the enginemen that they would still be paid on average 32s per week: the enginemen admitted 'that in all probability they could not do better anywhere else.' After some consideration, however, the Board agreed that the 5s rate for Sundays be reintroduced; other grievances were raised, including the long hours worked by the crews of the Banking Engines on the inclined planes which were passed on to the Management Committee for further consideration.[52] Having been informed of the letter written by the enginemen, the Chairman informed them: '… that the letter which they had written was an improper one, and cautioned them not to write another such letter in future.'[53]

Cost-cutting continued into April 1833: the Management Committee discussed 'The expediency of substituting Boys, (either apprenticed or not as may be thought desirable) for Men in the capacity of Firemen on the Engines.'[54] The discussion was to be adjourned after the next pay day (1 May), and at a committee meeting held the following day, after reviewing the pay bills, it was resolved:

> 'That in future Stout Boys, at the rate of Fifteen shillings per week, be employed to do the work of the Firemen at the Loco-Motive Engines – but that the present Firemen may retain their present situations at the reduced rate of Wages till they can meet with other situations.'[55]

Given Henry Booth's later (1840) comments deploring the use of boy firemen, it is likely that he was opposed to this cost-cutting measure.[56] The first two boys – William Daniel (recommended by Mr Earle) and Henry Brady (recommended by Mr Allcard) were appointed as firemen on 22 May 1833, and were paid 10s per week. Further boys were to be appointed as vacancies occurred, and the Board further resolved that only applicants who had been proposed by Dixon or Allcard were to be taken on as enginemen or firemen.[57] This penny-pinching was also extended to the fitters at the repair shops in Manchester and Liverpool; the fitters 'and other workmen' were instructed to 'be on the look-out for other situations' In the following spring, the Management Committee ordered that 'not more than <u>Quarter-Days, overtime</u> be allowed the mechanics in the Company's workshops', but an ale allowance was granted.[58] In other words, only a quarter day of overtime was allowed, presumably per week. Allcard was also ordered to reduce the establishment of all hands on the line between the summits of the Whiston and Sutton Inclines by one third and the number of brakesmen were also ordered to be reduced, and even Samuel Moss the time-keeper at the Manchester shed was 'let go'.[59] In order to prevent lateness or absence without leave, fines were introduced, some 2s 6d (or half a day's wages) 'for each offence.'[60]

Perhaps to make good the losses caused by the reduction of their wages, John Cropper Jr proposed in May 1833 the introduction of a bonus of £3 or £5 for those enginemen who 'shall take the most care of their engine for the space of six months.' After much discussion, the Board decided the idea was impractical, however, because of 'the different state of the tubes, fireboxes, &c. of the different Engines.' Instead, they placed £25 'at the disposal' of the Management Committee to reward enginemen and fireman 'at their discretion.'[61] By February 1834 the following men had been rewarded:

Thomas Scott	*Jupiter*	£5
John Wakefield	*Etna*	£5
Simon Fenwick	*Saturn*	£3
William McCrie	'sundry engines'	£3
John Robinson	*Sun*	£2
Barnard Rice	'sundry engines'	£2

A further bonus of £3 was ordered to be presented to 'Richard Callan of the Venus, on the Wigan Line for his satisfactory conduct during the same period.'[62] In October 1834, conscious of the long hours worked by the enginemen of luggage trains, the Directors resolved that enginemen of the luggage trains were to be paid 1s 6d on four trips per day instead of 1s 3d on *five* as heretofore.[63]

Labour relations

The Board originally had a paternal attitude towards its employers, no doubt through the influence of its Unitarian and Quaker members. Indeed, the Quaker James Cropper suggested in June 1831 that an 'Annuity Fund' for all railway staff be established 'to be Supported by a small weekly contribution out of the Wages of the Men.' The fund would pay out in case of injury, death or sickness. The Board agreed to the establishment of the fund, which was to be managed by Cropper.[64]

But after 1833 the Board became, on the one hand, increasingly dictatorial towards its employees, but on the other increasingly laissez-faire in terms of sick pay and caring for injured employees. The pay of the enginemen was a constant point of contention, eventually leading to the first railway strike in history. In order to encourage their locomotive crews to stay with the L&M, the Company's solicitors drew up an agreement in November 1834, to be signed by all newly-appointed enginemen to leave a surety of £10 with the Company and that they would give three months' notice if they intended to quit, and two of the longest-service enginemen resigned over the issue.

Reducing the running costs of the motive power department was a perennial concern; in September 1835 the pay of enginemen and firemen was discussed by the Directors, who authorised the Management Committee to give three weeks' notice to the enginemen that their pay was about to be reduced.[65] It was felt that the enginemen were too highly paid, taking home over 40s per week, whilst the firemen received less than half (15s). The Management Committee felt 'The Enginemen's wages were much too high and they agreed to recommend to the Board to reduce them, & perhaps to raise in some degree the Firemen's wages.'[66] A fortnight later, new rates of pay for the locomotive crews were adopted:[67]

	Enginemen	Fireman
Per trip with coach or picking-up trains	1s	8d
Per trip with luggage trains	1s 3d	10d
Sundays	5s	2s 6d
Waggons picked up (each)	1d	½d

Formally agreed to on 18 September 1835, the new rates would come into effect in three months' time. At the Management Committee meeting of 15 October 1834, the 'committee guarantee[d] of 30s per week for the next three months' so long as the enginemen were 'regularly employed.'[68]

As a result, the enginemen gave the Board three months' notice of their intention to quit 'if the Directors persevered in their resolution to reduce their wages.' The Board referred the matter to the Management Committee.[69] Three enginemen (William Cree, Barnard Rice and Charles Callan) attended the Management Committee on 29 October 1835 to urge them to abandon their planned cuts. They also raised other grievances, not least that they worked very long hours – especially those working the banking engines – and their clothes were destroyed 'by the nature of their work' which had to be replaced from their own pocket. Furthermore, the new rate of pay fell below the guaranteed 30s per week.[70] The first inkling of a strike came in December 1835. William Daniels (engineman) and Thomas Wainwright (fireman and 'occasional engineman') were before the Board on 14 December 1835 for having 'refused to go out with his Engine on Friday 11th inst., because of an alleged error in the settlement of his wages the previous for'night.' Daniels had been paid £4 10s but he claimed he was owed 'several shilling more, on account of the Extra trips up the Inline Planes.' Daniels' and Wainwright's refusal to work had meant that the 2pm coach train was delayed until a crew could be found for the engine; Daniels was immediately dismissed, and furthermore if any references were received from future employers they would be informed of 'the cause of his dismissal.' Wainwright was 'charged with purposefully getting out of the way and hiding himself' to avoid 'going in Daniels' place.' He was 'severely reprimanded, and lost his turn as Engineman;' his future as a fireman was dependent on his continued good character and conduct.[71]

The new rates of pay came into effect on Monday 30 January 1836, and as a result several enginemen gave verbal notice of their resignation. Henry Booth, the general superintendent, wrote to each man whether they 'persisted' in giving their notice, and giving them an opportunity to change their minds. The grievances between the enginemen and the Directors about their pay and conditions had been long-standing. The final straw appears to have been the sacking of one of the eldest of their number, John Hewitt, whereupon the regular enginemen came out on strike. The Management Committee resolved on 4 February that:

'Magistrates Warrants be obtained against such of the Loco-Motive Enginemen as have broken their engagements of service with the Company, and that they be dealt with according to Law.'[72]

The Directors' Minutes report that:

'The Treasurer reported that on Wednesday last there had been a turn out amongst the old Enginemen and firemen – on Monday last several of the enginemen had given verbal notice that unless the firemen's wages were increased they would leave on Friday evening. On Wednesday morning last, the Treasurer asked John Hewitt, one of the oldest enginemen, whether he persisted in that notice, and Hewitt answering that he did, the Treasurer discharged him instantly. – Upon this, the other enginemen refused to go with trains, and some slight delay was experienced …'[73]

Henry Booth acted swiftly to keep the trains moving:

'Other enginemen were however speedily engaged, some from Melling's Shed and some from Gray's Yard, and one or two new men who had been recently engaged. Some difficulty was experienced for the first day or two in despatching the luggage and picking-up trains, but matters were again pretty well arranged were now despatched as usual.'[74]

Booth praised those company employees who had stepped-in to break the strike:

'Several Fitters and Workmen from Melling's Shed and one or two Firemen from the Manchester end … conducted themselves very properly by taking the trains promptly, notwithstanding the persuasions and threats of the men who had struck.'[75]

The liberal *Manchester Guardian* reported that the strike was not only about pay, but also about the status of enginemen and firemen:

'The Directors, being desirous of increasing the number of Engine-men, and of having a few men of greater mechanical skill taught to manage the engines, gave directions that two or three mechanics from their workshops should go with the engines as firemen. The Engine-men, however, apprehending that the new regulation would diminish their importance, made strong objection to it; and on Wednesday two of them positively refused to start from Liverpool with their new assistants. They were therefore discharged on the spot; and the consequence was, that the whole of the engine-men, and a number of fire-men, left their employment as soon as they had implemented their first trips of that day.'[76]

This placed the Directors in a rather difficult situation, lacking [m]any locomotive crews so they:

'Filled up the places from the turn-outs from amongst the mechanics, whose previous knowledge of the construction of the engines very soon enabled them to overcome every difficulty in their new vocation; and we understand … are likely to make better engine-men than they predecessors.'[77]

The *Staffordshire Advertiser* believed that:

> 'The strike took place because the managers wished to have some men of greater mechanical skill to learn the duties of fire-men, which the latter thought would lessen their importance. The directors persevered, discharged the turn-outs, who earned on average 40s a week, – and have replaced them with a better set.'[78]

Sadly, despite the assertions of the press there was a serious accident during the strike on the Sutton Incline, resulting from the inexperience of the driver of the banking engine. Having assisted the coal train up the bank, the driver of the banking engine, contrary to regulations, continued to propel it on the Rainhill level, and as the train gathered speed the axle of a waggon in the middle of the train broke. This caused the coupling chain on that waggon to break, and the train engine was left to proceed with only half the train. The banking engine, which was still pushing from the rear with its regulator open, smashed several of the stranded waggons to pieces.[79]

The *Manchester Courier* of 13 February 1836 called the enginemen 'obstinate turn-outs' and 'in their refusal to work with the new firemen... they in the end will be the only sufferers in their folly.'[80] It further reported that:

> 'Three or four of the engineers employed on the railway have been sent to study practical mechanics on the rotary engine at Kirkdale House of Correction, commonly called the tread-mill, for having left their work, contrary to the terms of their several agreements.'[81]

The *Manchester Guardian* of the same date reported that the strike was still in progress, but that 'their places are now well supplied.'[82] Those men who were taken on to break the strike, in recognition of their service despite the 'persuasions and threats' from their colleagues, were awarded premiums of £5 and £3.[83] The four men sent to Kirkdale Gaol for one month's hard labour were Henry Weatherburn, Charles Callan, Peter Callan and George Massey. They were taken before the Bench, who:

> 'Considered the offence so grave a character, that if these men or any others were brought before them, and convicted of similar misconduct, they should commit them to prison, to hard labour, for not less than three months.'[84]

The four men wrote to the Directors 'expressing sorrow for their offence, and begging to be let out.' Henry Booth wrote in reply 'the Directors had no power to liberate them from confinement.'[85] A second letter from the men, delivered by the chaplain of Kirkdale Gaol, describing the harshness of their punishment – having to keep the treadmill turning for six hours a day – led the Directors to 'mitigate the severity of their labour for the remainder of their term of confinement.' Both Callans were subsequently re-employed and later worked on the London & Birmingham Railway. By their actions, the Directors hoped that:

> 'Their present enginemen should all enter into agreements of service, and they have every reason to believe that the strict measures adopted by this first display

of insubordination will tend powerfully to secure discipline and good conduct hereafter.'[86]

The strike by the enginemen was widely reported, not only across the North West but also as far afield as Newcastle, Sheffield and London.

The Management Committee was still in cost-cutting mode in the following year; in March 1837 they ordered a list of all the enginemen, firemen and fitters in the repairing shops to be made and further ordered that no additional staff be taken on, or bill paid without the express permission of the Directors and the Treasurer.[87] In May 1837 it was reported to the Management Committee that not all the enginemen had signed articles of agreement with the Company. As a result the committee ordered that 'every enginemen in the regular employ of the company' was to sign the 'usual memoranda of agreement.'[88] Cost-cutting measures also extended to medical practitioners and sick-pay: members of staff who were too sick to work or had been injured, had been paid half-rates until they could return to work, but in June 1837 the Management Committee dropped this. Instead they urged all enginemen and other members of staff to join a benefit club, and all new members of staff were to join one as a condition of service.[89] Similarly, the Board had paid the cost of a surgeons' fee for medical attendance on men who had been hurt whilst in the company's employ, but in August 1834 demurred to do so, ruling that they would only pay for a surgeon providing 'continuing medical aid' only if the situation had been reported to them and agreed by them.[90] By June 1841 some 833 men out of 1,180 were members of a benefit club or a sick society:[91]

	Enrolled	Not-enrolled	Total
Engineers' Department	525	59	584
Manchester Depot	149	140	289
Liverpool Depots	105	17	122
Carriage & Waggon	24	18	42
Coaching Department	30	13	43

Joseph Green, the Manchester Agent, was admonished by the Board for having so few of his men enrolled in a benefit club. They ordered him to 'make the proper Representation to the Men on the subject' as the Directors – in true laissez-faire management style – 'consider[ed] themselves absolved from any obligation to assist men under accidents or sickness' who were not members of a benefit club.[92]

Following a successful petition from 'Men in the Company's Employ in the Crown Street Yard' that they be allowed time off to celebrate the Coronation of Queen Victoria on 28 June 1838, the Board ordered that 'All men … not required to work on Thursday the 28th Inst.' were to receive full wages whilst those who were in work on Coronation Day (either full or half day) were to get double wages. Beer was also served out to the men.[93]

With the opening of the Grand Junction, London & Birmingham and the Great Western between 1837 and 1838, the Liverpool & Manchester no longer had the monopoly on enginemen or fireman, and indeed the locomotive crews recognised this, especially as it strengthened their bargaining power for better working conditions. Several enginemen in fact left the L&M to work for the GWR (and higher wages), resulting in the L&M Board writing a letter of complaint to the GWR. John Wakefield resigned to join the L&B, also resulting in a letter of complaint. In order to prevent this from happening again, the Board attempted to get their enginemen to sign articles of agreement binding them to the company, but in this they were ultimately unsuccessful. Recognising their stronger position, the enginemen sent a successful petition to the Management Committee in summer 1838, and again in 1839 'for advance of wages' when working on the bank engines and the 7.30pm coach train. It was ordered that the engineman on banking duty be paid 7s per day during the 14 days they were on banking duty and the fireman 4s 4d. Enginemen in charge of the 7.30pm coach train received an additional 6d and the firemen 4d.[94]

Whereas the Board had maintained discipline through a series of fines and punishments, Edward Woods, perhaps thanks to his Quakerism, whilst maintaining a series of fines for misconduct decided to reward meritorious service as a means of increasing loyalty amongst the enginemen, and as a means of promoting efficiency measures including time-keeping and coke usage. In February 1841 a bonus scheme of £10 per month was instituted, to be distributed amongst those enginemen and firemen who were the best time-keepers, payable at a rate of £2 per engineman and £1 5s per fireman.[95] By the early 1840s, the enginemen and firemen 'together' were taking home a wage of £10 per month (before any bonus), paid 'by the mile run.'[96] Bonus payments were also used to encourage more economical firing and driving, as a means to further reduce operating costs, especially the coke bill, which had markedly increased from 1836 onwards. Edward Woods states that whilst the 'actual work done' by locomotives 'had increased in the proportion of 100 to 112, the consumption of fuel increased in the proportion of 100 to 136' without any 'material difference' in the loads shifted. During summer 1839 Woods started to accurately measure the amount of coke burned, compared to actual work done by the locomotives. This was done during the 'ordinary routine of business' on both passenger and goods working with the L&M locomotives *Planet*, *Sun*, *Lighting*, *Firefly* as well as *Sirius* and *Phalares* of the GJR. With a load of twenty loaded waggons (100 tons gross) the average fuel consumption was 1/3lb of coke per ton per mile. Woods also observed that engines were kept in steam for up to 14 hours per day, but the actual 'useful work' they were doing was often less than half that amount, with as much as 14cwt of coke being burned per engine, per day. The performances of *Lion*, *Leopard*, *Rapid* and *Mammoth* were also examined, with Woods coming to a similar conclusion; there was massive wastage of fuel (and water) through the engines being kept in 'full steam' between trips whilst they were at rest.[97]

Therefore, in order to reduce operating costs, Woods established a Coke Bonus scheme in the autumn of 1839. Weekly returns were made for each locomotive and how much fuel was used per trip, but in Woods' opinion 'this served, to a certain extent' against extravagant usage of fuel, but 'was not so satisfactory as it could have been.' Thus, from 19 October 1839 instead of coke being placed loose in the tender, it was bagged; each bag was weighed and the number of bags loaded was duly recorded, and firemen were prohibited from opening a new sack of coke until the previous one had been emptied. Thus the number of bags, and therefore weight of coke used, could be more accurately measured. Woods notes that the scheme 'immediately roused an honourable and eager spirit of competition amongst the men' and had a marked effect on the weekly coke bill, falling by 100 tons per week. Woods noted that coaching engines were burning an average of 49lbs per mile and luggage engines

54lb per mile, and in the month before the introduction of the Coke Bonus 'the coke deliveries amounted to 826 tons 9 cwt' which fell 'during the four weeks succeeding … to only 717 tons 7 cwt, the work being done being precisely the same.' This success is demonstrated in the Disbursement Accounts: in the six-months ending 30 June 1839 the coke bill stood at 7,831 tons whilst for the corresponding period in 1840 it was 4,155 showing a reduction of 3,676 tons of fuel.[98] Following this unofficial trial, Woods raised 'his plan of Bonus arrangements … to economise the consumption of coke' with the Board in April 1840; the Board 'approved the principle' and instructed him to make an official 'trial of the scheme with such modifications in the detail as might be found expedient.'[99]

In August 1840 a 'coke premium' of 7½d per enginemen and 5d per firemen of luggage trains was instituted (coaching trains always having a lower fuel consumption), and once again, 'the result seems to have been an almost immediate reduction in the consumption of fuel': the amount of coke burned fell from an average of 45.5lb per mile to 33.6lbs per mile. The bonus payments were soon raised to 10d and 7d respectively, but after only one month the scheme was abandoned in September 1840, which then saw an almost immediate rise in fuel consumption. Consequently, bonuses for both coaching and luggage trains were re-adopted in November 1840. The bonus scheme was clearly a success, with 'both classes' of enginemen and fireman being awarded 'from 2d to 12.5d for luggage engines, 10d on coaching engines, 4.5d on bank engines and 1d on "Jobbing" engines.' By March 1841 'all drivers and firemen had premiums [paid to them] varying from 3d to 8½d' with coke consumption per mile standing at 23.3lbs for coaching engines and 32.3lbs for luggage engines.[100] Woods carried out trials with the newly-built *Stork* and the GJR *Hornet* on runs between Liverpool and Birmingham, each engine making one return trip per day, on alternate dates during a fortnight in July 1842. *Stork* was the most fuel efficient, burning 15.20lbs of coke per mile compared to the 15.91 of *Hornet*, hauling comparable loads at similar speeds, showing that through careful firing the coke bill could be reduced even further.[101]

In December 1840 the Board ordered that a list of every engineman and firemen be made 'in tabular form' showing their age, length of service and by whom they had been recommended to the company, to be 'filled up and corrected from time to time as vacancies take place.'[102] With the recession of the early 1840s, reductions were sought in wages of the engineers 'mechanics and other workmen' in the Company's employ. Edward Woods was requested to reduce the outgoings of the Engineers' Department by £76 15s per fortnight (equating to £2,000 per year) and the opinion of Edward Bury in his capacity as Running Superintendent of the London & Birmingham, was sought as to enginemen's wages.[103] Edward Woods presented a summary of the men in his employ:

Locomotive and Stationary Engine Department	271 men
Police and General Labourers	142 men
Maintenance of the Way	132 men
Millfield Yard	101 men
Coach Building Department	32 men

Woods was ordered to make as many 'reductions' amongst his staff as he saw fit to meet the cost-cutting of the Board.[104] In order to improve the lot of the enginemen, and perhaps to draw them away from public houses, a 'reading room for the use of the Enginemen, Mechanics and other Workmen of the Company' was established at Edge Hill in August 1843. The reading room was intended to improve the education of these skilled, technical, members of staff through reading and 'mutual improvement.' The books and periodicals were to be approved by the Directors before circulated 'or adopted by the men' and Henry Booth was instructed to find suitable literature, as well as draw up a list of rules and regulations.[105]

The enginemen and firemen were initially issued with short blue jackets, and blue caps with red embroidery (bearing the name of their locomotive and their duty) for the opening day in September 1830. How long the tradition of issuing uniforms to enginemen lasted is not known; one of the causes of the strike in 1836 was that the locomotive crews had to pay for their own clothing. It does appear, however, they were issued greatcoats for the winter months. In December 1841 it was reported that the enginemen's top coats 'were much worse for wear' and needed 'thorough repair.' The Management Committee granted 50s per engineman and fireman for new winter overcoats; they were of the opinion that each engineman or fireman should have two coats 'in wear' thus making one garment last for at least two years, rather than the year or so at present. The new winter coats cost a total of £102 11s 8d.[106]

Working to rule

The conduct of Enginemen and fireman was regulated through written rules and regulations, which went through various revisions between 1831 and 1841. A copy of the 1839 Rules & Regulations can be found as the appendix of The Liverpool & Manchester Railway: An Operating History by the present author, which also includes a section on signalling and safety. Locomotive crews were expected to be 'upright and sober', and to be on the alert at all times, and to keep a good look-out: sitting down on the job was prohibited! The engineman was responsible for the safe working of his engine whilst the fireman was responsible for the safe management of the boiler. Overall responsibility for the safety of the train was (then as now) vested in the guard. Crews probably had to sign-on at least forty-five minutes before 'train time' to prepare their locomotive;[107] Francis Whishaw describes that at the Ordsall Lane sheds there was:

> 'A black board for each workman, with white figures corresponding with figures on the time-boards. On the black boards are letters corresponding with days of the week; opposite to which, for each day, is set a mark if the man is at work, or if absent ... On the time-boards is noted down on what engine or engines each man has been engaged, and the result of each board is entered into a book daily.'[108]

Footplate rules

Enginemen and firemen were not allowed to carry passengers or 'unauthorised persons' on the footplate, one of the rules borrowed from the S&D. The failure to observe such instructions resulted in two accidents (one fatal) within weeks of the line opening.

The first accident was to a railway employee, John Tarbutt, a joiner who had been in the habit of cadging a lift on the tender of locomotives. On 14 October, he caught a lift on the engine of the 2pm train from Manchester as it passed the Water Street offices, saving him a walk to the engine shed at Ordsall Lane. Unfortunately, as he leapt off he lost his balance and fell, 'his left arm got under the wheel and was dreadfully crushed.' He was carried to the surgery of a Doctor in Oldfield Lane, and thence to the Manchester Royal Infirmary, where his arm was amputated.[109] As a result of this accident the Board ordered on 18 October 1830:

'That no person be allowed to ride on the Engine-tender, except the Engineman and Fireman: Mr Stephenson, Mr Dixon, Mr Allcard, Mr Gooch, Mr Melling, Mr Harding, and the Directors and Treasurer.'[110]

This became embedded in *Rules and Regulations* as part of Rule 1, prohibiting any person other than the crew 'without the special licence of the Directors, or of the Engineer of the Company' from riding on an engine.

The second, and this time fatal, accident happened a fortnight later when a local publican, Henry Hunter, who like Tarbutt was also in the habit of cadging a lift on a passing engine, was crushed to death when *Rocket* derailed whilst propelling a ballast train on Chat Moss. The 300-gallon water barrel on *Rocket*'s tender fell on him and he 'was killed on the spot'; his body 'presented a horrid spectacle.'[111] The Board requested a report from Stephenson as to the relative merits, and safety, 'of propelling as compared with drawing' a load; Stephenson concluded it was safer to draw a train rather than propel.[112] Thus, *Rules and Regulations* stated 'That no engine shall be allowed to propel before it a train of carriages or waggons, but shall in all cases draw the same after it' (Rule 11). Propelling a train also reduced the visibility of the train crew, especially the engineman and fireman who had no clear view of the road and who were thus unable to 'keep a proper look-out' (Rule 1). The prohibition against propelling a load was later enshrined in the 1839 *Rules and Regulations*. Written regulations, however, did not prevent the engineman of the *Samson* being reported to the Management Committee for 'propelling a Coach Train.'[113] The only allowable exception to the rule prohibiting propelling a train was for the banking engines. Furthermore, no engine was to run tender-first with a passenger train but Booth did note that the odd 'coal or ballast engines run occasionally tender foremost'.[114] The regulation against propelling a train was due to poor visibility and lack of sight-lines; practical experience with *Planet* and a restored 1840s first-class coach, and with the replica of *Rocket*, shows that the enclosed 'yellow coaches' in particular reduced visibility backwards to zero, and destroy any line of sight. But the official ban on propelling did not help prevent the death of a 'respectable surgeon' who, together with his horse, was knocked down and killed by a coal train using the Haydock crossing; the engineman of the coal train had not seen the deceased from his position at the back of the train, and furthermore had been moving at an 'improper speed.' Running tender-first resulted in *Victoria* derailing and falling down the embankment near Bag Lane when one of the tender wheels broke. The fireman, John Clowes, was killed on the spot and the engineman scalded. Quick action of the brakesman of the luggage train in putting his brakes on prevented the train of luggage waggons following the engine over the embankment.[115] The Board reiterated the regulation against any passengers or unauthorized persons on the footplate in 1832. Following a request from a Mr Turner that some of his agents or messengers might travel on the footplate or tender of an engine, the Board stated 'that they could not approve of any Passenger riding in the Tender with the Engineman.'[116]

There were no rules against footplate crews, brakesmen, guards or porters attempting to move from vehicle to vehicle whilst the train was in motion, or indeed alight from a train in motion. Following a series of accidents where personnel had been killed (in quick succession) the Board of Trade recommended to the Board 'a regulation to prohibit the irregularity of anyone jumping off or on any Engine, Waggon, or Carriage when in motion, except in cases of emergency.' Sadly, the Board refused to pass such a resolution, which might have prevented serious injury to Platelayer John Lea who fell whilst 'jumping out of a second class carriage' near Ordsall Lane, or the death of James Green a fireman who after coupling on some waggons to a luggage train at Broad Green Cattle Station was walking back to his engine over the top of the waggons, and slipped and fell. Michael Eccles a coach porter had his foot crushed when he fell from his perch on a cask he had placed on the tender of *Arrow*. By summer 1842, however, the Board had reversed this policy and had passed a regulation stating that 'Workmen [are] strictly ordered not to get, or attempt to get, on or off trains when they are in motion.' Despite this, however, Samuel Pownell, a joiner who was 'rather old and infirm', was killed in attempting to alight from a still-moving ballast waggon whilst making his way home from the Sankey Viaduct in August 1842. Charles Smith, Nightwatchman at Broad Green, was killed in September 1844 attempting to alight from a still-moving locomotive.[117]

Enginemen and firemen were expected to be sober; being found drunk at work meant instant dismissal, even in the case of Fireman Thorpe, who had been discharged for being intoxicated, despite the intercession of the Vicar of Huyton, Rev. Ellis Ashton who argued that 'Burton the Engineman was more to blame'. The Directors concluded 'that Intoxication whilst on Duty is an unpardonable offence [sic]' and were unable to reinstate Thorpe. They 'wished to make it known and understood' the penalty for drinking whilst on duty was immediate dismissal.[118] Drunkenness, particularly amongst the crews of luggage trains and on the banking engines, especially the latter from their long working days and amount of time spent idle, was a perennial problem.

Every engineman had to ensure he had the following tools and stores ready on his locomotive, and if any were missing had to pay for them out of his own pocket:

> 'A complete set of screw-keys, one large and one small monkey-wrench, three cold chisels and a hand hammer, one crow-bar, one long chain and two short coupling-chains with hooks, two spare ball-clacks, a quantity of flax, gaskin, and string for packing, &c.: oil-cans, large and small plugs for tubes and forcing mallet.'[119]

Nor were enginemen allowed to tamper with their locomotives; several of their number were reported by Mr Rigg for having 'introduced into the Blast Pipe of one of the Engines with a view to contract the apperture of the blast.' Upon examination William Allcard 'found no such thing', however. The device, known as a 'Jimmy' or 'Jemmy', was a crude attempt to improve the draughting by restricting the blast-pipe orifice.[120]

Before the advent of the steam whistle, it was the responsibility of the fireman to blow a horn when approaching every level crossing or stopping-place as a means of audible warning. The guards were also so equipped, so too the gatemen who were also to ring a warning bell.[121]

Enginemen and firemen were ordered to stand up and keep a good look-out at all times; failure to do this resulted in two collisions on the morning of 17 November 1833. Indeed, the majority of collisions occurred during autumn and winter due to poor visibility when extra vigilance was required. The first was on the Whiston incline, where a first-class train had stopped for an unknown reason and the following train ran into it; the concussion 'severely hurt several of the passengers.' The second was on the Warrington & Newton Railway. A Liverpool & Manchester train from Manchester had stopped at Newton 'owing to the cylinder covers coming loose' and whilst they were being repaired a Warrington & Newton train 'came up' and contrary to regulation was propelling its carriages 'and having no one on the look-out ran violently into the Mail of the Liverpool & Manchester train' causing considerable damage. The Board instructed Henry Booth to investigate the first accident, and was instructed to complain – in the strongest terms possible – to the Warrington & Newton 'of their great neglect of their servants in not keeping a proper look-out.'[122] As a result the Board issued the following regulation:

'Ordered and made known to all the Coach-Guards – That in case a coach train shall stop on any part of the Road, it shall be imperative to the Guards to keep a

A coloured magic lantern slide of Isaac Shaw's print of a Planet type locomotive passing underneath the skew bridge at Rainhill. Note the fireman blowing his horn to warn of the train's approach as ordered by the Board in June 1831. Failure to do so resulted in a fine of 6d. (Anthony Dawson collection)

good look-out behind, and if an Engine is perceived to be advancing on the same Line, the Coach Guards shall not trust to the Engineman of the coming Train keeping a good Look-Out, but shall run immediately <u>to warn him </u>not to advance on the stopped train.'[123]

A collision at Kenyon Junction resulted in the Management Committee suggesting that a Guard sit on the engine tender, whose sole responsibility was to keep a good look-out, acting as a Pilot would on board ship in order to relieve the enginemen from such a responsibility. Henry Booth's negative response to a similar suggestion made in 1840 suggests that the Board may not have acted upon this recommendation.[124] Following a rear-end collision at Broad Green, the Board ordered that if a train had to stop for any reason – such as ballast train discharging its load – the fireman was to go back 400 yards with a red flag and hand lamp as a warning to any on-coming trains running on the same line.[125] How useful this was in practice is not certain, given that the guard would have had to climb down from his perch on the carriage roof and, armed with a red flag and lamp, make his way as best and as fast as he could over the ballast, but it clearly showed the Board were conscious of safety and attempting to constantly improve their safety practices in the light of accidents and incidents. The press became interested in the safety (or lack thereof), in particular of passenger trains; the *Manchester Times* became quite strident following a series of accidents early in 1838, and demanded the presence of a pilot or conductor whose sole responsibility was the safety of the train and keeping a good look-out (an idea raised by the Board of Trade a few years later). The *Times* also urged for the involvement of Parliament to pass laws 'against persons driving locomotives in a rash or careless manner' and a prison sentence for the same.[126]

Incline Planes

The working of the Incline Planes presented an operational challenge during the first full year of working, not only in having sufficient motive power but also in how the inclines should be worked by trains. Hitherto incline planes had been worked by rope haulages, so locomotive working of them was an entirely new operational problem. Despite the purchase of *Samson* and *Goliath* as bank or 'help up' engines, delays to heavy luggage trains resulted in John Cropper Jnr suggesting to the Management Committee in July 1831 that they should invite Stephenson to prepare estimates for fixed engines at the top of the Sutton and Whiston Inclines.[127] The final figure of £9,000 was the equivalent of nine banking engines, and the proposal was dropped.[128] Until an engine shed and water tank had been built at Sutton, it was ordered in New Year 1833 that the 'Assistant Engine ... proceed to <u>Manchester</u> at <u>Night</u> after both of the Carriage and Merchandize trains shall have passed.'[129] The shed on the Sutton Incline was timber, and was blown down in a gale in November 1833, and the Directors ordered it be replaced by a brick structure.[130] Tenders for the replacement 'double Engine House and Smithy' were received in July 1834; the new engine shed was described as 'capacious, with a view to an increase in business, particularly in anticipation of a union with the Grand Junction Railway.' Unfortunately the cost

(£514 17s 10d) was too high, and the matter put on hold.[131] The smithy (and shed?) was under construction by September 1834, and the Management Committee thought it wise to modify the design, to accommodate a water tank 'above' to supply the Sutton Banker, rather than having it run forward to the head of the Whiston Incline to take water. In the same month, a siding and a cross-over were ordered to be installed 'about ½ a mile up the Sutton Inclined Plane, to communicate with the Up line, in which the assistant engine may wait the coming of the coach trains.' This was to prevent the 'necessity of galloping after them for so great a distance before over taking them.'[132] In December 1834, the timber engine shed for the Whiston Banker was reported to be 'too narrow … decayed and insecure' and a replacement was needed. Thus, land was purchased at the bottom of the Whiston Incline from Mr William Lees of Whiston on which to build 'a more commodious Engine House for the Bank Engine.'[133]

Stephenson reported to the Board the maximum loads for different train types: passenger trains were to consist of no more than six carriages, while ten loaded goods waggons was the maximum load for engines of the *Planet* class and eight waggons for those of the *Meteor* class. In September 1831 it was ordered that any coach train longer than eight carriages was to be always assisted up the Incline Planes.[134] Enginemen of luggage trains were ordered to always divide their trains, and never to take up a full load in one trip. But in so doing, the enginemen were in the habit of leaving half their load standing on the main line at the foot of the incline, whilst they took up the first half. Once at the top, they pinned down the brakes of the half load, and returned down the same line to pick up the remainder. This, however, led to complaints about 'coaches … detained … on the Whiston Incline Plane by a number of luggage waggons.' As a result, the Management Committee ordered on 19 October 1831:

> 'That every Engineman put half his Train of Waggons into the siding at the bottom of the Inclined Planes while he takes up the other half. That he place the first half of his load on the siding at the Top of the Plane, & return on the Down Line for the remainder of his load – And that any Engineman transgressing this order by leaving part of his load on the Main Line be discharged from the Company's service.'[135]

In other words, one half of the train was shunted off the main line, whilst the other half was taken up and the engine, in order to prevent running in the wrong direction, returned on the opposite line rather than running back down the same line. Not all enginemen adhered to this new rule, amongst them Mark Wakefield – one of the longest-serving L&M enginemen – and George Rogers of the Bolton & Leigh who were both dismissed on 3 November 1831 for 'direct disobedience of the Order'. William McCrie was discharged a week later for the same offence.[136]

The working of the Incline Planes, especially after dark, however, was still found to be unsatisfactory. A lengthy discussion took place between the Management Committee and William Allcard as 'to the most eligible mode of getting the Merchandize Trains up the Incline Planes.' Many of the enginemen had reported to Allcard that the practice of running back down the incline on the opposite line 'involved greater danger on dark mornings and evenings than leaving the load on the main line at the bottom and coming back down [on the same line].' Allcard agreed with the sentiments of the enginemen because of the danger of:

'While in the act of crossing at the Top an Engine coming in the opposite direction might run foul of her, which was not likely to occur by leaving part of the load at the <u>bottom</u> because the Engines which were <u>following in the same direction</u> knew what Engine were gone before and acted in concert and assisted each other.'[137]

In other words, practical day-to-day operation affected not only the working of the line but also its rule and regulations. As a result, it was ordered that the previous order 'be relaxed':

'To allow the Engines to leave part of their load on the Main Line at the Bottom of the Inclined Plane, and after having taken up the other half, to return on the <u>same line</u> – But on no account to leave part of the load on the Inclined Plane as they were formerly in the habit of doing.'[138]

These new working instructions were to be considered 'as a Trial & Experiment depending on its continuation on the success of its working' by reducing the number of accidents and delays caused to passenger trains working up the inclines. William Allcard was instructed to pass on the new working instructions to the L&M enginemen and policemen, as well those of the Bolton & Leigh and 'all other companies working on the line.' He was also to ensure that every L&M engineman and policeman, and the enginemen of other companies working on the line 'were provided with proper Signal Lamps and they use them as occasion required.' [139]

The working of the Inclines was raised again in September 1832. The 'Help Up Engine' was to keep to the 'proper lines' when working back to the foot of the Incline, in other words cross over at the top of the incline, returning on the opposite line, and never run 'wrong road'; furthermore, no engineman was allowed to leave part of their load on the incline. The Management Committee ordered that where the load had been divided, the train engine was to return back down the Incline 'wrong road' (i.e. going down the same line as they went up) to collect the remainder of their load:

'No Engine shall be allowed to leave any part of her load on the Line at the bottom of the Incline Plane <u>provided</u> the Help-Up Engine be there and ready to assist. But if the Help-Up Engine is not there, or ready, from any cause, the Engineer may leave a part of his load on the Incline and return down the <u>same line</u> unless there is a Coach Train following in which case he must shunt at the bottom in the first instance and come back down the other line.'[140]

In this way it was hoped to avoid collisions as 'an Engine proceeding with her Train cannot in any case <u>meet</u> an engine coming Down the Incline Plane.' Where part of the load had to be left on the main line, a brakesman with a red flag and hand lamp was to be sent back down the line at least 400 yards with a red flag and lamp to protect the train. No engineman was 'at any time or under any circumstances, leave his engine or train, or any part of his train, either on the inclined plane or elsewhere, without placing a man in charge of the same to cause the proper signals to be made to prevent other engines from running against them.' Enginemen working the banking engines were cautioned to buffer-up gently; despite this, complaints reached the Management Committee that two passengers had received 'violent shock' from the banking engine 'running against the coach train' on the Whiston Incline.[141]

Not all the enginemen obeyed the rules, of course. Engineman Simon Fenwick was brought before the Directors in February 1833 for having disobeyed these orders. He had 'left part of a train of waggons on the Sutton Inclined Plane ... without directing someone specially to warn any Train that might approach on the same line.' As a result the 7am coach train from Manchester had run into the waggons left on the main line, and several passengers were 'shaken and bruised.' Fenwick was thought to be culpably negligent in his duty especially as visibility was poor 'with a fog coming on.' He was severely reprimanded by the Board and fined £5. Later in the same year engineman Scott was reprimanded and fined 10s for having 'run the Pluto against the Venus train of Waggons' at the top of Whiston Incline.[142] *York* 'with a train of goods' ran into the rear of a slower-moving train headed by *Vesta* whilst working down the Whiston Incline in summer 1836. Both enginemen were thought 'much to blame.'[143]

Even returning 'right road' was fraught with danger, especially on dark mornings. Early on the morning of 6 March 1837, the duty Bank engine, *Lightning*, was involved in an accident with *Milo* and *Orion*. Engineman Murphy had assisted the early morning luggage train up the Whiston incline, and had then 'gone on to the top of the Sutton Incline'. As he was crossing over to the Down line to run back 'right road' toward Whiston, he heard the *Milo* and *Orion* 'close at hand coming up with the train' so 'started the engine forward again & had hardly got onto the main line' when *Milo* collided with *Lightning's* tender and was 'completely thrown off the road'. Murphy jumped off his engine but 'without shutting off the steam', and *Lighting* continued driver-less down the Sutton Incline, and on towards Eccles where the policeman on duty jumped on her footplate 'and brought her safely into Manchester.' Dick Cunliffe, engineman of the *Milo*; Markland (*Orion*) and Murphy (*Lightning*) were hauled before the Board later the same day and were severely reprimanded. The Board concluded that trains were 'too closely following one another from Rainhill to the Top of Sutton Incline' and Henry Booth was to instruct Melling to devise some system or signal 'for some plan of operation for the Luggage Engines at the Inclines Planes' in order to prevent a similar accident happening in the future.[144] Following yet another accident on the Whiston Incline in September 1837 – as a result of confusion as to priority – the Management Committee ruled that 'The Bank Engine should never go up the Incline in front of a train' which was to be embedded in *Rules and Regulations*.[145]

The March 1839 *Rules and Regulations* confirmed the practice of dividing the load, and specified the situation when an engine could return 'wrong road.' A brakesman was to be left in charge of the waggons, and in order to warn any on-coming trains, another was sent back at least 400 yards with a red flag and hand lamp. Furthermore:

> 'No luggage-engine shall leave any part of her load on the main line at the bottom of the Incline, provided the assistant engine be there; but if the assistant-engine be not there, or not ready, the luggage-engineman may leave part of his load at the bottom of the Incline, and return down the same line, provided that by so doing

he will not impede any coach-train that may be following ... If there be reason to expect a coach-train, the engineman must shunt at the bottom so many of his waggons as he cannot take up; and having shunted the remainder at the top, must return on the proper down line.'

Engines had to return 'wrong road' whilst working the Incline Planes, i.e. reversing back down the same line, rather than crossing over to run back on the opposite line. Engineman David Fletcher was suspended by the Board in November 1840 for:

'Gross Disobedience ... in bringing his engine the Buffalo down the wrong line of the Whiston Incline Plane ... on the evening of Tuesday last, in consequence of which, there had nearly been a violent collision between the Buffalo and a Grand Junction Engine that was ascending the Inclined Plane with a Luggage Train.'[146]

The Board thought his actions 'inexcusable' as he knew the GJR train 'was due' and they ordered a warrant be taken out against Fletcher and he be handed over to the County Magistrates under the provision of the 1840 Regulation of Railways Act. He was fined £5 and dismissed from the Company.[147] By 1845 whenever an engine had to run 'wrong road' the fireman was to be sent on ahead with a red flag and hand-lamp; failure to stick to these rules resulted in a collision in March of that year on the line between Ordsall Lane Junction and Hunt's Bank Station. Where a banking-engine was needed, 'the enginemen are ordered to be ready, on the signal being given, to follow the trains immediately after they pass, otherwise they will be fined for neglect of duty.' The bank engine was never to pilot a train up the incline, and was only to assist the load up to the top of the incline and no further.

The Directors ordered that all bank engines were to assist from the rear ('always go behind') and were not to continue to propel the train on the level. Failure to adhere to this resulted in two accidents, one in 1837 the second in 1840.

The first occurred near Collins Green around 6am on 16 June 1837; *Cyclops* was the engine on duty and after helping the double-headed early morning luggage train up Sutton Incline, had continued to propel the train 'at a rapid rate' when the leading engine dropped between the rails due to the track being out of gauge, 'the rails ... were new laid, the ballast not having been filled in around the blocks.' Everything came to a crashing stop, but Engineman J. Hurst on the *Cyclops* did not shut off, and ran into the wreckage: 'the waggons of goods were overthrown, one upon the other' five or six 'being totally destroyed', their contents scattered over the Up and Down lines. Hurst was immediately dismissed for 'Gross violation of their [the Directors'] orders': engines were 'not to Propel except up the inclines.'[148]

The second was on the Whiston Incline in June 1840. Instead of assisting from the rear, as per orders, it piloted a heavy train of 32 goods waggons up the incline: 'almost as soon as the engines had reached the summit, the [coupling] chain ... broke' resulting in the waggons careering down the Incline, running back as far as Huyton Lane Gate whereupon:

'They met the Bolton Luggage Train following from Liverpool. The Engineman with the Bolton train, hearing their approach, slackened his speed to 3 or

4 miles per hour, and then jumped off before the collision took place – Three or four waggons of both trains were smashed, and considerable damage done to the Goods, which consisted of sugars, raisins, wine, &c. The amount of damage … would no doubt be near several hundred pounds.'[149]

John Dewrance, 'Superintendent of the Locomotives', attended the Board Meeting and explained how written instructions stated 'that when an assistant Engine was required at the Bank, it must always go <u>Behind</u>', and furthermore he had verbally informed the engineman, John Guest, 'that he was to put <u>one</u> engine <u>before</u> the train and the other <u>behind</u>' working up the Incline Planes. Guest 'admitted the facts' and offered no explanation for such egregious breaking of standing orders; he was immediately discharged. His fireman, Joseph Rigby, was reprimanded by the Board as he was both party and witness 'to a breach of orders' and had neither reported Guest's offence nor done anything to prevent it. The Board ordered:

> 'That the Policemen on the Incline Planes be informed that if they witnesses any Engineman breaking the rule which required that when two Engines were employed in taking a Luggage Train UP the Bank, <u>one</u> shall always go <u>behind</u>.'[150]

As an upshot from this accident, the gateman at Huyton Gate, James Hunter, got uproariously drunk on 'wine from the casks which had been staved in' as a result of the accident and was immediately dismissed. On the same day engineman Thomas Leftwhich was killed by falling from the tender of his engine 'with the early morning train from Manchester, between 3 and 4 o'clock A.M.'[151] Working in the dark or bad weather with only the aid of a hand lamp presented operational dangers: J. Thelwell 'the nightwatchman at the foot of the Sutton Incline' was run over and killed about 7.30pm by the GJR Mail Train in March 1841; the Coroner ruled 'accidental death.'[152]

Failure to adhere to written regulations resulted in a collision on the Sutton Incline on a cold, dark, morning in December 1841 when a London Mail Train ran into the rear of an L&M luggage train. As per regulation, J. Sanderson the L&M engineman had divided his train at the foot of the Sutton Incline, and had placed the red tail-lamp on the waggon of the train at the foot of the incline. This meant, contrary to regulation, there was no red tail-lamp on the last vehicle of the half of the train being worked up the incline. Under examination, Sanderson and the brakesman John Greenwood revealed a complacent attitude toward regulations:

> 'It was the custom with all Luggage Trains, the Grand Junction, & Bolton, as well as the Liverpool & Manchester to leave the Red Light on the Waggon shunted, and for the Luggage Breaksman to ride on the last waggon of the portion going up the Incline with a hand lamp, to waive if any Engine appeared from behind.'[153]

Sanderson also noted that the GJR engineman would have known there was an L&M luggage train going up the incline which should have lessened the likelihood of an accident. Edward Woods was ordered to make sure the printed regulations were strictly adhered to, that there was a red tail lamp on the last vehicle of every train after dark, and that the local practice and custom hitherto in use cease immediately.[154]

Brakesman Richard Radcliffe was run over and fatally injured on the Whiston Incline on 9 October 1844. Edward Death, engineman of the bank-engine *Elephant*, spotted Radcliffe's body on the line. During the investigation, it was found that Radcliffe had been sat on the last waggon of the train being worked up the incline and had slipped and fallen from his perch on the waggon, and had been run over; 'legs and one arm across the rails ... one of his legs was torn asunder at the knee joint, the other was very much shattered; and his arm was smashed all to pieces.' He was 'placed upon the engine' which made all speed for Liverpool and rushed to the Infirmary where he later died. A verdict of accidental death was recorded.[155]

Coming down the inclines presented other problems: that of speed and insufficient braking power. In order to stop the heavy trains when descending the Inclines, the Directors ordered in June 1831:

'That only <u>one</u> Breaksman attend each train of Merchandize by the Planet Class of Engines & two Breaksmen the trains of the Goliath and Samson with instructions to Peg Down the Breaks on descending the Incline Planes.'[156]

Rules and Regulations further stated:

'That no engine, either with or without passengers, coals, goods, or luggage, shall go down any of the inclined planes at a greater speed than from twenty to twenty-five miles per hour; and that no engineman shall attempt to make up lost time in going down any inclined plane; and coming down Whiston Incline, no engineman shall begin to increase his speed till he gets to Huyton Quarry station.

    That, in going down any inclined plane, every engineman, or other person having charge of a luggage-train, shall take care that he has full and complete control over the speed of his train, by pinning down, or causing to be pinned down, his waggon-brakes, fewer or more according to the size or weight of the train, whether there be a luggage-brakesman with the train or not; and that in case of accident for want of this proper control over the speed, the engineman shall be held responsible. And the policemen at the top of the Inclines shall, and are hereby charged to, assist in pinning down the brakes when desired so to do by the engineman of the train.'

Firefly came to grief descending the Sutton Incline in February 1835. She was working the jobbing luggage train from Liverpool to Manchester, but owing to a 'crossing plate being out' was:

'Thrown off the Road and down the slope into the Hedge on the North side of the Road, and at the same time one of the luggage waggons taking the opposite direction, ran against some Waggons of Goods in front of the 8 o'clock Coach Train from Manchester ... at the same moment. Four or five waggons were badly broken, and the Luggage strewed on the ground.'

Both of *Firefly*'s axles were 'slightly bent' but no one was hurt. Charles Callan, the enginemen, was disciplined by the Board for 'not taking due care in descending the Incline Plane' and for doing so at 'an improper speed.' He was fined 20s. The policeman on duty, Murphy, was also fined (2s 6d) for 'not making more efficient signal of the danger.'[157] *Thunderer* broke an axle descending the Sutton Incline in autumn 1836 working a coal train belonging to the Haydock Colliery because the wheels of one of the coal waggons broke.[158] *Goliath* was involved in a collision at the foot of Sutton Incline whilst 'attempting to come out of the siding' at the same time a GJR passenger train was approaching; several of the coaches were damaged 'by rubbing against the Goliath engine'. Engineman John Haughton and Fireman James Blundell were thought to be 'much to blame' and were discharged.[159] Lack of brake power from the hand-brakes on the luggage waggons resulted in *York* being unable to stop running down the Sutton incline, and colliding with the GJR engine *Siroco* which had broken-down. Her Engineman had done everything he could to avoid the collision, but *York* was still moving at about 12mph when she hit *Siroco*. The L&M Board considered the GJR liable for the accident.[160]

Crime and punishment

Failure to adhere to company rules and regulations, which of course included the clause on sobriety, usually led to instant dismissal. The majority of those enginemen who were discharged were because of intoxication whilst on duty and 'negligence of duty' (the latter often a result of the former), invariably resulting in accidents which damaged company property (locomotives and rolling stock). Fatal accidents led to instant dismissal. Many of these enginemen were repeat offenders who had been previously let off with a severe reprimand and a heavy fine. Despite this, drunkenness amongst enginemen appears to have been a perennial problem. John Blackburn 'fireman of the Majestic' was discharged in May 1831 for 'Drinking and Neglecting his duty.' John Harding reported to the Management Committee that he had appointed Edward Wilson as his replacement and that:

> 'Martin Weatherburn had been appointed Engine-man to the Phoenix, and Edward Armstrong Fire-man to same; and that John Wakefield was appointed Engine-man to the Venus and Ralph Scott the Fire-man … confirmed by the Directors.'[161]

William McCrie, the 'engineman of the Majestic', was reported to the Management Committee by John Dixon at the end of August 1831 for 'approaching the Manchester Station at a very rapid and improper speed' resulting in him running 'against a waggon' which 'broke the front frames of his engine.' McCrie was ordered to pay the expenses of the repairs to *Majestic*.[162] He was brought before the Management Committee again in November 1831:

> 'Engine-man McCrie attended … and upon examination admitted that yesterday morning [9 November 1831] at half past 9 he left his load on the main line, and taking the other half up the bank came down again on the wrong line – contrary to the express orders of the Directors.'[163]

He was discharged for 'wilful disobedience of Orders.'[164] McCrie, however, petitioned the Directors for re-instatement. He attended the Management Committee meeting of 23 November 1831, and following an interview with them where he promised 'the most strict obeyance to the Directors' Orders in future.'[165] Simon Fenwick 'engineman of the Goliath' was discharged on 3 August 1831 for drunkenness and assaulting a workman; the Management Committee noted it was 'not the first time he had been drunk.'[166] Fenwick must have been re-appointed as he was brought before the Directors in February 1833 for having, contrary to regulation, left half of the waggons of his luggage train on the Sutton Incline, where they were run into by the 7am passenger train from Manchester. He was severely reprimanded.[167] Fenwick was brought before the Management Committee again on 17 July 1833 for having struck his fireman William Whitaker on the face – 'so that his face had bled considerably' – during a quarrel about 'filling up the firebox.' Henry Booth interviewed Fenwick, and reported 'that Fenwick had that morning allowed the *Liver's* boiler to run dry.' Fenwick was immediately suspended.[168] A week later, Fenwick was brought before the Management Committee and severely reprimanded; he was fined 20s: '10s for letting the Boiler of the *Liver* go dry and 10s for striking his fireman.'[169]

Not all accidents were due to the fault of the enginemen or firemen. The *Chester Chronicle* reported how:

'On Sunday morning last, as the locomotive engine, Jupiter, was proceeding with the second class train of carriages from Liverpool to Manchester, the engine stopped, as is customary, at Parkside, and took in water. After proceeding a short distance, the engineer found that the injection pump, which fills the boiler with water, refused its office, in consequence of which he stopped the engine, and proceeded to examine it. After taking off the union joint below the aperture, where the valve admits water into the boiler, he found, to his astonishment, the head of a live eel, which, on being drawn forth, measured 23 inches long, and 4 inches in circumference. This exhibition afforded considerable gratification to the passengers, who were all anxious to get sight of a fish caught by a locomotive engine.'[170]

In a similar vein, several newspapers reported that the enginemen of the L&M had taken to poaching, by collecting dead hares and rabbits which had established themselves on the slopes of the embankment and which had been 'knocked down and killed by the carriages.' On one occasion 'as one of the first-class train of carriages was proceeding at a rapid rate near Rainhill, a hare sprang up' between the rails, and 'after a race of three miles was over taken by the train' and killed, providing a quick, although illegal, meal.[171]

Engineman Robson of the *Vulcan* was suspended in March 1832 for bringing his train 'into the Manchester Station at an improper speed.' Upon examination by John Dixon it was found that *Vesta's* reversing gear had slipped on the crank axle, meaning that it 'act[ed] imperfectly.' Dixon considered Robson free from any misconduct and he was re-instated as soon as *Vesta* had been repaired.[172] Enginemen Robson and Scott were before the Committee in June 1834 for a quarrel whilst changing engines at Newton: 'Scott had used improper language toward Robson' but on the other hand 'Robson would not exchange engines when they met at Newton on Sunday as authorised.' Scott was admonished and Robson reminded that 'Enginemen must change engines when they met half way on a Sunday unless it was by mutual consent that each Engineman remained with his own Engine.'[173] Robson subsequently worked for the Manchester & Leeds Railway, but was brought before the Leeds Bench in March 1841 for being drunk in charge of a locomotive. At the trial Robson noted he had been 'ten years a driver of locomotive engines' during which time he 'had never had an accident.' He was sentenced to two months' hard labour and fined £10.[174] Enginemen Callan and Greenhough appeared before the Management Committee in August 1836 for fighting: 'Callan had given Greenhough some provocation by taunting him' whereupon Greenhough responded in kind and with fists. The committee considered 'both were to blame' but because both were of 'good character', they were let off with a caution.[175]

Alexander Fyfe was complaining in March 1832 that men at the Manchester Engine Shops were pilfering candles (and candle stubs); as a result 'coloured candles ... which might be recognised as railway candles' were ordered to be made and issued so that culprits might be identified.[176] In order to stop pilfering of tools and supplies a lock up store was ordered to be built at the Engine Station at Rainhill for £10.[177]

Martin Weatherburn was suspended in June 1832 for having run *Victory*, at the head of the 3pm coach train from Manchester, into the rear of a stationary coal train headed by the *Comet*. It transpired that one of the coal waggon wheels had broken 'which had delayed the coal train', but that *Victory* was 'running much too close behind' and the impact was inevitable. The last coal waggon was smashed and several others damaged, as was *Victory*'s 'cross beam'[buffer beam?].[178] Fireman John Bowen of Manchester was dismissed in November 1832 for brawling with John Dunn.[179] Engineman John Scholes was dismissed for being intoxicated and incapable 'and in consequence had got his Engine off the Way.' The policeman on duty at the time, Robert McCrie, was also dismissed for drunkenness.[180]

Engineman Abel Jones was cautioned and 'lost his turn on the list for promotion to Enginemen' after running the *Swiftsure* head-on into a stationary luggage train at Parkside Watering Station, killing a labourer 'who had been crushed between two waggons, and died in Manchester Infirmary.' Two of the porters at Parkside informed the Committee that Jones had been running at 'an improper speed' into the station, about five or six miles an hour, and considered his conduct was 'decidedly reckless'. The Committee reminded Jones that that trains should only enter 'a regular Water Station and Stopping-Place' at speeds less than even five miles per hour.[181] Engineman Millburn was cautioned for not keeping a proper look-out and running into a second-class carriage which was being shunted by hand from the Down to the Up line at Kendrick's Cross.[182] Fireman J. Slater also lost his position in the 'link': he was the oldest fireman at Manchester 'and occasional enginemen' and next due to promotion. He had been brought before the Manchester Petty Sessions for taking his banking engine out without a red signal lamp and fined £2 for misconduct. As he was a 'good character' the Board declined to discharge him, 'but allowed him to remain as fireman, though not as first fireman in line for promotion.'[183]

William Taburner (enginemen) and George Dixon (fireman) were both reprimanded by the Management Committee for running their banking engine into a Whitsun excursion train from Birmingham on the Sutton Incline. Taburner was 'in his cabin, taking his dinner' when Dixon 'without giving (him) notice' drove the engine, following the excursion up the incline and 'for want of proper management, ran into the train so violently, as to damage one of the carriages' causing great alarm amongst the passengers. Both were suspended following the incident: Taburner was allowed to return to work but losing three days' wages for those days he had been suspended. Dixon, however, was 'removed from his situation as fireman to that of cleaner ... in the sheds.'[184] Jasper Clarke (Bank Engineman) and James Rigby (Foreman) were fined 20s and 10s respectively following an incident on 30 August when Clarke ran the Sutton banker so violently against the last carriage of the 5.30pm train from Manchester that it was 'thrown off the rails' resulting in a bent axle and damaged steps. Both men were severely reprimanded by the Board for this misconduct.[185]

PART 4

MAINTENANCE AND REPAIR

CHAPTER 15

Engine Sheds and Workshops

The Liverpool & Manchester running sheds and workshops were at Brickfield Station, Liverpool, immediately east of the 'Moorish Arch' under the management of John Melling. Melling was faced with an uphill struggle; the workshops were poorly equipped and lacked sufficient capacity to repair the existing fleet. In the earliest days the engine shops even lacked something as simple as an inspection pit – but in November 1831 the Management Committee ordered them to be dug 'to enable the men to get under the Engines to repair them' and a lock-up store room was also provided by dividing the existing stores into two stories. A three horse-power engine supplied by Foster & Griffin had been installed in the workshops at Crown Street Yard in May 1830 to turn the lathes and other machinery.[1]

The first engine sheds

The first engine sheds and workshops were ordered to be built in June 1830, on land at the Liverpool end which had been purchased from Lord Salisbury and at Manchester on land acquired from Captain Barrow. Additional engine sheds at Liverpool were built in June 1831 when George Stephenson was asked to report on providing engine sheds at both ends of the line for the stabling of the locomotives at night. Hardman Earle informed the board that his wife was intending to 'make several communications between her land at Edge Hill and the railway, by means of tunnels cut into the rock for the purpose of engine houses.' Two of the rock-cut arched openings at the Edgehill Cutting have been tentatively identified as being engine sheds, and indeed T. T. Bury shows the use of such rock-cut arches as being used as engine sheds. Similarly the blind south tunnel was also used as an engine shed.[2] There were at least three lines passing the engine sheds at Brickfield as in May 1832 William Allcard was ordered to install a set of switches and crossing to enable the line outside the sheds to communicate with the south (Down) line so that 'the spare line' could be used for storing coal wagons.[3] The Ordsall Lane engine shed was built by David Bellhouse Jnr of Manchester, who also had the contract to build the Liverpool Road station buildings. It was brick-built with stone dressings. *The Manchester Courier* announced in July 1830:

> 'A building for an engine-house and sheds is in progress of erection, on the south side of the Line between Ordsall-Lane, and Oldfield-Lane. It will be a long building of single storey with a neat front, and will be capable of holding six engines and tenders.'[4]

Presumably this building proved to be too small, as a 'new' [additional?] engine shed was ordered to be built at Ordsall Lane in July 1831.[5] With the opening of the extension to Hunts Bank a replacement four-road engine shed was built, designed by Edward Woods.[6]

Locomotives were turned and serviced separately from their tenders; the first turntables were quite short, but with the introduction of the 6 wheeled Patentee types, longer 12 foot turntables were installed in September 1834, two at Manchester and one at Liverpool.[7] New turntables were provided at Edgehill and Brickfield Station in summer 1839. Installing a new 'large turntable' at Edge Hill Sheds cost £88 4s 7d, the turntable itself costing £79. 'Repairing turntables at Edgehill' in the same month cost £1 3s 9d.[8] A new turntable was laid at the GJR engine shed at Ordsall Lane in June 1841, costing £4 12s in labour for a foreman (five days); labourer (22¼ days), a smith and a striker (quarter day each).[9] Carriage sheds were built at Manchester (capable of holding twenty carriages) and at Parkside (1840) for the North Union Railway.

At the end of the day, locomotives had their fires dropped and were blown down, emulating marine and stationary engine practice. Blowing down would have helped scour out sediment and dirty water circulating within the boiler barrel, but it is not

Thomas Talbot Bury's depiction of the 'Grand Area' at Edgehill showing early rock-cut engine sheds and locomotives being turned separately from their tenders for servicing. (Anthony Dawson collection)

clear how often boilers were washed out. Whilst probably safe enough with an iron firebox, a copper firebox may not have welcomed such treatment on a daily basis. There were also complaints from some of the fitters when smaller boiler tubes were introduced with the suite of Planet locomotives that the tubes were harder to clean.

Watering facilities

Watering facilities were provided at Brickfield, Edge Hill Tunnel Station, Parkside (which irked Thomas Legh who wanted the watering facilities relocating to Newton where he had recently completed a lavish hotel), Eccles and Manchester but the facilities at Manchester were not completed by the opening day (15 September 1830) which meant that engines had to be despatched to Eccles and back to take water. A water tank, together with boilers to warm the water and pump it up to the high level tank, was built at Parkside. Water was drawn from a triangular-shaped reservoir to the north of the Up line, the outline of which can still be traced opposite the Huskisson Memorial. The memorial formed the base for an iron water tank. A new boiler was needed for the pumping engine at Parkside in February 1834 – the boiler plates being 'worn thin and hardly safe.' A new one was purchased at a cost of £15 to £20.[10] An engine shed was also built at Parkside. In Manchester, a monumental brick-built triumphal arch at Water Street disguised the water tank, and provided a suitable grand entrance to the town for those passengers alighting at the arrivals station between the Irwell and Water Street which was ordered to be built in August 1830. Messrs. Rothwell & Harrison who owned the dye works immediately to the north of the 'Arrivals Station' agreed to supply the Company with water, so long as the Company supplied a steam engine to the value of £1,000 with Rothwell & Harrison being responsible for its upkeep. Ultimately water was supplied by the Manchester & Salford Water Works Company for £70 per annum for 10,000 gallons per day. Boilers were provided to warm the water at each 'watering station' and a cylinder from Stephenson's *Twin Sisters* was used to work a pump to lift water to the top of the Manchester water tower. An additional boiler was provided at Manchester in 1834 'capable of heating the water for the Loco-Motive Engines, as well as pumping it' at a cost of £50 to £60. Water was subsequently taken from the mains supply at a cost of £70 per year, for 1,000 gallons a day. The mains water may not have been the cleanest, as in November 1832 the Management Committee discussed the possibility of filtering the water as boilers were being fouled with scale and sludge deposition.[11] The issue of dirty water was raised again in May 1833; John Dixon was instructed to obtain estimates for 'driving a drift under the river and half way across to form a filter for the water of the Loco-Motive engines' which was presumably being taken directly from the river. One French visitor to Manchester in 1831 had described the river Irwell as 'noisesome' and polluted: no wonder it needed filtering, and that boiler tubes were found to wear out so rapidly.[12] The state of the water taken from the river is shown by an incident to Jupiter in December 1831 when one of the water pumps was found to be blocked by a live eel two feet long! In July 1836 John Dixon reported that the water tank at Manchester was 'much corroded' and it was ordered to be replaced. There must still have been a problem with the quality of water as the Management

Sub-Committee ordered Dixon to 'consider the best plan for procuring a supply of pure water.' He was presented with several options: whether by a drift under the river; or by 'Rothwell & Harrison's Old Well'; 'or by purchase from the Manchester & Salford Water Works' which could cost 8d per 1,000 gallons. In order to overcome the problems associated with 'hard' water, Robert Stephenson had ordered that the Leicester & Swannington collect 'soft' rain water for its locomotives, to prevent scale and sludge deposition in boilers. The Leeds & Selby also experienced problems with using river water and had a large settling tank built to filter any impurities from the water, as well as had a chemical analysis of the water used in their locomotive as to its 'fitness' for use in locomotives. Eventually the Leeds & Selby collected rain water, directed from the roofs of its station buildings in Leeds and Selby into underground tanks.[13] It would appear a similar water-collection tactic was followed on the L&M when a large reservoir for the collection of rainwater for the feed water was ordered to be provided; a large 'trough or reservoir' was to be excavated at Brickfield to collect rain water, as the existing well was not capable of 'holding sufficient Water for the purpose of the Shops' and locomotives.[14] A new water tank capable of holding 12,000 gallons and able to supply twenty engines was built at Brickfield in September 1835.[15] At the recommendation of George Stephenson, four boilers were purchased

The water tank at Manchester was built to resemble a grand triumphal arch. Water was heated in a series of boilers and pumped to the elevated tank to fill locomotive tenders. The pumping engine incorporated a cylinder from *Twin Sisters*.

PARK - SIDE.

Parkside mid-way between Liverpool & Manchester where all trains stopped to take on hot water and coke. A boiler to heat the water and a pumping engine were erected here, so too an engine shed. Water cranes were provided on the Up and Down lines. The Huskisson Memorial was erected on the base of the water tank on the Down side. (Liverpool & Manchester Railway Trust)

in January 1830 to heat the feed water for the locomotives 'on their journey from Liverpool to Manchester.' A four-horse power engine and boiler was purchased in March 1830 from Wigan to pump water for the locomotives at Newton, and a second two-horse power engine for the 'Locomotive Boiler Station at Rainhill.'[16]

From 1833 water for the locomotives at Edge Hill 'Tunnel Station' was taken from wells in the cellars of the north and south engine houses; prior to that the well had supplied the winding engines only but in May 1833 Allcard was ordered to have the well of no. 1 engine house deepened by 30 or 50 yards and the pump gear enlarged to handle an increased volume of water. In November 1833 the well for No. 2 engine was ordered to be 'stopped' and instead a reservoir for the collection of rain water for both engines was to be 'hewn out of the rock between the two engines' and a pipe to deliver hot water for filling the boilers of the engines at John Melling's repair shops at Brickfield station was also ordered to be made.[17] The accumulation of sediment for both locomotive and stationary engine boilers was obviously a problem at Edge Hill, as in April 1833 an iron water tank 5 feet in diameter and 12 feet high was ordered to be made 'for the deposit of sediment from the water at Edge Hill previous to entering the boilers.'[18] A new, high-pressure pumping engine was installed at Edge Hill in 1835, which also had sufficient power 'to draw the coals up the little tunnel, and leave the present engines for no other duty than drawing up merchandize through the Old Tunnel from Wapping', reliving the winding engine from that duty. The new engine was considerably more compact than the low pressure engines and cost £280.[19] Two new cast iron 'Water pillars' were erected at Edge Hill by the L&M for use by the Grand Junction from Charles Tayleur & Co for £82 the pair.[20]

Melling's Shed, Brickfield Station

Upon taking responsibility for the workshops and locomotives in 1833, John Melling was not only short of equipment, but during his first eighteen months at was facing something of a motive power crisis. The fleet of locomotives purchased in 1830–1831 were worn out, and the cost of keeping them in operation was steadily rising. Five locomotives were out of action, and he reported to the Management Committee in February 1834 that:

> 'The <u>Planet & Atlas</u> would be repaired completely in <u>3 weeks</u> – and the Northumbrian in 6 weeks – and that the <u>Mercury</u> and <u>Majestic</u> would be repaired completely in 3 months if he be allowed a small Steam Engine; without which the work was done to great disadvantage.'[21]

With five locomotives going through the shops, there was not sufficient capacity for the repair of *Mars*, which was sent to the Vulcan Foundry.[22] *Goliath* had broken her crank axle, and was despatched to the Vulcan Foundry for repair. At the same time the opportunity was taken to lengthen the throw of the crank.[23] The cost of repairs to *Mars* totalled some £900 because, although only three years old, she was worn out and 'many of the parts were not fit for use.'[24] *Victory* had been sent to Foster & Griffin in November 1832 ostensibly for a new copper firebox, but was in such poor condition that the work was not completed until March 1833. The Management Committee were unimpressed with Foster & Griffin's 'very unreasonable charges' compared to the equivalent work carried out on *Venus* by Edward Bury & Co.[25] *Mercury* was out of action in March 1833,[26] and three other engines were under heavy repair by the end of 1834: *Saturn* was sent to Tayleur & Co. in October, whilst *Ajax* was sent to Edward Bury & Co. of Liverpool, and *Milo* to George Forrester as the L&M's own works were unable to cope.[27] The L&M works never seemed to be able to manage the amount of work required of them; in 1834 Booth had suggested that major repair work be 'put out' and in October 1838 the Board concluded it was more economical to 'get … the Loco Motive Engines now out of order, Repaired <u>out</u>, either at the Viaduct or Vulcan Foundry' rather than carry out major work 'in-house'.[28]

Repair work was only carried on from Monday to Saturday; in April 1832 one of the Directors, Robert Gladstone, had observed work taking place in the Engine shops on a Sunday and made a complaint to the Board. As a result, the Board ordered:

> 'That no Repairs or Other Work on the Line be done on a Sunday, except in Cases of an urgent necessity & that in such Case a Special Report thereof be made to the Board.'[29]

John Gray recommended to the Management Committee the purchase of a hydraulic wheel press in August 1832, but due to dithering over the cost, it was not ordered until September 1832 for £120.[30] Such was the pressure on Gray and his assistant Rotherham that the Management Committee ordered the 'turning engine ... be kept working night and day' during September 1832.[31] The shortage of locomotives was so severe that work was to take place 'night and day' on repairing *Mars* and *Fury* in order to get them back into service; John Dixon estimated that the two engines would be back in service in two or three days as a result of this all-out effort.[32]

William Allcard suggested that in order to reduce running costs, boiler repairs should be taken in-house and as such a punching machine for boiler plate be ordered. The Management Committee referred the decision to the Directors 'whether the Company should become Boiler Makers.' The Board obviously agreed with Allcard, as in September 1832 Melling sent a note to the Board recommending 'the purchase of sundry Machines for punching Boiler Plates, Planing Slides, Boring Cylinders etc etc, to be obtained from Sharp Roberts of Manchester.' Allcard was ordered by the Management Committee to 'procure a punching and paring engine for Melling's Shop, which was much needed, Price £70 – complete ready made.' Requests for additional machinery extended into the following year: John Gray requested the purchase of an additional lathe and new slide rest in order to prevent night working 'which was always done to disadvantage.' The cost of a new lathe was £250.[33] Two new 'punching and sheering machines ... one for the Manchester engine shop and the other for Gray's Yard' were ordered to be purchased in January 1834.[34]

The water pump at Melling's Shed was converted to steam power in January 1833, the Management Committee ordering 'that a connecting shaft be fixed to the Revolving Wheels ... to connect them with the pump now worked by hand' so that 'the power of the Locomotive Engines may be applied to pump water into the tanks for general use.' These 'revolving wheels' were probably a primitive form of 'rolling road' used to help with valve setting.[35]

In June 1833, 'in consideration of his long hours and ... Zealous attention' the Directors raised Melling's wages from three guineas per week to four, and he was authorised to take on four additional fitters.[36] In order to prevent night working, Melling had been repeatedly requesting a new (additional?) lathe and engine for his workshops, the Management Committee finally acceding to his request in August 1833 when they ordered a new 3 horse power steam engine 'for turning the lathes'.[37] A spare boiler was made by John Gray at Millfield Yard for the yard's engine in June 1833. It was to have a 'double fire place' one above the other as an experiment for burning coal. Coal was burned in the lower 'fire place' and coke in the upper, where it was hoped the coke would ignite the volatile gases from the burning coal 'to see how far coal might be burned without smoking.'[38] A new 'engine boiler for the repairing shed' was purchased in 1834 for £188; a new smithy and boiler house was built at the Manchester end in the same year for £83 10s 3d, whilst a new lathe and line shafting for the Liverpool repair shops were purchased for £126 2s 8d in January 1835.[39] A new planing machine, new screw-making machine and a 'new slide lathe' were purchased at the end of 1835 for £100 and £200 respectively.[40]

Some eight apprentices were taken on in the workshops at Millfield Yard under Gray late in 1835, clearly showing how extensive those premises were, including a foundry:[41]

Joseph Sefton	Joiner
John McNicoll	Engineer
William Bramwell	'who had been two years at business previously'
Richard Millard	'also had been 2 years or upwards at the business'
William Eaton	'now in the Foundry'
Thomas Sunderland	'in the Foundry'
Thomas Day	'moulding in the Foundry'
Thomas Weatherburn	Fitter

Some of the men and boys had previously been in the trade or, like William Bramwell, were already working for the company. They were indentured for a period of six years, with pay increasing year on year.

Working in the locomotive shops could be a dangerous job, as the *Liverpool Mercury* reported:

'On Wednesday night, a young man, employed in cleaning the wheels of the *Vulcan*, steamer, got his arm so entangled in one of them, that, before he was disengaged, it was crushed to a mummy above the elbow. The poor fellow was about a quarter or an hour in this perilous situation, and he bore it with extreme fortitude. He was sent to the Infirmary.'[42]

A new engine shed and new 'slate and timber roof' were ordered to be built at Brickfield in November 1836 for £1,055, and in February 1837 Edward Woods was to prepare plans and specifications for a new engine shed capable of holding twelve engines, and with attached forge, stores and offices for the accommodation of the Grand Junction Railway. John Melling proposed to amend this plan by requesting the space between his shed and the new GJR shed be roofed over, which was finally done in July 1838.[43] A 'Copper smiths & Brazier hearth' was built for the GJR at a cost of £11 8s in October 1837 and the smithy chimneys were taken down and completely rebuilt as they had 'been improperly built in the first instance.'[44]

In June 1838 Melling requested the construction of an office for himself as well as a drawing office and pattern store at Brickfield, the cost to be about £500, and at the end of October 1838 Melling repeated his usual litany for new or additional machine tools and equipment at Brickfield. Thus, Booth was authorised to purchase a new stationary engine 'to work the lathes and other machines lately put up' in 'Melling's shed.'[45] In 1839 the drawing office possessed three 'large' and one 'small' drawing table; two mahogany desks; one 'portable' desk; one board table; 3 squares and an oak rule as well as stools, chairs, cupboards and a wash-stand. Francis Whishaw toured the workshops in November 1839 and was suitably impressed:

'About thirty yards beyond the Edge-Hill Passenger station ... The Locomotive-engine repairing-shops are on the right side of the wide space at Edge Hill; and are fitted up with lathes and other requisites in a very competent manner. About fifty men, including fitters and smiths, are said to be here employed; there is a 12-horse power engine for giving motion to the lathes and other machinery throughout this department.'[46]

Whilst at Millfield Yard there was a smithy with 36 hearths 'a spacious foundry, a boiler maker's shop, a waggon-building and repairing shop' and amongst the workmen at Millfield were 'smiths, strikers, boiler-makers, and spring-makers.'[47] A useful comparison can be made between Brickfield and up-to-date engine wrights such as Bourne & Bartley of Manchester, who possessed a 21 inch 'back geared' slide lathe with a 25 feet long bench which was capable of turning 5ft locomotive driving wheels; an 18 inch 'back geared' slide lathe; a 13 inch slide lathe 'with change wheels for screw-cutting'; a 9 inch 'single geared lathe'; four 9 inch 'back geared' lathes 'with facing plates', and an 8 foot planing machine, all driven from a 4hp stationary steam engine. In addition was a brass foundry, and smith's shop. This suggests that Melling's works were on a level with those of commercial engine-builders and quite capable of turning out new locomotives.[48]

In December 1839 and January 1840 an additional 10,000 square yards of land at Wavertree Lane was purchased in order to expand the works. Tenders were invited for enlarging the Brickfield engine shops in spring 1840, including a new smithy, 'engineman's waiting room' and additional storage sheds at a cost of £898 and another engine shed for the GJR for £640. At the recommendation of Edward Woods, additional machine tools were purchased, including a screw-making machine (£90); 'double-acting wheel lathe' (£480); and a slotting machine (£120). The first two were ordered from Messrs. Whitworth & Co whilst the latter came from Sharp Roberts & Co.[49]

The staff at Brickfield Station in the summer of 1837 included two braziers and two 'assistant boys'; four smiths and four 'strikers'; two boilermakers and two assistant boilermakers; two joiners and two painters; one brass caster and four brass fitters; and eighteen fitters.[50] It appears that the wage bill for the fitters and other employees in the engine shops was higher than that for the engine crews. During the second half of 1836 the wages of the men in the repair shops totalled £4,683 12s 3d, whilst the engine crews were paid £1,115 4s 4d. An additional £454 12s 4d was spent on the wages for the men who watered the engines and loaded the tenders with coke; £300 8s 11d on gas for lighting the workshops as well as oil, tallow and hemp for packing glands; £541 15s 3d for brass, iron and copper 'for repairs', and over £1,000 was spent on new wheels and axles.[51]

According to Francis Whishaw, the staff were on duty from 6am to 8pm, having on average an 84-hour week. They were allowed thirty minutes for breakfast, an hour for lunch and another thirty minutes for their evening meal. The 'Locomotive & Stationary Engine Department' was always the largest department of the railway; Francis Whishaw estimated in November 1839 that John Melling employed 50 men whilst Alexander Fyfe had over 100 at Manchester but these figures are not borne out from the pay lists of fitters at either repair shop. In 1842 Edward Woods reported that he employed 271 men in the locomotive department; 32 men were employed in the carriage and waggon shops and 101 at Millfield Yard. The Management Committee thought Woods' establishment excessive and desired Henry Booth to make inquiries of Edward Bury as to how he ran the London & Birmingham works at Wolverton, with an eye to reducing the number of fitters on the pay roll.[52]

CHAPTER 16

Workshop Costs

Due to the working agreement between the L&M and the Grand Junction, the latter's locomotives were repaired in the workshops of the L&M by L&M staff. Although not referring to L&M locomotives, the bills and costed work presented to the L&M give an insight into the hours of labour and cost involved in keeping these early locomotives running. The most frequent entry for repair are the gauge glasses, on average three needing replacement per month: in July 1837 six locomotives needed replacement water gauges, the cost of which included 1s 3d for the glass tube; '2 pieces 2-inch brass pipe' 1s 4d. A gauge cock cost 6s 6d. Nine locomotives needed replacement gauge glasses in October 1837 and four in November. Due to the high number of broken gauge glasses, it appears protectors were introduced, costing 2s for 'three squares of glass' and a 'brass frame.' This, however, does not appear to have solved the problem of bursting gauge glasses, as by April 1839 glass tubes were being purchased by the dozen. On 29 October 1839 a fireman was injured when the gauge glass of the engine working the 5.30pm train from Liverpool burst at Broad Green 'with a loud explosion – the lamp had been thrown out of the socket and the man had been stunned by the blow and knocked down onto the railway.' Edward Woods, however, suspected foul play as a Grand Junction Mail Train was passing in the opposite direction at the same moment the glass burst. He was of the opinion that something must have been thrown from the GJR engine 'which had broke the Glass tube, forced off the lamp, and nocked down the fireman.' Henry Booth was instructed to remonstrate with the GJR.[1]

Feed pipes, force-pumps and clack valves all must have given trouble as they constitute the second most frequent entry for repair; those of GJR *Hecate* must have been particularly temperamental – on 2 September 1837 it took two men half a day to repair *Hecate*'s feed pipe at the Manchester repair shops (£6 3s for labour, and materials). Her pump was repaired again four days later in Liverpool for 8s 4d. *Hecate*'s pumps were under repair again at Manchester during the following month, two men taking one day to dismantle and repair the pump and fit a new ram (12s) and a further two men to make and fit new copper feed pipes (12s for labour; 5lbs of copper for the pipes costing 6s 8d). A replacement ball clack and seat cost 12s. The flexible cloth hose pipes running between the tender and locomotive were 3 feet long and cost 3s each whilst a 'Brass cock & Union Joint for hose feed pipes' cost £4 2s 8d.[2] 'India Rubber' feed pipes had been experimented with in 1834, costing £75 17s 7d, whilst replacement feed pipes in the period July–December 1835 came to £214 3s.[3]

Leeds was under repair in April 1838 after being run into by a Grand Junction locomotive at Edge Hill which resulted in a broken frame:[4]

Making new Pedestal to fore axle	)
New Brass Step	} £22

Dissecting the hinder part of framing; fitting and planing iron plates, & c.	)
Fitting new step and Axle Guard to Tender; repairing broken step and hand rail	£5

Repairs to *Patentee* in October 1838 (following a fatal accident at Newton Junction) totalled:

Safety guards, front stays, knees & framing	£3
Lifting framing and examining axles	£2
New Blow-off cock and piping	£2
Refitting feed-pipe and pumps	£2 5s
Straightening connecting rods & new keys provided	£1 15s
Repairing and Fitting ash box	£1[5]

There was sufficient capacity at Edge Hill and Manchester for larger repairs to be carried out. John Melling's insistence on using machine tools meant that valves and port faces were able to be planed and cylinders could be bored accurately. GJR *Stentor* and *Hecla* were obviously undergoing a serious rebuild March to May 1838 involving the fitting of new valve gear. The cost of 204lbs of iron for new 'iron work ... for valve gearing' in March 1838 was £4 5s; 'Lathes for turning and boring rod ends' £7 5s and the 'machine planing of Rod ends' cost a further £4 10s. In April, '2 strong wrought Iron levers and 4 crank rod ends' (£3 7s 8d) were made, the machine work ('lathes, planing machine, turning, & boring') costing £6 10s and in May 'boring and turning Gearing Stentor & Hecla' cost £5 2s 6d and 'machine planing £2 2s 6d.' New eccentric brasses with collar and bolt were fitted to *Hecla* in June (£2 5s). A pair of cast bronze slide valves cost £2 10s and the 'planing & machining' of slide valves and port faces cost £1 10s in October 1838. There is no contemporary evidence to suggest how valves and cylinders were lubricated, and bronze slide valves were probably adopted as they have a lower friction coefficient compared to iron on iron with little or no lubrication present, and were then thought to be largely self-lubricating. Furthermore, with a bronze and iron pair, there would no associated judder (or 'stick-slip') associated with iron on iron. That said, with iron being harder than bronze, the valves probably wore out quite quickly unless properly lubricated using the animal or vegetable lubricants which were then available. The replica of *Planet* uses cast iron slide valves, and although fitted with a modern lubrication system using displacement lubricators to introduce oil into the valve chest and cylinders, the slide valves suffered from 'stick-slip' early in the locomotive's career, until the valve faces had been worn to a mirror-like finish. By 1839 Alexander Fyfe is noted as apparently using case-hardened cast-iron slide valves and steel-faced valve ports. Lubrication was introduced into the cylinders of the original L&M locomotive *Lion* using brass 'trumpets' mounted on the front of each cylinder cover, activated by a three-way cock. Tallow was put into the upturned mouth of the trumpet and would melt and run into the cylinder. Such 'trumpets' are depicted on Nasmyth's sketch of Northumbrian.[6]

Boiler work also took place, John Jepson, Joseph Jepson, Peter Parnell, and Richard Wilson being employed as boilermakers on a daily rate varying from 5s (John Jepson) to 1s 3d (Joseph Jepson). The GJR also employed their own boiler maker at Edge Hill, one J. Evans. The most common boiler work was replacing and plugging tubes; making and fitting six brass tubes with twelve steel ferrules cost £7 13s 7½d in July 1837; the cost of an individual rolled brass tube, 1 5/8 in diameter and 8ft 4in long, and weighing 20lbs, was £1 4s 2d. Irregular payments were also made for Low Moor iron and sheet copper for 'linings' (i.e. inner fireboxes) suggesting work on fireboxes was also undertaken. Payments were also made to 'strikers' and their assistants suggesting riveting was also taking place. Edge Hill was also set up for soldering; salamoniac – a rare compound of aluminium chloride – was purchased for cleaning surfaces to be soldered, and spelter solder, i.e. solder for soldering copper, iron and brass, consisting of one part brass and two parts spelter (zinc), was also purchased.[7]

The Edge Hill shops were also capable of making and fitting just about every component of a locomotive: for example a new cast iron chimney with wire mesh spark arrester cost £3 6s 8d; an ash buffer plank (7ft 6ins x 16¼ins x 6¼ins) plus two iron mounting brackets cost £1 13s; a pair of leather buffers with iron rings cost £4 12s 3d; a brass blast pipe cost 42s whilst a copper blast pipe was 23s 7d; a copper and brass regulator cost £6 10s 4d. A brass steam whistle cost £1 16s. The Edge Hill shops had a set of taps and dies as well as a screw making machine to make fixings such as nuts, bolts, screws and washers. They were made to suit each locomotive as needed. A lot of reliance was placed on different shaped files and cold chisels for making parts fit, and many tools such as chisels and hammers, were made 'in house.' One fireman was clearly over-enthusiastic, jettisoning his shovel into the firebox, as the accounts show a new fireman's shovel had to be made (4s 6d, paid for by the fireman) whilst a wrought iron ash pan rake cost 6s. Despite the presence of a lathe and other machines, a lot of work still went on by hand, with purchases of flat and round files and 'valve facing files' for finishing the surfaces of slide valves and valve chests. Upwards of £100 per half year was spent on 'Shop Tools, files, chisels, etc' 1835–1836.[8]

Consumables included lubricants and materials for cleaning (cotton waste, bath brick) as well as paint and turpentine. 'Gallipoli Oil' – a crude form of olive oil – was the most widely used lubricant (between 50 and 100 gallons a month costing 4s 6d per gallon), together with Rape Oil (three to four gallons per month at 4s per gallon). Grease was also used as a lubricant, 216lbs being purchased at 3d per pound in October 1837. Sperm Oil (around thirteen gallons per month, costing between 8s and 8s 3d per gallon) was used for lamps. Black and green paint and red lead were purchased, together with 'whiting', turpentine and varnish. Over a hundred pounds of cotton waste was purchased per month for cleaning purposes, usually for 2¼d per pound. An individual bath brick for cleaning metal cost 6d.[9] The lubrication of axle boxes was either with a mineral oil such as white lead mixed with linseed or rapeseed oil, or by vegetable oil alone from oil pots mounted over the journal, using a worsted wick. Mineral grease or tallow would have been used on the axle box under keeps. High quality Russian tallow (clarified mutton fat) was used to lubricate the slide valves and cylinders, as tallow best resisted the 'washing' effect of steam and any condensed water in the valve chest and cylinder. However, it had a tendency to leave deposits which could carbonise. Furthermore as it decomposed in the presence of oxygen, it created fatty acids which would corrode the pistons, valves and other moving parts.[10]

Booth was perennially in a cost-cutting mood. He had reported to the Board in December 1834 that there was 'great waste' in the use of oil 'to the principal journals and moving parts of the Locomotive Engines' and recommended instead the use of a grease of his own devising, consisting of a mixture of palm oil and tallow, which was being successfully used in the axle boxes of the carriages and waggons. It was ordered to fit one locomotive up with grease boxes rather than oil pots and comparative trials to take place between the two lubricants.[11] This axle grease was later patented by Booth. Whilst grease was adopted for the carriage and waggon axle boxes, it does not appear to have been suitable for the locomotives.[12] Indeed, the *Planet* replica was originally fitted with grease lubrication, but very early on this was found to be unsuitable with fine particulates entering the axle boxes and disrupting the film lubrication.

Locomotives for hire

The close working relationship between the L&M and GJR lead to the former hiring-out locomotives (and rolling stock) to the latter concern, as well as sending its locomotives to rescue GJR trains which had broken down; *Milo* was sent to assist a GJR passenger train from Edge Hill to Newton Junction at 5s per mile on 7 July 1837 whilst *Firefly* worked a GJR train from Edge Hill through to Birmingham and back on the following day, '194 miles at 5/- per mile … £4 5s.' On the same day *Ajax* took a GJR train from Liverpool to Warrington and back, and the *Sun* made the same trip on 12 July. *Mars* worked a GJR train to Warrington and back at the end of the month.

Vesta, *Milo* and *Speedwell* were hired to the GJR to work their trains to Warrington during August 1837, and in September 1837 two GJR locomotives failed on or near the Whiston Incline: *Milo* was sent on 13 September to bring a train back to Newton Junction whilst *Comet* brought a failed GJR train back to Edge Hill ten days later. Similarly, the GJR hired engines to assist the L&M; *Scorpion* and *Alecta* were hired to 'lead passenger trains' from Manchester to Liverpool and *Scorpion* and *Hecla* had been hired as 'assisting engines.' The GJR's *Caliban* had to be sent to rescue *Hercules* when she failed in October 1837 and in the following month *Ajax* was sent out twice to rescue GJR trains which had failed on the Whiston Incline. This practice of mutual help – no doubt aided through the familial ties between the GJR and the L&M locomotive department – continued for several years: on 29 November 1839 *Tiger* was sent to recover a GJR train 'which had been disabled on the road' on Barton Moss, due to the failure of the *Tamerlane*. Similarly, the GJR engine *Prospero* was hired by the L&M to 'lead coals' from Warrington to Edge Hill, at a charge of 3d per ton.[13]

CHAPTER 17

Locomotive Working

Keeping the locomotives in running order, as well as supplying coke and water, was one of the biggest expenses, with an upward trend throughout the early 1830s:

Half year ending	Locomotive Expenses	Cost/Train Mile
31 December 1831	£12,203 5s 6d	
30 June 1832	£10,582 16s 3d	9.3d
31 December 1832	£12,646 9s 8d	10.8d
30 June 1833	£14,715 16s 9d	10.75d
31 December 1833	£13,965 8s 1d	11.17d
30 June 1834	£15,641 17s 10d	13.1d

In October 1833 the board considered putting the operation and maintenance of its locomotive fleet out to tender and Charles Tayleur (of the Vulcan Foundry) proposed to take over this role from the Company. In other words, the Vulcan Foundry would undertake design and specification work, as well as the construction (or licensed construction) of the locomotives, including operation and maintenance of them. In reply to this overture, Booth was instructed to inform Charles Tayleur:

'That the Directors looked forward to contracting for their moving power, but at present while so many changes had recently taken place, and the Mechanical operation of the company still be considered as Experimental, the Directors felt unable to enter into the proposed contract.'[1]

The ever-increasing expenditure in the motive power department was presented in a report to the Directors on 24 March 1834. The rising costs were detailed as being due to 'First – increase in speed; 10 miles an hour having been assumed, whereas it is more than double'; secondly locomotives working empty (and therefore non-remunerative) waggons back to Manchester; and that locomotives were also being expected to work higher mileages: 'In the half-year, ending 31st December 1831, they travelled 66,044 miles; in the half-year ending 31st December, 1833, they travelled 95,851 miles.' In order to reduce the coke bill, coal was 'being tried' but with indifferent success. The report also noted that locomotive availability had improved during the same period:

'Three engines … were in active operation in both periods, viz. the Jupiter, Saturn, and Etna, and that their performances were upwards of 50 per cent (that of Etna, indeed, 100 per cent) better in the latter than in the former period; and secondly, that with respect to the performances in the six months ending December, 1833, the three best were old Engines, which had undergone thorough repairs by the

Company. The Ajax and the Firefly are comparatively new Engines, this last one being the best the Company ever received from the hands of the maker.'[2]

That the annual mileage run by the locomotives was increasing is shown in the half-yearly reports:[3]

No. of trips of 30 miles					
Year	Passenger	Goods	Coal	Total	Mileage
31 Dec.1831	2,944	2,298	150	5,392	161,760
30 June 1832	2,636	2,248	234	5,118	153,540
31 Dec. 1832	3,363	1,676	211	5,250	157,500
30 June 1833	3,262	2,244	/	5,506	165,180
31 Dec. 1833	3,253	2,587	/	5,840	175,200
30 June 1834	3,317	2,499	/	5,816	174,480

Increased expenditure in the locomotive department in the same period was due to the adoption of brass tubes and steam pipes rather than copper; the 'introduction of copper and steel where only iron was used'; and also 'stronger and more durable wheels and axles.' It was hoped that although costly, this process would ultimately lower locomotive running costs through needing fewer replacements and repairs.[4] Colburn (citing de Pambour) estimates the cost of repairs per train mile averaged 13.1d, and that the 'sum paid for repairs in 1833 would have purchased twenty new engines at £778 each' whilst the repair bill for the first half of 1834 was 'equal to twelve new engines.'[5] By the end of December 1835, motive power expenses stood at £15,681 17s 9d and six months later in June 1836 at a staggering £20,425, which was apparently due to:

'Some bad accidents which had occurred to the waggons, and also in consequence of the strike of locomotive enginemen, which had obliged the Directors to employ extra hands.'[6]

Part of this high expenditure was because repairs were carried out 'in house'. The workshops were already at capacity, working through the night 'which was always done to great disadvantage & at considerable extra Cost to the Company.' As a result, Henry Booth suggested that anything other than running repairs be contracted for.[7] De Pambour suggests that the main reason for the high cost of repairs was because of the repair policy then in place:

'When an engine requires a repair, unless it be for some trifling accident, it is taken to pieces and a new one is constructed which receives the same name as the first, and in the construction of which are made to serve all such parts of the old engine as are still capable of being used with advantage. The consequence of this is, that a new re-constructed or repaired engine is literally a new one. The repairs thus amount to considerable sums.'[8]

De Pambour also notes that of the thirty engines on the L&M, ten of them were out of action as 'useless'; ten were under repair with the remainder in service. He also details locomotive reliability and availability for a three-year period (1831–1834): of the ten locomotives available during 1831, six had been operational for a full 52 weeks, whilst four had been out of service for periods varying between 15 weeks (*Sun*) and 2 weeks (*Mars*). The locomotives had run 182,675 miles between them, each averaging 380 miles per week, a figure which remained constant into the late 1830s/ early 1840s. Edward Woods estimated that the life-expectancy of a locomotive was based on mileage, calculated from the cost of a locomotive in pennies, divided by three, and that deprecation was equal to 3d per mile run. Thus a locomotive which cost £1,500 would be expected to run 120,000 miles, or approximately six years based on annual mileages.[9]

Hardman Earle described in 1837 that it was policy to work an engine every other day ('we consider that an engine ought to be allowed to rest every other day') for maintenance work to take place, and this is borne out by the purchase policy of the Company where locomotives were delivered in pairs, so that one locomotive of a particular type or class would be running whilst the other was 'allowed to rest.' The shortage of motive power, however, meant that this was not always strictly adhered to, so that 'we have run engines which have sometimes not been in sufficiently good order' which subsequently failed whilst out on the line, increasing operational costs and placing the burden more heavily on the locomotives in service, which in turn would be more likely to fail.[10]

Earle also presented a list of failures which contributed to delays to 139 out of 1,120 trains on the L&M between 9 July and 25 November 1837, which included:

Broken axles of engines, tenders and waggons	5
Failure of pumps, eccentrics, connecting-rods, cotters, &c.	19
Bad coke, and fire-bars burnt out, &c.	9
Engine more or less out of order	28
Rails slippery	11
Detention in watering	7

He further notes that the broken axles 'happened more particularly to one make of engine by most highly respectable persons, and to show that they do not think it any fault of our specification, they have allowed for the fractures in settling accounts.'[11]

Woods shows that for the period 26 October 1839 to 21 August 1840[12] he had on average fourteen locomotives for 'coach' turns; eight locomotives employed working 'luggage' turns; three 'bank' engines and four 'jobbing' engines working the pick-up goods and ballast trains. The engines selected to work the jobbing turns appear to have been either very elderly, such as *Planet* or *Leeds*, or those engines which were spare. Locomotives from other builders which were under trial also appear to have been used on jobbing turns: during the week-ending 15 February 'Atlas, J & Es' was on such a turn, presumably referring to the firm of Jones, Turner & Evans of Newton Le Willows. Nasmyth, Gaskell & Co. also used the L&M for testing its locomotives, officially and unofficially – in March 1839 a disgruntled Henry Booth wrote to Nasmyth, Gaskell & Co. for having not obtained permission to test one of their locomotives for the London & Southampton Railway. Thereafter trials were supervised by Edward Woods and indeed a siding was laid to serve the Bridgewater Foundry at Patricroft.

One (or several) of Nasmyth's locomotives are noted at work on the L&M between January and May 1840.[13]

The distinction between the different classes of engine/engine working do not appear to have been hard and fast; coaching engines could be found working all four turns (coach, luggage, bank and jobbing) but the slower-moving luggage engines never have appeared to have worked coach trains. Analysis of Edward Woods' detailed logs of locomotive performance suggests there is no discernible pattern for how long locomotives were worked before being stopped to undergo repair, either in times of weeks worked or mileage run; it is presumed that where locomotives are absent from his logs that they were in the workshops. Locomotives were usually absent for a fortnight during these periods. Thus, it would appear that locomotives were worked until they failed rather than being stopped and taken into the shops to a set pattern, which also explains the high cost of repairs and maintenance.

Locomotive policy

If the Liverpool & Manchester Railway can be said to have had a locomotive policy, it can be divided into two phases which saw the locomotive fleet almost completely renewed: the 'experimental phase' from 1830 to 1838; and a 'mature phase' from 1838–1845 (culminating with the delivery of the Bird class), which roughly coincides with the appointment of Edward Woods as 'Principal Engineer.' The appointment of Woods saw the start of a dynamic period for the L&M with the introduction of several of John Melling's patent improvements but also some of Woods' own ideas, including the unsuccessful short-stroke locomotives. Under Woods and Melling the workshop facilities (despite the penny-pinching attitude of the Board) were continually expanded, and it is likely that Melling had more machine tools available to him at Brickfield than Robert Stephenson & Co. had at Forth Street.[14] The locomotive fleet was completely renewed (1836–1838) with larger six-wheel locomotives, and, under Woods' direction, the first systematic study of fuel consumption and action of steam in the cylinder took place. This was done with the full support of the Board primarily because it offered promised economies in working the line, requiring fewer, larger locomotives (and therefore fewer crews) which were more fuel and steam efficient. Experiments with using coal and anthracite during a period of high coke prices were also supported by the Board to reduce working costs. Finally, with the appointment of John Dewrance in 1840, the L&M found its first true Locomotive Superintendent, and together with Woods saw another complete renewal of the locomotive fleet, first by rebuilding the earlier Melling locomotives to conform with Woods' ideals in valves and valve gear, and secondly the introduction of a standard fleet of locomotives (1842–1845). The standard fleet of Bird class locomotives would have made maintenance and repair considerably easier, and therefore cheaper, through having a standard design and layout, interchangeability of parts, and a single design ethic, rather than having a collection of locomotives built by a variety of builders, which more or less conformed to specifications published by the Company.

Prior to 1836 it would appear that every effort was made to keep the locomotives purchased in 1830 running, even if this meant spending more money repairing and rebuilding them than they had either originally cost, or than buying a replacement locomotive. This policy made perfect sense given the very small number of locomotive building concerns, and those engineering firms which could undertake maintenance and repair work. Indeed the demand for locomotives had resulted in Robert Stephenson establishing with Charles Tayleur of the Vulcan Foundry, and later sub-contracting work to Fenton, Murray & Jackson of Leeds. Disagreements with Edward Bury of Liverpool over the form of firebox and type of frame only resulted in a single locomotive from that firm, but Bury & Co. were still contracted to repair L&M locomotives. Pressure on its own repair facilities lead to the L&M having to out-source overhaul and rebuilding of locomotives, several being sent to engineering firms with little or no locomotive building experience. From the mid-1830s onwards, thanks to a proliferation of locomotive builders, locomotives were built for the cheapest tender (invariably around the £1,000 mark), worked hard and then scrapped after three or four years of work. Woods' policy was one of constant improvement and renewal; together with John Dewrance his policy during the 1840s mirrors that of First Sea Lord Jackie Fisher in 1901: 'Scrap the Lot.'

The L&M had a 'small engine' policy, and showed considerable conservatism in terms of design. Both Henry Booth and Edward Woods stated that train weights were rarely more than 100 tons; Booth preferred to run several lighter trains in close succession after each other rather than double-head, whereas Woods when faced with loads greater than 100 tons resorted to double-heading. Thus, L&M locomotives tended to be small, with low-pressure boilers and small wheels (5 feet). Boiler pressure was no more than 50psi even into the 1840s when other builders, such as Bury, were pushing far higher. The Gauge Commissioners remarked upon the short, light nature of L&M trains in 1845. Failure to adopt higher boiler pressure was a result of 'early adoption':[15] having found a locomotive design in *Planet* (1830) with outside frames, inside cylinders, 5 feet driving wheels, and a 50psi boiler, and other than in size never deviating from that basic design. Despite the high failure rate of crank axles, outside cylinders only ever featured on a single locomotive (*Swiftsure* by Forrester & Co.). Where locomotives did break this mould, such as those by Edward Bury, the Board – no doubt influenced by Henry Booth and the long-shadow of both Stephensons – viewed them with suspicion as being dangerous. Indeed Hardman Earle's comments to Dionysius Lardner in 1833 that *Planet* represented perfection could have been said as late as 1840. There was little room to experiment or deviate from the Stephenson 'norm' established with *Planet*: the 5ft 6in driving wheels of *Leopard* and *Panther* being an unusual innovation; one which was in breach of the Company's own bye-laws, and never repeated. Within the design envelope of a 50psi boiler, outside frames, and 5 foot wheels, there was little room for innovation, other than in improving fuel efficiency both through refinement of valve gear and choice of fuel. John Melling's patent improvements were all directed toward increased efficiency, such as pre-heating the feed water; increasing track adhesion when necessary, and a more user-friendly valve gear. Similarly, Edward Woods' short-stroke engines had been promised to reduce expenditure; his experiments with valve events, and also the coke bonus scheme, lead to considerable cost savings. The innate conservatism of the Board was shown by their response to Dewrance's proposal to increase boiler pressure to 70psi: they were aghast, despite the increased power output and resulting reduced running costs. By 1845 Woods had got his way with increased boiler pressure (70psi), but probably only after amalgamation with the Grand Junction whose engines were working at 70–75psi.

PART 5

ROLLING STOCK

CHAPTER 18

Passenger Carriages

The passenger carriages were designed by the father-and-son team of Thomas Clarke Worsdell II (1788–1862) and Nathaniel Worsdell (1809–1866); Thomas Clarke had been appointed as 'Superintendent of the Carriage Department' in 1828 upon the recommendation of their fellow Quaker, James Cropper.[1] Thomas Clarke had moved his family north to Lancaster around 1812 to work for the Quaker coach-builder Jonathan Dunn, to whom Nathaniel was articled; Dunn later moved over to building railway coaches, supplying four for the North Union Railway in 1838.[2] George Stephenson referred to Thomas Clarke as 'the best coachmaker I ever knew' and according to Nathaniel in his old age:

'In 1828 ... I and my father in consultation with George Stephenson ... planned the first railway carriage ... Stephenson produced a sketch of what he thought might possibly do for a railway carriage. My father and I being practical coachbuilders ... we suggested certain improvements ... the first carriage that ever travelled between Manchester and Liverpool was built from that sketch.'[3]

Early carriages

The earliest carriages involved various experimental prototypes, but generally fall into three types: fully-enclosed 'yellow' or 'glass' coaches, of which one variation had a fully-glazed central compartment whilst the end compartments were closed with leather curtains; open (later semi-open) second-class 'blue coaches'; and the

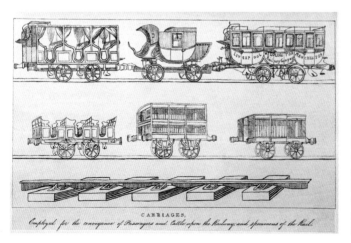

CARRIAGES,
Employed for the conveyance of Passengers and Cattle upon the Railway; and specimens of the Rail.

A lithograph by Crane showing early rolling stock, depicting L-R, a second-class coach with roof and curtains; Lacey & Allen's road-rail carriage; a fully enclosed 'glass coach.' In the second row is an open second-class coach with turn-over tramcar type seats; a double-decker sheep waggon and a pig waggon. That the sleeper blocks were square-on rather than diagonal is confirmed through surviving blocks. (Liverpool & Manchester Railway Trust) 'four-inside' Mail coaches. Due to the Liverpool & Manchester Act stating that no loaded rail vehicle was to weigh more than four tons, these carriages were exceptionally light, and as a result perhaps somewhat flimsy. It was estimated that twelve adult passengers constituted one ton; and with a weight limit of 60lbs of luggage per passenger (equating to ½ton) a fully-laden first-class coach probably weighed in at 4 tons. The Chevalier de Pambour notes in 1834 that a first-class carriage weighed 3.65 tons; second-class 2.23 tons and a Mail 2.71 tons. By 1845 Edward Woods described carriages as being marginally heavier, with a first-class weighing 4 tons 7 cwt, and a second-class 3 tons 16cwt.

First class and mail

There are no known working drawings for Liverpool & Manchester carriage stock. One contemporary description notes the bodies of a first-class coach as only 14 feet long with a maximum width of 7 feet (probably including door and commode handles, suggesting a body width of around 6ft 6in).[4] The model of the first-class coach *Experience* made in 1911 (which replaced Nathaniel Worsdell's original model of c.1838 that was lost in a fire in Brussels in 1910) suggests a body length for a first-class coach of 15 feet 6 inches. Worsdell's original model was built as a specimen or 'model' carriage for the London & Birmingham Railway, who offered him £200 for it. This was a third-scale model, and was 6 feet long overall suggesting a length of 18 feet over buffers. The replica first-class coaches built by the LMS at Derby in 1929–1930, built with reference to the 1911 drawings and replacement model, are 15 feet 6 inches long over head-stocks and 6 feet 7 inches wide; the bodies are 5 feet 6 inches high with a maximum width of 6 feet 6 inches. They are 18 feet 8 inches over the buffers.[5] A body length of 15 feet 6 inches is also suggested by the carriages of the London & Birmingham Railway which were built with reference to those of the L&M.[6] The semi-open second-class carriages depicted by S. C. Brees and Francis Whishaw on the London & Birmingham Railway are shorter than the first-class coaches, only 13 feet long, which, if based on earlier L&M practice, would also account for L&M second-class carriages being considerably lighter than the enclosed first-class. The replica second-class L&M vehicles share a common underframe with the firsts, are standing-only (despite the L&M never having standing-only passenger accommodation), and are probably based on the long print by Rudolph Ackermann rather than any known contemporary model or technical drawing. Indeed, *The Engineer* noted their unreliability in November 1930, through lack of seats and third-class designation. They probably tell us more about the 1930s idea of 1830s travel than 1830s sources and are best treated as unreliable.[7]

Three types of underframes are depicted in the period 1830–1831 by contemporary artists:

Solid timber with inside bearings, the bodies between the wheels (Crane; Austen; Baird Colyer)

Solid timber with outside bearings, the bodies above the wheels (Colyer)

An open frame work, with outside bearings and bodies above the wheels (Ackermann; Shaw)

Variations on a theme: enclosed 'glass' or 'yellow' coaches as depicted by Ackermann (top left and right) with outside bearings; and by T. T. Bury with inside bearings (bottom left) and a 'curtain coach', the central compartment of which was glazed, the two other compartments having leather curtains (bottom right). (Anthony Dawson collection)

Two lithographs by Henry Austen (one of *Planet* and a train of carriages; the second 'Sketch of the carriages') show outside wheels/inside bearings for the first-class carriages, but details of the underframe are not clear. His shading implies that the carriage sides bowed out slightly in stage coach fashion, the wheels being placed under the middle pair of seats. Colyer in his lithograph of *Caledonian* shows similar carriages with the addition of a splasher over the wheels and stirrup-shaped steps, whilst his depiction of Parkside shows outside bearings but in both instances a solid timber frame. Those carriages with outside wheels/inside bearings must have had correspondingly narrow bodies probably little over 4 feet wide. It is also likely that the 'four inside' carriages, which were all converted to Mail coaches (below) had narrow bodies also, a tradition which perhaps persisted with later Mail coaches. The patent Mail coach of Nathaniel Wordsell (which was also *coupé*-ended and sat 'four inside') had a narrow body, so too those of the Grand Junction. Queen Adelaide's saloon also has a narrow body.

The most familiar Underframe is that depicted by Ackermann, with an open framework supported by brackets and with outside bearings. This design of underframe was principally designed to save weight, to keep the vehicles below the 4 ton maximum stipulation of the Liverpool & Manchester Act, despite it being considered 'dead letter' very soon after. It was finally repealed in summer 1842.[8] Weight would also have been saved by cladding the sides with *papier-mâché*, as evidenced on the preserved Manchester & Birmingham Coach at the Science & Industry Museum, Manchester, and on Queen Adelaide's saloon at the National Railway Museum, York.[9]

The most usual description of the first-class coaches is by comparison with contemporary road-vehicles; the three-compartment 'glass coaches' being invariably likened to French *Diligences*. A *Diligence* was a large, three-compartment road coach with two full compartments and a *coupé* at the leading end, a design reminiscent of later railway Mail coaches. A *Diligence* had space for luggage on the roof, along with the *Impériale* or mail-box, and one or two passengers on the box with the driver. They were painted chrome yellow and black; yellow being the colour of the fastest 'crack' stage coaches and also the traditional colour of the French post office and its mail coaches. Yellow was also a colour associated with speed, so it is little wonder that the L&M adopted the same colour scheme. Whereas a stage-coach or *Diligence* body was carried between their wheels and thus restricted in terms of width, the body of railway carriages was carried over the wheels meaning that they were more spacious, something which was agreed upon by many commentators. The degree of extra room compared to a road coach is one of the most frequently remarked upon descriptions of these carriages. This is not surprising, given how the comfort, build quality and safety of stage-coaches were then being hotly debated, and that the railway was marketing itself as being superior to road travel in terms of speed, comfort and safety.[10] Each compartment sat six, making a total of eighteen passengers per coach. The contemporary press described the interior:

'The seats which accommodate three persons each are at least twice as wide as a four-inside stage-coach, so as to allow the same space for three as is now allotted to four.' [11]

The windows were plate glass, and 'were so constructed that the glass in the coach doors and at the sides will slide down, so as to leave them as open and as airy' as a second-class but 'far more comfortable.' The 1911 LNWR-built model of *Experience* also shares this feature, with all the windows being drop-lights. Lamps were hung on the outside at night.[12] An experiment took place in 1834 to light the carriages with 'portable gas', the equipment being supplied by Mr Taylor of the Manchester Gas Works at the suggestion of Daniel Hodgson, one of the Directors. Two gas lamps were used, each housed in a frosted glass shade 10 inches in diameter. One lamp was mounted in the partition between the first and second compartment, so as to light both, and the second lamp mounted in the end wall of the carriage to light the third compartment and illuminate the guard. They gave sufficient light 'to enable any person to read the smallest print.'[13]

The *coupé*-ended vehicles had a central compartment which sat six but with two half compartments or *coupés* (literally meaning cut off) at each end, sitting three, with each end being fully glazed:

'The Steam Carriages vary in their size and plan; some are intended to accommodate four persons in each body, and others six; and some have a central compartment which will contain six persons, with seats before and behind, and two other compartments, one in front and one in rear, each of them resembling a post-chaise, with windows in front, containing only three persons. The seats which accommodate three persons are at least as wide as a four inside stage coach... Between each sitting is a rest for the arms, and each passenger has a cushion to himself; there is also a little projection against which he may rest his head; and the backs are covered and padded'[14]

Three replica first class 'glass coaches' were built by the LMS at Derby in 1930 for the Railway Centenary. They were built using second-hand materials, inspired by the 1911 LNWR model of Worsdell's *Experience*. They provide an excellent impression of the 'elegant discomfort' of first-class travellers in the 1830s.(Lauren Jaye Gradwell)

James Scott Walker waxed lyrical:

> 'The most costly and elegant contain three apartments, and resemble the body
> of a coach (in the middle) and two chaises, one at each end, the whole joined
> together. [They are] handsome and commodious coaches, all of which are hung
> on springs, and run each on four equally sized wheels.'[15]

The 'standard' first-class coach had three compartments, each sitting six, as one early
traveller wrote in September 1830:

> 'The carriages which consisted of … three bodies, similar in interior arrangements
> to the French diligence, lined and fitted up in the most airy and elegant manner, and
> constructed with reference to the unobstructed view of passengers whilst on the road.'[16]

Worsdell's original model shows that the upholstery reached to head-height only,
whilst the 1911 model and the 1930 replicas are upholstered to the height of the
ceiling. The 'second generation' of coaches delivered by Melling & Co. had 'Among
the contrivances which tend to augment the comfort of the passengers, we would
particularly mention the additional elbows at the sides and in the lining of the lights
and doors in French grey cloth.' In other words there were additional arm rests and the
sides and internal face of the doors were lined with cloth, suggesting that the previous
coaches lacked both of these details.[17] Each first-class coach was individually named
and a list of 34 has been reconstructed. Mail coaches were not named.

The L&M ran five Mail coaches: four were conversions from 'four inside' first-class
coaches, whilst the fifth was a new-build. They were painted 'scarlet lake' with black
upper panels; 'the doors decorated with the arms of the four orders of knighthood'
and had long boxes called 'Imperials' (emblazoned with the royal arms) on the roof
to carry the mail and a seat for the Mail Guard perched behind.[18] The Board ordered
in February that 'a Guards' seat be placed behind the 'last carriage of the Train that
Carriage the Mail' suggesting hitherto the Mails were not so fitted. The *Duke of
Wellington* and *Lord Derby* were ordered to be so converted in April 1831; so too
the *Fly* in August 1831, and an anonymous 'yellow coach' which had been damaged
in an accident at Newton in March 1832. A fifth purpose-built Mail was delivered in
1837 from Melling & Co. of Manchester.[19] The *Manchester Guardian* describes how
the central compartment of a Mail coach could be converted into a divan bed:

> 'The backs are taken out of the seats on one side, opening into a sort of boot,
> lined with black leather and cushioned, and are then laid down across the space
> between the back and front seats, into which they fit, thus forming a complete
> bed. The cushions on the opposite side are buttoned up and form a pillow; the legs
> are put into the boot, and the passenger may thus sleep or recline comfortably.'

There were at least four 'curtain coaches' which were used in the summer months;
Queen Adelaide and *Royal William* were ordered to be converted into 'glass coaches'
in January 1832, whilst in March 1833 the leather curtains of *Croxteth* and *Fair
Trader* were ordered to be taken off, and the coaches re-painted and re-varnished.[20]

The Liverpool & Manchester Railway Mail Coaches by Ackermann. Note they show the use of solid and 'open' frames, as well as the use of inside and outside bearings for the wheels. All three agree on the colour scheme (red/black bodies with yellow wheels and underframe) and the carrying of the *Impériale* on the roof. (Anthony Dawson collection)

The curtain coach *Queen Adelaide* is depicted in a print by Crane and again by T. T. Bury.[21] Both Isaac Shaw and Crane show an alternative form of curtain coach, which resembled a second-class *char-à-banc* type vehicle but fitted with a roof and curtains at the side in case of inclement weather. Are these the mysterious 'yellow Open coaches' which were ordered to be attached to first-class trains in the summer months?[22]

One of the more unusual vehicles was the *Chinese* coach which was depicted by Bury, and also appears in his print of Crown Street. The *Chinese* coach had a central entrance on each side, and presumably longitudinal bench seats, the passengers sitting back to back, facing outwards. The body of the carriage narrowed considerably above the waist, with the passengers' legs and feet being accommodated in the wider part of the body. Another unusual, and unique, experimental vehicle was that designed by Lacey & Allen which consisted of a stagecoach body which could be lifted from its road wheels, placed on a set of railway wheels, and back again.[23]

The first-class coaches were painted 'deep chrome yellow' (so somewhat darker than the 'primrose yellow' of the 1930 replicas) and each was individually named. They also carried 'the coats of arms of Liverpool and Manchester on a shield' on the centre door on each side.[24] Chrome yellow can vary from lemon (pale chrome yellow) to rich mustard colour (deep chrome yellow). The shade of yellow would have been darkened again through several coats of turpentine-based varnish, and indeed contemporary painter's manuals note that chrome yellow was 'liable to change' and darken – even turning black – in the presence of

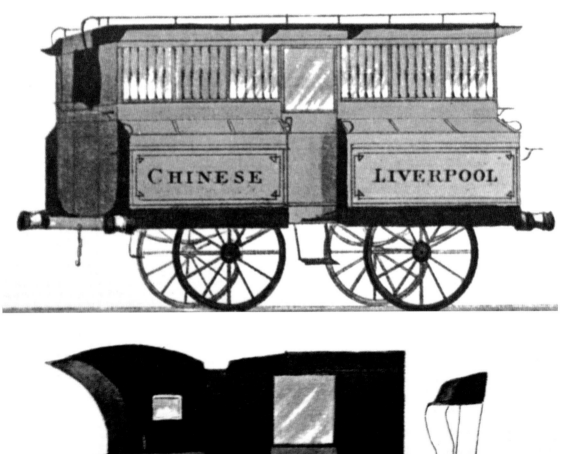

4

Two of the oddest vehicles to run on the L&M were the *Chinese* coach and Lacey & Allen's experimental road-rail carriage which could be lifted from a set of road wheels onto railway wheels and back again. (Anthony Dawson collection)

sulphur, ash and moisture (all of which would be emitted from a locomotive chimney) so was perhaps not ideal for a railway carriage.[25] Worsdell's original model has a quite simple yellow and black livery with the name of the company in Times New Roman lettering in black, with the name of the carriage also in black. The 1911 model, and indeed 1930s replicas, have the name in gold leaf; the latter also have a far more ornate paint scheme. But, for all their splendour, thanks to the effects of the pollutants from a locomotive chimney reacting with the varnish and the type of paint used, they may not have retained their pristine finish for long; Worsdell was several times instructed by the Board to keep on top of the cleaning of the carriages (inside and out) and to take on extra men to help do so.[26] The *Marquis of Stafford* was re-painted and the interior re-upholstered in September 1833.[27]

Second-class

It would appear it took some time for a working design of second-class carriage to evolve. Whilst Worsdell and his team at Crown Street had contemporary road coaches, especially the French *Diligence*, upon which to base their enclosed 'glass coaches', due to the expensive nature of travel there were fewer contemporary vehicles upon which to take inspiration from for the less well-off, other than the old-fashioned 'long coach', 'Irish cars' and '*chars-à-bancs.*' Some of the early second-class carriages were clearly experimental and built with reference to contemporary road vehicles. The *Liverpool Albion* (20 July 1829), and others, whilst recording a recognisable three-compartment first-class carriage, some of the second-class vehicles are less familiar. Of these experimental prototypes, the first example was based on an 'Irish car':

> 'Without any covering overhead, the passengers sit in two rows, (parallel with the road), back to back, a common rail serving for a support to their backs, and their feet resting on foot-boards, in the manner of a double Irish car, the four wheels being under the seats.'

An 'Irish car' alias 'Bianconi Car' was a horse-drawn road vehicle developed by Charles Bianconi (1786–1875), who established the first public transport system in Ireland. Passengers sat on longitudinal benches, back to back, facing outwards, with luggage often piled in the gap between the benches.[28]

A second example was more familiar, being akin to a 'block of church pews' with turn-over seats, without any doors but 'boxed in at the front and back, with panelled work' surmounted by an iron rail. The third experimental vehicle was a composite of some sort, rather like the 'long coaches' used on the roads:

> 'On the outside of the body, and overhanging the wheels, are seats for outside passengers, who will sit sidewise, in the Irish car fashion, with a projecting roof over their heads. This coach will carry sixteen inside and sixteen outside passengers.'

From this description it appears that there was a long, narrow, compartment for 'inside' passengers who sat on longitudinal benches eight per side facing inwards. Benches were mounted on the outside of the body, with the eight passengers sitting facing outward. Presumably access to the compartment was via end doors. It is unclear whether this unusual vehicle was ever more than a one-off demonstrator.

One of the most common descriptions of second-class carriages is of them resembling church pews, panelled and 'railed around', and with turnover seats 'so that the passengers may face which way they please, and the machine never requires to be turned around.' Contemporary prints show them with elaborate wrought iron work arm rests. Ackermann also shows carriages of *char-à-banc* type, both with and without roof, and Fanny Kemble also describes them: 'A long-bodied vehicle with seats placed across it back to back; the one we were in had six of these benches, and it was a sort of uncovered *char-à-banc*.' A second variation had doors in the centre, and longitudinal bench seats, the passengers sitting on benches, facing each other in each compartment, an arrangement similar to a contemporary wagonette. Wagonettes were small, completely open passenger-carrying road vehicles with longitudinal, inward-facing benches. Carriages of this type are depicted in the well-known Ackermann long prints, and a similar vehicle was depicted by Dempsey as late as 1855 as a third-class carriage.[29]

The most well-known second-class coaches are those depicted by Ackermann (both with and without roofs) and which probably formed the basis for replicas built in 1930 to accompany *Lion*, and which sat eight persons per compartment. The *Liverpool Mercury* describes the second-class carriages as having transverse bench seats and:

'About as high as a common cart, and having four or six rows of seats, under which there are receptacles for the luggage; the passengers on these conveyances

A variety of second-class carriages were in use in the early days of the L&M: the most familiar being those 'resembling a block of church pews' both with and without canopies (bottom L and R). Top left has a body style resembling a contemporary wagonette whilst its companion resembles a *char-à-banc* with benches in rows. (Anthony Dawson collection)

will not be nearly so elevated, nor so much exposed to the danger of falling off, as the outside passengers on a stagecoach.'[30]

That luggage was carried in boots formed underneath the bench seats is confirmed by one traveller writing in October 1830 and by a drawing sent by George Stephenson to the Boston & Lowell Rail Road in 1835; a practice continued by the GJR and London & Birmingham in their seconds.[31] Henry Austen shows a similar carriage in use in 1832, and fitted with a roof. Following the receipt of several complaints that falling cinders burnt passenger's clothing, roofs were ordered to be fitted to second-class carriages in August 1831. Whishaw describes them as having roofs and 'open at each side, but closed at the ends', an observation confirmed by Booth in 1842:

> 'Second class coaches are composed of three compartments, the seats being arranged as in first class carriages. They are roofed, and boarded-up close at each end; and at the sides are closed as high as the elbows; and they have buffers and draw springs, the same as on first class carriages.'[32]

Unfortunately the 1930 replicas – described at the time as third-class – are standing-only, despite the Liverpool & Manchester never having used such crude accommodation and therefore do not provide a wholly accurate depiction of second-class travel. The sides are also far too tall, hardly the 'panelled up to the elbow' of a seated passenger and the lack of seats means there is no luggage provision. The replica second-class coaches at the Science & Industry Museum, Manchester, were built according to drawings in Nicholas Wood's *Treatise* and are thus perhaps more representative of early 1830s second-class carriages, although they lack the boots formed under the seats.[33] The second-class carriages were painted a colour described as 'waggon blue' or 'cart blue.' This shade was

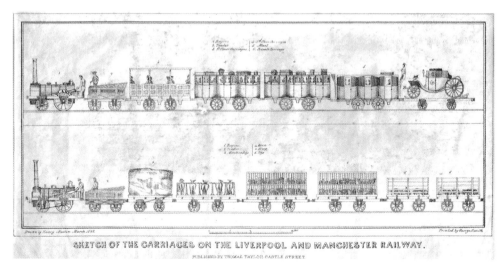

A measured and scale drawing of Liverpool & Manchester Rolling Stock by Henry Austen dated March 1832. Note the use of inside and outside bearings for passenger carriages. The wheelbase scales at only 5 feet with bodies 16 feet long. Goods waggons have the same short wheelbase and measure 10 feet long. The three larger cattle waggons scale at 15 feet. (Anthony Dawson collection)

A near contemporary drawing of a second-class coach, reputedly by George Stephenson, dated 1835. Although roofless, it has seats with luggage stowed in 'boots' formed beneath the seats. Neither the buffers nor draw-hook appear to be sprung. (Anthony Dawson collection)

One of the three replica open carriages built at Derby in 1930. They are inaccurate in many respects, particularly being standing only and denominated third-class. (Matthew Jackson)

mixed up from ultramarine and black, so was quite a deep, strong shade of blue quite unlike the blueish-grey of the 1930 replicas. However, a cheaper version of this paint could be made using synthetic ultramarine (invented in 1828 using a mixture of soda ash, charcoal and sulphur) which tended toward 'a pale greyish blue tint'. Unlike the chrome yellow of the first-class coaches, 'waggon blue' was very hard-wearing and 'not liable to change' in the presence of the various pollutants, especially sulphides, from a locomotive chimney. Internally they were painted 'drab', a dull pale brown or buff, and varnished.

These semi-open vehicles remained in use into the 1840s, by which point they were increasingly old-fashioned and crude compared to the enclosed seconds run by the Grand Junction or Manchester & Leeds. It was only in April 1844 that the Management Committee 'took into consideration the expediency of improving the 2nd Class Carriages' through the addition of 'windows and closed sides.' Instead, however new enclosed second-class carriages were ordered and the existing stock downgraded to third-class. During the first half of 1845 some £1700 was spent on new carriages. It is unclear what these new second-class carriages looked like, but by November 1845 the Company possessed 34 second-class and 61 third-class carriages, the latter presumably being the old, down-graded, second-class.[34]

Buffers, brakes, and wheels

Buffing gear was initially supplied for the first-class coaches only, consisting of a 'strong leather muffler'; this consisted of a leather tube stuffed with horse hair containing a coil spring to absorb some of the shock. They were apparently only provided for first-class carriages, as in his evidence to a Parliamentary Select Committee in 1841 Henry Booth admits that for the first two years sprung buffing gear was not in use on second class carriages, leading to a very uncomfortable ride. Each carriage was coupled by chains, the draw-gear being initially unsprung. The 'Stephenson' drawing of a second-class carriage shows a forged round iron draw-bar running longitudinally through the entire length of the carriage to which the coupling chain was secured, flanked by safety-chains. The wheels are sprung and have outside bearings, the axle boxes and guard irons being similar to those on the replica *Rocket*.[35] Booth notes in an accident report that the carriages were coupled by three rows of chains, which meant in case of a derailment the carriages would not topple over.[36] By 1833 (if not earlier) the first class coaches had been fitted with sprung draw-gear and buffers, as in that year it was ordered that the second-class coaches be so fitted as well.[37] This sprung buffing and draw-gear, and three link screw-coupling, was patented by Henry Booth in January 1836, although this was apparently a refinement of a design of Thomas Worsdell, and the contemporary press thought 'The buffer work underneath is very ingenious, and does great credit to the inventors, Mr Henry Booth and Mr John Gray' tending toward increased safety and comfort.[38]

Thomas Bergin (of the Dublin & Kingstown Railway) observed the behaviour of the L&M carriages and buffing gear which led him to develop his own system of buffing gear which he patented in March 1835.[39] This, together with criticism of Booth's buffing gear by the *Mechanics' Magazine* – and its high praise of Bergin's system – led to the Board seeking the opinion of 'Mr [John] Dixon, the Company's engineer, and some of our practical Mechanics, on the subject.' Whilst Hardman Earle was in favour of Bergin's system because of its simplicity and low cost, Dixon was opposed to it. So too Henry

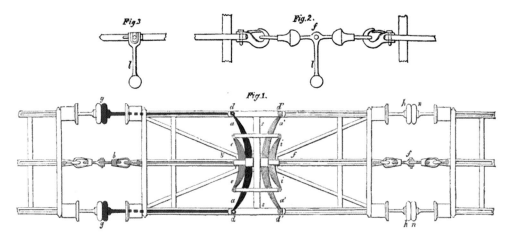

Henry Booth's patent buffing- and draw-gear of 1836 which was adopted for first- and second-class carriages. Springing was provided using elliptical leaf springs and a complicated system of rods: buffers (red) and draw-hook (blue). Booth is also credited with the invention of the three-link screw-coupling. (Andrew Mason)

Booth who wrote his own reply to the *Mechanics' Magazine* in November 1835 giving a detailed criticism of Bergin's buffer. Booth had provided a pair of sprung buffers and a sprung draw-hook, using a complicated system of rods and leaf springs; Bergin used a single, central buffer-cum-coupling using a coil rather than leaf spring. Booth thought that this system was unsafe in case of collision; it was not safe to propel a train; it was difficult to fit to locomotives and their tenders. Furthermore, whilst Booth's more complicated arrangement cost £20 per vehicle, Bergin's cost £26, excluding a £10 patent fee. The L&M Board finally approved the use of Booth's buffing and draw-gear on 13 March 1837 (although it had been use on first-class carriages for four years), which was ordered to be fitted to 'all Engines and Carriages … for the use of the Liverpool & Manchester Railway'. The Board also ruled it must be fitted to those carriages on hire to the Company and those of other companies who wished to run over L&M metals. The Board voted Booth a handsome purse of 150 guineas for the 'free use' of the patent.[40]

The ash or oak frames were formed from an 'open' or 'double frame' secured by wrought-iron brackets. Joseph Locke was critical of the 'double frame'. He thought the design was insubstantial; they often shook themselves apart; and in the case of accident were more liable to break-up than a carriage with a solid underframe. The contemporary press agreed: L&M carriages were 'too slightly built' and not strong enough to resist impact damage in the case of a collision. The use of the 'double frame', however, allowed for the use of Booth's patent buffing- and draw-gear and its complicated system of rods and leaf springs below the carriage floor. One report noted that the 'double frame' was 'for the purpose of applying buffer apparatus' and therefore introduced with Henry Booth's buffing gear.[41]

Brakes were an 'optional extra' fitted 'in the proportion of two out of every five' so that the front and rear vehicle of a train of five carriages had brakes, each manned by a guard perched on his roof seat. In September 1840 the Directors ordered the number of brakes increased so that 'one half the number of coaches composing any train shall be supplied with Breaks of the best-construction, and made to the satisfaction of the Company.' The resolution was to be issued to other companies running trains on L&M metals for them to comply.[42]

First- and second-class vehicles were fully sprung; the *Liverpool Albion* refers to the first-class coaches having elliptical 'grasshopper springs' and the Ackermann long prints show the use of leaf springs mounted beneath the frames. Wheels were at first cast iron with wrought-iron tyres, but following a series of breakages, were later changed to having a cast iron hub with ash spokes and elm felloes and wrought iron tyre which included the flange. They also gave a quieter ride and 3 feet diameter wooden wheels were purchased from Stephenson & Co., presumably for carriages. By November 1833 iron wheels with wrought iron tyres are mentioned but Worsdell's model has wooden spokes and felloes.[43]

Carriage builders

Carriages were built 'in-house' at Crown Street construction beginning in 1828. In August 1828 Thomas Lowe of Birmingham was paid £18 14s 3d for 'brass coach furniture'; William Barton £10 17s 6d for 'coach fringe'; John Williams & Co for 'broadcloth for Coach Linings' (£6 10s 6d). Ash timber for coach bodies was had from W. B Harrop. The Company had 33 passenger carriages in operation on opening day (15 September 1830) which included the three special vehicles for the Duke of Wellington and other VIPs. This initial stock was obviously insufficient as Worsdell was ordered by the Board on 27 September 1830 to 'take measures for building more Coaches, as on consideration, they may deem most expedient.' Worsdell's team was not necessarily always able to cope; in June 1831 two first class coach bodies (*London* and *Auxillium*) were supplied by Lacey & Allen of Manchester for a total cost of £456 10s 6d. The underframe was to be supplied by the Company.[44] Five more first class bodies were supplied by Liverpool coach makers. John Gorst delivered two costing £210, so too Richard R Jones for the same price in February 1831. A fifth first class body was supplied by John R Johnson of Torbock Street, Liverpool in March 1831 costing £210 8s 6d of which £190 had already been 'paid on account.' In December 1831, Worsdell was ordered to build '3 or 4 additional First Class Coaches – to be ready for the next season' and two more were to be put in hand in January 1832. Another was ordered in September 1833.[45] Evidence of coach building comes from the minutes of the Finance Committee: payments were made for both oak and ash timber and William Barton of Manchester was paid for 'Coach Lace' costing between £14 15s 3d and £17 4s 4d between April 1830 and March 1831. Messrs. T & R Williamson of Ripon were paid for 'coach varnish' (£14 9s 3d) in January 1831; Thomas Rowly & Son for 'coach lamps' (£6 2s 8d) and Wilson & Foster for 'curtains for coaches' (£33 15s). Samuel Sykes supplied drab cloth for coaches costing £21 5s in December 1829. Thomas & Henry Porter supplied paint (£17 19s). Iron castings including wheels and steps were supplied by John Bates and 'steel for springs' from William Hunt & Son of Oldbury. Old carriages were either broken up for such materials as could be re-used, or sold: ten passed to the North Shields Railway for £1,105 in April 1839, and others were sold to the North Union Railway or St Helens Railway for £100 to £125 each.

In September 1836 it was resolved to approach the long-established coach builder Richard Melling of Chorlton on Medlock, Manchester,[46] to build six first-class and one Mail coach because the Company carriage works were at capacity. These coaches were named: *Stanley, Melbourne, Duchess of Kent, Zephyra, Sylph* and *Ariel*. Upon delivery they were described as 'far superior' to Company-built carriages. The French-grey upholstery was carried 'to a considerable height above the seats', included padded head-rests and arm-rests and the carriage sides and doors were also upholstered. The Manchester press had long been a critic of the L&M passenger accommodation, especially its second-class carriages, describing them as little better than pig pens; one disgruntled passenger referred to them as 'travelling pneumonia waggons'. Seconds, from their lighter construction, were also thought to be more liable to break-up in the case of an accident. Having travelled many miles as a Guard on the railway at the Science & Industry Museum in the replica second-class coaches, the author can personally vouch for them being cold, wet and miserable in anything other than bright sunshine.[47]

With the opening of Lime Street, a new carriage works costing £3,176 was ordered to be built at Liverpool; Whishaw toured it in 1839, describing it as being of two storeys with 'four lines of way, extending from end to end of the ground-floor.' By the use of trapdoors in the floor above 'the bodies and other parts of carriages' were easily raised from their underframes into the workshops above. There was a certain amount of controversy associated with the building of the carriage works; despite Messrs. John Kilsham offering the lowest tender, the contract was awarded to Messrs. Samuel & James Holmes. Messrs. Kilsham wrote in protest, but the Board replied that that firm had previously carried out work for the Company but had not 'executed [them] satisfactorily.'[48] Thomas Clarke Worsdell handed in his notice in January 1837 and John Pownall was appointed as 'Superintendent of the Coach Building and Repair Shops' a month later. Pownall had previously been a journeyman for Henry Whalley, a local coachbuilder. Thomas Clarke Worsdell moved to Germany to superintend the locomotives and rolling stock of the Leipzig and Dresden Railway, whilst Nathaniel took employment with the Grand Junction Railway.[49] This employment was only short-lived as both Thomas Clarke and Nathaniel Worsdell were invited by the Manchester & Leeds Railway to submit designs for rolling stock in October 1838, and in November 1838 Thomas Clarke was appointed as 'inspector of the carriage department' of the M&L, with Nathaniel being employed in an advisory capacity.[50]

As in other areas, the L&M provided technical expertise through the sharing of ideas or personnel for carriage building. The little Leeds & Selby Railway had initially ordered a very mixed-bag of passenger carriages, including some designs where the 'outside' passengers quite literally sat outside on the roof, despite the presence of numerous road bridges over the line! Advice was sought from the L&M for carriage designs, and with the appointment of William Williams as Superintendent, the L&S approached Beeston & Melling, alias Richard Melling & Co., of Manchester to build first- and second-class coaches, to the same design as those built for the L&M and at the same cost of £210 for a first-class carriage and £85 for a second-class. They were painted yellow and black (first) and green (second) respectively green being thought to be more handsome than the 'cart' or 'waggon blue' of the L&M; the firsts were lined in drab broadcloth and had plate-glass windows. The demand for railway carriages is shown by the fact that other coach builders, such as William Carr of Deansgate,

Manchester, and Unsworth of Liverpool also entered the trade.[51] It is unsurprising that there was a family resemblance between early Grand Junction carriages and L&M vehicles given the role the Worsdells played with both companies; the contemporary press thought the GJR carriages, particularly the second-class, far superior to those of the L&M. The London & Birmingham had also studied the rolling stock of the L&M in order to design its own passenger carrying vehicles.[52]

Table 9: Known first-class coaches 1830–1845

Ariel	Melling & Co, 1837
Aurora	
Auxilium	Lacey & Allen, 1831
Clarence	
Conservative	
Croxteth	Curtain coach; converted to glass coach 1833
Delight	
Despatch	
Duchess of Kent	Melling & Co, 1837
Duke of Wellington aka *Lord Wellington*	'four inside', converted to Mail 1831
Earl of Wilton	
Experience	
Fair Trader	Curtain coach; converted to glass coach 1833
Fly	'four inside', converted to Mail 1831
Greyhound	
Harlequin	
Huskisson	
London	Lacey & Allen, 1831
Lord Derby	'four inside', converted to Mail 1831
Marquis of Stafford	
Melbourne	Melling & Co, 1837
Queen Adelaide	Curtain coach, converted to glass coach 1832
Reformer	
Royal William	Curtain coach, converted to glass coach 1832
Sir Robert Peel	
Stanley	Melling & Co, 1837
Sovereign	
Sylph	Melling & Co, 1837
The Lark	
The Times	
Treasurer	
Velocipede	
Victory aka *Victoria*	
Zephyra	Melling & Co, 1837

CHAPTER 19

Goods Stock

By far the largest amount of rolling stock belonging to the Company were merchandize, aka luggage, waggons; some 200 had been ordered to be constructed in June 1828. The Board ordered in May 1830 that every waggon and passenger carriage was to have springs, and every waggon was to have a brake, and any company which wished to run their rolling stock over the L&M would have to comply. In February 1833 an audit was made showing there were 301 waggons, but 'the highest painted number was 312'. This was probably because three waggons had been destroyed by fire and others 'so thoroughly repaired after breakages as to be numbered afresh as new.'[1] The Directors ordered a further fifty new goods waggons, in two batches: the first a batch of twenty, and the second a batch of thirty in December 1833 as the existing stock was thought to be insufficient.[2] A further fifty new goods waggons were ordered in November 1835.[3] Whishaw notes in November 1839 there were 428 'waggons and trucks' with cast-iron wheels and wrought-iron tyres, and in 1844 Edward Woods states the line had 516 goods waggons, three horse boxes and six carriage trucks.[4] The owners of merchandize waggons were responsible for the accurate weighing of their loads carried, and any discrepancy meant a possible fine of as much as 40s per ton; the Company also had the right to weigh all waggons and their loads. Furthermore every waggon or carriage which was used on the railway had to be approved by the Board before it could be run on the L&M and also was to be individually named and/or numbered, in white letters ('Two Inches high at least') on a black background on 'some conspicuous Part of the Outside every such Waggon'; the weight and gauge of each vehicle also being so recorded. Failure to comply could result in a maximum fine of 40s. No loaded waggon or carriage was to weigh more than 4 tons.

Merchandise waggons

Goods vehicles were simple four-wheeled platform waggons. The cast-iron wheels were 3 feet diameter and were all sprung. Nicholas Woods describes one example in 1838 as being approximately 14 feet long overall, 'with a superficial surface of platform area of seventy-five square feet' being able to carry 'a considerable quantity of light goods', usually 'about four tons weight.'[5] Henry Booth notes in 1841 they had dumb-buffers and three coupling chains. Four years later Edward Woods describes the platform as being 13 feet long and 7 feet 9 inches wide 'about 100 square feet platform.' They had a short wheel-base, and loose sides measuring 'perhaps two feet high' could be fitted so that they could be used to carry coal.[6] Sundry 'axle shafts, Oak timbers, &c.' for building goods waggons were purchased in May 1831.[7] Cast iron wagon wheels, and wrought iron axles were supplied by a variety of outside contractors, including Edward

General Merchandise Waggons were small platform waggons which could be fitted with low sides or crib rails. They were used for a variety of loads, the loads being secured with rope and tarpaulins. (Anthony Dawson collection)

Bury and Foster & Griffn of Liverpool; Parkinson & Waddington of Bradford; Robert Stephenson & Co of Newcastle, and the Bedlington Iron Works. There was obviously a problem with waggon wheels and axles ordered from the Bedlington iron works, as Stephenson reported to the Management Committee in October 1831 that there were twenty-eight iron waggon wheels with broken tyres and twelve with broken spokes. He recommended that the Company held back half the 'invoice price' for them.[8]

With the opening of the Manchester & Leeds in 1844, goods waggons were 'run through' from Liverpool to Leeds and back to avoid transhipment of goods. But the M&L vehicles had a longer-wheel base which presented many problems:

> '[The Leeds waggons were] longer between the wheels than ours, and they would not turn on our turn-tables at the station at Wapping; they were therefore stopped at Manchester and [the cargo] loaded on Manchester waggons; but there was immense inconvenience.'[9]

The L&M was therefore obliged to 'refuse goods' going through to Liverpool from Leeds (and vice versa), and instead they were sent by water presenting a considerable loss of revenue. The M&L had proposed building a number of goods vehicles to L&M specifications, but 'the demands upon them were so great from the increase of the traffic that they were not able to meet their engagement.' Ultimately, the L&M installed larger turn-tables enabling them to handle the longer M&L waggons, and furthermore, adopted the larger M&L style waggons which were thought to be 'better adapted to the trade.'[10] Henry Henson, who was in charge of the rolling stock workshops of the London & Birmingham Railway at Camden from 1841–1847 and later head of the LNWR Carriage Department (March 1847–1855), described early goods vehicles as weighing about 2 to 2½ tons, and costing about £65 each including wheels. They were:

'Nothing more than a platform upon wheels, about 10 feet long, with sides varying from four to ten inches high above the floor level. Indeed, many of them are still employed, and for certain portions of traffic, such as minerals, casks, ... sundries, they were as well adapted as they are unfit, unprofitable and dangerous if employed in the conveyance of merchandise generally ... The addition of portable sides and ends, which were merely portable open crib-rails, dropped in staples at the sides and ends ... and secured at the corners by hooks and eyes. To this slight improvement was soon added the worst evil of all, the inflammable and expensive tarpauling, the use of which had involved such costly contingencies. The most striking defect ... is the facility with which large bales fall from the trucks ... whereby numerous accidents have arisen. In shunting and starting the train, it is clearly impossible that the goods can keep their position.'[11]

Henson further thought that tarpaulins were more trouble than they were worth, both in keeping them in good repair and the time taken in ensuring they were properly secured. Similarly, he thought the removal 'crib-rails' not only dangerous but equally 'inconvenient' 'from the great labour of taking down and refixing' and the 'trouble of loading and unloading.' All in all the open platform waggon was 'the most imperfect' vehicle, yet even by the early 1850s were still used in large numbers.[12]

Loose goods like corn and grain were loaded into weighed bags – the bags being provided by the Company, rather as the canal carriers did. Andrew Comber, the Goods Agent at Liverpool, was ordered to purchase '500 new corn sacks' in August 1831 'in order to extend the Company's business in corn' but in October of the same year, the Management Committee resolved that they would no longer loan corn sacks to merchants 'at the Manchester end' due to pilferage.[13] In order that they earned revenue, empty coal waggons which were being returned to the various colliery branches along the line were used to convey corn and flour as 'back carriage'. The toll on the carriage of corn and flour from Crown St to St Helens Junction was reduced in April 1833 to 1s 6d per ton.[14]

Coal waggons

The Liverpool & Manchester used two types of coal waggon, which reflected different unloading arrangements at either end of the line due to the specific geography of the dépôts. The waggons used to carry coal to Liverpool each carried two 'loose boxes' which were carried on a 'skeleton waggon.' They were filled at the pit-head and loaded on to the skeleton waggons, and once at the Liverpool coal depot 'would be transferred to Cart Wheels.' The waggons used to carry coal to Manchester, where coal-drops were used to load waiting road carts, had 'bottoms that would open to let out the coals into the stores underneath the railway.'[15] In order to facilitate road/rail transhipment, in November 1829 George Stephenson was instructed to prepare drawings for 'two coal carts as specimens, to receive the loose bodies of the coal Waggons' for the supply of coal around Edge Hill and environs.[16]

The use of different types of coal waggon lead to complaints from various colliery owners, including Mr William Turner esq of Shrigley Hall, on behalf of Thomas Legh MP of Lyme, who enquired 'Whether with the help of cranes to lower the moveable coal Boxes, the same type of waggon might be used at the Manchester Station and Liverpool.'

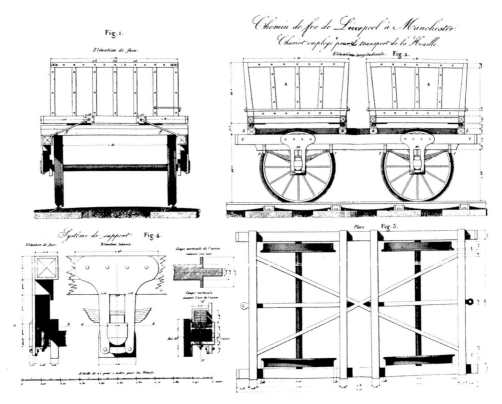

The L&M used two types of coal waggon: the first had a hopper-shaped body and trap-door in the floor to discharge coal. The second type, designed by George Stephenson, used loose coal boxes which were readily interchanged from railway waggons to road carts. (Anthony Dawson collection)

The Management Committee did not think it expedient to do so, due to the 'different levels and different descriptions of coal Depot at the two ends.'[17] The Bolton & Leigh Railway and Messrs. Bourne & Robinson also adopted loose 'coal boxes' which could be lifted on and off 'skeleton waggons.' In October 1831 Bourne & Robinson approached the Management Committee whether, instead of having to purchase additional 'skeleton waggons', the Board would allow them to transport these 'new' boxes on Company cotton waggons, which was declined.[18] Similarly, the Board declined to loan ten cotton waggons to Thomas Legh for the carriage of coal boxes.[19]

From May 1831 the colliery owners themselves were considered responsible for transporting their coal, so the Management Committee began disposing of many of the loose 'coal boxes': Messrs. Smith & Unsworth offered £200 for sixty coal boxes, but the Management Committee declined the offer, as they expected at least £5 per box, which Smith & Unsworth declined to pay.[20] In October 1831, the Management Committee again affirmed that colliery owners 'find their own waggons' and as a result the L&M continued its disposal of old coal waggons. Three old cotton trucks were sold to the Bolton & Leigh Railway for use as coal waggons, and Bourne & Robinson purchased another three 'to convert into coal trucks' (presumably to carry 'coal boxes') at £45 each 'on the same terms as three sold to the Bolton Company.' Another three 'old' cotton trucks were sold to Bourne & Robinson in December to carry coal and a dozen coal boxes for £5 each in August 1831. The Management Committee also agreed to sell them twelve 'skeleton waggons for the moveable boxes.' Bourne & Robinson purchased another three coal waggons in February 1832. Turner & Evans also requested to purchase old coal waggons, whilst John Hargreaves the Lessee of the Bolton & Leigh Railway, noted he would have to build an additional sixty coal waggons as a result of the decision of the Management Committee that colliery owners supply their own locomotives and waggons.[21] Ten coal waggons were loaned to Hargreaves (to tide him over) in January 1832 as ten of his had been smashed in an accident on the Chequerbent Incline.[22] Stephenson reported to the Board in early 1832 that some of the coal proprietors at Manchester were using coal waggons which were 'too heavy & that the wheels were at improper distances from each other.' Upon investigation, it transpired that Thomas Legh had had thirty-six new coal waggons built, but William Allcard reported that they were 'considerably more than the allowed weight of 32cwt' and as a result the Management Committee forbade Legh from running them on L&M tracks.[23]

By 1838 it was reported there were thirty or forty L&M coal waggons on the Bolton & Leigh, and 300 coal waggons working over the L&M to Liverpool or Manchester and that in order to maximise their revenue earning 'we make a double use of them … by filling them with merchandize one way, and coal the other'. Whishaw in November 1839 describes the coal waggons at Manchester as being long and narrow: 10 feet long overall, with a body 3 feet 9 inches wide and 1 foot high carried on cast-iron wheels 3 feet in diameter. They weighed, fully loaded, 5 tons 17 cwt 2qrs.[24]

Cattle waggons and horse boxes

Three types of cattle waggon were in use: those for 'cows' and other 'beasts and large cattle' were a platform waggon, railed around on all four sides with the animals loaded transversely; pigs were carried in a similar but smaller vehicle; whilst sheep were crammed into cruel-looking double-decker waggons. The first sheep waggons were ordered in May 1831, when tenders were advertised for '10 or 15 Sheep Carriages' to a design by John Gray; the Company was to supply the wheels, axles and springs with the bodywork being supplied by contractors.[25] Tenders were received by 1 June from Foster & Stewart, Haigh & Franklin, and H. P. Hughes. It was resolved to order:

   7 carriages from Foster & Stewart
   7 carriages from Haigh & Franklin
   5 carriages from H. P. Hughes
   'The price to be £60 each, delivered.'

Foster & Stewart had previously supplied 27 merchandise waggons costing £486 in October 1830. John Gray also designed the larger cattle waggons, but the first cargo of 'beasts' was carried in December 1831 in old cotton trucks, five per truck presumably because none of the 'large cattle' waggons had yet been delivered.[26] A further dozen pig waggons were ordered in 1832.[27] The sheep waggons were in poor repair by 1834 and

Sheep were carried in double-decker waggons, sometimes with a waterproof tarpaulin thrown over the top. (Anthony Dawson collection)

Pigs and cows were carried in larger, open, waggons; in 1841 the Society for the Prevention of Cruelty to Animals complained about the way the L&M treated animals in its care. (Anthony Dawson collection)

For the wealthiest of travellers their private road coach could be loaded onto a flat 'carriage truck' with their horses travelling in a horse box. Carriage loading docks were provided at Liverpool, Manchester and Newton. Any accompanying servants had to travel in a second-class carriage. (Anthony Dawson collection)

John Dixon was instructed to inspect them as to the 'soundness of the timbers' and ascertain whether they needed re-painting.[28] By 1839 however, the sheep waggons were 'much decayed ... and no longer safe.' Many of the older waggons had been broken up, but the Directors declined to purchase new sheep waggons and instead resolved to use pig waggons instead.[29]

The Company owned at least six horse boxes if not more. One was destroyed whilst transporting an elephant (!) and another damaged by a spooked horse kicking its side out. Ackerman shows horse boxes as being open-sided and carrying two horses, whilst Whishaw describes them as being fully enclosed, measuring 12 feet 3½ inches over the buffers. The body was 9½ feet long, 7 feet 7 inches wide and 7 feet 5 inches high. Access was via flapped side panels.[30]

Private-Owner Waggons

One of the most unusual pieces of rolling stock on the L&M was owned and operated by Messrs. Pickfords. Pickfords began running a daily 'contract waggon' in November 1830 for 'London goods' at 40s per trip, making one trip each way per day, six days a week. This vehicle had a 'moveable body to be transferred to cart wheels at each end of the line', somewhat similar to the road-rail coach body devised by Lacey & Allen of Manchester. It was probably some form of pantechnicon (i.e. box van), perhaps painted blue, and no doubt carried Pickfords' name.[31]

Loads of timber up to 50 feet long were carried on purpose-built bolster wagons. The bolsters were able to swivel 'to allow the waggons to have proper play in going round curves.' The load was secured with chains. Seen here depicted by Ackermann, c.1831.(Anthony Dawson collection)

Conclusion

The Liverpool & Manchester Railway lived up to its unofficial title 'The Grand Experimental Railway', learning from the earlier colliery lines and the Stockton & Darlington to create the first inter-city main line. Nor was the Board afraid to share it's own experiences and lessons learned. This appears to have been a matter of policy set by the Board: Charles Lawrence noted at the General Meeting of 21 January 1835 that the Board were aware that they and their endeavours would inspire 'similar Enterprises' and would be minutely scrutinised. Therefore 'every step ... in their proceedings, whether with reference to the extent of traffic, mechanical improvements ... was interesting, as well as to the Public.' Information was liberally provided to other fledgling railways, both nationally and internationally. Furthermore the Board were not afraid to experiment themselves, and welcomed any suggestion which could improve the operations or efficiency of their railway, but moreover reduce running costs. This is especially true during the first six or so years of the company running trains. Experiments included burning coal and anthracite; various experimental (and often patented) fireboxes; and valve gears which were intended to improve the economy of Stephenson-type locomotive by reducing the fuel bill and making better use of the steam (longer travel valves, expansive working). The weird and wonderful locomotives by Braithwaite and Ericsson, or Galloway & Bowman did little to influence the development of the Stephenson-type locomotive regionally or nationally, and these experimental machines had no effect on the day-to-day operation of the railway in the long term, although the failure of Braithwaite & Ericsson's locomotives delayed the commencement of freight carrying by the L&M. Ultimately, however, there was little scope to innovate within a restrictive design envelope established by the track system and the Stephensons for locomotives and rolling stock. But that is not to say the Board did not welcome innovation; as noted in Part 2, the L&M was open to any suggestion to improve the working of the railway, and treated many inventors and engineers fairly. Whilst the role of Robert Stephenson in the development of the main line locomotive in the crucial period 1830–1833 has often been emphasised, it was men such as John Melling or John Dewrance who had the day-to-day job keeping these early machines in working order so that they could operate the first timetabled passenger and goods service.

The rapid development of a timetabled passenger and goods service demanded a high-level of locomotive reliability, and devoid of any test facilities, the L&M became a locomotive laboratory for Stephenson & Co. with the design team responding to feed-back from men 'on the ground' such as Melling, Dixon or Allcard. The rapid development of the locomotive had perhaps over-taken materials technology, with wheels, axles, boiler tubes and fireboxes being particularly failure-prone and therefore expensive for the end-user. A process of observation and development by John Dixon saw iron boiler tubes replaced first by copper and then brass and the substitution of copper for iron for inner fireboxes. Repeated failure of wheels led to the ultimately successful patent 'gas pipe' wheel and more durable axle designs using better materials.

Despite its success, the L&M suffered from what Rogers has described as 'early adoptionism' – a problem which affects all those innovators who adopt a new technology or ideas. The L&M began life as the vision of a group of imaginative 'Innovators' who are defined by Rogers as belonging to a small, usually well-educated, socially elite and exclusive group of individuals with close contact to sources of scientific progress and innovations; this certainly sums up the L&M Board in terms of social make-up and their relationship with the Stephensons.[1]

Once these 'innovators' had demonstrated the advantages of the railway, and indeed steam power, they took a technological leap forward by adopting steam locomotives to work their railway from the outset (becoming as Rogers terms it 'early adopters'). But, once the new technology had been adopted, they were in turn over-taken by what Rogers describes as the 'early majority' – all those other railways, such as the London & Birmingham or Grand Junction, which were based on detailed study of the L&M, identifying what the L&M did well, did badly, and where improvements could be made, making a leap ahead from the 'early adopters'. The great 'Railway Mania' of the 1840s would be defined by Rogers as the 'late majority' when the ideas and technology proposed by the 'early adopters' became accepted, and adopted by the majority, but only after most of the major problems had been ironed-out. The problem for 'early adopters' was that they were initially 'ahead of the curve' but were now 'behind the curve' of adoption, and often left behind in terms of innovation. Furthermore, whilst initially being 'venturesome', early adopters often acted as 'gate keepers' to further innovation; they had 'put their stamp' on the innovation, with a high degree of 'ownership' and either distrusted, or at least controlled, further innovation. Such a pattern is observable for the Liverpool & Manchester Railway, for example, with regards to emphasising the Stephenson-type locomotive with outside frames, 5 feet diameter wheels, and square fireboxes.[2]

The history of the L&M falls into two distinct phases: the 'experimental' (1830–1838) and the 'mature' (1838–1845), as defined by Henry Booth in 1836, and delineated with the completion of the relaying of the main line with 75lb rails.[3] Indeed, the sentiments expressed by Charles Lawrence in January 1835, when it was felt that the time had come to stop publication of detailed reports for the public and indeed rivals to read, marks the beginning of the end of his 'experimental' phase. Indeed, this first, 'experimental' phase can be equally divided into two sub-phases, a 'pioneer' phase (1830–1833) and 'developmental' (1833–1838), the two being delineated with the appointment of Booth as general superintendent. After 1833 the management of the Company had become settled, so too its mode of operations. The majority of the experimental work in terms of locomotive development (for example) had taken place in that early 'pioneer' phase; such as the controversy surrounding the shape of the firebox and the various one-off experimental locomotives by Braithwaite and Ericsson or Galloway & Bowman.

Whilst there were innovations regarding valves and valve gear, and alternative fuels (for example), this was carried out within a restrictive design envelope, which had been established by the Stephensons: a 50psi boiler; 5 foot driving wheels; and outside sandwich frames. There was little deviation from this norm, because the 'standard' Stephenson locomotive as established by *Planet* in October 1830 demonstrably worked, and any digression from this model was considered to be unsafe, and unproven. Innovation which did take place was to further refine the Stephenson locomotive.

The same is true of passenger rolling stock, the only major innovation being the universal adoption of Booth's sprung buffing- and draw-gear by 1837. It persisted in using short, flat-bed 'platform waggons' for the conveyance of goods and merchandise into the 1840s, despite such waggons having many short-comings, and neighbouring – and connecting railways such as the Manchester & Leeds – having adopted larger vehicles which had necessitated the L&M installing larger waggon turntables, and later building new waggons to conform with the new standard. Similarly, passenger rolling stock had not appreciably evolved; second-class passengers rattled along in semi-open vehicles into the 1840s when lines such as the Grand Junction, London & Birmingham and others had adopted fully-enclosed second-class vehicles. The L&M continued to use very light weight, perhaps insubstantial underframes designed by the Worsdells to overcome a clause of the Liverpool & Manchester Railway Act, but one which was effectively 'dead letter' by the end of the 1830s. This was a form of underframe which Joseph Locke of the GJR, and indeed the Press, had condemned as being prone to breaking-up in the case of an accident. Again, the type and form of passenger carriage had been achieved early-on in the line's history and had failed to evolve until, as with goods waggons, it was influenced by external factors. The upgrading of its own second-class stock, and provision of third-class, came due to pressure from the Manchester & Leeds Railway as well as the Gladstone Act of 1844.

Select Bibliography

1.1 Primary – Archival

Institute of Mechanical Engineers, London
STE/1/5/3 Letters from George and Robert Stephenson, via https://archives.imeche.org/archive/industrial/stephenson/letter-book-1/586534

Liverpool Record Office & Local Studies385 STE 1 - 17 letters and papers of George Stephenson.

National Museums Liverpool
Vulcan Foundry Collection
B/VF/15/1/9 1836/1 Liverpool & Manchester Railway Locomotive *Star*, 18 February 1836.
B/VF/15/12/7 1835/3 Liverpool & Manchester Railway Locomotive *Rapid* & *Speedwell*, 1835.
B/VF/15/21/15 1834/1 Liverpool & Manchester Railway Locomotive *Titan* & *Orion*, September 1834.

Salford City Archives, Salford Museum & Art Gallery, Salford
Ref. U268/C1/1-6 Letter books, Nasymth, Gaskell & Co.

Senate House Library, University of London
Charles Lawrence papers (MS584)
2343 Names and numbers of Liverpool & Manchester locomotives to 1 March 1836.
2345 Names and numbers of Liverpool & Manchester locomotives to 18 January 1837.
2346 Abstract of locomotive working expenses, 1841.
2347 Letter Edward Woods to Charles Lawrence re. locomotive stock, 16 December 1842.

The National Archives, Kew, London
Grand Junction Railway
RAIL 220/11 Report from Henry Booth on rails and chairs, July 1835.
RAIL 220/37 Fragments of Miscellaneous Bills and Receipts, August 1839–June 1840.
RAIL 220/41 Reports on locomotives *Rokeby*, *Hecate* and *Cyclops*. No date.

Leeds & Selby Railway
RAIL 351/1 Directors' Meeting, Minutes June 1833–April 1835.
RAIL 351/3 Management Committee, Minutes November 1836–April 1839.

RAIL 351/8 General Ledger: Accounts 1834–1840.
RAIL 351/14 Correspondence Folio, 1834–1836.

Liverpool & Manchester Railway Company
RAIL 371/1 Directors' Meeting, Minutes May 1826–June 1830.
RAIL 371/2 Directors' Meeting, Minutes June 1830–February 1833.
RAIL 371/3 Directors' Meeting, Minutes February 1833–February 1836.
RAIL 371/4 Directors' Meeting, Minutes February 1836–December 1838.
RAIL 371/5 Directors' Meeting, Minutes December 1838–March 1842.
RAIL 371/6 Directors' Meeting, Minutes March 1842–August 1845.
RAIL 371/7 General Meeting, Reports May 1826–May 1845.
RAIL 371/8 Management Sub-Committee, Minutes April 1831–March 1833.
RAIL 371/9 Finance Committee, Minutes September 1824–August 1838.
RAIL 371/10 Management Sub-Committee, Minutes March 1833–August 1839.
RAIL 371/11 Management Sub-Committee, Minutes August 1839–September 1845.
RAIL 371/12 Report by Henry Booth on accident to *Patentee* Locomotive, 20 June 1836.
RAIL 371/16 Agreement with Manchester & Salford Water Works to supply water, 16 March 1838.
RAIL 371/22 Agreement with John Blundell for employment as fitter.
RAIL 371/24 Disbursement Accounts, July 1833–June 1845.
RAIL 371/29 Monthly accounts for cost of repairs on locomotives, carriages and wagons, June 1837–May 1841.
RAIL 371/35 Miscellaneous bills and receipts, Grand Junction Railway to L&M Railway, June 1839–June 1841.
RAIL 371/36 Miscellaneous Accounts, Bills and receipts, June 1838–September 1845.
RAIL 371/40 Performances of locomotives and coke consumption, 1839–1840.
RAIL 371/41 Roll of drawings of locomotives.
RAIL 371/42 Extracts from Liverpool & Manchester and Grand Junction Railway minutes.
RAIL 371/50 Memorandum re. Loan of chairs, rails, etc. 22 November 1834.

London & Birmingham Railway
RAIL 384/115 Report by Edward Woods on forms of rail, 20 October 1834.
RAIL 384/188 Specification of Rails and Chairs, c.1835.
RAIL 384/260 Report from Henry Booth on Bergin's buffing gear, 20 November 1835.

London & North Western Railway
RAIL 1008/95 Report from John Dixon on rails and chairs, 29 June 1835.
Report from Rathbone and Sinclair on rails and chairs, 24 July 1835.
Particulars of Rails and chairs, examination of James Scott, 18 December 1834.

London & North Eastern Railway
RAIL1021/8/24 Type-written notes on Thomas, Nathaniel, George, and Thomas William Worsdell, compiled for the L&NER in 1928.

Railway Rulebooks
RAIL 1134/221 Liverpool & Manchester Railway, Rules & Regulations, December 1840.
RAIL 1134/222 Liverpool & Manchester Railway, Rules & Regulations, September 1841.

The National Railway Museum, York:
British Railways, London Midland Region
Drawing No. D14/1667, L&M Centenary Vehicles, first class carriages, 5 August 1930.

Hackworth Papers
Hack/1/1/25 Timothy Hackworth to L&M Directors, no date but October 1829.

London & North Western Railway
DS/2/TOP/13 Drawings of Model Coach '*Experience*', LNWR Wolverton 5 January 1911.

John Melling Papers
MEL/1 Letters patent granted to John Melling.
MEL/2 Names and numbers of Liverpool & Manchester locomotives to January 1837.
MEL/3 List of locomotives fitted with 'patent gear' and 'old hand gear', 10 April 1839.
MEL/4 Note, number of locomotives built with patent gearing.
MEL/7 Letter from Edward Woods to Thomas Melling re. *Rocket*.

Robert Stephenson & Co.
ROB/2/1/1 Robert Stephenson & Co., Order Book No. 1, March 1832.
ROB2/1/2 Robert Stephenson & Co., Order Book No. 2.
ROB/2/2/1 Robert Stephenson & Co., List of engines finished.
ROB/2/2/2 Robert Stephenson & Co., List of engines finished.
ROB/2/3/1 Robert Stephenson & Co., List of engines delivered.
ROB/2/4/1 Robert Stephenson & Co., Description Book 1831.
ROB/2/4/2 Robert Stephenson & Co., Description Book No. 1.
ROB/2/5/1 Robert Stephenson & Co., Particulars of Locomotive Engines.
ROB2/6/1 Robert Stephenson & Co., Engine Record Book 1828-1903.
ROB/2/7/2 Robert Stephenson & Co., Weight Book No. 1.
ROB/3/2/ Robert Stephenson & Co., Locomotive drawings, nos. 14–25, nos. 31–37.
ROB/4/1 Robert Stephenson & Co., Works Ledger No. 1, 1824–1831.

1.2 Primary – Printed

Anon, *Description des Locomotives Stephenson circulant sur les chemins de fer en Angleterre, et en France, et … Bruxelles* (Bruxelles: J-B. Champeron, 1835).
'A Tourist', *The Railway Companion, describing an Excursion along the Liverpool Line* (London: Effingham Wilson, 1833).

W. B. Adams, *English Pleasure Carriages* (London: Charles Knight & Co, 1837).

Armengaud & Armengaud, *L'Industrie des Chemins De Fer* (Paris: L. Mathias, 1839).

H. B. Barlow, *A Comparative Account and Delineation of Railway Engine & Carriage Wheels* (London: John Weale, 1848).

Prof. P. Barlow, *Second Report Addressed to the Directors and Proprietors of the London & Birmingham Railway Company…* (London: B. Fellowes, 1835).

H. Booth, *An Account of the Liverpool & Manchester Railway* (Liverpool: Wales and Baines, 1830).

J. Bourne, *A Treatise on the Steam Engine in its Application to Mines, Mills, Steam Navigation, and Railways* (New York: D. Appleton & Co., 1851).

N. P. Burgh, *Link Motion and Expansion Gear Practically Considered* (London: E. & F. N. Spon, 1872).

T. T. Bury, *Coloured views on the Liverpool and Manchester Railway* (London: R. Ackermann, 1831).

D. K. Clark, *Railway Machinery: A Treatise on the Mechanical Engineering of Railways* (London: Blackie & Son, 1855), vol. 1.

Z. Colburn, *Locomotive Engineering and the Mechanism of Railways* (London: William Collins, Sons, & Co., 1871).

L. Coste & A. Perdonnet, 'Machine Locomotives', *Annales des Mines* Vol. VI (1829).

L. Coste & A. Perdonnet, *Mémoire sur les Chemins à Ornières* (Paris: Bachelier, 1830).

G. D. Dempsey, *The Practical Railway Engineer* (London: John Weale, 1847).

J. Farey & J. Field, 'Report of John Farey and Joshua Field: Respecting Boilers for Steam Engines', *The Artizan*, vol. 3, pp. 19–20.

E. Flachat & J. Petiet, *Guide du Mécanicien Conducteur des Machines Locomotive* (Paris: Mathias, 1840).

L. Hebert, *The Engineers and Mechanics Encyclopaedia* (London: Thomas Kelly, 1836).

Lieutenant P. Lecount, *A Practical Treatise on Railways* (Edinburgh; Adam & Charles Black, 1839).

C. E. Lee & K. R. Gilbert, eds., *C. von Oeynhausen and H. Von Dechen Railways in England 1826 and 1827* (Cambridge: W. Heffer & Sons Ltd, 1971).

W. P. Marshall, *Description of the Patent Locomotive Engine of Robert Stephenson* (London: John Weale, 1838).

A. Notré & P-J Moreau, *Description raisonnée et vues pittoresques du chemin de fer de Liverpool à Manchester* (Paris: Carillan-Goeury, 1831).

F. M. G. de Pambour, *Traité Théorique et Pratique des Machines Locomotives* (Paris: Bachelier et Co., 1835), 1e edition.

F. M. G. de Pambour, *Traité Théorique et Pratique des Machines Locomotives* (Paris: Bachelier et Co., 1840), 2e edition.

J. S. Russell, *A Treatise on the Steam Engine* (Edinburgh: Adam & Charles Black, 1851).

I. Shaw, *Views … on the Line of the Liverpool and Manchester Railway* (Liverpool: I. Shaw, 1831).

W. Templeton, *The Engineer's Common-place Book of Practical Reference* (London: William Simpkin, 1839).

T. Tredgold, ed., *Principles and Practice … of Locomotive Engines* (London: John Weale, 1850).

J. S. Walker, *An accurate description of the Liverpool & Manchester Railway* (Liverpool: J. F. Cannell, 1830).

F. Whishaw, *The Railways of Great Britain and Ireland* (London: Simpkin, Marshall & Co, 1840), first edition.

E. Woods, 'On Certain Forms of Locomotive Engines', *American Railroad Journal and Mechanics' Magazine*, vol. VIII (1839), pp. 376–379.

E. Woods, 'Expansion of Steam in Locomotives', *The Artizan*, vol. I (1844), pp.57–60.

E. Woods, 'The Consumption of Fuel in the Locomotive Engine', *Quarterly Papers on Engineering*, Vol. II (1844), pp. 1–21.

E. Woods, 'On the Consumption of Fuel and the Evaporation of Water in Locomotive and other Steam Engines,' in T. Tredgold, ed., *The Principles and Practice … of Locomotive Engines* (London: John Weale, 1851), pp.1–44.

N. Wood, *Practical Treatise on Railways* (London: Longman, Rees, Orme, Brown, & Green, 1832), second edition.

N. Wood, *Practical Treatise on Railroads* (London: Longman, Orme, Brown, Green & Longmans, 1838), third edition.

2.1 Secondary – Technical

J. Addyman & V. Haworth, *Robert Stephenson: Railway Engineer* (The North Eastern Railway Association and Robert Stephenson Trust, 2005).

E. L. Ahrons, *The British Steam Locomotive 1825–1925* (London: Locomotive Publishing Co., 1927).

M. R. Bailey, ed., *Robert Stephenson – The Eminent Engineer* (London: Routledge, 2017).

M. R. Bailey, *Locomotion. The World's Oldest Steam Locomotives* (Stroud: History Press, 2014).

M. R. Bailey & J. P. Glithero, *The Engineering and History of Rocket* (London: Science Museum, 2001).

M. R. Bailey, 'Learning Through Replication: The *Planet* Project' in *Transactions of the Newcomen Society*, vol. 68 (1996–1997), pp. 109–136.

M. R. Bailey, 'George Stephenson – Locomotive Advocate' in *Transactions of the Newcomen Society*, vol. 52 (1980–1981), pp. 171–179.

M. R. Bailey, 'Robert Stephenson & Co. 1823–1829' in *Transactions of the Newcomen Society*, vol. 50, (1979–1980), pp. 109–138.

P. S. Bagwell, *The Transport Revolution 1770–1985* (London: Routledge, 1988).

P. Chatham, 'Henry Henson and the Early Wagon Stock of the Southern Division', *The L&NWR Society Journal*, vol. 6, No. 6 (September 2010), pp. 3–5.

A. L. Dawson, *Lion: The Story of the Real Titfield Thunderbolt* (Stroud: Amberley Publishing, forthcoming).

A. L. Dawson, 'Planet: Instructions not included', *The L&NWR Society Journal*, vol. 9, no. 3 (December 2018), pp. 110–123.

A. L. Dawson, *Planet, Lion and Burys: Experiences of early Locomotive Management*, paper presented to The L&NWR Society, Kidderminster Railway Museum, 29 July 2017.

A. L. Dawson, *Working on the Victorian Railway* (Stroud: Amberley Publishing, 2017).

A. L. Dawson, *Travelling on the Victorian Railway* (Stroud: Amberley Publishing, 2017).

C. F. Dendy Marshall, *A History of Railway Locomotives down to the end of the year 1831* (London: Locomotive Publishing Co., 1953).

A. Dow, *The Railway. British Track Since 1804* (Barnsley: Pen & Sword Transport, 2014).

M. C. Duffy, 'Technomorphology and the Stephenson Traction System', *Transactions of the Newcomen Society*, vol. 54 (1982–1983), pp. 55–74.

N. Ferguson, 'Anglo-Scottish Transfer of Railway Technology in the 1830s', in M. R. Bailey, ed., *Early Railways 3* (Sudbury: Six Martlets, 2006), pp. 176–190.

R. Gibbon & R. Lamb, 'Runnin' wi' your breeks down': An investigation of coupling-rod resistance in a four-coupled locomotive', in M. J. T. Lewis, ed., *Early Railways 2* (The Newcomen Society, 2003), pp. 232–240.

Rev. Dr. R. L. Hills, 'The Development of Machine Tools in the Early Railway Era', in M. R. Bailey, ed., *Early Railways 3* (Sudbury: Six Martlets, 2006), pp. 242–259.

Rev. Dr. R. L. Hills, *Life and Inventions of Richard Roberts 1789–1864* (Landmark: 2002).

J. Macaulay & C. Hall, *Modern Railway Working. A Practical Treatise* (London: The Gresham Publishing Company, 1912), 12 vols.

S. Murfitt, 'The English Patent System and Early Railway Technology 1800–1852' in M. Chrimes, ed., *Early Main Line Railways 2* (Croydon: CPI, 2019), pp. 151–198.

J. B. Snell, *Railways: Mechanical Engineering* (London: Arrow Books, 1973).

J. G. H. Warren, *Century of Locomotive Building by Robert Stephenson & Co.* (Newcastle: Andrew Reid & Co., 1923).

J. G. H. Warren, 'John Nuttall's Sketch Book with Notes on Wrought Iron Details and Wheels for Early Locomotives', *Transactions of the Newcomen Society*, vol.11 (1930), pp. 70–71.

2.2 Secondary – General and Social

H. Booth, *Henry Booth. Inventor; Partner in the Rocket; Father of Railway Management* (Ilfracombe: Arthur H. Stockwell Ltd., 1980).

G. Hill, *The Worsdells. A Quaker Engineering Dynasty* (Glossop: Transport Publishing Co., 1991).

S. Hylton, *The Grand Experiment. The Birth of the Railway Age 1820–1845* (Hersham: Ian Allen, 2007).

P. W. Kingsford, *Victorian Railwaymen. The Emergence and Growth of Railway Labour 1830–1870* (London: Frank Cass Ltd., 1970).

L. T. C. Rolt, *George and Robert Stephenson* (London: Penguin Books, 1978).

3. Parliamentary Papers

Report from the Select Committee on Railroad Communication (London: 1838).

Report from the Select Committees on Railways, Vol. 1 and Vol. 2 (London: 1839).

Minutes of Evidence Taken before the Selected Committee on Railways (London: 1841).

Parliamentary Papers, House of Commons, vol. 41. Accounts and Papers: Railways (London: William Clowes, 1842).

Sessional Papers of the House of Lords. Vol. XIII. Accounts and Papers: Railways (London: HMSO 1843).

Fifth Report from the Select Committee on Railways (rates and fares) (London: 1844)

Gauge Commissioners Reports. Minutes of Evidence (London: William Clowes & Sons, 1846)

'Returns of Accidents on Railways', *Parliamentary Papers vol. 39: Accounts and Papers: Railway Department* (London: 1846)

Report … on the Atmospheric Railway (London: William Clowes & Sons, 1846).

4. Contemporary Journals and Newspapers

American Railroad Journal and Mechanics' Magazine.

Annales des Ponts et Chaussées.

Journal des Chemins de Fer.

Mechanics' Magazine.

The Artizan.

The Engineer.

The Practical Mechanic and Engineer's Magazine.

The Railway Magazine alias *Herapath's Railway Journal.*

Newspapers were searched digitally via www.britishnewspaperarchive.co.uk and on microfilm. Space does not permit a complete list of every newspaper consulted.

Endnotes

Introduction

1. M. R. Bailey, 'George Stephenson – Locomotive Advocate' in *Transactions of the Newcomen Society*, vol. 52 (1980-1981), pp. 171-179; M. R. Bailey, ed., *Robert Stephenson: The Eminent Engineer* (London: Routledge, 2017), p. 169 and pp. 176-180. See also: A. L. Dawson, 'Rocket, the Liverpool & Manchester Railway, and Public Relations', Railway & Canal Historical Society Railway History Research Group, Occasional Paper 12 (2020).

2. RAIL 371/1 Directors' Meeting, Minutes 30 April 1827, 7 January 1828, 21 April 1828, 12 October 1829, 7 December 1829, 4 January 1830.

3. J. G. H. Warren, *A Century of Locomotive Building by Robert Stephenson & Co, 1823-1923* (Newcastle: Andrew Reid & Co. Ltd., 1923), Chapter IX. For a discussion on different blast characteristics, see P. Davidson, 'Early Locomotive Performance', in A. Coulls (ed.) Early Railways 6 (Six Martlets, 2019), pp. 136-141.

4. F. Satow, M. G. Satow, and L. S. Wilson, *Locomotion: Concept to creation… the story of the reproduction, 1973-1975* (Beamish: The Locomotion Trust, 1976), passim.

5. RAIL 371/1 Directors' Meeting, Minutes 29 September 1828.

6. RAIL 371/1 Directors' Meeting, Minutes 29 September 1828, 6 October 1828, 13 October 1828, 20 October 1828, 5 November 1828; B. Thompson, *Inventions, Improvements and Practice of Benjamin Thompson …* (Newcastle: M. & M. W. Lambert, 1847), pp.38-42; S. J. Jeans, *Jubilee Memorial of the Railway System* (London: Longmans, Green & Co., 1875), pp. 48-49; Bailey, 'George Stephenson', pp. 175-176.

7. Institute of Mechanical Engineers, London: *Report to the Directors of the Liverpool and Manchester Railway*, 5 November 1828.

8. RAIL 371/1 Directors' Meeting, Minutes 6 November 1828.

9. RAIL 371/1 Directors' Meeting, Minutes 1 December 1828.

10. J. C. Jeaffreson, *The Life of Robert Stephenson* (London: Longman, Green, Longman, Roberts, and Green,1864), vol. 1, p. 121.

11. RAIL 371/1 Directors' Meeting, Minutes 16 March 1829, 6 July 1829, 13 July 1829, 17 August 1829; Liverpool Record Office & Local Studies, 385 STE/13, George Stephenson to Michael Longridge, 23 August 1829; 'The New Loco-Motive Carriage', *Chester Chronicle* (31 July 1829), p. 3; 'Progress on the Railway', *Manchester Mercury* (25 August 1829), p. 2; 'Mr Huskisson's visit to Liverpool', Manchester Courier (29 August 1829), p. 3; 'Melancholy Accident', *Liverpool Mercury* (11 February 1831), p. 6. See also C. F. Dendy Marshall,

A History of Railway Locomotives down to the end of the year 1831 (London: Locomotive Publishing Co., 1953), pp. 141-142; Warren, *A Century*, pp. 155-157.

12. RAIL 371/1 Directors' Meeting, Minutes 6 November 1828, 17 November 1828, 24 November 1828.

13. RAIL 371/1 Directors' Meeting, Minutes 17 October 1828.

14. RAIL 371/1 Directors' Meeting, Minutes 1 December 1828, 8 December 1828, 15 December 1828, 22 December 1828, 29 December 1828, 5 January 1829, 12 January 1829. Thompson, *Inventions*, pp.40-41.

15. RAIL 371/1 Directors' Meeting, Minutes 7 September 1829.

16. RAIL 371/1 Directors' Meeting, Minutes 6 April 1829, 13 April 1829.

17. NRM HACK 1-1-22, Hackworth to R. Stephenson, 9 April 1829.

18. Ibid.

19. R. Stephenson & J. Locke, *Observations on the Comparative Merits of Locomotive and Fixed Engines* (Liverpool: Wales & Baines, 1830), passim.

20. Bailey, 'George Stephenson', pp. 176-178.

21. J. Walker & J. U. Rastrick, *Report to the Directors on the Comparative Merits of Locomotive and Fixed Engines* (Liverpool: Wales & Baines, 1830), pp. 29-30.

22. RAIL 371/1 Directors' Meeting, Minutes 20 April 1829.

23. RAIL 371/1 Directors' Meeting, Minutes 13 April 1829, 20 April 1829, 4 May 1829; Dawson, *Rainhill*, passim.

24. D. Pennington, 'The Lime Street Tunnel Experience', *The L&NWR Society Journal*, Vol. 4, No. 4 (March 2004), pp.144-148; C. E. Mountford, *Rope & Chain Haulage. The forgotten element of Railway History* (Melton Mowbray: Industrial Railway Society, 2012), pp. 46-47.

25. RAIL 371/2 Directors' Meeting, Minutes 21 July 1830, 23 August 1830, 30 August 1830, 6 September 1830.

26. A. L. Dawson, *The Liverpool & Manchester Railway: An Operational History* (Barnsley: Pen & Sword Transport, 2020), pp. 10-21.

27. Ibid.

PART 1: THE STEPHENSON LOCOMOTIVE

Chapter 1. From *Rocket* to *Northumbrian*

1. M. R. Bailey & J. P. Glithero, *The Engineering and History of Rocket* (London: Science Museum, 2001), chapter 1.

2. 'Links in the History of the Locomotive', *The Engineer* (6 February 1885), p. 95, letter from E. Woods, 28 January 1885; 'Further Experiments on the Railway', *Manchester Courier* (7 November 1829), p. 4. For a complete history of *Rocket* see Bailey & Glithero.

3. Dendy Marshall, *A History*, p. 152; RAIL 371/1 Directors' Meeting, Minutes 26 October 1829, 1 February 1830, 15 February 1830; 'New Steam Engine', *Durham County Advertiser* (9 January 1830), p. 2; 'A new locomotive carriage',

Manchester Courier (16 January 1830), p. 4; 'The New Locomotive Engine' *Newcastle Courant* (23 January 1830), p.4.

4. 'New Locomotive Engine', *Carlisle Patriot* (23 January 1830), p. 4, citing *Liverpool Courier;* 'The Wildfire', *Manchester Courier* (26 January 1830), p. 2.

5. NRM, Acc. ROB/2/4/1 Robert Stephenson & Co., Description Book 1831, p. 5.

6. Warren, *A Century,* p. 232. However, John Rastrick notes that *Arrow* had 90 boiler tubes, whilst other sources indicate 92 tubes: Nicholas Wood (second edition (1832), p. 400) states that *Meteor* had 90 tubes and *Arrow* 92. This is confirmed in his third edition (1838), p. 518. One Belgian source (*Description des Machines Locomotive Stephenson* (Bruxelles: J-B. Champeron, 1835), p. 48.) also describes *Arrow* with 92 boiler tubes. Z. Colburn *Locomotive Engineering and the Mechanism of Railways* (London: William Collins, Sons, Co., 1871), vol. 1, p. 30, also suggests *Arrow* had 92 tubes.

7. ROB/2/4/1 Description Book 1831, p. 5.

8. RAIL 371/1 Directors' Meeting, Minutes 14 June 1830; NRM Acc. 1945-108 John Rastrick, Rainhill notebook; Warren, *A Century,* pp. 232-237; Bailey & Glithero, *Rocket,* pp. 55-75, 88-91, 131-135, 135-155; Colburn, *Locomotive Engineering,* p. 30. See also: NRM ROB/3/2/14 'Plan of Rockett [sic] Engine', ROB/3/2/15 'first after Rockett [sic]'.

9. Rail 371/2 Directors' Meeting, Minutes 11 October 1830, 9 December 1830, 'The Manchester and Liverpool Railway', *Manchester Mercury* (14 December 1830), p. 4.

10. Dendy Marshall, *A History,* pp. 153-156; RAIL 371/1 Directors' Meeting, Minutes 1 February 1830; RAIL 371/2 Directors' Meeting, Minutes 21 June 1830, 23 August 1830.

11. ROB/2/4/1 Description Book 1831, p. 6.

12. Colburn, *Locomotive Engineering,* p. 30.

13. Warren, *A Century,* pp. 234-237; Bailey & Glithero, *Rocket,* p.89.

14. 'The Railway', *Manchester Courier* (23 October 1830), p. 3.

15. 'The Railway', *Manchester Courier* (23 October 1830), p. 3, 'Railway Accident', *Manchester Courier* (6 November 1830), p. 2; 'Fatal Accident on the Railway', *Manchester Courier* (30 October 1830), p. 2. RAIL 371/2 Directors' Meeting, Minutes 11 October 1830, 18 October 1830, 8 November 1830.

16. Institute of Mechanical Engineers, Letter from George Stephenson to Michael Longridge, 11 October 1830 via https://archives.imeche.org/archive/industrial/stephenson/michael-longridge/586474, accessed 20/05/2019 at 18:51.

17. 'Fatal Accidents on the Railway', *Manchester Times and Gazette* (2 April 1831), np.

18. RAIL 371/1 Directors' Meeting, Minutes 13 December 1830. See also Wood. *Practical Treatise,* third edition, pp.515-520*ff.*

19. Warren, *A Century,* pp. 239-241. See also Dendy Marshall, *A History,* pp. 155-156. See also ROB/3/2/18 'Liverpool Locomotive No. 9', ROB/3/2/19 'Liverpool Engine No. 2 End View.', ROB/3/2/20 'Northumbrian.'

20. RAIL 371/2 Directors' Meeting, Minutes 21 June 1830, 5 July 1830, 9 August 1830.

21. ROB/2/4/1 Description Book 1831, p. 6 to 7; RAIL371/41/3 Locomotives and Rolling Stock. Comparison Statement Northumbrian and Planet; Warren, *A Century*, p. 239.

22. ROB/3/2/18 Robert Stephenson & Co., locomotive drawings, 'Liverpool Locomotive Engine No 9 [Northumbrian]'.

23. 'Messrs. Braithwaite and Ericsson's Engines' *Mechanics' Magazine* (25 September 1830), pp. 69-70; 'Liverpool & Manchester Railway', *Mechanics' Magazine* (2 October 1830), p. 88; 'The Liverpool and Manchester Railway', *The Glasgow Mechanics' Magazine* (No. CXXXII), pp. 287-289; 'The William the Fourth', *Mechanics' Magazine* (22 January 1831), p. 365; 'Messrs. Braithwaite and Ericsson's Steam-Carriages. To the Editor', *Mechanics' Magazine* (5 February 1831), pp. 414-415.

24. 'Liverpool and Manchester Railway – Further Particulars. Performance of Engines', *Mechanics' Magazine* (2 October 1830), pp. 87 – 88; 'Liverpool and Manchester Railway – Further Particulars. Performance of Engines, continued.', *Mechanics' Magazine (16 October 1830)*, pp. 114-116; 'The Manchester Guardian and the Mechanics' Magazine', *Mechanics' Magazine* (20 November 1830), pp. 211-213.

25. *'A Report to the Directors of the Liverpool & Manchester Railway...'* (Philadelphia: Carey & Lee, 1831), p. 260 'Liverpool and Manchester Railway', *Liverpool Mercury* (28 January 1831), p. 6.

26. A. R. Bennet, *The Chronicles of Boulton's Siding* (London: Locomotive Publishing Company Ltd., 1926), p. 268; Dawson, *Rainhill*, pp. 74-75.

27. RAIL 371/8 Management Sub-Committee, Minutes 30 November 1831.

28. F. D. Smith, 'Were these two locos the first contractors' locos to be sold?', *The Industrial Locomotive*, No. 68, Vol. 6 (1993), p. 227; RAIL 351/1 Leeds & Selby Railway, Directors' Meeting, Minutes 3 October 1834, 10 October 1834; RAIL 351/14 Leeds & Selby Railway, Correspondence Folio, letters dated 1 October 1834, 3 October 1834, 6 October 1834, 9 October 1834, 21 November 1834.

29. Smith, 'Contractors Locos', p. 227.

30. ROB/4/1 Robert Stephenson & Co., Works Ledger 1824-1831, p. 288, entry dated 20 November 1830.

31. RAIL 371/1 Directors' Meeting, Minutes 16 November 1829; RAIL 371/2 Directors' Meeting, Minutes 14 February 1831, 21 May 1832, 25 June 1832, 2 July 1832, 9 July 1832, 16 July 1832, 10 September 1832; RAIL 371/3 Directors' Meeting, Minutes 25 March 1833. See also, E. A. Forward, 'Gurney's Railway Locomotives 1830', *Transactions of the Newcomen Society*, vol. 2 (1921), pp.127-129; D. H. Porter, *The life and times of Goldsworthy Gurney, gentleman scientist and inventor* (London: Associated Universities Press, 1998), chapter 7.

32. 'Robbery at the Railway Station', *Manchester Courier* (14 June 1834).

33. RAIL 371/8 Management Sub-Committee, Minutes 23 May 1832, 31 May 1832, 24 October 1832.

34. RAIL 384/68 London & Birmingham Railway. Birmingham Committee Minutes, 15 January 1836; RAIL 371/4 Liverpool & Manchester Railway, Directors' Meeting, Minutes 24 October 1836. Thompson family tradition suggests *Rocket* was purchased on 15 April 1837 – unless that is the date *Rocket* started work at Kirkhouse. Tradition also records how *Rocket* ran, on 8 August 1837 (being election day), at an unrealistic speed of 4 miles in 4 ½ minutes ('Fete at Kirkhouse. Messrs. Thompson and their workpeople', *Carlisle Patriot* (16 August 1889), p. 6.) A contemporary account of *Rocket*'s high-speed run suggests a speed no greater than 35mph (*Carlisle Journal* (12 August 1837), p. 2). A later version of events notes a speed of 60mph ('The late George Stephenson, Esq.' *Carlisle Journal*, (15 September 1848), p. 2.).

Chapter 2. The Planet class

1. 'Links in the History of the Locomotive No. X', *The Engineer* (18 March 1881), p. 193.
2. M. R. Bailey, 'Leaning Through Replication: The *Planet* Project' in *Transactions of the Newcomen Society*, vol. 68 (1996-1997), p. 113.
3. 'Improvements in Locomotive Engines', *Manchester Guardian* (4 March 1831), p. 4.
4. D. K. Clark, 'Railway Locomotive Stock, and reduction of working expenses', in C. Manby, ed., *Minutes of Proceedings of the Institute of Civil Engineers*, vol. XVI (1856-1857), p. 22.
5. Ibid, p. 23.
6. Dendy Marshall, *A History*, chapter X, chapter XII, and chapter XVII. See also Warren, *A Century*, pp. 260-262.
7. 'The Journey from Manchester to Liverpool', *Liverpool Mercury* (26 November 1830), p. 6; see also *Gore's Liverpool General Advertiser* (25 November 1830).
8. RAIL 371/2 Directors' Meeting, Minutes 29 November 1830.
9. 'Extraordinary performance on the Railway', *Liverpool Mercury* (10 December 1830), p. 6.
10. RAIL 371/2 Directors' Meeting, Minutes 6 November 1830.
11. RAIL 371/2 Directors' Meeting, Minutes 6 December 1830.
12. 'The Railway', *Preston Chronicle* (12 February 1831), p. 3.
13. RAIL 371/10 Management Sub-Committee, Minutes 27 April 1837; D. K. Clark, *Railway Machinery: A Treatise on the Mechanical Engineering of Railways* (London: Blackie & Son, 1855), vol. 1, p. 11.
14. RAIL 371/2 Directors' Meeting, Minutes 30 May 1831, 22 August 1831.
15. *Chester Chronicle*, (3 June 1831).
16. NRM1998-11384/70 colour-wash drawing of Vulcan; ROB/4/1 Robert Stephenson & Co, Ledger 1824-1831, p. 304 entry 28 February 1831.
17. RAIL 371/2 Director's Meeting, Minutes 3 October 1831, 10 October 1831.
18. RAIL 371/2 Directors' Meeting, Minutes 21 November 1831.

19. RAIL 371/2 Directors' Meeting, Minutes 3 December 1832.
20. RAIL 371/3 Directors' Meeting, Minutes 4 February 1833.
21. RAIL 371/3 Directors' Meeting, Minutes 3 February 1834, 10 February 1834.
22. RAIL 371/10 Management Sub-Committee, Minutes 5 September 1833.
23. RAIL 371/24 Disbursement Accounts, 1833-1845, p. 23.
24. ROB/2/1/1 Robert Stephenson & Co., Order Book No. 1, pp. 13-19, p. 39, pp. 48-49.
25. RAIL 371/8 Management Sub-Committee, Minutes 11 April 1832; RAIL 371/10 Management Sub-Committee, Minutes 27 April 1837.
26. *Edinburgh Review* cited by *Wolverhampton Chronicle* (19 December 1832).
27. RAIL 371/8 Management Sub-Committee, Minutes 4 July 1832, 11 July 1832.
28. Bailey, 'Planet Project', pp. 122-123.
29. Matthew Jackson, *Pers. Comm.*, 5 January 2018.
30. RAIL 371/3 Directors' Meeting, 25 August 1834, Minutes 1 December 1834, 8 December 1834, 29 December 1834; RAIL 371/10 Management Sub-Committee, Minutes 2 October 1834; RAIL 351 Leeds & Selby Railway, Directors' Meeting, Minutes 30 August 1834.

Chapter 3: Engine Building

1. C. E. Jullien, *Nouveau Manuel Complete du constructeur de machines locomotives* (Paris: La Librairie Encyclopédique de Roret, 1842), pp.291-293. J. G. H. Warren, 'John Nuttall's Sketch Book with Notes on Wrought Iron Details and Wheels for Early Locomotives', *Transactions of the Newcomen Society*, vol.11 (1930), pp. 70-71. Warren cites Jullien but blends the five methods described into three and muddies the waters somewhat.
2. Rev Dr. R. L. Hills, 'The Development of Machine Tools in the Early Railway Era', in M. R. Bailey, ed., *Early Railways 3* (Sudbury: Six Marlets, 2006), p. 255.
3. ROB/2/4/1 Robert Stephenson & Co., Description Book 1831, passim.; Rob/2/1/1 Robert Stephenson & Co., Order Book No. 1, p. 13; ROB/2/4/2 Robert Stephenson & Co., Description Book No. 1, pp. 8- 9, p.12.
4. Institute of Mechanical Engineers, Letter from George Stephenson to Michael Longridge, 11 October 1830 via https://archives.imeche.org/archive/industrial/stephenson/michael-longridge/586474, accessed 20/05/2019 at 18:51.
5. RAIL 371/2 Directors' Meeting, Minutes 5 September 1831, 12 September 1831; 'Railway Accidents', *Liverpool Mercury* (2 September 1831), p. 8; 'Accident on the Railway', *Liverpool Mercury* (18 November 1831), p. 3; on various types of iron, Dr. S. Summerfield, Loughborough University, *pers. comm.*
6. RAIL 371/8 Management Sub-Committee, Minutes 7 December 1831; 'Railway Accident', *Liverpool Mercury* (9 December 1831), p. 6; 'Railway Accident', *Gore's Liverpool General Advertiser* (8 December 1831), p. 3.
7. 'Railway Accident', *Liverpool Mercury* (9 December 1831), p. 6.
8. Ibid.

9. RAIL 371/8 Management Sub-Committee, Minutes 21 December 1831.

10. RAIL 371/8 Management Sub-Committee, Minutes 7 December 1831.

11. RAIL 371/2 Directors' Meeting, Minutes 12 December 1831; 'Four-wheeled and Six-wheeled Locomotive engines. To the editor', *Railway Times* (4 December 1841), p. 1257.

12. RAIL 351/8 Leeds & Selby Railway, Ledger, entry dated 31 December 1835.

13. RAIL371/8 Management Sub-Committee, Minutes 4 April 1832.

14. ROB2/1/1/1, Memoranda, p.2

15. RAIL 371/3 Directors' Meeting, Minutes 3 June 1833.

16. Bailey, 'Planet Project', pp. 118-120; M. E. Jackson, *pers. comm.*; Prof. B. Pardoe, University of Salford, *pers comm.*

17. Ibid.

18. RAIL 371/2 Directors' Meeting, Minutes 20 June 1831, 27 June 1831.

19. ROB4/1 Robert Stephenson & Co, Works Ledger 1824-1831, p. 276, p. 288.

20. RAIL 371/8 Management Sub-Committee, Minutes 30 May 1832. See also ROB/2/1/1, Memoranda, p. 2 '1832 1st June. Mr Booth wishes the next two engines for Liverpool to be sent without wheels.'

21. RAIL 371/8 Management Sub-Committee, Minutes 8 August 1832.

22. RAIL 371/2 Directors' Meeting, Minutes 30 September 1832; ROB/2/1/1 p. 13.

23. RAIL 371/8 Management Sub-Committee, Minutes 4 January 1832; RAIL 371/2 Directors' Meeting, Minutes 12 September 1831, 12 March 1832.

24. RAIL 351/1 Leeds & Selby Railway, Directors' Meeting, Minutes 6 February 1835, 20 February 1835; Engineers' Report February 1835.

25. H. B. Barlow, *A Comparative Account and Delineation of Railway Engine & Carriage Wheels* (London: John Weale, 1848), p. 16. See also Dr. R. L. Hills, *Life and Inventions of Richard Roberts 1789-1864* (Landmark: 2002), p.169ff.

26. 'Report of the Chief Engineer: To the President and Directors of the Portsmouth and Roanoke Rail-Road Company', *Journal of the House of Delegates of the Commonwealth of Virginia* (Richmond: Samuel Shepherd, 1835), p.60.

27. ROB/2/1/1 Robert Stephenson & Co., Order Book No. 1, pp.15-16, p.19; Bailey, 'Robert Stephenson & Co.', p. 125.

28. ROB/2/1/2 Robert Stephenson & Co., Order Book 1831, pp.7-8.

29. Colburn, *Locomotive Engineering*, pp. 36-37; Bailey, 'Planet Project', p. 124.

30. ROB/2/4/1 Robert Stephenson & Co., Description Book 1831, passim.

31. Warren, *A Century*, pp. 272-273.

32. ROB/2/1/1 Robert Stephenson & Co., Order Book No. 1, Memoranda, p. 2, pp. 13-15. See also: M. R. Bailey, 'Robert Stephenson and the Horseley Company', *Transactions of the Newcomen Society*, Vol. 58 (1986), pp. 139-140.

33. RAIL 371/8 Management Sub-Committee, 9 February 1832.

34. RAIL 371/8 Management Sub-Committee, 17 May 1832.

35. ROB/2/1/1 Robert Stephenson & Co., Order Book No. 1, pp. 15-16; ROB/2/4/2 Description Book 1, p. 3, p.13, p. 17.

36. 'Liverpool and Manchester Railway', *Liverpool Mercury* (15 February 1833), p. 6.

37. 'Railway Engines', *Carlisle Journal* (7 September 1833), p. 4; ROB/2/4/2 Robert Stephenson & Co, Description Book No. 1, pp. 15-16.

38. RAIL 371/8 Management Sub-Committee, 14 June 1832; Warren, *A Century*, pp. 273-275.

39. RAIL 371/8 Management Sub-Committee, 12 July 1832.

40. Warren, *A. Century*, p. 275

41. Ibid.

42. Ibid

43. RAIL 371/8 Management Sub-Committee, Minutes 23 May 1832, 31 May 1832.

44. RAIL 371/8 Management Sub-Committee, Minutes 24 October 1832.

45. RAIL 371/8 Management Sub-Committee, 20 September 1832.

46. S. Timmins, ed., *The Resources, Products, and Industrial History of Birmingham* (London: Robert Hardwicke, 1866), pp. 321-328.

47. RAIL 371/8 Management Sub-Committee, 18 October 1832.

48. RAIL 371/3 Director's Meeting, Minutes 8 April 1833.

49. RAIL 371/2 Directors Meeting, Minutes 6 August 1832; ROB/2/4/2 Description Book No. 1, p. 9.

50. RAIL 371/10 Management Sub-Committee, Minutes 10 April 1833.

51. De Pambour, *Traité*, 1e edition, pp. 172-173.

52. ROB/2/4/2 Robert Stephenson & Co, Description Book No. 1, p. 9; 'Perkins's Steam Generator', Liverpool Standard and General Commercial Advertiser (1 February 1833), p. 6.

53. RAIL 371/2 Directors' Meeting, 3 December 1832; RAIL 371/3 Director's Minutes, 25 February 1833, 29 April 1833, 2 September 1833, 16 September, 14 October 1833, 21 October 1833, 28 October 1833.

54. 'Railway Engines', *Carlisle Journal* (7 September 1833), p. 4.

55. RAIL 371/10 Management Sub-Committee, Minutes 10 April 1833; ROB/2/1/1 Order Book No. 1, Memoranda, p. 9.

56. RAIL 371/10 Management Sub-Committee, Minutes 15 April 1833, 24 April 1833.

57. RAIL 371/10 Management Sub-Committee, Minutes 16 May 1833, 27 June 1833, 5 September 1833.

58. RAIL 371/3 Directors' Meeting, Minutes 6 January 1834.

59. RAIL 371/24 Disbursement Accounts, passim.

60. RAIL 371/3 Directors' Meeting, Minutes 8 June 1835.

61. ROB/2/1/1/ Order Book No. 1, Memoranda, p. 13.

62. RAIL 371/10 Management Sub-Committee, Minutes 27 March 1833.

63. RAIL 371/10 Management Sub-Committee, Minutes 16 October 1834.

64. RAIL 371/3 Directors' meeting, Minutes 7 April 1834.

65. RAIL 371/3 Directors' Meeting, Minutes 21 April 1834, 21 July 1834; RAIL 371/10 Management Sub-Committee, Minutes 10 July 1834.

66. RAIL 371/8 Management Sub-Committee, 11 July 1832.

67. RAIL 371/8 Management Sub-Committee, 7 March 1833.

68. RAIL 371/10 Management Sub-Committee, Minutes 23 June 1836.

69. RAIL 371/10 Management Sub-Committee, Minutes 8 December 1836.

70. Ibid.
71. Warren, *A Century*, p. 265; NRM 1945-108 John Rastrick, Rainhill notebook.
72. Pambour, *Traité*, p. 47
73. ROB/2/1/1 Order Book No. 1, Memoranda, p. 2.
74. RAIL 371/8 Management Sub-Committee, Minutes 27 July 1831.
75. Pambour, *Traite*, p. 47.
76. RAIL 371/8 Management Sub-Committee, Minutes 3 May 1832.
77. Colburn, *Locomotive Engineering*, pp. 35-36
78. RAIL 371/8 Management Sub-Committee, Minutes 4 April 1833.
79. RAIL 371/10 Management Sub-Committee, Minutes 3 April 1833.
80. P. Brown, *Pers comm.*, 30-1-2018.
81. E. Flachat & J. Petiet, *Guide du Mécanicien Conducteur des Machines Locomotive* (Paris: Mathias, 1840), p. 151.
82. W. P. Marshall, *Description of the Patent Locomotive Engine of Robert Stephenson* (London: John Weale, 1838), p. 45.
83. ROB2/1/1 Order Book No. 1, p. 13 and p. 88; Memoranda p. 1; Flachat & Petiet, *Guide*, p. 151.
84. *The Engineer* (7 November 1884).

Chapter 4: Luggage Engines

1. RAIL 371/2 Directors' Meeting, Minutes 20 September 1830, 6 December 1830.
2. RAIL 371/2 Directors' Meeting, Minutes 12 December 1831.
3. ROB/2/4/1 Description Book 1831, pp. 8 to 10.
4. 'The Railway', *Preston Chronicle* (12 February 1831), p. 3.
5. 'Improvements in Locomotive Engines', *Manchester Guardian* (26 February 1831); see also 'Extraordinary performance on the Railroad', *Chester Courant* (1 March 1831), p. 3.
6. Ibid.
7. 'Improvements in Locomotive Engines', *Chester Courant* (4 March 1831), p. 4, citing *Manchester Guardian*.
8. 'Extraordinary Performance on the Railway', *Preston Chronicle* (9 April 1831), p. 4; 'Manchester, Saturday Evening', *Chester Courant* (12 April 1831), p. 4.
9. Edinburgh Review cited by *Wolverhampton Chronicle* (19 December 1832).
10. RAIL 371/10 Management Sub-Committee, Minutes 27 June 1834.
11. RAIL 371/2 Directors Meeting, Minutes 30 April 1832.
12. Warren, *A Century*, p. 285*ff*.
13. ROB/2/4/1 Description Book 1831, pp. 27-28; Pambour, *Traite*, 1e edition, pp. 120-122, 171-174, 242-244, 356-359; 2e edition p, 444.
14. Pambour, *Traite*, 1e edition, p. 167 and pp. 356-357.
15. RAIL 371/2 Directors Meeting, Minutes 27 February 1832.
16. Dendy Marshall, *Centenary History*, p, 86.
17. Pambour, *Traité*, 1e edition, p. 337.

18. RAIL 371/10 Management Sub-Committee, Minutes 11 June 1835.
19. N. Ferguson, 'Anglo-Scottish Transfer of Railway Technology in the 1830s', in M. Bailey, ed., *Early Railways 3* (Sudbury: Six Martlets, 2006), p. 186.
20. RAIL 371/2 Director's Meeting, Minutes 23 April 1832.
21. RAIL 371/8 Management Sub-Committee, Minutes 16 May 1832.
22. RAIL 371/2 Directors Meeting, Minutes 11 June 1832, 18 June 1832.
23. RAIL 371/2 Directors' Meeting, Minutes 11 June 1832, 18 June 1832, 9 July 1832.
24. RAIL 371/8 Management Sub-Committee, Minutes 26 September 1832.
25. Warren, *A Century*, p. 274; RAIL 371/3 Directors' Meeting, Minutes 10 November 1834, 17 November 1834; RAIL 371/10 Management Sub-Committee, Minutes 16 October 1834, 13 November 1834.
26. 'Liverpool and Manchester Railway', *Manchester Courier* (7 February 1835), p. 2.
27. RAIL 371/8 Management Sub-Committee, Minutes 28 December 1831.
28. RAIL 371/8 Management Sub-Committee, Minutes 20 September 1832.
29. RAIL 371/10 Management Sub-Committee, Minutes 18 September 1835.
30. RAIL 371/3 Directors' Meeting, Minutes 3 February 1834.
31. RAIL 371/3 Directors' Meeting, Minutes 15 September 1834, 15 October 1834; 16 February 1835; RAIL 371/10 Management Sub-Committee, Minutes 27 November 1834, 19 February 1835.
32. National Museums Liverpool: Locomotive Drawings, Vulcan Foundry Collection B/VF/15/21/15, drawing no. 1834/1 'Titan' and 'Orion'; RAIL 371/41, Drawing No. 12 'Titan' and 'Orion'.
33. RAIL 371/3 Directors' Meeting, Minutes 2 March 1835.
34. RAIL 371/3 Directors' Meeting, Minutes 12 January 1835.
35. RAIL 371/29 Monthly accounts for cost of repairs on locomotives, carriages and wagons 1837-1839, 31 January 1838.

Chapter 5. The Patentee Type

1. A. Dow, *The Railway. British Track Since 1804* (Barnsley: Pen & Sword Transport, 2014), p. viii.
2. M. C. Duffy, 'Technomorphology and the Stephenson Traction System', *Transactions of the Newcomen Society*, vol. 54 (1982-1983), pp. 55-74; S. Smiles, *The Life of George Stephenson* (London: John Murray, 1858) 5th edition, p. 136.
3. RAIL 371/3 Directors' Meeting, Minutes 18 November 1833.
4. RAIL 371/8 Management Sub-Committee, Minutes 8 June 1831.
5. RAIL371/2 Directors' Meeting, Minutes 9 April 1832; RAIL 1008/95 Report of John Dixon, Manchester 29 June 1835.
6. RAIL1008/95 Particulars of Rails and Chairs, &c. Examination of James Scott.
7. RAIL 384/115 Report of Edward Woods, Liverpool 20 October 1834; RAIL 1008/95 Report of John Dixon, Manchester 29 June 1835;RAIL220/11 Grand Junction Railway. Report of Henry Booth, July 1835; RAIL 1008/95 Report of

Rathbone and Sinclair, 24 July 1835.R. Stephenson, 'Remarks and Calculations on the best form for Railway Bars, and on the defects which exist in the present method of supporting the same', *Mechanics' Magazine and Register of Inventions and Improvements*, Vol. V (January – June 1835), pp. 269-278.

8. RAIL 371/3 Directors' Meeting, Minutes 19 January 1835, 9 February 1835, 24 August 1835, 5 October 1835, 4 January 1836; RAIL 371/10 Management Sub-Committee, Minutes 5 February 1835; RAIL 371/4 Directors' Meeting, Minutes 11 July 1836; Prof. P. Barlow, *Second Report Addressed to the Directors and Proprietors of the London & Birmingham Railway Company...* (London: B. Fellowes, 1835).

9. RAIL 371/2 Directors' Meeting, Minutes 5 November 1832, 26 November 1832.

10. RAIL 371/8 Management Sub-Committee, Minutes 21 February 1833.

11. Ibid.

12. 'Locomotive Engines', *Westmorland Gazette* (13 February 1836), p. 1.

13. E. Woods, 'On certain forms of Locomotive Engines', *American Railroad Journal and Mechanics' Magazine*, vol. VIII (1839), pp.330-332.

14. RAIL 371/10 Management Sub-Committee, Minutes, 19 February 1835; RAIL 371/3 Directors' Meeting, Minutes 7 December 1835.

15. RAIL 371/4 Directors' Meeting, Minutes 6 February 1837; Whishaw, *Railways*, Appendix X, p. xviii.

16. RAIL 371/10 Management Sub-Committee, 4 April 1833.

17. RAIL 371/3 Directors' Meeting, Minutes 19 May 1834, 7 July 1834, 29 September 1834.

18. RAIL 371/10 Management Sub-Committee, Minutes 12 December 1833.

19. RAIL 371/10 Management Sub-Committee, Minutes 12 December 1833.

20. RAIL 371/10 Management Sub-Committee, Minutes 26 December 1833.

21. RAIL 371/10 Management Sub-Committee, Minutes 4 February 1834.

22. RAIL371/10 Management Sub-Committee, Minutes 31 March 1836; RAIL 371/4 Directors' Meeting, Minutes 18 April 1836.

23. RAIL 371/12 Report by Henry Booth on Patentee Locomotive 30 June 1836, passim.

24. J. Gray, 'Four-wheeled and six-wheeled Engines. To the Editor', *The Railway Times*, vol. IV (1841), p. 1256.

25. *Manchester Courier* (17 November 1838).

26. Ibid.

27. Ibid.

28. RAIL 371/4 Directors' Meeting, Minutes 19 November 1838.

29. W. K. Hall, 'On the Cause of the Explosion of Steam Boilers', *Minutes of Proceedings of the Institution of Civil Engineers*, vol. 15 (1855-1856), p. 301.

30. 'Specification of Patent granted Robert Stephenson', *Repertory of Patent Inventions*, New Series Vol. II (July-December 1834) (London: John Weale, 1834), p. 261.

31. ROB/2/4/2 Description Book, pp. 27-28; ROB/2/4/1 Description Book 1831, pp. 42-43.

32. Marshall, *Patent Locomotive*, p. 16.

33. RAIL 371/3 Directors' Meeting, Minutes 5 May 1834, 12 May 1834, 19 May 1834, 2 June 1834.

34. 'On the relative Heating Powers of Coal and Coke', *Proceedings of the Institution of Civil Engineers*, Vol. 1 (1838), pp. 39-40; 'Mr Parkes on Steam Boilers and Steam Engines', *Transactions of the Institute of Civil Engineers*, Vol. 3 (1842), pp. 33-35.

35. ROB/2/4/1 Description Book 1831, p. 43.

36. 'Specification Robert Stephenson', p.266.

37. Marshall, *Patent Locomotive*, p. 54.

38. RAIL 371/3 Directors Meeting, Minutes 3 June 1833.

39. RAIL 371/3 Directors' Meeting, Minutes 24 February 1834.

40. RAIL 371/3 Directors' Meeting, Minutes 3 March 1834.

41. RAIL 371/4 Directors' Meeting, Minutes 2 May 1836.

42. RAIL 371/3 Directors' Meeting, Minutes 10 March 1834.

43. 'Patent Suspension Wheels by Theodore Jones of Vauxhall', *Register of Arts and Journal of Patent Inventions*, vol. 2, new series (1828), pp. 65-66.

44. RAIL 371/10 Management Sub-Committee, Minutes, 19 February 1835.

45. RAIL 371/24 Disbursement Accounts 1833-1845, *passim*.

46. Marshall, *Patent Locomotive*, pp. 48-49.

47. 'Specification Robert Stephenson', p. 265.

48. RAIL 371/10 Management Sub-Committee, Minutes 6 August 1835.

49. RAIL 371/3 Directors' Meeting, Minutes 3 August 1835, 14 September 1835; RAIL 371/10 Management Sub-Committee, Minutes 3 September 1835.

50. E. Woods, 'On the Consumption of Fuel in the Locomotive Engines of the Liverpool & Manchester Railway', in *Weale's Quarterly Papers on Engineering*, Vol. II. (1844), p.5; E. Woods, 'On the Consumption of Fuel and the Evaporation of Water in Locomotive and other Steam Engines', in T. Tredgold, ed., *The Principles and Practice and Explanation of the Machinery of Locomotive Engines* (London: John Weale, 1850), p. 24.

51. RAIL 371/3 Directors' Meeting, Minutes 22 February 1836; RAIL 371/4 Directors' Meeting, Minutes 28 March 1836.

52. RAIL 371/41 Drawing No. 15 'Star'.

53. RAIL 371/4 Directors' Meeting, Minutes 11 April 1836.

54. RAIL 371/4 Director's Meeting, Minutes 6 June 1836; RAIL 371/10 Management Sub-Committee, Minutes 9 June 1836.

55. RAIL 371/4 Directors' Meeting, Minutes 27 March 1837; 'Improved Loco-Motive Engine', *Newcastle Journal* (4 March 1837), p. 3; 'Improvement on Loco-Motive Machinery', *Newcastle Journal* (11 March 1837), p. 3; 'Railway at Speed', *Liverpool Mercury* (22 June 1868), p. 6.

56. RAIL 371/4 Directors' Meeting, Minutes 24 April 1837, 16 April 1838.

57. RAIL 371/3 Directors' Meeting, 8 December 1834, 15 December 1834.

58. RAIL 371/3 Directors' Meeting, Minutes 15 December 1834, 29 December 1834; RAIL 371/10 Management Sub-Committee, Minutes 26 December 1834.

59. RAIL 371/3 Directors' Meeting, Minutes 8 December 1834; RAIL 371/10 Management Sub-Committee, Minutes 26 December 1834; 8 January 1835.

60. RAIL 371/10 Management Sub-Committee, Minutes 8 January 1835.

61. RAIL 371/10 Management Sub-Committee, Minutes 2 April 1835.

62. RAIL 371/3 Directors' Meeting, Minutes 16 March 1835, 28 December 1835; RAIL 371/10 Management Sub-Committee, Minutes 27 November 1834.

63. 'Locomotive Engines', *Westmorland Gazette* (13 February 1836), p. 1.

64. 'Locomotive Engines', *Westmorland Gazette* (13 February 1836), p. 1.

65. RAIL 371/3 Directors' Meeting, Minutes 2 November 1835.

66. RAIL 371/3 Directors' Meeting, Minutes 28 December 1835.

67. RAIL 371/4 Directors' Meeting, Minutes 2 May 1836.

68. RAIL 371/3 Directors' Meeting, Minutes 7 December 1835.

69. 'Locomotive Engines', *Westmorland Gazette* (13 February 1836), p. 1.

Chapter 6. Melling's Patent Locomotives

1. RAIL 371/10 Management Sub-Committee, Minutes 24 November 1836, 6 December 1836.

2. 'To Engineers and Engine Builders', *Gore's Liverpool General Advertiser* (22 June 1837), p. 1.

3. RAIL 371/4 Directors' Meeting, Minutes 8 May 1837, 21 May 1838.

4. RAIL 371/24 Disbursement Accounts, 1833-1845, p. 8, p. 17.

5. RAIL 371/4 Directors' Meeting, Minutes 2 October 1837.

6. RAIL 371/4 Directors' Meeting, Minutes 1 October 1838, 3 December 1838, 24 December 1838; RAIL 371/10 Management Sub-Committee, Minutes 20 December 1838; 'On Sale: Two New Powerful Locomotive Engines', *Manchester Courier* (13 October 1838), p. 1.

7. National Railway Museum, York: Melling Papers. MEL/3, list of locomotives fitted with Melling's patent improvements, 10 April 1839; MEL/4 note, 'Number of locomotives fitted with the Patent Gearing', 6 December 1838.

8. 'Specification of Patent granted to John Melling', *The Repertory of Patent Inventions 1838*, new series, vol. X (July -December 1838) (London: J. S. Hodson, 1838), pp. 8-9. See also NRM MEL/1, Specification of Letters Patent Granted to John Melling.

9. RAIL 371/3 Directors' Meeting, Minutes 15 July 1833.

10. 'Specification of Patent granted to Robert Stephenson', *The Repertory of Patent Inventions*, vol. XIII (1832) (London: Effingham & Wilson, 1832), pp. 1-9.

11. RAIL 371/8 Management Sub-Committee, Minutes 2 January 1833.

12. 'Specification John Melling', pp. 2-3.

13. RAIL 371/4 Directors' Meeting, Minutes 12 February 1837.

14. RAIL 1008/88/1/2 Letter from R. Stephenson to H. Booth, 3 August 1829; E. Woods, 'On Certain Forms of Locomotive Engines', *American Railroad Journal and Mechanics' Magazine*, vol. VIII (1839), pp. 376-379. Paper originally

presented to the Institute of Civil Engineers, 30 January 1838; R. Gibbon & R. Lamb, ''Runnin' wi' your breeks down': An investigation of coupling-rod resistance in a four-coupled locomotive', in M. J. T. Lewis, ed., *Early Railways 2* (The Newcomen Society, 2003), pp. 232-240.

15. De Pambour, *Traité*, 1e edition, p. 337.

16. De Pambour, *Traité Théorique et Pratique des Machines Locomotives* (Paris: Bachelier et Cie., 1840), 2e edition, p. 37 and pp. 490-491.

17. 'Specification John Melling', pp. 2-3.

18. RAIL 371/10 Management Sub-Committee, Minutes 23 November 1837; RAIL 371/42 Grand Junction Railway. Extracts from Minutes of the Board, Minute 11 October 1837.

19. 'Scraps from a Manuscript Volume', *Liverpool Chronicle* (2 September 1882), np.

20. D. K. Clark, *Railway Machinery: A Treatise on the Mechanical Engineering of Railways* (London: Blackie & Son, 1855), vol. 1, p. 23.

21. J. S. Russell, *A Treatise on the Steam Engine* (Edinburgh: Adam & Charles Black, 1851), p. 135.

22. Clark, *Railway Machinery*, p. 23; N. P. Burgh, *Link Motion and Expansion Gear Practically Considered* (London: E. & F. N. Spon, 1872), p. 13.

23. 'Specification John Melling', pp. 9-10.

24. Burgh, *Link-Motion*, p. 13; J. Bourne, *A Treatise on the Steam Engine in its Application to Mines, Mills, Steam Navigation, and Railways* (New York: D. Appleton & Co., 1851), pp. 238-239.

25. Pambour, *Traite*, 2e edition, p. 27.

26. RAIL 371/4 Directors' Meeting, Minutes 11 December 1837, 18 December 1837, 1 January 1838, 8 January 1838, 15 January 1838.

27. RAIL 371/42 Grand Junction Railway. Extracts from Minutes of the Board, Minutes 24 January 1838. NRM MEL/3 list of Grand Junction Locomotives, 10 April 1839.

28. NRM MEL/4 note 'locomotives fitted with the Patent Gearing', 6 December 1838.

29. RAIL 371/10 Management Sub-Committee, Minutes 1 March 1838.

30. Whishaw, *Railways*, Appendix X, p. xvii.

31. RAIL 371/10 Management Sub-Committee, Minutes 16 March 1838.

32. RAIL 371/29 Monthly accounts for cost of repairs on locomotives, carriages and wagons 1837-1839, Bills dated 30 March 1838, 30 June 1838, 31 August 1838, 31 May 1839.

33. E. Woods, 'Evaporation of water', pp. 22-23.

34. NRM, MEL/3, list of locomotives with patent gearing, 10 April 1839.

35. T. R. Pearce, *The Locomotives of the Stockton and Darlington Railway* (The Historical Model Railway Society, 1996), pp. 87-88; B. Reed, *The Norris Type* (Windsor: Profile Publications, ND) p. 264.

36. De Pambour (p. 369), however, describes goods wagons as weighing 1.5 tons and carrying 3.5 tons, making 5 tons gross; Booth in his evidence to the Gauge Commissioners suggests an average unladen weight of 2 tons 12cwt.

37. Woods, 'Evaporation of Water', p.22.

38. L. E. Morris, 'The Restoration of Lion', *Railway World* vol. 41, no. 481 (May 1980), p.251; J. G. H. Warren, *Liverpool & Manchester Railway Lion. Exhibition notes*, September 1930.

39. Woods, 'Evaporation of Water', p.22*; Gauge Commissioners Report*. Minutes of Evidence (London: HMSO, 1846), p. 303, para 5923.

40. Woods, 'Evaporation of Water', p.22; RAIL 371/40 Performances of Locomotives, 1839-1840, *passim*.

41. De Pambour (p.370) suggests a first-class coach weighed 3.65 tons; a second-class 2.23 tons and a mail 2.71 and that 15 passengers constituted one ton. Edward Woods in 1845 describes a first-class coach weighing 4 tons 7cwt; second-class 3 tons 16cwt. Thus, a fully laden coach would weigh approximately 5 tons.

42. 'Locomotive Performance', *The Engineer* (15 October 1880), p. 291.

43. 'Quick Travelling', *Leeds Times* (1 October 1842), p. 5.

44. J. Gray, 'Four-wheeled and six-wheeled Engines. To the editor', *The Railway Times*, vol. IV (1841), p. 1257.

45. RAIL 371/5 Directors' Meeting, Minutes 14 February 1842.

46. RAIL 371/4 Directors' Meeting, Minutes 1 October 1838.

47. 'Links in the History of the Locomotive, No. XV', *The Engineer* (28 December 1883), p. 500.

48. William Greener, 'Strength of Iron, in reply to a Correspondent', *The Railway Magazine* vol. 5 (new series), 1839, pp. 377-378.

49. Ibid.

50. Ibid, p. 501.

51. Whishaw, *Railways*, Appendix X, p. xviii.

52. RAIL 371/4 Directors' Meeting, Minutes 22 October 1838, 29 October 1838.

53. RAIL 371/4 Directors' Meeting, Minutes 20 December 1838, 24 December 1838.

54. RAIL 371/5 Directors' Meeting, Minutes 17 June 1839.

55. 'Notice to Engine Builders', *Manchester Courier* (15 June 1839), p. 1.

56. M. R. Bailey, *Locomotion: The world's oldest steam locomotives* (Stroud: The History Press, 2014), p. 95.

Chapter 7. Edge Hill Comes of Age

1. RAIL 371/4 Directors' Meeting, Minutes 13 August 1838.

2. RAIL 371/11 Management Sub-Committee, Minutes 23 September 1839.

3. RAIL 371/11 Management Sub-Committee, Minutes 10 October 1839.

4. RAIL 371/5 Directors' Meeting, Minutes.

5. RAIL 371/5 Directors' Meeting, Minutes 2 December 1839.

6. RAIL 371/5 Directors' Meeting, Minutes 18 November 1839; 2 December 1839; 23 December 1839; 27 January 1840.

7. RAIL 371/11 Management Sub-Committee, Minutes 9 September 1841.

8. *Gauge Commissioners 1846*, p. 305, para. 5990.

9. 'Reports to the Committee of the Privy Council', *Parliamentary Papers*, Vol. 41 (February – August 1843) p. 206, evidence of Edward Woods.

10. RAIL 3741/11 Management Sub-Committee, Minutes 16 November 1843.

11. RAIL 371/11 Management Sub-Committee, Minutes 16 November 1843; RAIL 371/11 Directors' Meeting, Minutes 20 November 1843.

12. RAIL 371/11 Management Sub-Committee, Minutes 14 December 1843, 28 December 1843, 8 February 1844.

13. British Transport Commission, *Handbook for Railway Steam Locomotive Enginemen* (London: British Transport Commission, 1957), pp. 81-82.

14. Ibid, pp. 80-86 and pp.98-103.

15. E. Woods, 'Consumption of fuel', p. 8. See also Woods, 'Evaporation of water', p.25-29*ff*.

16. Woods, 'Consumption of Fuel', pp. 8-9; Woods, 'Evaporation of Water', p. 27.

17. Woods, 'Consumption of Fuel', pp. 9-10. See also Woods, 'Evaporation of water', p.29*ff*.

18. Woods, 'Consumption of Fuel', pp. 11-12.

19. E. Woods, 'Expansion of Steam in Locomotives', *The Artizan*, vol. I (1844), p.59.

20. Woods, 'Consumption of Fuel', pp. 13-14; see also D. K Clark, *Railway Machinery*, p. 25.

21. Colburn, *Locomotive Engineering*, vol. 1 p.67; D. K. Clark, *The Steam Engine: A treatise on Steam Engines and Boilers* (London: Blackie & Son, 1891), p.76.

22. RAIL 351/5 Directors' Meeting, Minutes 9 December 1839.

23. Woods, 'Evaporation of Water', p. 29.

24. RAIL 220/41 Grand Junction Railway. Report on "Rokeby" and "Cyclops", nd.

25. 'Lead of the Valve' in W. Templeton, *The Engineer's Common-place Book of Practical Reference* (London: Simpkin Marshall & Co, 1839) pp. 60-6; Woods, 'Consumption of Fuel', p. 29.

26. RAIL 220/41 Grand Junction Railway. Report on "Rokeby" and "Cyclops", nd.

27. RAIL 220/41 Grand Junction Railway. Report on "Cyclops" and "Hecate" 11 January 1840; RAIL 371/29 Monthly accounts for cost of repairs on locomotives, carriages and wagons 1837-1839, 30 November 1839. See also 'Scraps from a Manuscript Volume', *Liverpool Courier* 2 September 1882, np.

28. Woods, 'Consumption of Fuel', p. 30; Colburn, *Locomotive Engineering*, p. 50.

29. Woods, 'Expansion of Steam', pp.57-60.

30. RAIL 371/11 Management Sub-Committee, Minutes 9 September 1841.

31. *Handbook for the Railway Steam Locomotive Engineman* (London: British Transport Commission, 1957), pp. 23-25; *Good Firemanship* (London: British Transport Commission, 1956), *passim*.

32. Colburn, *Locomotive Engineering*, p. 54.

33. RAIL 371/3 Directors' Meeting, Minutes 30 November 1835.

34. RAIL 371/3 Directors' Meeting, Minutes 31 October 1836; 7 November 1836.

35. RAIL 371/3 Directors' Meeting, Minutes 14 November 1836; 'On the relative Heating Powers of Coke and Coal', *Proceedings of the Institute of Civil Engineers*, Vol. 1 (1838), p. 40.

36. RAIL 371/3 Directors' Meeting, Minutes 21 November 1836, 5 December 1836.

37. RAIL 371/3 Directors' Meeting, Minutes 16 January 1837; RAIL 371/10 Management Sub-Committee, Minutes 19 January 1837.

38. RAIL 371/4 Directors' Meeting, Minutes 23 January 1837, 20 February 1837.

39. RAIL 371/4 Directors' Meeting, Minutes 3 April 1837.

40. RAIL 371/4 Directors' Meeting, Minutes 18 September 1837, October 1837.

41. RAIL 371/4 Directors' Meeting, Minutes 28 July 1838.

42. RAIL 371/4 Directors' Meeting, Minutes 15 May 1837.

43. Lieutenant P. Lecount, *A Practical Treatise on Railways* (Edinburgh: Adam & Charles Black, 1839), p. 389.

44. Ibid.

45. 'Trial of Anthracite Coal', *Manchester Courier* (28 July 1838), p. 2; 'Anthracite Coal', *Northampton Mercury* (4 August 1838), p. 4.

46. 'Anthracite Coal', *Northampton Mercury* (4 August 1838), p. 4. See also 'Trial of Anthracite Coal in Locomotive Engines', *The Mechanics' Magazine*, vol. XXIX (April-September 1838), p. 302; 'Trials of Anthracite Coal for Locomotive Engines', *The Civil Engineer and Architect's Journal*, Vol. 1 (October 1837-December 1838), p. 320.

47. RAIL 371/6 Directors' Meeting, Minutes 26 September 1842; 'Locomotive Smoke Consumer', *Leicestershire Mercury* (22 May 1841), p. 3: 'Mr Samuel Hall's Smoke-Burner', *Mechanics' Magazine*, vol. XXXVII (July-December 1842), pp. 227-229.

48. *Description of the Operation of Samuel Hall's Patent Condensers and ... Improvements on Steam Engines ... and Patent Smoke Consuming Apparatus* (London: John Weale, 1843), pp. 13-14.

49. 'Mr Samuel Hall's mode of admitting air to furnaces', *The Mechanics' Magazine*, vol. XXXVII (July-December 1842), p. 227.

50. 'Dewrance's Firebox: to the Editor of the Engineer', *The Engineer* (18 December 1857), pp. 456-457; D. K. Clark & Z. Colburn, *Recent Practice in the Locomotive Engine* (London: Blackie & Son, 1860), p. 26.

51. 'Dewrance's Patent Boiler: to the Editor of the Engineer', *The Engineer* (15 February 1856), p. 77; 'Letters to the Editor: Improvement in Locomotives', *The Engineer* (27 November 1857), p. 399; 'An Improved Locomotive Engine', *Worcester Journal* (30 October 1845), p. 4.

52. 'To the Editor of the Engineer', *The Engineer* (29 February 1856), p. 108 and p. 113; Z. Colburn, & A. L. Holley, *The Permanent Way and Coal Burning Boilers of European Railways* (New York: Holly & Colburn, 1858), p. xvii.

53. Woods, 'Consumption of Fuel', p. 13.

54. Ibid.

55. Ibid.

56. *Gauge Commissioners* 1846, p. 513.

57. University of London, Senate House Library: Charles Lawrence Papers MS584, 2347 letter Edward Woods to Charles Lawrence 16 December 1842.

58. Ibid.

59. Ibid.

60. 'The London & North Western Railway and Crewe Works', *The Engineer: Supplement* (11 December 1908), p. iv.

61. C. F. Dendy-Marshall, *Centenary History of the Liverpool & Manchester Railway* (London: Locomotive Publishing Co., 1930), p.86.

62. Woods, 'Consumption of Fuel', pp. 13-14.

63. 'The "Lion" Locomotive', *The Engineer* (14 November 1930), p. 335 and direct observation of the locomotive.

64. Woods, 'Consumption of Fuel', pp. 13-14, p. 19; see also *Gauge Commissioners 1846*, p. 303, para. 5923.

65. Ibid.

66. 'The London & North Western Railway and Crewe Works', *The Engineer: Supplement* (11 December 1908), p. iv; A. R. Bennet, *The Chronicles of Boulton's Siding* (London: Locomotive Publishing Co., Ltd., 1926), p. 59*ff.*

67. 'Liverpool & Manchester Railway. Cost of Motive power for six months, Ending 20 December 1844', *The Engineer* (6 February 1885),p. 97.

68. Colburn, *Locomotive Engineering*, p. 50ff.

69. 'Liverpool & Manchester Railway. Cost of Motive power for six months, Ending 20 December 1844', *The Engineer* (6 February 1885),p. 97.

70. Ibid; P. Eckersley, *Railway Management* (London: Simpkin, Marshall & Co., 1848), p. 31.

71. RAIL 371/29 Monthly accounts, *passim*.

72. Salford City Archives, Ref. U268/C1/1-6 Nasmyth, Gaskell & Co, Letter books. U268/C1/5 letter from Nasmyth Gaskell to Mr Gordon of Manchester 5 June 1839 ordering numbers for each engine 'similar to those on the chimneys of the Liverpool & Manchester engines.'

73. RAIL 371/2 Directors' Meeting, Minutes 7 February 1833.

PART 2: BREAKING THE MOULD

1. Warren, *A Century*, pp.79-85. See also Bailey, *Robert Stephenson*, pp.176-182.

2. RAIL 371/2 Directors' Meeting, Minutes 24 September 1832; RAIL 371/3 Directors' Meeting, Minutes 6 January 1834.

3. RAIL 371/1, Directors Meeting, Minutes 7 September 1829, 22 March 1830, 24 May 1830; RAIL 371/4 Directors' Meeting, Minutes4 July 1836, 18 July 1836.

Chapter 8. Braithwaite and Ericsson

1. P. Davidson & J. Glithero, 'Learning from Replication', in M. R. Bailey, ed., *Early Railways 3* (Sudbury: Six Martletts, 2006), pp.284-292.

2. RAIL 371/1 Directors' Meeting, Minutes 2 November 1829.

3. 'The Rival Carriages', *Liverpool Mercury* (30 October 1829), p.6; 'Rail-way Experiments', *The Staffordshire Advertiser* (26 December 1829), p. 2, citing *Liverpool Courier*; RAIL 371/1 Directors Meeting, Minutes 11 January 1830; J. Locke & R. Stephenson, Account of the Competition of Locomotive Engines... (Liverpool, 1830) pp. 81-82.

4. *Lancaster Gazette* (2 January 1830).

5. For example: 'Rail-ways', *The Cork Constitution* (2 January 1830), p. 4; 'Experiments making on the Railway', *Nottingham Review* (8 January 1830), p. 4; 'To the Editor of the Aberdeen Journal' *The Aberdeen Journal* (13 January 1830), p. 4.

6. National Railway Museum, York: John Rastrick MSS, Rainhill Notebook, Acc. 1945-108, passim.

7. RAIL 371/1 Directors' Meeting, Minutes 1 February 1830.

8. K. H. Vignoles, *Charles Blacker Vignoles: Romantic Engineer* (Cambridge: Cambridge University Press, reprint 2010), p. 47.

9. RAIL 371/1 Directors' Meeting, Minutes 15 February 1830.

10. RAIL 371/2 Directors' Meeting, Minutes 19 July 1830, 26 July 1830.

11. RAIL 371/2 Directors' Meeting, Minutes 2 August 1830, 16 August 1830, 23 August 1830, 30 August 1830.

12. 'Messrs. Braithwaite and Ericsson's Engines' *Mechanics' Magazine* (25 September 1830), pp. 69-70; 'Liverpool & Manchester Railway', *Mechanics' Magazine* (2 October 1830), p. 88.

13. 'Experiment with a ... Boiler on Messrs. Braithwaite and Ericsson's Exhausting Principle', *Mechanics' Magazine*, (5 June 1830), pp.235-236. See also, ICE, London, report of Alexander Nimmo and C B Vignoles, 29 May 1830.

14. M. R. Bailey, 'Brunel's Fan: His Locomotive Draught Experiments 1840/1841', *Transactions of the Newcomen* Society, vol. 87 (2017), pp.20-41.

15. RAIL 371/2 Directors' Meeting, Minutes 27 September 1830; 'The Liverpool and Manchester Railway', *Mechanics' Magazine* (2 October 1830), pp. 88-89; 'The Liverpool and Manchester Railway', *The Glasgow Mechanics' Magazine* (No. CXXXII), pp. 287-289.

16. RAIL 371/2, Directors' Meeting, Minutes 4 October 1830.

17. 'The Locomotives', *Manchester Mercury* (26 October 1830), p. 4; 'The Railway', *Birmingham Journal* (2 October 1830), p. 4 citing the *Liverpool Chronicle*.

18. RAIL 371/2 Directors' Meeting, Minutes 24 January 1831.

19. 'The William the Fourth', *Mechanics' Magazine* (22 January 1831), p. 365.

20. 'Messrs. Braithwaite and Ericsson's Steam-Carriages. To the Editor', *Mechanics' Magazine* (5 February 1831), pp. 414-415.

21. 'Braithwaite and Ericsson's Engine', *Preston Chronicle* (26 February 1831), citing the *Manchester Guardian*; 'Braithwaite and Ericsson's Steam-Carriages v. Those of Mr Robert Stephenson', *The Register of Arts and Journal of Patent Inventions*, vol. VI (1832), pp.20-21.

22. 'Braithwaite and Ericsson's Steam-Carriages v. Those of Mr Robert Stephenson', *The Register of Arts and Journal of Patent Inventions*, vol. VI (1832), pp.20-21.

23. Ibid, pp. 21-22.
24. 'Final Trial of Braithwaite and Ericsson's Engine', *Manchester Guardian* (26 February 1831), p. 3; also cited by *The Preston Chronicle* (5 March 1831), p. 4.
25. 'Braithwaite and Ericsson's Steam-Carriages', p. 23.
26. 'Improvements in Locomotive Engines', *Manchester Guardian* (26 February 1831) p.3; 'Experiments on the Liverpool and Manchester Railway', *Aris's Birmingham Gazette* (2 May 1831), p. 4.
27. Dawson, *Rainhill Trials*, pp. 82-83.
28. RAIL371/3 Directors' Meeting, Minutes 18 November 1833, 2 December 1833, 23 December 1833, 20 January 1834; 'The Ericsson Caloric Engine', *The Mechanics' Magazine,* No. 535 (9 November 1833), pp. 81-83. See also J. Ericsson, *The Caloric Engine invented by J. Ericsson* (London: 1833), passim. Although' Ericsson claimed to have invented the hot air engine, it had in fact been patented by Stirling in 1816.

Chapter 9: *Sans Pareil*

1. M. R. Bailey, 'Robert Stephenson & Co. 1823-1829' *Transactions of the Newcomen Society*, vol. 50 (1978), pp. 112-113.
2. RAIL 371/1 Directors' Meeting, Minutes 18 May 1829.
3. Dawson, *Rainhill*, chapter 3.
4. NRM HACK 1-1-25. Timothy Hackworth to Liverpool & Manchester Board of Directors, no date but probably October 1829; Bailey, 'Robert Stephenson', p. 125.
5. HACK 1-1-25. Hackworth to Liverpool & Manchester Board.
6. HACK 1-1-25. Timothy Hackworth to Liverpool & Manchester Board.
7. RAIL 371/2 Directors' Meeting, Minutes 3 October 1831, 12 October 1829, 19 October 1829; NRM ROB/4/1 Robert Stephenson & Co, Works Ledger 1823-1831, p. 214, entry dated 28 September 1829.
8. RAIL 371/1 Directors' Meeting, Minutes 19 October, 7 December 1829, 4 January 1830.
9. RAIL 371/1 Directors' Meeting, Minutes 8 March 1830, 15 March 1830.
10. *Liverpool Mercury* (9 April 1830).
11. RAIL 371/2 Directors' Meeting, Minutes 3 October 1831.
12. RAIL 371/8 Management Sub-Committee, Minutes 4 January 1832; C. F. Dendy Marshall, A *History of Railway Locomotives down to the end of the year 1831* (London: Locomotive Publishing Co., Ltd. 1953), p. 176.
13. 'Engineering Archaeology – The Historical Locomotives at South Kensington', *Journal of the Franklin Institute* Vol. LXXIX (January – June 1865), p. 307; J. Liffen, 'The Beginnings of Railway Locomotive Preservation' in M. J. T. Lewis, ed., *Early Railways 2* (London: The Newcomen Society, 2003), pp.208-213.

Chapter 10. Edward Bury

1. J. Bourne, 'Recollections of Improvements which have been made in the steam engine during the last half century. No. IV', *The Engineer* (24 December 1875), p. 441.

2. *Recollections of Edward Bury by his Widow*, (Windermere: John Garnett, ND) p. 2.

3. 'To the editor: George Stephenson and his detractors', *The Engineer's Journal* (3 January 1861), p. 7.

4. Lecount, *Treatise*, p. 377; J. S. Walker, *An accurate description of the Liverpool & Manchester Railway* (Liverpool: J. F. Cannell, 1830), p. 46; Bourne, 'Recollections of Improvements', p. 441; Ahrons, 'History of famous firms', *The Engineer* (2 February 1923), pp. 111-112.

5. 'Dreadful Accident on the Bolton & Leigh Railway', *Gore's Liverpool General Advertiser* (23 June 1831), p. 4.

6. D. K. Clark, 'On the Improvement of Railway Locomotive Stock and Reduction in Working Expenses', *Minutes Proceedings of the Institute of Civil Engineers*, vol. XVI (1856-1857), p. 24.

7. Bourne, 'Recollections of Improvements' p. 441; Clark, 'On the Improvement', p.24; *Recollections* p. 3.

8. *Recollections*, p. 3; Clark, 'On the Improvement', p. 25; Lecount, *Treatise*, p.477; RAIL 371/2 Directors' Meeting, Minutes 25 October 1830, 22 November 1830; Vignoles, *Vignoles*, p. 44.

9. RAIL 371/2 Directors' Meeting, Minutes 20 June 1831, 27 June 1831, 4 July 1831.

10. *Recollections*, p. 3; 'Railway Accident', *Lancaster Gazette* (30 July 1831), p. 4; Clark, 'On the Improvements', p. 24.

11. RAIL 371/2 Directors' Meeting, Minutes 1 August 1831.

12. RAIL 371/2 Directors' Meeting, Minutes 8 August 1831.

13. RAIL 371/2 Directors' Meeting, Minutes 15 August 1831.

14. Ibid.

15. RAIL 371/8 Management Sub-Committee, Minutes 4 December 1831.

16. RAIL 371/8 Management Sub-Committee, Minutes 1 January 1832.

17. RAIL 371/8 Management Sub-Committee, Minutes 1 January 1832; RAIL 371/2 Directors' Meeting Minutes, 2 January 1832, 9 January 1832.

18. RAIL 371/2 Directors' Meeting, Minutes 2 April 1832.

19. ROB Memoranda, p. 6; see also ROB2/4/2 Robert Stephenson & Co, Description Book No. 1, p.10.

20. RAIL 371/2 Directors' Meeting, Minutes 2 April 1832, 16 April 1832, 2 July 1832.

21. RAIL 371/2 Directors' Meeting, Minutes 10 December 1832.

22. RAIL 371/2 Directors' Meeting, Minutes 28 May 1832.

23. RAIL 371/2 Directors' Meeting, Minutes 18 June 1832.

24. Ibid.

25. RAIL 371/2 Directors' Meeting, Minutes 2 July 1832.

26. RAIL 371/2 Directors' Meeting, Minutes 23 July 1832.
27. RAIL 371/2 Directors' Meeting, Minutes 30 July 1832.
28. Rail 371/8 Management Sub-committee, Minutes 6 September 1832.
29. RAIL 371/2 Directors' Meeting, Minutes 10 September 1832.
30. RAIL 371/2 Directors' Meeting, Minutes 10 September 1832.
31. RAIL 371/2 Directors' Meeting, Minutes 24 September 1832, 1 October 1832, 8 October 1832.
32. RAIL 371/2 Directors' Meeting, Minutes 12 October 1832, 22 October 1832, 29 October 1832.
33. RAIL 371/2 Directors' Meeting, Minutes 22 October 1832, 29 October 1832.
34. RAIL 371/2 Directors' Meeting, Minutes, 14 January 1833.
35. RAIL 371/2 Directors' Meeting, Minutes, 21 January 1833.
36. RAIL 371/2 Directors' Meeting, Minutes 28 January 1833.
37. Ibid.
38. RAIL 371/3 Directors' Meeting, Minutes 4 February 1833.
39. RAIL 371/3 Directors' Meeting, Minutes 18 February 1833.
40. RAIL 371/3 Directors' Meeting, Minutes 25 March 1833, 22 April 1833.
41. RAIL 371/3 Directors' Meeting, Minutes 3 February 1834, 10 February 1834. RAIL 371/3 Directors' Meeting, Minutes 23 December 1833, 30 December 1833, 3 February 1834, 10 February 1834; RAIL 371/10 Management Sub-Committee, Minutes 24 January 1834.
42. RAIL 371/3 Directors' Meeting, Minutes 31 March 1834; RAIL 371/10 Management Sub-Committee, Minutes 28 May 1834.
43. RAIL 371/3 Directors' Meeting, Minutes 7 April 1834, 21 April 1834, 21 July 1834, 8 December 1834; RAIL 371/8 Management Sub-Committee, Minutes 20 March 1833; RAIL 371/10 Management Sub-Committee, Minutes 10 July 1834.

Chapter 11. Built in Manchester

1. C. F. Dendy Marshall, 'Locomotive No. 28, Liverpool & Manchester Railway', *The Engineer* (4 July 1924), p. 20. For a discussion on these three locomotives see also: A. L. Dawson, 'Three Liverpool & Manchester Curiosities', *R&CHS Journal*: forthcoming.
2. 'New Locomotive Engine', *Manchester Times* (3 September 1831), p. 5.
3. D. A. Farnie & W. O. Henderson (eds.), *W. H. Challoner Industry and Innovation. Selected Essays*, pp. 104-107.
4. 'New Locomotive Engine', *Manchester Times* (3 September 1831), p. 5.
5. Farnie & Henderson, *Industry and Innovation*, pp. 107-108.
6. RAIL 371/3 Directors' Meeting, Minutes 4 March 1833.
7. RAIL371/8 Management Sub-Committee, Minutes 6 March 1833.
8. Ibid.

9. RAIL 371/3 Directors' Meeting, Minutes 18 March 1833; 'Fatal Accident on the Railroad', *Liverpool Advertiser* (7 March 1833), p. 6. Also reported as 'Fatal Accident on the Rail Road', *Lancaster Gazette* (9 March 1833), p. 3.

10. A. L. Dawson, *The Early Railways of Manchester* (Stroud: Amberley Publishing, 2017), p. 13.

11. 'New Locomotive Engine', *Manchester Courier* (29 September 1832), p. 2.

12. RAIL 371/2 Directors' Meeting, Minutes 19 September 1831, 31 October 1831, 10 September 1832, 22 October 1832, 29 October 1832.

13. Obituary, 1884 via https://www.gracesguide.co.uk/Isaac_Dodds accessed 12-06-2019 @18.51. See also 'The First Locomotive on the Sheffield and Rotherham Railway' *Sheffield Daily Telegraph* (9 October 1875), p. 8.

14. RAIL 371/ Directors' Meeting Minutes 2 March 1835.

15. RAIL 371/4 Directors' Meeting, Minutes 29 May 1837; Dawson, *Early Manchester*, pp.10-14.

16. RAIL 371/2 Directors' Meeting, Minutes 15 August 1831.

17. RAIL 371/2 Directors' Meeting, Minutes 22 August 1831.

18. RAIL 371/2 Directors Meeting, Minutes 29 August 1831.

19. RAIL 371/2 Directors' Meeting, Minutes 24 October 1831.

20. RAIL 371/3 Directors' Meeting, Minutes 20 May 1833; RAIL 371/8 Management Sub-Committee, Minutes 29 November 1832; RAIL 371/10 Management Sub-Committee, Minutes 16 May 1833.

21. RAIL 371/3 Directors' Meeting, Minutes 7 October 1832, 24 June 1833, 24 February 1834; RAIL 371/4 Directors' Meeting, Minutes 19 October 1836; RAIL 371/10 Management Sub-Committee, Minutes 16 October 1834; Dendy Marshall, *Centenary History*, p. 91.

Chapter 12: Outside Cylinders

1. RAIL 371/3 Directors' Meeting, Minutes 17 November 1834; RAIL 371/10 Management Sub-Committee, Minutes 19 March 1835; 'Links in the History of Railway Locomotives: No. 14' *The Engineer* (2 March 1883), p. 160; E. L. Ahrons, *The British Steam Locomotive 1825-1925* (London: Locomotive Publishing Co., 1927), pp. 29-30; Dendy Marshall, *Centenary History*, p. 94.

2. RAIL 371/10 Management Sub-Committee, Minutes 1 March 1838; Woods, 'Consumption of Fuel', p. 13.

3. 'Wonders of Steam', *Liverpool Mercury* (4 July 1834), p. 6.

4. RAIL 371/10 Management Sub-Committee, Minutes 26 November 1835.

5. RAIL 371/3 Directors' Meeting, Minutes 18 November 1833, 2 March 1835, 16 March 1835, 27 July 1835, 23 November 1835.

6. 'Improvements in Locomotive Engines', *Manchester Courier* (31 December 1836), p. 2; RAIL 371/4 Directors' Meeting, Minutes 6 February 1837.

7. RAIL 374/4 Directors' Meeting, Minutes 11 April 1836, 2 July 1838; 'Alarming Accident on the Liverpool & Manchester Railway', *Kendal Mercury* (14 January 1837), p. 1; 'Scraps from a Manuscript Volume', *Liverpool Chronicle* (2 September 1882), np. A *St David* by the same maker is recorded as being at work on the Bolton & Leigh in 1841.

8. 'Lathes, High-pressure Steam Engines, &c.' *Manchester Courier* (14 March 1840), p.8.

9. RAIL 351/5 Directors' Meeting, Minutes 24 June 1839; 'Rowley's Patent Rotary Engine', *Mechanics' Magazine* (18 August 1838), pp. 321 -323; 'New Rotary Steam Engine', *Mechanics' Magazine* (29 June 1839) p. 224; 'New Rotary Engine', *Manchester Courier* (9 February 1839), p. 5; 'New Rotary Steam Engine', *Preston Chronicle* (8 June 1839), p. 3.

10. 'New Locomotive Engine', *Manchester Courier* (5 October 1839), p. 4.

11. Ibid: 'Scraps from a Manuscript Volume', *Liverpool Chronicle* (2 September 1882), np.

12. S. Murfitt, 'The English Patent System and Early Railway Technology 1800-1852', in M. Chrimes, ed., *Early Main Line Railways 2* (Croydon: CPI, 2019), pp. 154-156.

PART 3: ENGINEMEN AND FIREMEN

Chapter 13. Locomotive Foremen

1. Warren, *A Century*, p. 271.

2. RAIL 371/3 Directors' Meeting, Minutes 4 January 1836; 'Reports to the Committee of the Privy Council', *Accounts and Papers. Railway Department*, vol. 39 (January – August 1846) p. 90; 'The Fog in Manchester', *Manchester Courier* (4 January 1845), p. 2; 'Dense Fog in Manchester. Fatal Railway Accident', *London Evening Standard* (1 January 1845), p. 4. 1845 was a bad year for the Forsyth family: John and Thomas had attended the funeral of a family member (a daughter/sister) only that morning; another daughter had been burned to death only twelve months previously.

3. F. Dickinson, 'The Mellings of Rainhill', *Journal of the Historic Society of Lancashire and Cheshire*, Vol. 121 (1969), pp. 59-75.; T. C. Fyfe, letter to the editor, 'Links in the History of the Locomotive', *The Engineer* (25 March 1881), p. 216. RAIL 371/8 Management Sub-Committee, Minutes 22 March 1832, 5 April 1832.

4. 'The Manchester Fog', *Manchester Courier* (4 January 1845), p. 2; 'Forsyth's Patent Railway Signal', Illustrated London News (21 February 1846), p. 4; 'Forsyth's Night Signals', Bradshaw's Railway Gazette, vol. II (1846), p. 706; 'Frightful Boiler Explosion', *Lancaster Gazette* (10 July 1858), p. 7; 'The Boiler Explosion at the Atlas Works', *Manchester Courier* (10 July 1858), p. 7; Fyfe, 'Links in the History of the Locomotive', p. 216.

5. Thomas, The L&M, p. 35; L. T. C. Rolt, *George and Robert Stephenson* (London: Penguin, 1978), p. *5ff*; A. Holt, *A Pennine Pioneer. The History of Summit Railway Tunnel* (Littleborough: George Kelsall, 1999), p. 81.

6. RAIL 371/8 Management Sub-Committee, Minutes 18 May 1831, 2 November 1831.
7. RAIL 371/8 Management Sub-Committee, Minutes 27 April 1831.
8. RAIL 371/2 Directors' Meeting, Minutes 28 February 1831.
9. RAIL 371/2 Directors' Meeting, Minutes 4 April 1831.
10. RAIL 371/8 Management Sub-Committee, Minutes 1 February 1832.
11. RAIL 371/8 Management Sub-Committee, Minutes 18 January 1832.
12. RAIL 371/2 Directors' Meeting, Minutes 16 July 1832; RAIL 371/3 Directors Meeting, Minutes 29 April 1833, 30 April 1833.
13. Holt, *Pennine Pioneer*, pp. 44-45 and p. 81; 'Testimonial to Robert Stephenson', *The Railway Times*, vol. 2 (1839), p.451; C. R. Clinker, *The Leciester & Swannington Railway* (Bristol: Avon-Anglia Publications, 1977), p. 18, p. 21, p. 48; https://www.gracesguide.co.uk/Copeland_and_Harding accessed 3-09-2020@ 11.27.
14. RAIL 371/8 Management Sub-Committee, Minutes 26 July 1832; M. R. Bailey, 'Robert Stephenson & Co., 1823-1829' *Transactions of the Newcomen Society*, vol. 50 (1980), p. 115.
15. RAIL 371/3 Directors' Meeting, Minutes 17 June 1833, 18 June 1833, 21 June 1833, 22 June 1833, 29 June 1833; RAIL 371/4 Directors' Meeting, Minutes 4 July 1836.
16. RAIL 371/3 Directors' Meeting, Minutes 15 July 1833, 22 July 1833, 14 October 1833.
17. RAIL 371/2 Directors Meeting, Minutes 13 August 1832; RAIL 371/10 Management Sub-Committee, Minutes 2 May 1833, 16 May 1833; RAIL 371/3 Directors' Meeting, Minutes 11 May 1835.
18. RAIL 371/8 Management Sub-Committee, Minutes 27 December 1832; RAIL 371/3 Directors' Meeting, Minutes 3 June 1833.
19. RAIL 371/3 Directors' Meeting, Minutes 1 September 1834, 8 September 1834.
20. RAIL 371/3 Directors' Meeting, Minutes 1 September 1834, 8 September 1834.
21. RAIL 371/10 Management Sub-Committee, Minutes 24 December 1853, 7 January 1836.
22. RAIL 371/5 Directors' Meeting, Minutes 17 February 1840, 2 March 1840.
23. RAIL 3741/5 Directors' Meeting, Minutes 27 April 1840, 4 May 1840.

Chapter 14. The First Enginemen

1. P. W. Kingsford, *Victorian Railwaymen. The Emergence and Growth of Railway Labour 1830-1870* (London: Frank Cass Ltd., 1970), pp. 3-4.
2. *Ibid*, pp. 4-5.
3. N. W. Webster, *Joseph Locke. Railway Revolutionary* (London: George Allen & Unwin Ltd., 1970), p. 54.
4. A. L. Dawson, *Working on the Victorian Railway* (Stroud: Amberley Publishing, 2017), p. 11.
5. 'Veritas Vincit', *Railway Locomotive Management* (Birmingham: H. Winnall, 1847), p. 23; 'The Rocket', *The Engineer* (7 November 1884) p. 359; 'The Rocket' *The Engineer* (14 November 1884), p. 378.

6. 'To the Editor', *Bell's Weekly Messenger* (29 November 1851), p. 3.

7. 'Reedwater', *Hexham Courant* (28 December 1889), p. 5.

8. 'Obituary' *Sheffield Evening Telegraph* (9 September 1895), p. 2.'Obituary', *Grantham Journal* (14 September 1895), p. 7.

9. 'The First Engine Driver', *Cumberland Paquet* (18 November 1851), p. 4.

10. *The Safety Valve*, vol. 10 (1896), p. 329; 'The Man who Drove the Rocket', *The Strand Magazine*, vol. 24 (1902), p. 786; 'The Oldest Engine-Driver', *Leamington Spa Courier* (29 July 1904), p. 2; 'Driver of the Rocket. Exciting Trial', *Daily Telegraph* (7 October 1907), p. 7; 'Entwistle and Stephenson;', *Globe* (8 April 1909), p. 5; W. Wood, 'Survivors' Tales of Great Events: No. LIV – The "Rocket" and the world's first railway', *The Royal Magazine*, vol. XXII, no. 16 (1909), pp. 248-254.

11. 'The Rocket', *The Engineer*, (14 November 1884), p. 378.

12. RAIL 371/8 Management Sub-Committee, Minutes 3 November 1831.

13. RAIL 371/10 Management Sub-Committee, Minutes 4 May 1835;RAIL 371/3 Directors' Meeting, Minutes 25 May 1835.

14. RAIL 371/10 Management Sub-Committee, Minutes 24 December 1835.

15. RAIL 371/8 Management Sub-Committee, Minutes 17 August 1831; RAIL 351/3 Leeds & Selby Railway, Management Committee, Minutes 9 December 1836, 16 June 1837.

16. The L&M had no locomotive of such name; presumably it was a nickname.

17. 'A Railway Veteran', *Northampton Mercury* (25 August 1893), p. 6.

18. 'Death of an Old Engine-Driver', *Grantham Journal* (6 February 1904), p. 7.

19. 'Jubilee of the Manchester and Liverpool Railway', *Manchester Courier* (29 June 1880), p. 6; Thomas, *L&M*, p. 238.

20. *Locomotive Management*, p. 23 and p.30; 'The Rocket', *The Engineer* (7 November 1884), p. 359; 'The London & North Western Railway and Crewe Works', *The Engineer: Supplement* (11 December 1908), p. ii.

21. RAIL 371/8 Management Sub-Committee, Minutes 1831-1833, *passim*.

22. RAIL351/14 Leeds & Selby Railway, Correspondence Ledger, letter from William Williams to Robert Kirkup, 31 October 1834.

23. 'The Rocket', *The Engineer* (14 November 1884), p. 378; https://www.gracesguide.co.uk/Robert_Weatherburn_(1811-1880) accessed 12-02-2018 @ 12.18.

24. 'The Rocket', *The Engineer* (7 November 1884), p. 359.

25. Bennet, *Boulton's*, p. 268.

26. RAIL 371/4 Directors' Meeting, Minutes 3 September 1838, 10 September 1838; RAIL 371/10 Management Sub-Committee, Minutes 13 September 1838.

27. 'Railway Accident', *Liverpool Mercury* (5 May 1837), p. 6.

28. 'The London & North Western Railway and Crewe Works', *The Engineer: Supplement* (11 December 1908), p.ii.

29. RAIL 371/8 Management Sub-Committee. Minutes, 27 July 1831.

30. RAIL 371/3 Directors' Meeting, Minutes 8 September 1834.

31. RAIL 371/5 Directors' Meeting, Minutes 7 December 1840; RAIL 371/10 Management Sub-Committee, Minutes 26 November 1835.

32. RAIL 371/10 Management Sub-Committee, Minutes 13 June 1833.
33. 'Prevention of Railway Accidents', *The Railway Times*, (2 January 1841), p. 19.
34. Ibid.
35. RAIL 371/8 Management Sub-Committee. Minutes, 14 September 1831.
36. RAIL 371/8 Management Sub-Committee. Minutes, 23 November 1831.
37. RAIL 371/8 Management Sub-Committee. Minutes, 29 February 1832.
38. RAIL 371/10 Management Sub-Committee, Minutes 8 August 1833; RAIL 371/3 Directors Meeting, Minutes 12 August 1833, 19 August 1833.
39. RAIL 371/10 Management Sub-Committee, Minutes 15 May 1834, 18 July 1839.
40. RAIL 371/8 Management Sub-Committee. Minutes, 26 January 1832.
41. RAIL 371/8 Management Sub-Committee, Minutes 17 November 1831.
42. RAIL 371/8 Management Sub-Committee, Minutes 19 April 1832.
43. RAIL 371/8 Management Sub-Committee, Minutes 25 April 1832.
44. RAIL 371/8 Management Sub-Committee Minutes 3 May 1831, 16 May 1832.
45. RAIL 371/8 Management Sub-Committee, Minutes 14 June 1832.
46. RAIL 371/8 Management Sub-Committee, Minutes 25 July 1832.
47. RAIL 371/8 Management Sub-Committee, Minutes 21 February 1833.
48. RAIL 371/10 Management Sub-Committee, Minutes 13 June 1833.
49. RAIL 371/2 Directors' Meeting, Minutes 7 February 1833.
50. RAIL 371/8 Management Sub-Committee, Minutes 21 February 1833.
51. RAIL 371/3 Directors' Meeting, Minutes 1 March 1833.
52. Ibid.
53. Ibid.
54. RAIL 371/10 Management Sub-Committee, Minutes 24 April 1833.
55. RAIL 371/10 Management Sub-Committee, Minutes 2 May 1833.
56. 'Prevention of Railway Accidents', *The Railway Times*, (2 January 1841), p. 19.
57. RAIL 371/10 Management Sub-Committee, Minutes 22 May 1833; RAIL 371/3 Directors' Meeting, Minutes 3 June 1833.
58. RAIL 371/10 Management Sub-Committee, Minutes 16 May 1833; 6 March 1834.
59. RAIL 371/8 Management Sub-Committee, Minutes 12 January 1832; RAIL 371/3 Directors' Meeting, Minutes 1 September 1834.
60. RAIL 371/10 Management Sub-Committee, Minutes 13 June 1833.
61. RAIL 371/3 Directors' Meeting, Minutes 20 May 1833.
62. RAIL 371/10 Management Sub-Committee, Minutes 20 February 1834.
63. RAIL 371/10 Management Sub-Committee, Minutes 16 October 1834.
64. RAIL 371/2 Directors' Meeting, Minutes 27 June 1831.
65. RAIL 371/3 Directors' Meeting, Minutes 7 September 1835.
66. RAIL 371/10 Management Sub-Committee, Minutes 3 September 1835.
67. RAIL 371/10 Management Sub-Committee, Minutes 18 September 1835.
68. RAIL 371/10 Management Sub-Committee, Minutes 15 October 1835.
69. RAIL 371/3 Directors' Meeting, Minutes 28 September 1835.
70. RAIL 371/10 Management Sub-Committee, Minutes 28 October 1835.
71. RAIL 371/3 Directors' Meeting, Minutes 14 December 1835.
72. RAIL 371/10 Management Sub-Committee, Minutes 4 February 1836.

73. RAIL 371/3 Directors' Meeting, Minutes 8 February 1836.

74. Ibid.

75. Ibid.

76. 'Turn-out of Engine-men on the Railway', *Kendal Mercury* (13 February 1836), p. 1, citing *Manchester Guardian*.

77. Ibid.

78. 'A General turn-out of the Enginemen', *Staffordshire Advertiser* (13 February 1836), p. 3.

79. RAIL 371/3 Directors' Meeting, Minutes 15 February 1836, 22 February 1836.

80. 'Turn-Out of the Engineers on the Railway', *Manchester Courier* (13 February 1836), p. 2.

81. Ibid; see also *Manchester Guardian* (13 February 1836), p. 3.

82. 'Turn out of Engine-men on the Railway', *Manchester Guardian* (13 February 1836), p. 3.

83. RAIL 371/3 Directors' Meeting, Minutes 7 February 1836.

84. Thomas, L&M, p. 141.

85. RAIL 371/3 Directors' Meeting, Minutes 15 February 1836.

86. RAIL 371/3 Directors' Meeting, Minutes 22 February 1836.

87. RAIL 371/10 Management Sub-Committee, Minutes 30 March 1837; 31 March 1837.

88. RAIL 371/10 Management Sub-Committee, Minutes ND May 1837.

89. RAIL 371/10 Management Sub-Committee, Minutes 8 June 1837.

90. RAIL 371/3 Directors' Meeting, Minutes 11 August 1834.

91. RAIL 371/5 Directors' Meeting, Minutes 14 June 1841.

92. Ibid.

93. RAIL 371/4 Directors' Meeting, Minutes 18 June 1838.

94. RAIL 371/3 Directors' Meeting, Minutes 25 May 1835; RAIL 371/4 Directors' Meeting, Minutes 11 September 1837; RAIL 371/10 Management Sub-Committee, Minutes 4 May 1835, 30 August 1838, 15 August 1839.

95. RAIL 371/11 Management Sub-Committee, Minutes 11 February 1841.

96. *The Engineer*, Supplement 1908, p. iv.

97. 'Scraps from a Manuscript Volume', *Liverpool Courier* (2 September 1882), np; Woods, 'Evaporation of Water', p. 22.

98. E. Woods, 'On the Consumption of Fuel in the Locomotive Engines of the Liverpool and Manchester Railway', in *Weales' Quarterly Papers on Engineering*, vol. II (1844), p.*16ff*; E. Woods, 'On the Consumption of Fuel and Evaporation of Water in Locomotive and other Steam Engines', in T. Tredgold, ed., *Locomotive Engine* (London: John Weale, 1850), pp. 17-18; RAIL 371/24 Disbursement Accounts 1833-1845, p.17.

99. RAIL 371/5 Directors' Meeting, Minutes 20 April 1840.

100. 'The Performance of Locomotive Engines', *The Engineer* (15 October 1880), p. 291; 'The London & North Western Railway and Crewe Works', *The Engineer: Supplement* (11 December 1908), p. ii – iii.

101. RAIL 371/3 Directors' Meeting, Minutes 18 July 1842; 1 August 1842.

102. RAIL 371/5 Directors' Meeting, Minutes 7 December 1840.

103. Rail 371/6 Directors' Meeting, Minutes 14 November 1842, 12 December 1842; RAIL 371/11 Management Sub-Committee, Minutes 1 December 1842.

104. RAIL 371/11 Management Sub-Committee, Minutes 1 December 1842.

105. RAIL 371/6 Directors' Meeting, Minutes 24 July 1843, 7 August 1843.

106. RAIL 371/11 Management Sub-Committee, Minutes 10 December 1841; RAIL 371/24 Disbursement Accounts 1833-1845, p. 23.

107. Dawson, *Working*, pp. 14-22.

108. Whishaw, *Railways*, p. 202.

109. 'Accident on the Railway', *Manchester Courier* (16 October 1830), p. 2; 'The Railway' *Manchester Mercury* (19 October 1830), p. 4.

110. RAIL 371/2 Directors' Meeting, Minutes 18 October 1830.

111. Dawson, *L&M*, p. 50; 'Fatal Accident on the Railway', *Manchester Mercury* (2 November 1830), p. 2.

112. RAIL 371/1 Directors' Meeting, Minutes 19 April 1830, 26 April 1830.

113. RAIL 371/8 Management Sub-Committee, Minutes 12 September 1832.

114. *Parliamentary Accounts and Papers: Railways*, vol. XLI (Session February – August 1842), (London: 1842), p. 206.

115. 'Shocking Accident on the Railway', *Lancaster Gazette* (4 May 1833), p. 3; 'Fatal Railway Accident', *Manchester Courier* (8 February 1838), p. 4.

116. RAIL 371/2 Directors' Meeting, Minutes 27 February 1832.

117. RAIL 371/5 Directors' Meeting, Minutes 26 July 1841, 11 October 1841; RAIL 371/6 Directors' Meeting, Minutes 8 August 1842, 17 April 1843, 2 September 1844; *Sessional Papers of the House of Lords, vol. XIII, Accounts and Papers* (London: HMSO 1843), p. 31, p. 44.

118. RAIL 371/3 Directors' Meeting, Minutes 27 January 1834.

119. *Rules and Regulations*, Rule 3.

120. RAIL 371/3 Directors' Meeting, Minutes 4 March 1833.

121. RAIL 371/5 Management Sub-Committee, Minutes 18 June 1831, 29 June 1831.

122. RAIL 371/3 Directors' Meeting, Minutes 18 November 1833.

123. RAIL 371/3 Directors' Meeting, Minutes 25 November 1833.

124. RAIL 371/10 Management Sub-Committee, Minutes 13 September 1837.

125. RAIL 371/4 Directors' Meeting, Minutes 7 May 1838.

126. 'Railway Accident', *Manchester Times* (10 February 1838), p. 3.

127. RAIL 371/8 Management Sub-Committee, Minutes 27 July 1831.

128. RAIL 371/2 Directors' Meeting, Minutes 2 January 1832.

129. RAIL 371/8 Management Sub-Committee, Minutes 24 January 1833.

130. RAIL 371/3 Directors' Meeting, Minutes 2 December 1833.

131. RAIL 371/10 Management Sub-Committee, Minutes 10 July 1834.

132. RAIL 371/10 Management Sub-Committee, Minutes 18 September 1834.

133. RAIL 371/3 Directors' Meeting, Minutes 15 December 1834; RAIL 371/10 Management Sub-Committee, Minutes 11 December 1834.

134. RAIL 371/2 Directors' Meeting, Minutes 12 September 1831.

135. RAIL 371/8 Management Sub-Committee, Minutes 19 October 1831.

136. RAIL 371/8 Management Sub-Committee, Minutes 3 November 1831; 10 November 1831.
137. RAIL 371/8 Management Sub-Committee, Minutes 17 November 1831.
138. Ibid.
139. Ibid.
140. RAIL 371/8 Management Sub-Committee, Minutes 12 September 1832.
141. RAIL 371/8 Management Sub-Committee, Minutes 21 November 1832.
142. RAIL 371/3 Directors' Meeting, Minutes 4 February 1833; RAIL 371/11 Management Sub-Committee, Minutes 3 July 1833.
143. RAIL 371/4 Directors' Meeting, Minutes 11 July 1836; 25 July 1836.
144. RAIL 371/4 Directors' Meeting, 6 March 1837.
145. RAIL 371/10 Management Sub-Committee, Minutes 28 September 1837.
146. RAIL 371/5 Directors' Meeting, Minutes 23 November 1840.
147. RAIL 371/5 Directors' Meeting, Minutes 23 November 1840; 30 November 1840.
148. RAIL 371/4 Directors' Meeting, Minutes 19 June 1837.
149. RAIL 371/5 Directors' Meeting, Minutes 6 July 1840.
150. Ibid.
151. Ibid.
152. RAIL 371/5 Directors' Meeting, Minutes 22 March 1841.
153. RAIL 371/5 Directors' Meeting, Minutes 20 December 1841.
154. RAIL 371/5 Directors' Meeting, Minutes 20 December 1841.
155. 'Fatal Railway Accident', *Manchester Courier* (12 October 1844), p. 5.
156. RAIL 371/8 Management Sub-Committee, Minutes 18 June 1831.
157. RAIL 371/3 Directors' Meeting, Minutes 23 February 1835.
158. RAIL 371/4 Directors' Meeting, Minutes 24 October 1836.
159. RAIL 371/5 Directors' Meeting, Minutes 12 August 1839.
160. RAIL 371/4 Directors' meeting, Minutes 26 March 1838.
161. RAIL 371/8 Management Sub-Committee, Minutes 25 May 1831.
162. RAIL 371/8 Management Sub-Committee. Minutes, 25 August 1831.
163. RAIL 371/8 Management Sub-Committee. Minutes 10 November 1831.
164. Ibid.
165. RAIL 371/8 Management Sub-Committee. Minutes 23 November 1831.
166. RAIL 371/8 Management Sub-Committee. Minutes 3 August 1831.
167. RAIL 371/3 Directors Meeting, Minutes 4 February 1833.
168. RAIL 371/10 Management Sub-Committee, Minutes 17 July 1833.
169. RAIL 371/10 Management Sub-Committee, Minutes 25 July 1833.
170. 'The Mighty Power of Steam', *Chester Chronicle* (2 December 1831).
171. 'Hunting by Steam', *Leeds Times* (28 June 1834), p. 3; 'Sporting on the Railway', *Chester Chronicle* (27 June 1834), p. 3; 'A few days ago', *The Globe* (27 June 1834), p. 3.
172. RAIL 371/8 Management Sub-Committee, Minutes 28 March 1832, 4 April 1832.
173. RAIL 371/10 Management Sub-Committee, Minutes 12 June 1834.
174. 'Committal of an Engine-Driver for Drunkenness', *Leeds Times* (6 March 1841), p. 3.

175. RAIL 371/10 Management Sub-Committee, Minutes 4 August 1836.

176. RAIL 371/8 Management Sub-Committee, Minutes 22 March 1832.

177. RAIL 371/8 Management Sub-Committee, Minutes 13 June 1832.

178. RAIL 371/8 Management Sub-Committee, Minutes 6 June 1832.

179. RAIL 371/8 Management Sub-Committee, Minutes 21 November 1832.

180. RAIL 371/8 Management Sub-Committee, Minutes 30 January 1833; 6 February 1833.

181. RAIL 371/10 Management Sub-Committee, Minutes 10 November 1835.

182. RAIL 371/10 Management Sub-Committee, Minutes 22 May 1833.

183. RAIL 371/5 Directors' Meeting, Minutes 14 December 1840.

184. RAIL 371/11 Management Sub-Committee, Minutes 2 June 1842.

185. RAIL 371/6 Directors' Meeting, Minutes 4 September 1843.

PART 4: MAINTENANCE AND REPAIR

Chapter 15. Engine Sheds and Workshops

1. RAIL 371/1 Directors' Meeting, Minutes 3 May 1830; RAIL 371/8 Management Sub-Committee, Minutes 30 November 1831.

2. RAIL 371/1 Directors' Meeting, Minutes 31 May 1830, 7 June 1830; RAIL 371/2 Directors' Meeting, 6 June 1831, 11 July 1831; P. Rees, 'Excavations at Chatsworth Street Cutting, Part of the Original Terminus of the Liverpool and Manchester Railway', *Industrial Archaeology Review*, Vol. 4, No. 2 (Spring 1980), pp.160-161.

3. RAIL 371/8 Management Sub-Committee, Minutes 17 May 1832.

4. 'Local Intelligence', *Manchester Courier* (27 July 1830), p. 2.

5. RAIL 371/2 Directors' Meeting, Minutes 18 July 1831.

6. RAIL 410/2109 Roll of drawings: Liverpool & Manchester Extension Railway through Salford and Manchester, Engine Shed.

7. RAIL 371/10 Management Sub-Committee, Minutes 18 September 1834.

8. RAIL 371/29 Monthly accounts for cost of repairs on locomotives, carriages and wagons 1837-1839, Bills dated 1 July 1839, 31 July 1839; RAIL 371/35 Miscellaneous Receipts and Bills Grand Junction Railway to Liverpool & Manchester Railway, Bill dated April 1839.

9. RAIL 371/35 Miscellaneous Receipts and Bills Grand Junction Railway to Liverpool & Manchester Railway, Bill dated 14 June 1841.

10. RAIL 371/10 Management Sub-Committee, Minutes 6 February 1834.

11. RAIL 371/1 Directors' Meeting, Minutes 7 June 1830; RAIL 371/2 Directors' Meeting, Minutes 9 August 1830, 20 September 1830, 7 October 1831; RAIL 371/8 Management Sub-Committee, Minutes 15 November 1832; RAIL371/3 Directors' Meeting, Minutes 14 April 1834.

12. RAIL 371/10 Management Sub-Committee, Minutes 16 May 1833.

13. Clinker, *Leicester & Swannington*, p. 33; RAIL 351/1 Leeds & Selby Railway, Directors' Meeting, Minutes 6 February 1835, 20 February 1835.

14. RAIL 371/8 Management Sub-Committee, Minutes 17 May 1832.

15. RAIL 371/10 Management Sub-Committee, Minutes 18 September 1835.

16. RAIL 371/1 Directors' Meeting, Minutes 28 December 1829, 8 March 1830, 29 March 1830.

17. RAIL 371/10 Management Sub-Committee, Minutes 16 May 1833, 30 May 1833, 8 November 1833.

18. RAIL 371/10 Management Sub-Committee, Minutes 5 April 1833.

19. RAIL 371/10 Management Sub-Committee, Minutes 18 September 1835.

20. RAIL 371/29 Monthly accounts and bills, Bill dated 30 September 1837.

21. RAIL 371/10 Management Sub-Committee, Minutes 4 February 1834.

22. Ibid.

23. RAIL 371/10 Management Sub-Committee, Minutes 27 June 1834.

24. RAIL 371/10 Management Sub-Committee, Minutes 21 August 1834, 2 October 1834.

25. RAIL 371/10 Management Sub-Committee, Minutes 21 March 1833.

26. RAIL 371/10 Management Sub-Committee, Minutes 27 March 1833.

27. RAIL 371/10 Management Sub-Committee, Minutes 16 October 1834.

28. RAIL 371/4 Directors' Meeting, Minutes 29 October 1838.

29. RAIL 371/2 Directors Meeting, Minutes 23 April 1832.

30. RAIL 371/8 Management Sub-Committee, Minutes 1 August 1832, 5 September 1832.

31. RAIL 371/8 Management Sub-Committee, Minutes 12 September 1832.

32. RAIL 371/8 Management Sub-Committee, Minutes 15 November 1832.

33. RAIL 371/2 Directors' Meeting, Minutes 10 September 1832; RAIL 371/8 Management Sub-Committee, Minutes 5 September 1832, 26 September 1832, 16 January 1833.

34. RAIL 371/10 Management Sub-Committee, Minutes 9 January 1834.

35. RAIL 371/8 Management Sub-Committee, Minutes 16 January 1833.

36. RAIL 371/3 Directors Meeting, Minutes 3 June 1833, 19 June 1833.

37. RAIL 371/10 Management Sub-Committee, Minutes 8 August 1833.

38. RAIL 371/10 Management Sub-Committee, Minutes 5 June 1833.

39. RAIL 371/24 Disbursement Accounts, *passim.*

40. RAIL 371/3 Directors' Meeting, Minutes 23 November 1835.

41. RAIL 371/10 Management Sub-Committee, Minutes 12 November 1835.

42. 'Accident at the Railway', *Liverpool Mercury* (2 November 1832), p. 6.

43. RAIL 371/10 Management Sub-Committee, Minutes 10 November 1836, 20 February 1837, 16 March 1836, 5 July 1838.

44. RAIL 371/29 Monthly Accounts and Bills, Bill dated 31 October 1837.

45. RAIL 371/4 Directors' Meeting, Minutes 4 June 1838, 29 October 1838.

46. Whishaw, *Railways*, p. 203.

47. *Ibid*, p. 195.

48. 'Lathes, High-pressure Steam Engine' *Manchester Courier* (14 March 1840), p. 8.

49. RAIL 371/5 Directors' Meeting, Minutes 18 November 1839, 2 December 1839, 23 December 1839, 27 January 1840, 1 June 1840, 19 October 1840.

50. RAIL 371/29 Monthly accounts for cost of repairs on locomotives, carriages and wagons 1837-1841, *passim*.
51. RAIL 371/24 Disbursement Accounts 1833-1845, p. 8.
52. Whishaw, *Railways*, pp. 202-203; RAIL 371/11 Management Sub-Committee, Minutes 1 November 1842.

Chapter 16. Workshop Costs

1. RAIL 371/11 Management Sub-Committee, Minutes 7 November 1839.
2. RAIL 371/29 Monthly accounts for cost of repairs on locomotives, carriages and wagons 1837-1841, *passim*.
3. RAIL 371/24 Disbursement Accounts 1833-1845, p. 3, p. 8.
4. RAIL 371/29 Monthly accounts, bill for repairs 30 April 1838.
5. RAIL 371/35 Miscellaneous Receipts and Bills Grand Junction Railway to Liverpool & Manchester Railway. Cost of repairs, 6 November 1838.
6. RAIL 371/29 Monthly accounts, Bills 31 March 1838 to 31 December 1838. F. Sims, *Engineering Formulas Interactive: Conversions, Definitions, and Tables* (New York: Industrial Press, 1999), vol. 1, p. 151. See also I. V. Kragelsky & V. V. Alisin, *Friction Wear Lubrication* (Oxford: Pergamon Press, 1982), *passim*.;Bailey, 'Planet Project', p. 121; author's examination of the locomotive; E. R. Clark, 'Early Locomotive Building in Lowell, Mass.,' *The Railway & Locomotive Historical Society Bulletin* No. 7 (1924) p. 35.
7. RAIL 371/29 Monthly accounts, Bills 30 June 1837 to 31 December 1837.
8. RAIL 371/29 Monthly accounts, *passim*; RAIL 371/24 Disbursement Accounts 1833-1845, p. 8.
9. RAIL 371/29 Monthly accounts, *passim*.
10. Dawson, *Working*, pp. 23-24. See also C. J. Bowen Cook, *British Locomotives* (London: Whittaker & Co, 1894), chapter XVII.
11. RAIL 371/3 Directors' Meeting, Minutes 22 December 1834.
12. Dawson, *Working*, pp. 24.-25.
13. RAIL 371/29 Monthly Accounts and Bills, 1837-1840, *passim*.

Chapter 17. Locomotive Working

1. RAIL 371/3 Directors' Meeting, Minutes 14 October 1833.
2. 'Liverpool and Manchester Railway', *Leicester Journal* (18 April 1834), p. 4.
3. 'Extracts from the Reports of the Liverpool & Manchester Railway', *The Mechanics' Magazine*, vol. VIII (July-December 1836), pp. 57-62.
4. 'Liverpool and Manchester Railway', *Leicester Journal* (18 April 1834), p. 4.
5. Colburn, *Locomotive Engineering*, p. 37.
6. 'Meeting of the Proprietors of the Liverpool and Manchester Railway', *Manchester Courier* (30 July 1836), p. 3.

7. RAIL 371/3 Directors' Meeting, Minutes 13 October 1834.

8. F. M. G. De Pambour, *Traité Theorique et Pratique des Machines Locomotives* (Paris: Bachelier, 1835), 1e edition, p. 368; Colburn, *Locomotive Engineering*, p. 37.

9. Pambour, *Traité*, 2e edition, pp.610-615; RAIL 371/40 Performance of locomotives, *passim*; *Gauge Commissioners*, p. 304, para 5957, 5958.

10. *Report from the Select Committee on Railroad Communication* (London, 1838), pp. 62-63, paras. 690-692, 698.

11. Ibid.

12. RAIL 371/40 Performance of Locomotive Engines, *passim*.

13. SCA Ref. U268/C1/4 Nasmyth Gaksell to Henry Booth, 11 March 1839; NG to Henry Booth 16 April 1839; U268/C1/5 NG to Joseph Woods (London & Southampton Railway), 29 July 1839; RAIL 371/40 Performance of Locomotive Engines, *passim*.

14. Rev. Dr. R. Hills, 'The development of Machine tools in the early railway era', in M. Bailey, ed., *Early Railways 3* (Sudbury: Six Martlets, 2006), pp. 254-255.

15. As defined by E. M. Rogers, *Diffusion of Innovations*, fifth edition (New York: Free Press 2003), *passim*.

PART 5: ROLLING STOCK

Chapter 18. Passenger Carriages

1. RAIL1021/8/24 North Eastern Railway, type-written notes on Nathaniel, Thomas, George, and Thomas William Worsdell. See also: 'Railway Carriages Past and Present', *Soulby's Ulverston General Advertise*r (10 December 1896), p. 6.

2. G. Hill, *The Worsdells. A Quaker Engineering Dynasty* (The Transport Publishing Company, 1991), pp. 22-23; A. L. Dawson, *Travelling on the Victorian Railway* (Stroud: Amberley Publishing, 2017), p. 54.

3. Hill, *The Worsdells*, p. 24.

4. Anon, *The Railways of England* (London: E. Grattan, 1839), p. 89.

5. RAIL 1021/8/24, Type-written notes on Thomas, Nathaniel, George, and Thomas William Worsdell; 'Railway Carriages Past and Present', *Soulby's Ulverston General Advertise*r (10 December 1896), p. 6; NRM DS/2/TOP/13 Model coach 'Experience', drawings made by LNWR Wolverton 5-1-1911; 'Rolling-Stock for the Liverpool & Manchester Railway Centenary Exhibition', *The Railway Gazette* (22 August 1930), pp. 242-243;'Locomotives and Rolling-Stock for the Liverpool & Manchester Railway Centenary Proceedings', *The Railway Gazette* (5 September 1930), pp. 314-317. See also NRM, Drawing No. D14/1667 'L&M Centenary Vehicles. First Class Carriages. BR, London Midland Region, Derby.'

6. RAIL 384/263 London & Birmingham Railway, Specification for a First-Class Coach, London 1836.

7. Dawson, *Travelling*, p. 57; P. Chatham, 'Early London & Birmingham Railway Carriage Stock', *The L&NWR Society Journal*, vol. 6 no. 9 (June 2011), pp. 10-21; S. C. Brees, *Fourth Series of Railway Practice* (London: John Williams & Co., 1847), plate 1, and plate 2; 'The "Lion" Locomotive Liverpool & Manchester Railway', *The Engineer* (14 November 1930), p. 535. See also 'Locomotives and Rolling Stock for the Liverpool & Manchester Railway Centenary Proceedings', *Railway Gazette* (22 August 1930), pp. 242-243; 'Locomotives and Rolling Stock for the Liverpool & Manchester Railway Centenary Proceedings', *Railway Gazette* (5 September 1930), pp. 315-316.

8. Parliamentary Papers of the House of Commons, Report of Major General Pasley on Railway Carriages 5 July 1842, p147; RAIL 371/6 Directors' Meeting, Minutes 1 August 1842.

9. Dawson, *Travelling*, p. 49ff; A. L. Dawson, 'Manchester & Birmingham Railway First Class Coach', *The L&NWR Society Journal*, Vol. 8, No. 11 (December 2017), pp. 404-412.

10. Bagwell, *Transport Revolution*, pp. 36-37; A. L. Dawson, 'Rocket, the Liverpool & Manchester Railway and 'Public Relations" R&CHS Railway History Research Group, Occasional Paper 12 (2020).

11. 'Railway Coaches', *Manchester Mercury* (15 June 1830), p. 4; 'Railway Coaches', *Liverpool Mercury* (11 June 1830), p. 6; 'Railway Coaches', *Chester Chronicle* (11 June 1830), p. 3. See also: Dawson, *Travelling*, pp. 33-36.

12. *York Herald* (27 September 1834), p. 4; 'Railway Carriages Past and Present', *Soulby's Ulverston General Advertiser* (10 December 1896), p. 6.

13. 'Steam Carriages Lit with Gas', *Manchester Times* (8 February 1834), p. 2.

14. 'Railway Coaches', *Liverpool Mercury* (11 June 1830), p. 4. The same report was reproduced verbatim by the *Manchester Mercury* (15 June 1830), p. 6.

15. J. S. Walker, *An accurate Description of the Liverpool & Manchester Railway* (Liverpool, 1830) p.24.

16. 'Liverpool & Manchester Railway', *Gore's Liverpool Advertiser* (16 September 1830), p. 3.

17. 'New First-Class Train of Carriages', *Gore's Liverpool Advertiser*, 31 August 1837, p. 4.

18. 'New First-Class Train of Carriages', *Gore's Liverpool Advertiser*, 31 August 1837, p. 4.

19. RAIL 371/2 Directors' Meeting, Minutes 14 February 1831; RAIL 371/8 Management Sub-Committee, Minutes 14 April 1831, 24 August 1831, 14 March 1832; RAIL 371/10 Management Sub-Committee, Minutes 15 September 1836.

20. RAIL 371/8 Management Sub-Committee, Minutes 26 January 1832; RAIL 371/10 Management Sub-Committee, Minutes 27 March 1833.

21. Dendy Marshall, *Centenary History*, plate XXIII.

22. RAIL 371/8 Management Sub-Committee, Minutes 18 May 1831.

23. Dawson, *Travelling*, pp.8-9.

24. 'New First-Class Train of Carriages', *Gore's Liverpool Advertiser*, 31 August 1837, p. 4.

25. T. H. Fielding, *On the Theory of Painting* (London: Ackermann & Co., 1846), pp. 179-180; *The Technical Educator* (London: Cassell & Co Ltd., 1844), vol. 1 p. 236. see also: https://www.tandfonline.com/doi/abs/10.1080/00393630.2015.1131478?journalCode=ysic20 accessed 19-02-2019 @09:40.

26. RAIL 371/8 Management Sub-Committee, Minutes 15 April 1832, 23 January 1833; RAIL 371/10 Management Sub-Committee, Minutes 27 March 1833.

27. RAIL 371/10 Management Sub-Committee, Minutes 5 September 1833.

28. http://www.oughterardheritage.org/content/topics/19th-century-coach-travel-bianconi-galway-oughterard-clifden, accessed 19-1-2019 @ 13.13.

29. *Description of the Tunnel of the Liverpool & Manchester Railway* (Liverpool: T. Bean, 1830), pp. 10-11; J. S. Walker, *Accurate Description*, p. 24; Dendy Marshall, *Centenary History*, p. 67; Dawson, *Travelling*, pp. 72-73.

30. 'Railway Coaches', *Liverpool Mercury* (11 June 1830), p. 6.

31. 'Railroad Travelling' *Sheffield Independent* (2 October 1830), p. 1; W. S. Kennedy, *Wonders and Curiosities of the Railway* (Chicago: S. C. Griggs & Co., 1884), pp. 10-11; Dawson, *Travelling*, pp.65-67 and p. 70.

32. *Parliamentary Papers, House of Commons*, vol. 41 (1842), p. 231.

33. 'Railway Travelling', *Sheffield Independent* (2 October 1830), p. 1; Whishaw, *Railways*, p. 204; Dawson, *Travelling*, pp. 55-69.

34. RAIL 371/6 Directors' Meeting, Minutes 4 April 1844, 22 April 1844; RAIL 371/11 Management Sub-Committee, Minutes 18 April 1844; RAIL 371/24 Disbursement Accounts, p. 32; *Gauge Commissioners 1845*, p. 513.

35. Kennedy, *Wonders and Curiosities*, p. 11.

36. 'Railway Accident', *Liverpool Mercury* (11 November 1831), p. 6; 'To the Editor of the Liverpool Mercury', *Liverpool Mercury* (18 November 1831), p. 5; 'Accident on the Railway', *Liverpool Mercury* (18 November 1831), p. 3.

37. Dendy Marshall, *Centenary History*, p.65; 'Railway Travelling', *Sheffield Independent* (2 October 1830), p. 1; 'To the Editor of the Liverpool Mercury', *Liverpool Mercury* (18 November 1831), p. 5; RAIL 371/8 Management Sub-Committee, Minutes 24 January 1833.

38. 'Railway Carriages Past and Present', *Soulby's Ulverston General Advertiser* (10 December 1896), p. 6; 'New First Class Train of Carriages', *Gore's Liverpool Advertiser* (31 August 1837), p. 4.

39. 'The Railway Buffing Apparatus of Mr Bergin', *Mechanics' Magazine* No. 615 (23 May 1835), p. 144; 'Bergin's Patent Railway Buffing-Apparatus', *Mechanics' Magazine* No. 634 (3 October 1835), pp. 1-6.

40. RAIL 384/260 Henry Booth. Report on Bergin's Buffers, 20 November 1835; RAIL 371/4 Directors' Meeting, Minutes 13 March 1837; *The Repertory of Patent Inventions*, new series, Vol. V (January -June 1836)(London: J. S. Hodson, 1836), pp. 349-351; N. Wood, *A Practical Treatise on Railroads* (London: Longman, Orme, Brown, Green & Longman, 1838), third edition, pp. 225-226ff.

41. *Gauge Commissioners 1845*, p. 33, paras.453 to 463; 'New Railway Carriages', *Manchester Times* (3 June 1837), p. 2; 'Dreadful Accident on the Manchester & Liverpool Railway', *Manchester Times* (16 September 1837), p. 3, 'Dreadful

Accident on the Manchester and Liverpool Railway', *Manchester Times* (1 December 1838), p. 2.

42. Dawson, *Travelling*, p.48; RAIL 371/5 Directors' Meeting, Minutes 14 September 1840.

43. ROB4/1 Robert Stephenson & Co, Works Ledger 1824-1831, p. 288, p. 302; RAIL 371/2 Directors' Meeting, Minutes 11 October 1830; RAIL 371/3 Directors' Meeting, Minutes 4 November 1833.

44. RAIL 371/8 Management Sub-Committee, Minutes 27 June 1831.

45. RAIL 371/2 Directors' Meeting, Minutes 19 December 1831; RAIL 371/8 Management Sub-Committee, Minutes 26 January 1832; RAIL 371/10 Management Sub-Committee, Minutes 5 September 1833.

46. For more on Richard Melling, see A. L. Dawson, 'Three Early Tourist Carriages', *R&CHS Journal* No. 237 (March 2020), pp.47-52.

47. RAIL 371/10 Management Sub-Committee, Minutes 15 September 1836; 'New Railway Carriages', *Manchester Times* (3 June 1837), p. 2; 'New First-Class Train of Carriages', *Gore's Liverpool Advertiser*, 31 August 1837, p. 4.'Opening of the Grand Junction Railway', *Manchester Courier* (8 July 1837), p. 3; 'Railway Accidents: Collision of the Manchester and Liverpool and Grand Junction Railway Trains', *Suffolk Chronicle* (1 December 1838), p. 4 citing the *Liverpool Times*; Dawson, *Travelling*, pp. 87-89.

48. Whishaw, *Railways*, p. 192; RAIL 371/4 Directors' Meeting, Minutes 20 March 1837, 27 March 1837.

49. RAIL 371/4 Directors' Meeting, Minutes 16 January 1837, 30 January 1837; RAIL 371/10 Management Sub-Committee, Minutes 16 February 1837; G. Hill, *The Worsdells*, p. 29; RAIL 1021/8/24, Obituary George Worsdell, December 1912.

50. J. Marshall, *The Lancashire and Yorkshire Railway* (Newton Abbott: David & Charles, 1972), volume 3 p. 24.

51. RAIL 351/1 Leeds & Selby Railway, Directors' Meeting, 3 December 1833, 10 January 1834, 4 February 1834, 14 March 1834; RAIL 351/8 Leeds & Selby Railway, Correspondence Folio, letters 7 June 1834, 5 July 1834, 4 August 1834.

52. RAIL 384/182 London & Birmingham Railway. Extract from the Minutes of the Sub-Committee for Carriages 7 September 1837; RAIL 384/263 London & Birmingham Railway. Specification for a first-class coach.

Chapter 19. Goods Stock

1. RAIL 371/1 Directors' Meeting, Minutes 16 June 1828, 24 May 1830; RAIL 371/10 Management Sub-Committee, Minutes 10 February 1833.

2. RAIL 371/3 Directors' Meeting, Minutes 23 December 1833.

3. RAIL 371/3 Directors' Meeting, Minutes 23 November 1835.

4. Whishaw, *Railways*, p. 204; *Gauge Commissioners 1846*, p. 513.

5. Wood, *Practical Treatise*, 3rd edition, pp. 209-211 and plate VII fig. 10, fig. 11.

6. *Gauge Commissioners 1846*, pp.304-305, paras 5946, 5962.

7. RAIL 371/8 Management Sub-Committee, Minutes 6 May 1831; 25 May 1831.
8. RAIL 371/8 Management Sub-Committee, Minutes 26 October 1831.
9. *Gauge Commissioners 1846*, p. 305, para. 5972.
10. *Gauge Commissioners 1846*, p. 305, paras 5975 – 5987.
11. P. Chatham, 'Henry Henson and the Early Wagon Stock of the Southern Division', *The L&NWR Society Journal*, vol. 6, No. 6 (September 2010), pp. 3- 5.
12. Ibid, p. 5.
13. RAIL 371/8 Management Sub-Committee, Minutes 31 August 1831; 12 October 1831.
14. RAIL 371/3 Directors' Meeting, Minutes 8 April 1833.
15. RAIL 371/2 Directors' Meeting, Minutes 16 August 1830.
16. RAIL 371/1 Directors' Meeting, Minutes 16 November 1829.
17. RAIL 371/8 Management Sub-Committee, Minutes 16 November 1831.
18. RAIL 371/8 Management Sub-Committee, Minutes 6 October 1831.
19. RAIL 371/2 Directors' Meeting, Minutes 2 January 1832.
20. RAIL 371/2 Directors' Meeting, Minutes 16 August 1830; RAIL 371/8 Management Sub-Committee, Minutes 15 June 1831, 27 June 1831, 6 July 1831.
21. RAIL 371/2 Directors' Meeting, Minutes 8 August 1831; RAIL 371/8 Management Sub-Committee, Minutes 30 November 1831, 7 December 1831, 14 December 1831, 4 January 1832, 1 February 1832.
22. Rail 371/8 Management Sub-Committee, Minutes 11 January 1832.
23. RAIL 371/2 Directors' Meeting, Minutes 27 February 1832; RAIL 371/8 Management Sub-Committee, Minutes 1 March 1832.
24. 'Second Report of the Commissioners appointed to consider and recommend a general system of railways for Ireland', *Sessional Papers of the House of Lords*, vol. XLVII (London: 1838), p. 82; Whishaw, Railways, p. 205.
25. RAIL 371/8 Management Sub-Committee, Minutes 11 May 1831.
26. RAIL 371/8 Management Sub-Committee, Minutes 1 June 1831, 7 December 1831; 'Early Cattle Traffic on the Liverpool & Manchester Railway', *The L&NWR Society Journal*, vol.5., no. 5 (December 2006),p. 21.
27. RAIL 371/8 Management Sub-Committee, Minutes 11 January 1832.
28. RAIL 371/10 Management Sub-Committee, Minutes 7 August 1834.
29. RAIL 371/5 Directors' Meeting, Minutes 25 February 1839.
30. See A. L. Dawson, *The Liverpool & Manchester Railway: An Operational History* (Barnsley: Pen & Sword Transport, 2020), for more information on the cattle trade.
31. RAIL 371/2 Directors' Meeting, Minutes 22 November 1830.

Conclusion

1. E. M. Rogers, *Diffusion of Innovation* (New York: Free Press, 2003), fifth edition pp.280-289, pp. 316-320ff.
2. Ibid, pp. 280-283.
3. 'Second Report', p.77.

Index